Life on the Edge –
Adventures of a Travelling Surgeon

Sam Ramsay Smith

Published by New Generation Publishing in 2022

Copyright © Sam Ramsay Smith 2022

First Edition

The author asserts the moral right under the Copyright, Designs and Patents Act 1988 to be identified as the author of this work.

All Rights reserved. No part of this publication may be reproduced, stored in a retrieval system or transmitted, in any form or by any means without the prior consent of the author, nor be otherwise circulated in any form of binding or cover other than that which it is published and without a similar condition being imposed on the subsequent purchaser.

ISBN
Paperback ISBN: 978-1-80369-260-9
Hardback ISBN: 978-1-80369-261-6

www.newgeneration-publishing.com

A DEDICATION

I dedicate this book to the memory of Dr Jack Payne MD, the surgeon who first inspired my love of surgery.

ACKNOWLEDGEMENTS

Many different people have helped contribute to my story, and I thank them all. I offer particular thanks to……..
All the teachers and mentors who have helped to shape my life.

Raymond Russell of Tartarus Press for his invaluable early advice.

My cousins Peter, Rosalind and Simon, who have always been at my side with wise advice and support during this long project.

TARGET AUDIENCE

My primary target audience is anyone who aspires to a career in medicine and healthcare, in the hope that my story will inspire them.

My secondary audience is anyone who is not aware, that once upon a time, a career in medicine could also be a load of fun, and the gateway to all sorts of interesting opportunities.

A NOTE ON GLOSSARY AND REFERENCES

Today, through the internet it is possible to obtain data on any subject, in any language, at the touch of a plastic key. No longer is it necessary to peruse thick tomes. Wikipedia and YouTube are both excellent portals to further information about many of the things I have written about, including translations.

CONTENTS

1. THE EARLY YEARS 1
   From choral scholar in Ely cathedral to teenage bomb-maker in the Sussex Weald and embryo fighter pilot in Hampshire

2. SAVANNAH DAYS IN CAMEROUN 1964 25
   From Lewes Grammar to the Collège Protestante and my first taste of Africa. Big game hunting on horseback. My first Caesarian section.

3. JUNGLE DAYS IN CAMEROUN 1965 57
   From how not to hunt elephants to performing my first operations, age 19. Living amongst the pygmies. First dose of malaria. Dinner and prayers with Dr Albert Schweitzer at Lambaréné

4. FROM AFRICA TO LIVERPOOL 1965 – 74 82
   Learning Scouse and Anatomy, Liverpool in the '60s. Taking tea with Tutankahmen, and wine with Charlie Chaplin.

5. TO WAR IN BIAFRA 1968 105
   From playing HighLife jazz with Fela Ransome Kuti in Lagos to gas gangrene and the surgery of war on the eastern battle front

6. CLINICAL YEARS TO FINALS 1968 – 71 123
   The long hard road to Final MB,ChB…. but it did not stop me playing live in the Cavern Club, nor hitch-hiking to Marrakech.

7. EAST TO ARABIA 1971 138
   Hitch-hiking through five countries in 10 weeks, from the Valley of the Kings to the Wailing Wall and beyond

8. DOCTOR AT LARGE - THE HOUSEMAN YEARS 1971 – 74 167
   Your life in my hands, finally. Sleepless nights and endless days

on the wards. A small taste of fame and fortune in the Liverpool nightclubs

9. FROM CAMEROUN TO THE CONGO 1974 – 5................... 194

   Back to Ebolowa as head of Paediatrics…… six to a bed, and two under it……plus much surgery. Then to The Congo as single- handed surgeon and physician to Munangu, King of the Bakuba

10. WEST TO AMERICA 1973... 217

    A caustic taste of consumer society and racism, alcoholic professors, bullets in the brain and my first heart transplant with De Bakey

11. TO KENYA WITH THE FLYING DOCTORS 1975.................. 237

    Surgeon volante in East Africa, a dream come true… my pilot was a beautiful 26-year-old nun. Chasing giraffe from above, how to operate on a crocodile, and the lady with five breasts.

12. BRIGHTON: THE LONG HOT SUMMER OF 1976 267

    When Brighton became Mediterranean, and I became a Fellow of the Royal College of Surgeons

13. THE ROAD TO MOMBASA 299

    Three months overland to Kenya via Iran in revolution and across the Gulf in a dhow to Arabia, and into Mecca by mistake

14. GENERAL SURGERY IN EAST AFRICA 1978 – 81 331

    Surgeon to a million patients, trauma galore and much blood, living with the lions of George Adamson

15. TO LESOTHO AND THE MAGIC MOUNTAINS 1981 – 84..375

    Skiing in Africa, how to build a hospital, ritual murders by the score. Living and working dangerously under apartheid

16. FROM LESOTHO TO LONDON AND TRAGEDY 1984........ 413

    Down and out in London facing a family tragedy. My move from bush surgery to academia and public health

17. FROM TRIBULATION TO TRIUMPH 1986 – 2000 446
    Squeezing triumph from tragedy with HALO and COITIS, and back to general surgery in East Sussex

18. MAKING IT WITH LOS MEDICOS (1) 476
    War surgeon and trainer with MSF in West Africa

19. MAKING IT WITH LOS MEDICOS – (ii) 2007 506
    Third mission with MSF. Not a tourist in sight.

20. EPILOGUE 534
    From Socrates to Hippocrates, Ibn-al-Khatib and the Black Death, via the Quakers to coronavirus.

1.   The Early Years

Prologue

Republic of Cameroun, West Africa. September 4th 1964

It was 3 a.m. and I was mesmerised. Even the scary trip through the dark African night to the hospital had not fazed me for, at the age of just 18 I had been invited to watch my very first operation.

The day before, Tak Braaten, the Director of the Collège had taken me all round the Mission Protestante, introducing me along the way to Dr Nils Carlson the surgeon in charge of the Lutheran hospital at N´Gaoundéré mission. I told Dr Carlsson I hoped to become a surgeon and he immediately took me under his wing. He was a man of his word, and just a few hours later I found myself in the operating suite with him.

"No time to start like now", he said in a thick Norwegian accent as he showed me how to scrub up and clothe myself in theatre greens. I could not quite believe my luck, for on the operating table was a woman in obstructed labour and I was about to witness my first Caesarian Section.

Dr Carlsson made the classic vertical skin incision between the umbilicus and the pubis, and then a horizontal incision into the lower segment of the uterine wall. The gush of blood and amniotic fluid which poured out of the incised uterus was impressive in its volume and colour. Even with the sucker going full bore the floor of the OT was soon awash with blood, and so were we at the operating table. I soon learned that this was normal in a Caesarian section, which was why we were also wearing rubber aprons and wellington boots.

The baby's body emerged, all shiny, the head covered in membranes, half-strangled by the umbilical cord around its neck. A new life begun, and an older life saved, thanks to the power of surgery.

That magical moment, over half a century ago, is as vivid to me now as it was then.

By dawn I had learned what a Duval´s forceps was, and how to use it to clamp off the bleeding edges of the uterine incision, as well as the importance of completely separating the bladder from the lower uterine segment. I had also learned how to suck out the throat and larynx of a new-born baby, allowing it to draw its first breath, which was a lesson that saved many neonatal lives during my years as a tropical surgeon.

When I finally fell into bed, I knew that my dream of becoming a surgeon was the right one, and it remains a path I have never regretted taking.

Nils Carlsson was the first of many surgical mentors, a brave surgeon as well as a generous teacher. It is thanks to him and all the other wonderful teachers I have been privileged to study under that I have enjoyed such a rich and fulfilled life.

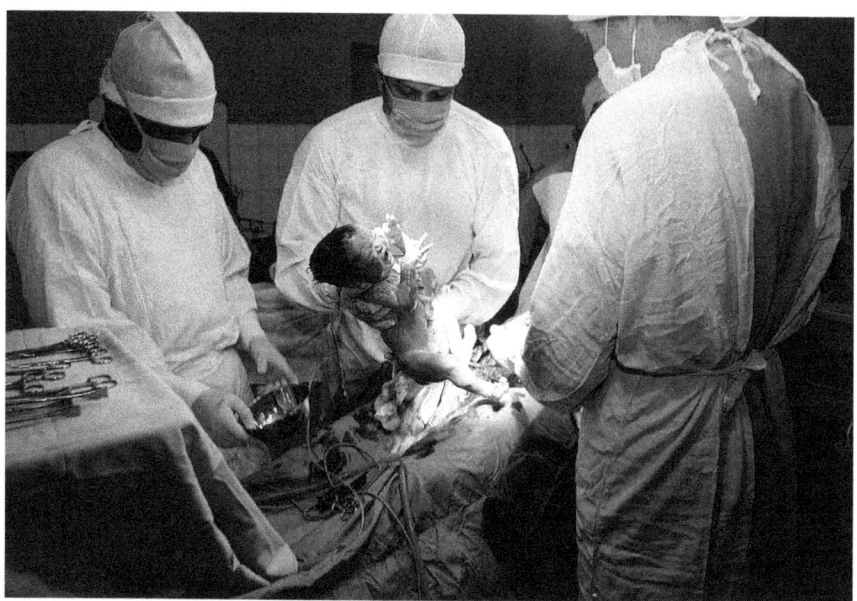

Mannar.2008. Forty-two years later.... my last Caesarian section

My story follows.

Gibraltar 1948.

My first memory: I am a two-year-old boy sitting atop a handcart piled high with oranges, lemons, garlic, and onions as it passed through the Airforce base at Gibraltar, where my father was a senior Royal Air Force officer. The handcart belongs to Carlos, a friendly local vendor who gives me rides and speaks in guttural Spanish. In my mind I can still smell those fruits and see his kindly, weather-beaten face.

I also remember Corporal Moss, my father´s batman. He used to let me ride on the crossbar of his grey Air Force bicycle, a Senior Service cigarette hanging out of his lips, as we careered around the base. He used to make me laugh by putting his fag in his mouth backwards and blowing through it until I choked in the smoke. I can still feel the fear as he leaned the bike over, cornering at quite a lick just to give me a thrill, and me thinking we were bound to fall into the dirt. But we never did.

Romadia was my dark, vivacious Spanish nanny and it was with her that my two sisters and I spent most of our time. It was 1948 and in those post-war days Gibraltar was still a vital outpost of the British Empire with all the trappings of a major military base as well as huge docks. One day Corporal Moss showed me three captured German submarines amongst a fleet of deadly looking British destroyers, frigates, and gun boats, and I was fascinated.

There were parades and receptions my parents attended, along with many high social occasions where the officers wore dress uniform, and the women wore long ball-gowns. I remember my mother looking beautiful in her gown with her stole around her shoulders.
Then, from the Mediterranean to Newquay on the Atlantic coast of Cornwall, where my father was posted to the airfield of St.Mawgan

and Coastal Command. The Cornish peninsula is a peculiar part of Britain, with its massive granite cliffs and wild winds blowing in from the Atlantic. I would make my way home from school along the cliff road with Lizzie, my little sister, and sometimes the Atlantic storms blew so fiercely that we might have been swept over the cliff had not some kindly passing adult taken us in hand.

There were also endless rockpools along the sandy beaches containing a multitude of interesting creatures to entertain us. We spent hours enjoying the Cornish coast as well as swimming in the frigid waters for much of the year. One day my father appeared with a wooden surfboard and thus it was I learned to enjoy the delights of surfing at a very early age. It was a healthy upbringing for us children, even with post-war food shortages and ration books still in use. My father made good use of the RAF camp farm at St Mawgan, and he was able to supplement our diet with fresh fruit and vegetables in between hunting for enemy submarines.

My father flew 4-engined Lancaster bombers and later Shackletons. The noise of their four Rolls Royce Merlins thrilled me. I liked to imagine him in his leather flying helmet, looking for spies and enemy soldiers whilst doing his coastal reconnaissance. At events like Battle of Britain Day in early September, the whole squadron did a fly-past, the massive aircraft flying low over the airfield making the ground below shake, dropping small bombs and blowing up phantom villages. There was a feeling of something majestic and awe-inspiring about these lumbering bombers which has never left me.

My father (second left) was a bomber pilot and navigator

The Seeds of Pyromania

It was at Newquay in 1953 that the first seeds of my pyromania took root. I am not sure what ignited my early interest in flames and explosions at such a young age, but it must have been inherited – probably from my paternal grandfather.

David Livingstone Ramsay had been by all accounts, not just an inventive Victorian engineer, but eccentric to the point of madness and there is good evidence that some of his genes passed on to me.

I was only seven years old when I set fire to a small Cornish forest, known by my mother as 'The Bluebell Wood'. Every weekend in Spring she loved to drive out there to pick bluebells with Frances and Elizabeth, my sisters. I, on the other hand, had more destructive ideas in mind.

With a couple of Swan Vesta matches I soon had a minor

conflagration going, which pleased me greatly, until I could see it begin to spread uncontrollably. Small fir trees were even exploding as my mother arrived, looking somewhat vexed, with my two sisters in tow.

"You're going to get into trouble", was Frances's contribution to this festive scene.

"Daddy's going to be very angry", said Lizzie, as my mother rushed around beating out flames. They were not wrong, and I went to bed that night with bread, water and a sore backside.

Soon afterwards, with great ease I successfully set fire to the family coal bunker, which burned quite merrily until father arrived. Once again it was my own arse which was later burning, after a dose of the old man's version of CBT – Corrective Behavioural Therapy, and it was not the last time. I received countless beatings from my old man during my formative years, but I forgive him every one, for as often as not he was justified. Some of my relatives have even suggested that I was a 'difficult child'.

1953. Officers Married Quarters, Medmenham. With Lizzie and Frances. We were a typical, aspiring, middle-class family

On Becoming Educated

I began my formal education at Crantock Street Primary School in Newquay and it was there that I started to learn about Music. My singing lessons began under the tutelage of the jovial Canon Peake, the rector at St Michael's church. These would prepare me for a choral scholarship to an English public school. This was the dream and aspiration of my very middle-class parents, that I should have a 'proper' education in such an environment, far away from the 'oiks' of downtown Newquay. Their great hope was that this would make a gentleman of me.

I did get the choral scholarship, but I'm still not too sure about the outcome, though it was certainly modified by the books I devoured at that time.

You could not read of the timeless adventures of Beau Geste and Biggles without stimulating that inherent manly sense of derring-do, dangerous desperados and destruction. These were the adventure stories we were brought up on during the 1950's and '60's. There was also Bulldog Drummond and Jock of the Veld, each one a brave hero and role model to a youth like me. In later years I also took up with Flashman, the product of George MacDonald Fraser's powerful imagination, and possibly the greatest hero of them all as he fought and fornicated his way around the world. As spell-binding accounts of the evolution of the British Empire during the 19th century the adventures of Flashman are hard to beat. I believe they should be included in the History syllabus of every school. It was these books which became my companions when I left Newquay in 1955 for the flat fens of Ely and five years as a choral scholar in that massive cathedral.

Choral scholar at Ely

I still remember my mother, standing alone on Platform 2 at Newquay railway station, her face damp with tears, as I struggled to wedge an enormous pig-skin case and my wooden tuck box onto the carriage seat. At the age of just eight years that was the last I saw of my family for over four months.

When I arrived at Liverpool Street station hours later a kindly porter helped me to extricate my massive baggage from the carriage and dump it onto the platform. I was both amazed and terrified at the masses of people I saw everywhere around me, scurrying up and down the platform, shouting for porters and waving their umbrellas. I had never seen the like before, and the scene reminded me of images of Bedlam I had seen in books. I had never felt so alone.

It was at the ticket barrier that my Uncle George met me and probably saved me from a terrible fate. He became my London saviour over the next five years meeting me off the trains to and from Ely to Newquay and introducing me to his wife, Aunt Chris and their three children at 33, Westhill Road, Wandsworth as well as showing me some of the wonders of London town. One day he even took me into the Houses of Parliament. He was married to my father's elder sister, Christiana, and they had three children, my cousin Roger, who sadly died prematurely, his sister Rosalind and their little brother, Cousin Peter. And we three have been friends ever since.

This frightening and traumatic rupture in my young life, removed from my immediate family at the age of eight years, was considerably softened by the love and kindness of Chris and George, to whom I am always indebted. It also engendered in me an early sense of independence and travel which has never left me.

As well as learning the theory of music and how to sing canticles correctly in Ely cathedral, I was also honing my skills as an inventor and troublemaker.

1957 Ely. Choral scholar and embryo pyromaniac

Together with my best friend Swabs, we would spend weeks creating KielKraft model aeroplanes, constructed of balsa wood and doped paper. Then we would go up the West tower of the cathedral, some 200 feet high, and set fire to them as we launched them over the ecclesiastical dwellings and the Canonry, which was our House at the Kings School, Ely.

This amusing form of entertainment came to an abrupt end one July evening in 1959 as I celebrated the completion of the Dolphin, a 36-inch wingspan glider with a bird-like dihedral to the wing and a fuselage curved in the sagittal plane which actually did make this glider look quite similar to a dolphin. It had taken me three months to construct and was the best plane I ever made.

Together with Swabs and a few other choristers we climbed the hundreds of steps up to the West tower after evensong in our cassocks, clutching this flying work of art. In the pocket of my blue cassock, I also had my tinderbox. All true heroes carried tinderboxes, from Biggles to Flashman, and I was no exception. It was an old tobacco tin, sequestered from my father, which I still possess. It contained inside all the requirements to produce fire and explosions. There was a big ball of cotton wool and a vial of surgical spirit – these recovered from Sister Cotton´s extensive First Aid box in the Canonry. There was also a small tin of gunpowder, created from a mixture of bangers and Swan Vesta matches.

When we stood breathless on the lead roof looking down onto the comfortable accommodations of the Dean, the Bishop, the Precentor and all the other religious acolytes and hangers-on, there was a palpable sense of expectation as we imagined the flaming glider cruising gently down above the gilded gables of the priests who so loved to play with us in the showers during Choristers Holidays.

I took a small ball of cotton wool and pulled it onto the tow-hook of the glider. Then, a few drops of surgical spirit, and it was Swabs who had the honour of lighting this as I launched the Dolphin over the castellated wall of the tower.

She flew just like a bird at first, until the growing cloud of flame began to interfere with the structural aerodynamics. Then its flight took a turn for the worse as it spun onto the left wing and began its final plunge earthwards in an incandescent ball of fire which careered drunkenly straight for a window in the side of the bishop´s mansion, disappearing within to the sound of shattering glass.

"God Almighty!", said Nigel, who later became one of the original King´s Singers, "that was impressive".

"I say", said Swabs, ever tactful even in those early days, "we could be in trouble".

"Let's go", said I, and we scarpered down those hundreds of stairs, rushing through the graveyard by St Etheldreda´s chapel to gain the south wall of the Canonry, and the freezing granite cell which was our dormitory. It was not five minutes before we heard the sound of sirens outside, and only a minute later when the door of the dormitory burst open to expose the livid face of 'Slipper' Crowe, our very physical assistant housemaster.

"Everyone out of bed and feet on the floor" came his brusque command, and it was only when I saw 19 pairs of striped pyjamas and my own bright blue cassock that, with sinking heart I realized that I was in a spot of bother once again.

It was shortly after this painful episode that I was invited to attend Lewes County Grammar School for Boys. My mother said it was because my voice had broken, my father gave me another dose of corporal just in case it wasn't. Covey-Crump, my genial housemaster whom we all thought wise, shook my hand as we said goodbye, and shared his wisdom with me. "You could do well", he said, "but if you carry on setting fire to bishops and other servants of the Lord, you will only find yourself in more trouble", which proved to be exactly the case.

I bade a fond farewell to Swabs, who still remains my oldest schoolboy friend from those Ely days. I said goodbye to the green fields around the Deanery where we had played rugby and cricket for five good years in the shadow of that huge cathedral, now more than 700 years old, where I had learned two things of great value, Latin and Music. Thus it was that I left the privileged ranks of the upper classes and joined the more earthy fraternity of the local grammar school in Lewes, East Sussex.

An Introduction to Practical Physics

Public school days were over for me, and it was back to East Sussex where my father had now retired from the RAF to become a gentleman farmer on a small farm 10 miles north of Eastbourne. This is where I grew up and enjoyed some of my most memorable childhood experiences.

Newly arrived also was a baby brother, 10 years after my little sister Elizabeth, with my mother now in her 40´s. Undoubtably a fractured condom, for both my parents had seemed non-plussed at this unplanned pregnancy.

It was great fun for all three of us older kids to have a baby brother. The girls could play real-life dolls with him, and I could use him in my evolving experiments with physics, electricity and high explosives. That´s the thing about little kids. They are naturally curious, so Mark was always a naïve and eager subject for my advancing experiments.

When Sid Pierce, our chain-smoking Physics master introduced our 'O'-level class to Ohm´s Law, I was already working on a primitive form of electro-detonation for my home-made bombs and rockets. It was shortly afterwards that Mark, aged five, found himself in the woodshed with me one afternoon, connected to the high-voltage terminal of the magneto on one of the old man's antique mowing machines. When I kicked the engine over it was quite amazing to see my little brother's hair rise vertically as his howl split the tranquil air.

So that was what high-tension voltage was really about.

Sid Pierce´s pathetic experiment in the Physics lab had nothing on the sparkling, shrieking sight in front of me. The massive electric shock I had just given my little bro almost certainly fused a few central neurons, because he has never mentioned this great experiment again. It may come as some surprise that Mark and I are still the best of buddies, some 60 years later. But in those intervening years he has become a lot wiser to my ways.

Mark took over the farm where we all grew up after our parents retired to Eastbourne some 30 years ago, and we have seen yet one more generation grow up in this beautiful Sussex valley, all enjoying the same healthy atmosphere which we four kids all enjoyed back in the ′50s and 60s - the woods, the fields and vales of East Sussex, the lake where we have all fished over the years. The barn owl roosting in a huge old oak tree bordering the lake and the squirrels, who my brother hates, for the damage they cause on the farm. But I find them hilarious as they jump like acrobats from tree to tree on the far side of the lake.

East Sussex was a wonderful part of Britain to grow up in during those post-war years and is still always a pleasure to revisit during my rare forays from the Spanish Costa Tropical where I now live. Every time I do come back to England you will find me and Mark, fishing rods in one hand, a pint of Harveys in the other, looking over the lake, half-covered with the yellow and white lilies my mother sowed over 60 years ago, both of us at perfect peace with the world.

1962. Deanlands Farm. We led a healthy, outdoor life

On Teenage Sex in the Countryside

I am not sure whether it is more dangerous for a teenager to grow up in the country than the city. All I can say is that on a farm there are endless opportunities for all sorts of escapades, without much chance of being caught, and I took full advantage.

My mother was an intelligent and aspiring woman. In order to supplement the family income, through the Classified section in *'The Lady'* she started to invite foreign children who were studying in English schools to spend their school holidays at 'Deanlands Farm', whilst learning English, and other British social skills.

Thus, it was that a steady file of really beautiful, sophisticated young ladies, as well as the occasional youth, began spending months at a time with us. George was a boarder at King's School, Canterbury, whose parents were in the diplomatic service in Nigeria, and he became a long-time stayer and a good friend of mine. During school holidays there were sometimes 12 of us at the old oak dining table at Deanlands farmhouse. It was roast beef on Sundays, lots of healthy outdoor activities - and the chance to go fishing and boating on the lake with me, especially the girls.

Something was stirring inside me. Hormones were circulating in my 15-year-old body which were quietly turning me from an innocent young arsonist into a sexual predator.

I had been busy building tree houses and fortresses in various oak trees around the farm during my many free moments. There was one at the side of the lake where we pitched the tent every summer, but the best one was in a big oak tree in the Stream field, where it bordered on the Lake field. I had spent hours and days perfecting this hidden refuge in the canopy of old oaks which bordered the Stream field. I had even created a fantastic, retrievable ladder made of ivy vines and cut branches, and there were three spy holes in the floor of pine planks which I had relocated from Pa's store in the piggery.

When the Icelandic maidens arrived to learn English, things began to get a bit out of hand. Hilde was the first of my severe problems, for she was far more of a predator than I. She was 15 years old, blonde and beautiful, with a never-ending smile, sensuous thick lips, and a sense of innocence which was nothing to do with the puritanical British.

"Can we go fishing in the lake?", she asked so sweetly, on Day Two after her arrival at Deanlands Farm.

And that was how, some 30 minutes later I was to be found in the Tree House, charged up with testosterone, languishing in the arms of Hilde when I received the shock of my life.

"Are you there?", came the thunderous voice of my father.

Cripes!! Gadzooks!! This was a real crisis. Minutes passed before the angry farmer moved off, leaving me and Hilde speechless with fear.

I was not looking forward to the near future.

Sure enough, I was sitting in the playroom next to the grape conservatory, a dusty tome of Practical Biology on my knees when the old man burst in and shouted, "Where's that child?", then gave me such a whack around the head from which I have still not properly recovered.

On Becoming a Teenage Pilot

My parents became so concerned at my predatory behaviour that I was banished to Uncle Dave's pig farm in Hampshire for two weeks. He was my father's elder brother and was a flying instructor at Thruxton airfield as well as the owner of a luxuriant, tobacco-stained, standard RAF moustache, and a large herd of fat pigs.

He and Aunt Cherry lived in an old, thatch-roofed cottage hidden in the Hampshire hills not far from Andover. When I arrived, they did not even have any mains electricity, but a series of beautiful oil lamps illuminated their comfortable abode. It was their smell which greeted me every morning as Uncle Dave cooked up a fearsome full English breakfast, including home-cured bacon and sausages, whilst listening to BBC Radio 4. It was he who introduced me the 'The Archers', a programme I still occasionally enjoy.

Knowing of my unfortunate circumstances, he offered me a deal. If I mucked out the pigs every day, he would lend me his old RAF bike to ride to the pub at Cholderton every night and he would also take me flying and go-karting. Which is how, at the age of 15, I came to be piloting a De Havilland 'Jackaroo' biplane.

In the mid-1950's the Jackaroo company, based at Thruxton, developed this strange variant of the original De Havilland Tiger Moth. It had a widened fuselage with four seats and a dual-control system. I was the pilot in control as Uncle Dave and I flew over the thatched roof of 'Curlews', his farmhouse, waving at Aunt Cherry in the garden. It was a thrilling moment, the precursor to many others, and I could never thank Uncle Dave enough for introducing me to the joys of manned flight.

Thruxton had been a World War 2 airfield and was still used for training pilots, but a go-kart racing track had recently been developed on part of the runway, and that is where I learned the thrills of karting. As an entrée into the world of speed it was unbeatable, and whilst there was little chance of death or injury, there was always enough to make it exciting.

One day at Thruxton, Uncle Dave took me into one of the original hangars, a huge, black tin construction. Inside were three of the most beautiful planes in the world. The De Havilland Mosquito, a twin-engine monoplane, which I already knew much about from my readings. It was a very fast fighter-bomber with twin Merlin Mk 23 or 25's to power it. These three aeroplanes were still in perfect condition, under covers, having been requisitioned by the RAF during the Suez Crisis, but never called on.

Uncle Dave lent me his leather flying helmet and let me sit inside one, in the pilot's seat. He could well imagine the thrill I was feeling as I swung the control column and leant on the red firing button, blasting the four 20mm Hispano cannons into the approaching enemy. Dave was a great uncle in every sense.

After two weeks in Wiltshire, not only was I in great physical shape, with visible biceps after shovelling uncountable tons of pig manure, but I was an embryo pilot and a possible Formula 1 champion. Looking back, I can see that my stimulating two weeks with Uncle Dave were to play a major part in the rest of my life. I was really sorry to leave Dave and Cherry, who had given me such a good time – even though it was supposed to be part of a punishment regime.

The luscious young girls were still on the farm when I got back, but this time I kept my distance, fearing more parentally induced brain damage. Instead, George and I started to develop water-launched rockets, whilst I recounted my recent exciting adventures in Wiltshire with Uncle Dave.

In retrospect, I would advise parents to think carefully before inviting female teenagers from Mexico, Sweden, Germany and Iceland into their houses where teenage sons may be lurking.

Other Teenage Diversions

Apart from the girls, there was also booze to be had at the War-Bil-in-Tun just a mile up the road at the tiny hamlet of Warbleton, which derived its name from the halberd in a barrel which was the pub's logo, from where Bert Sellins dispensed pints of Harvey's Best from wooden firkins. I drank my first glass of mild ale there aged 13, in the company of my school friend, Nick Russell after choir practice one Friday night.

In those early days this hidden rustic ale house was just a tiny, plank-floored room in the shadow of St Mary's Church, Warbleton, and the bar always had a tall jar of Ma Sellins pickled eggs fermenting on top.

She ran the kitchen, where there was a Rayburn wood-fired stove on top of which there was always a broody hen sitting on a hessian sack with a clutch of eggs to hatch. I found this most amusing back then, but today that gentle, country mode of life is history.

Bert Sellins has now passed on. His pub has evolved into a place where the local burghers come to fill their bellies with locally sourced, organic, gluten-free dishes at some considerable price, affordable only to the richer inhabitants of south-east England. But Mark and I still always go and have a pint there when I am back, just for old time´s sake.

As well as beer, there was song and dance every Tuesday night up at the Goward Hall outside Heathfield, which was our local Youth Club. That is where I learned to love Chubby Checker and The Twist. And there was also Janet, the sloe-eyed daughter of the local estate agent. I used to cycle up five miles of hills just to touch her immaculate body, and bike home with an over-dose of testosterone.

We all need a special pal, especially during those fragile formative years, and in George I found the perfect partner for my pranks.

I always looked forward to the arrival of George during the holidays, for he was a willing accomplice to my various home-entertainment projects. His parents always gave him excellent birthday and Christmas presents, which included the Jettex rocket-powered boat one year - 'the fastest boat in the world for its size', as it was advertised. With it came rolls of fine Jettex fuse-wire to ignite the tiny rocket engine. This fuse wire was also perfect for igniting my own rockets and bombs.

Christmas 1961, and a two-metre-long box from Harrods arrived for George. "I hope that is not what I think it is", said my mother. But her hopes were dashed, for it was indeed a beautiful BSA Meteor .22 air-rifle with telescopic sights that George unwrapped on Christmas Day.

After a stupendous Christmas lunch, topped off with the alcoholic

Christmas pudding which mother and Frances had concocted George and I went upstairs to further investigate his new gun, whilst Pa sank into his siesta in front of the glowing log fire in the dining room.

It took us an hour to read through the instructions, and more time to prepare the rifle and set up the sights, but finally we were ready. Directly opposite our bedroom window was the cowhouse with its ancient small windows, half of which were already damaged or missing.

"I´ll aim for the centre one", I told George, and pulled the trigger. This was followed by the sound of shattering glass, swiftly accompanied by the enraged voice of my father who, having awoken from his siesta, had been milking Jester, our placid Jersey cow. "How was I to know?", I asked George mutely.

The rifle was confiscated for a week, and I went to bed with an achingly full stomach and blazing buttocks once again.

One week later, George and I took the Meteor down to the Stream field for a bit of target practice in order to set the sights once again on this powerful weapon, the target this time being me.

I had chalked a target onto the back of my gaberdine mac, which I had stylishly cut short to waist length. George stood at the gate while I strode 50 paces towards the stream, then shouted "Fire". I should not have been so surprised when the lead slug missed the shortened gaberdine mac and tore through my jeans into my left buttock, which was still recovering from a recent dose of CBT from my father.

I screeched and jumped around like a psychotic rabbit at the pain. Only a miracle prevented fatal septicaemia after George´s amateur efforts to retrieve the bullet with my rusty penknife. I was sitting on my right buttock only in class 5B for several weeks afterwards.

I am still not quite sure whether it was just down to George´s poor aim.

1964. On the Road to Adventure

At Lewes County Grammar school, we were fortunate to have good teachers dedicated to turning us into useful citizens. The facilities were excellent, including a big new gymnasium, two rugby fields, a swimming pool and even two tennis courts. Sport and exercise were an important part of our curriculum, even extending to night patrols and sleeping out on the Downs during a weekend's 'wide games', as they were called. I enjoyed all these outdoor activities and became competent in reading a map and setting a compass course and other survival techniques, all of which later proved invaluable skills during my years of travel.

Early in 1964 during my final year at school a competition was announced, open to all sixth formers. The simple aim was to get as far from Lewes as possible – and back again, in teams of two during the course of one week during the Easter holidays, and to present a log of the journey for scrutiny. Pete Hill and I formed a team, and duly set off with high hopes and £10 in our pockets. We hitch-hiked towards London, which we reached quite late at night, hungry and damp. Neither of us knew anything about London and we had no idea where we were going to sleep, so when I spotted an open door, we entered and found ourselves in a richly furnished room. Thinking no further we both collapsed exhausted into sleep on top of a large Persian carpet.

Breakfast with the Lord Mayor of London

My first vision as I awoke was of a pair of highly polished black, patent leather boots. These belonged to the butler of the Lord Mayor of London, into whose chambers we had unwittingly strayed. He had brought us two cups of tea, as well as an invitation from the Lord Mayor to have breakfast with him. The Mayor was highly amused when he heard our story, and it was his own writing which covered the first page of our journey log which he then stamped with his impressive seal.

That was just the beginning of our good fortune. Three days later we slept the night inside the Edinburgh barracks of the Argyll and Sutherland Highlanders and had breakfast with the Colonel before we headed back to Lewes. He also wrote some encouraging words in our log, stamping them to prove their authenticity. Back in Lewes, after examination of our journey log, which I had written every day in ´real time´, Pete and I were awarded the prize, and our adventure was even reported in the East Sussex Gazette and Herald.

I am sure that it was these educational opportunities which also helped to form my character. The freedom and responsibilities we were given at Lewes Grammar allowed us to evolve from children into adults, whilst still enjoying life.

On Music

It was my mother who first instilled in me a love for music, and it was she who propelled me to Ely cathedral. All choral scholars were obliged to learn a musical instrument – but only the piano or violin, neither of which interested me. I bought my first guitar with the royalties we were given from the first LP the choir made, and before I left Ely we already had a primitive form of skiffle group on the go. The guitar was the instrument for me. I had no serious interest in classical church music, but a great deal of interest in rock and roll.

After my years as a choral scholar at Ely I was adopted into the school choir at Lewes, which was another important component of the school in those days. At that time the choir was considered good enough to be invited every year to sing with the chorus inside the world-famous Glyndebourne opera house. But what mostly impressed us schoolboys at Glyndebourne were the lines of Rolls-

Royces and Bentleys and the champagne and caviar picnics which the guests were enjoying.

Music was still in my bones, and it was during my 6th form years that we started a rock and roll group. My friend Pete Hill was a natural lead guitarist and even made his own beautiful copy of an early Fender during the woodwork class. I played rhythm guitar and sang vocals. We also had a tea-chest bass. Tragically, I was prevented from ever becoming a teenage sensation as the group members declared that my voice was 'too posh' and banned me from singing. After five years at public school, I really did speak posh, and inside the grammar school I stood out on account of that expensively gained accent.

Friday evenings after school Pete, Barry, Ronuk and I used to go down to the Cliffe High Street in Lewes and take coffee in The Polar Bear café, a revolutionary coffee bar in those days. The coffee was grey and insipid and came in brown glass Duralex (or Durex as we liked to call them) cups. It had the first juke box I had ever seen. I used to always play Lonnie Donnegan singing 'The Rock Island Line' at 6d a shot. Then we would get into Ronuk's mother's Mini for the ride home.

The Mini was yet another British revolution in 1964. Issigonis had designed a wonder for the travelling public. It even had a radio which occasionally crackled into life, and being a Mark 1, it had the weird long, bent gear lever. The freedom that it gave us turned me on to motors forever.

My father's younger brother, Arthur was a second-hand car salesman in Esher, and it was he who got me my first motorbike when I was just 14 years old. I have rarely been without a motorbike ever since. 60 years later I still enjoy doing the ton on my 600F Suzuki Bandit up the old Granada Road. When I wind her up to 7000 revs we are doing 160 kms an hour, and all I can hear is the banshee wail of four cylinders going flat out as the force of the wind tries to tear me off the bike. That is what I mean by a cheap thrill.

Going out with a Bang!

Late summer in 1964 there was a big celebration party at Deanlands Farm, Vines Cross, to which were invited a dozen of my school mates. We had finished our 'A-levels' and our schooldays were over. For most of us our next step was university.

Four years earlier I had stepped out of the cinema in Hailsham having just seen 'The World of Suzie Wong', somehow magically knowing I was going to become a surgeon. That germ had lain dormant since then but was always there. I had serious plans for medical school, but before that I had decided to explore a bit more of the world and was shortly off to Cameroun Republic in West Africa with Voluntary Services Overseas to spend one year working as a teacher in a college.

The party we had that night was a memorable gathering of friends. Much ale was drunk and charred meat consumed, and as a grand finale I blew up the dead oak tree at the corner of the lake where we were all camped out. But once again I had over-cooked the goose.

The bomb was amongst the most powerful I had yet made and consisted of a one-foot length of two-inch diameter copper tubing. I had packed inside a mixture of sodium chlorate, ammonium nitrate with magnesium and aluminium powder, which gave a great flare to the explosion. My last bit of Jettex fuse wire spluttered as I thrust the bomb into the empty starling's nest inside the hollow trunk, and then there was silence.

Oh God! I thought. If the fuse had failed, then things could get very dangerous indeed. But to my huge relief a sheet of flame suddenly appeared at the base of the tree. This was followed by a massive explosion and a sudden storm of fractured wood, flaming branches and debris flying across our campsite. Fortunately, everyone was already horizontal on the ground, comfortably inebriated beside the empty firkin of Harvey´s Best, and nobody was injured. But the tree had disappeared and as I slid into coma, I could hear its carcass still crashing into the still waters of the lake. At that moment I was too happy and too drunk to care.

Two days later, whilst the rest of the gang were still celebrating the end of their school days, I was to be found, stripped to the waist, half-buried in the dank waters of the lake, armed with only a small hand saw, attacking the multitudinous branches of the recently deceased oak tree. As my father had so wisely stated to me the next morning, following my rather pale explanation, "It may well have been a lightning strike, as you say, dear son. However, whether it was God or the Devil, we now have fire-wood for the coming winter – on the understanding that you will cut every piece to size for the fire". And with that my father strode off to milk the two cows who provided the daily provender for our family.

It was the end of my secondary school days, where at Lewes Grammar I had gained an enduring interest in all the Natural Sciences as well as making some life-long friends. It was also the end of my daily existence at the farm where I had enjoyed a wonderful childhood, as well as learning a few vital things about Life.

Looking back on my early years I am still not sure why I did so many crazy things, many of which were dangerous. Only last year, Lizzie said to me, "I am amazed that you are still alive", and she had a point. It was not just a case of thumbing my nose at authority, but more a desire to explore the universe and all it had to offer. Yet throughout these stimulating formative years I never lost my dream of becoming a surgeon.

As I sawed my way through the oak tree I was ruminating on the years of childish pranks and fun I had enjoyed on the farm, whilst regretting that very soon these simple childhood pleasures were all coming to an end. In two weeks' time I was to be on an aeroplane, bound for West Africa for a year with Voluntary Service Overseas as a school teacher in the Republic of Cameroun.

It was to be the first of many voyages to the Dark Continent.

2. SAVANNAH DAYS IN CAMEROUN 1964

To Africa

Barely a month after leaving Lewes County Grammar School for Boys I found myself sitting in an Air France DC-6 bound for West Africa. It was the beginning of an adventure that was to change my life.

I was planning on going to medical school but felt a strong compulsion to learn more about the wider world before I started my medical studies. It was not to be some commercialized gap year, but a branch of the Ministry of Overseas Development, Voluntary Service Overseas which provided the means.

In 1964 it was still possible to leave school not knowing much, and then spend a year in a far-away land working with people and taking on responsibilities which would have stretched a full-grown man.

Thus, at the same moment my old school friends were starting their university studies I found myself heading in the opposite direction, south and east to Africa.

I bade farewell to my parents at Heathrow, and in a brand-new tropical suit set off for Paris. It was to be the first stop on my three-day voyage to the Republic of Cameroun, West Africa where I was to become a ´professor´ at the College Protestante, N'Gaoundéré at the tender age of 18.

Tripoli. Libya. 03.09.64

The DC-6 was a piston-powered aircraft. When it touched down just as the sun was setting after a 6-hour flight from Orly airport every passenger was still shaking to the throb of the four Rolls-Royce engines as we disembarked into the hot air of Tripoli airport. There I was met by the VSO representative, a kindly chap called Mr Bennett who gave me a bed for the night.

I was used to waking up at my parents' farm in East Sussex to the clarion call of Bilko the cockerel, but next door to Mr Bennett's residence was a mosque, and the amplified call to prayer at 5 a.m. was quite a shock to my system. It was impossible to sleep so I made my way outside and into the awakening streets of Tripoli.

The sights and sounds which greeted me and the smell of exotic spices cooking over charcoal fires on the streets were a world away from East Sussex. The men were in flowing white robes and kaffiyahs, the women covered in hijab or burkhas. It was easy to imagine I was in Arabia rather than the Maghreb. I knew no Arabic but by the time I returned to the house I had already learned my first word, *'Inshallah!'*, the exhortation to God, which I still use today.

I found I had a full day to spend in Tripoli before the onward flight to Fort Lamy in Chad. Mr Bennett was kind enough to spend the day taking me on a grand tour of this ancient north African city where he had lived for four years. Of all the wonderful sights I saw that day the Grand Mosque was the most impressive, and in some way reminded me of Ely Cathedral where I had been a choral scholar for five years. The grandeur and the extraordinary decoration with Islamic tiles were something I had never seen before except in a book and made me realize that there was another world outside that of the white, Anglo-Saxon protestants who ruled the remnants of the British Empire in those days.

The Phoenicians founded Tripoli during the 7th century BC and since then it had been ruled by the Romans, Vandals, Arabs, Spanish, the Knights of St John, the Ottoman Turks and Italians. It also became the base for the Barbary pirates during the 18th century and most recently it was a main base for the Allied forces during World War 2. So it really was an ancient city with a long history. I had never seen such a rich variety of buildings in so many different styles, from Ottoman palaces to the modern villas where the rich people and diplomats lived, and a multitude of mosques stretching their minarets to the sky.

I was also introduced to the delights of Arabian cuisine, enjoying couscous, the subtle cumin-flavoured falafel, and shish-kebabs cooked over an open fire. I enjoyed every moment in this new environment and was already looking forward to more new sights when we took off in a DC-4 the next morning, heading south to Chad.

The flight over the Sahara desert was interminable, just miles and miles of nothing but sand until we landed in the blazing heat of Fort Lamy, the capital of Chad now known as N'Djamena. It was a town straight out of Beau Geste, with French legionnaires in kepis marching around amidst the fantastically attired Africans from every corner of the Sahara.

There were Touaregs, their faces hidden by huge indigo turbans, leading long trains of camels and donkeys laden with blocks of salt and goat-skins full of water, as well as dried fish from Lake Chad which stank abominably. Ebony black negroes were everywhere, some dressed in fine robes, but the majority were wearing rags. They were all shouting in strange dialects and laughing as they carried their loads and wheeled their primitive handcarts through the teeming streets splattered with manure.

Standing out above the buildings was the Fort, a colonial structure housing the French Camel Corps with a castellated wall holding ancient cannon poking out into the desert and stables for all the camels.

Having been brought up on Biggles and Beau Geste I quite expected to see these heroic characters as I walked mesmerized amongst these wonderfully attired desert warriors on their camels, all of whom carried large leather holsters bearing long rifles. The only camels I had seen before had been locked up in a zoo, so it was impressive to be in a place where most of the transport seemed to be by camel. There were hundreds of them all over the place, snorting and spitting as they were led along, often by a child who barely came up to the camel´s knee.

On the west flank of the fort was the camel market which I briefly visited. It was like a huge gypsy encampment with a thousand tethered animals, goats and donkeys as well as the ubiquitous camels and a mass of shady tents under which were gathered families cooking over open fires. One of these families invited me in and soon I was sharing fermented camel milk and millet gruel with these people I had never met before. I found this wherever I travelled in Africa. However poor the people, they were always generous and always kind to me, a stranger from a strange land.

The French arrived here in the late 19th century and by 1920 Chad had become the largest colony in French Equatorial Africa. There was still a lot of French influence to be seen, from ancient Citroen lorries to the smell of Gauloise, the cigarettes my mother used to smoke. Most of Chad is desert with a population then existing on subsistence farming of maize, millet and pulses and the export of salted fish from Lake Chad. But there were also economic reasons for the French presence, most of them lying below the Saharan sands, including uranium, tungsten and other strategic minerals. There was also talk of Total hunting for petroleum under those desert sands.

It seemed that the further south into the Sahara we flew, the more we left any trace of familiar civilization behind. When the ancient DC-3 arrived to take the few of us travellers on the last leg south to N'Gaoundéré in the north of Cameroun I knew that I really was in Wonderland, for this old battle-horse was no normal passenger plane. It was divided into two separate halves; up front we were 10, and I was the only white person amongst my colourful travelling companions. Behind us swinging gently from a beam were the eviscerated carcasses of 13 cattle, sheep and goats. There was no evident refrigeration and as the ambient temperature on the tarmac of Fort Lamy was approaching 40 Centigrade, the atmosphere inside the plane was ripe to say the least.

In the front seat sat someone who I felt must have been a chief of some sort. He was swathed in a rich, red robe and had a white turban the size of a small tower around his head. I noticed that all the other passengers deferred to him, and when we landed some hours later at N'Gaoundéré under a late afternoon sun I saw a huge phalanx of mounted warriors, each one with a long lance, ride out and surround the plane. As we descended behind this grand old man these dusky cavaliers reared their horses up onto their hind legs and gave a mighty salute.

I later found out that this royal salute was known as the *'Défile'*, and these grandly attired chevaliers were the royal guard of the Emir of N'Gaoundéré, who indeed had been the old chap with the turban.

Welcoming the Emir - the 'Défile' at N'Gaoundéré

And that is how I became a friend of the Emir, spending many of my free hours exploring northern Cameroun on the back of one of his fine Arabian steeds. The old man was intrigued to know what such a young *mzungu* was doing in his town and was delighted to know I had come for a year to teach at the Collège Protestante.

Even though he was a Mohammedan Fulani and the spiritual leader of the mosque and several Koranic schools in the town, he also had respect for the two Christian missions in N'Gaoundéré. These were the Catholic College Mazenod and my own Collège Protestante which also ran the Hôpital Protestante, a most valuable resource in this remote community at the interface of the Bantu Christian and *animist* south and the Nilo-Hamitic peoples of the Moslem north.

When I hitch-hiked into Nigeria later that year, I was interested to note that the same historic divide occurred. The Christian Yorubas and Ibos in the south were separated from the Muslim Hausas and Fulanis in the north by the mighty Niger river flowing east from the southern Guinea highlands. However, during the last century the French and British colonialists had chosen to re-define these natural boundaries, and in so doing had divided families, tribes and whole cultures in their search for economic and political dominance.

N'Gaoundére, Northern Cameroun, West Africa. September 1964

Tak Braaten, who was waiting to meet me was the director of the Collège Protestante and its 84 pupils, which was run under the evangelical auspices of the American-Norwegian Lutheran mission. It was here that I passed some of the most agreeable months of my life up until then. It was my introduction to the magical world of the Dark Continent, and I could not have been in a better place.

N'Gaoundéré was not only well north of the sweaty southern jungles but was also nearly 1000 metres above sea-level, so the climate was perfect, and in those days the seasonal rains were like they had always been. Incredibly, during the small rains of autumn the rain arrived on the dot at 1400hrs every day. It was usually a short downpour, but its constant regularity I found astonishing after the unpredictable weather of England.

I was to be lodged with the mission dentist, Kjeld, who was the only other bachelor on the mission compound. The house was a simple single-storey block with two bedrooms, a kitchen with a wood-fired range and a bucket shower which invariably ran out leaving me half-covered in soap.

It was inside the kitchen the first night that I had my first encounter with that marvel of the animal world, the cockroach. They crunched under my feet as I entered the kitchen and when I looked around there were literally hundreds of these 'beetles' covering every surface. I was even more shocked to see tiny nematode worms wriggling out of the body of one crushed cockroach. It was my first sight of parasitic worms, but not my last.

My mother ran a spotless household, so it came as a shock to find myself sharing my abode with such house mates. And the roaches were not the only insects I met that night. When I switched on the meagre bedroom light, I suddenly started having to dodge massive flying torpedoes which made a sound like a machine gun as they crashed blindly around the room. It was my introduction to the world of *dudus* as they are known in Swahili. These are the flying insects which populate the African nights, usually heading for any source of light, many of them carrying nasty disease such as 'Nairobi eye', malaria and dengue fever. It was certainly not what I had been used to during the frigid evenings on the farm in East Sussex.

When I walked outside to Tak's house where I was to dine that first evening, I was startled to see what appeared to be a large rock moving across my path. Closer examination proved this to be a huge snail. I had never seen such an animal in my life before. This is just how it was being in Africa. Every single sensation was a revelation to me, but I was thirsty for it all. I fell asleep that first night on the Dark Continent, far from home, but happy and full of exciting dreams.

The next morning, I awoke to brilliant sunshine and a clear blue sky, and a smell so sweet I have never forgotten it. Outside my bedroom window was growing a big shrub with many creamy white flowers, from which emanated this beautiful scent. Kjeld taught me many things during my stay with him, and the first was the name of this remarkable plant. The fragrance of frangipani still ranks with ylang-ylang as the scent I would want in my nostrils when I eventually take my last breath on planet Earth.

The town itself was a marvel to me. It was a mixture of beautiful traditional architecture and tin sheds. Koran schools were taking place on the sidewalks, goats and donkeys were patrolling the streets, some of them completely hidden by their loads. There was a fine smell of wood smoke in the air, as well as the sound of throbbing drums. I could easily have been on another planet, and I had never seen such a mixture of people in my life. From the beautiful and lissome Fulanis and Hausas dressed in their colourful embroidered cotton robes, to the many Bantu Africans from different tribes, the town was a hive of activity.

Entrance to the Emir's palace

Fulani woman

Thus, I enjoyed the miracle of Africa for six glorious months in N'Gaoundéré. The origin of this town's name is also interesting. Overlooking this Fulani outpost was a minor mountain whose form was exactly that of an umbilical hernia, so common amongst all the Bantu tribes of Africa. The town took its name from this mountain – umbilicus in the Fulbé dialect.

The savannah highland of northern Cameroun was a fertile area watered by the Benué river, which rises in the Adamoua plateau north of N'Gaoundere. It is the main tributary of the Niger river, meeting it at Lokoja, north of Port Harcourt in eastern Nigeria. As it flows west it forms a natural, geographic divide between the southern Bantu and the northern Nilo-Hamitic tribes. Through these fertile lands meandered the herds of cattle and goats of the MBorroro, the nomadic cousins of the urban Fulanis. Horses were also an integral part of this community and the Emir owned dozens of sleek Arab steeds on which he mounted his 100-strong cavalry, most wonderfully attired in rich robes and finely tooled leather.

By the time I left N'Gaoundére I had explored a large part of the Benué plateau, mostly on the back of a fine Arab steed from the Emir´s stables. I was often accompanied by some of his chevaliers, dressed most splendidly in their *djebellas*. They all spoke Fulani and taught me much of that musical language as we galloped through the endless miles of open country dotted with acacias, fever trees and full of all sorts of wild animals. It was in their company that I saw my first lions, barely 50 metres away. This was not Regents Park Zoo and there was no enclosure, but my companions were all heavily armed with spears as well as guns. They showed no fear, so I stiffened my upper lip and dug my heels in a bit harder, imagining I was Jock of the Veld on safari.

On the work side life was also interesting. Tak Braaten was an ex-Marine and a real red neck as well as an evangelical Christian, so perfect discipline was the order of the day. When he realized that I knew hardly one word of French and had only my A-levels in Biology and Chemistry to offer his college, in true military fashion I found myself next day mixing concrete blocks in a bilharzia-infested river with a small gang of Africans. Every evening until the generator was switched off at 10 pm I was to fervently study French until Tak considered me fluent enough to converse with my students.

In those pre-and post-colonial days it was quite typical to be sent to some foreign outpost by VSO without the means to actually communicate, except in English. However, I was particularly fortunate to have this ex-marine commando-cum-missionary as my tutor in French, for Tak's mother had been French and Tak remains to this day the only American I have ever heard speaking a foreign language faultlessly. He taught me well, so that within three months I was fairly fluent and was already teaching my first classes in English, Music and Sport.

After a relatively sheltered upbringing in England there was still a lot to learn about the world outside, and Tak was a good teacher. His only problem was that he thought any non-Christians to be less than whole, and the worst of all these heathens were the Communists, wherever they were. Some of them obviously hung out in Vietnam, for not long after I arrived, I saw on the front cover of Time magazine, which was another piece of America, like VOA – Voice of America radio, which Tak introduced me to, a picture of American soldiers in the Vietnam jungle.

"Why are American soldiers fighting in Vietnam?", I asked him.

"They are not soldiers, they are Military Advisors!", he replied definitively.

"But Tak, why are they there?", I continued, not understanding that this really was the very beginning of the Vietnam War.

"To kick out the Communists!", and that was that. This fervently religious man who had already honed his killing skills in Korea was utterly convinced that going to war in Asia again was the way to go.

Life on the mission was new to me, who had been raised in moderate Anglicanism by my parents. My new acquaintances were Norwegian and Americans and were utterly devoted to Jesus, and nobody was excluded. Such that unless I showed up for Sunday church I did not get fed. The boss of the whole mission, Pastor Bendt regularly walked 25 miles a day in order to reach those Africans whom he thought would benefit from a dose of Christianity – as well as the education and health care which these proselytizing missionaries held out like candy to these impoverished people.

Prayers went before everything, before classes started, before their own day started, and before any surgical operation began. Even amongst some of the Catholics I occasionally worked with, before they got high on communion wine and incense I saw lots of interesting human behaviour within the missionary communities before I got to medical school. Including what happened to pregnant nuns, and it was not always so pleasant.

To me, young though I was, I could see the conflict between religious beliefs and natural human behaviour and the hypocrisies it often generated. This is something which has always distanced me from any formal religion.

The first Sunday I was at the mission Tak invited me to go water-skiing, a sport I had never even heard of until then. After church and then Sunday lunch, a gang of sporting missionaries would head the 30 minutes out of town to a volcanic lake, hidden in a mesmerizing tropical forest, towing a 16 ft speedboat loaded with life-vests and skis. They would then spend hours being plunged into this bilharzia - infested water at regular intervals. In spite of the high risk of catching this lethal parasitic disease I took the plunge as well, and learned the thrills of water-skiing.

Periodically one of them would get schistosomiasis, as this disease is otherwise known, and then they would suffer the trauma of the treatment, which in those days was not only less-than efficacious, but also very toxic with quite severe side-effects, and often had to be repeated. Thank God I never got attacked by those lethal little worms.

On Parasites

I learned about the life cycle of this parasite from the pages of Manson's Tropical Diseases, a weighty tome which was an essential part of every tropical doctor's armoury in those days. I have always had an interest in all things biological, and the life of this small parasite was impressive. There are 4 stages in the development, the first occurring within a fresh-water snail from which escape the larval stage, the cercariae. These are great swimmers, although only possessing one cell, and they swim until they find something similar to a bare human leg, and then start boring in through the skin. This is the point at which infection occurs, and it is much more common in still waters such as volcanic lakes than it is in flowing waters. It is once inside the human body that the maturation cycle is completed, and an adult worm eventually evolves. It is this adult which causes so much chronic pathology and even death across the equatorial belt of the world.

Schistosomiasis was also a huge problem in China during the time of Mao Tse-Dung, but he took a very pragmatic, communistic approach to the problem, which also proved very effective as well as very cheap. He sent out an order, and from that day on every school child took one snail into school with them. It did not completely remove the scourge of schistosomiasis, but it significantly reduced its incidence amongst the rural Chinese.

So, whatever else has been said about Mao, I think he must have been quite clever.

Another interesting problem which arose with the disease was the incidence of it in completely remote ponds, which were often only seasonal. For years scientists pondered how this snail could find its way across the desert and end up suddenly infecting people. It was the wading birds who turned out to be the culprits. As they foraged in one infected waterhole, mud accumulated on their feet, and within this wet mud survived some of the infected snails. Later these would be flown to a new site, and once free in the water would infect that. Schistosomiasis was only one of hundreds of tropical medical conditions which I began learning about that year as well as many other aspects of life in the tropics.

Living with the Evangelists

The proselytizing of the Christians took little regard of the indigenous culture, which was predominantly Moslem, and this led to tragedy one day. Hamid was one of only four Moslem students in the Collège and the day he capitulated under the duress of the missionaries and became a Christian there was a great celebration throughout the

Mission Protestante. A special service was even dedicated to this triumph of evangelical persuasion. Things went muted a week later when poor Hamid was found in a ditch with an arrow through his heart. He was only 15.

If this murder gave the Christians any pause for thought, it did nothing to stop them from trying to convert Moslems to their faith. That was what seemed to be their prime aim where I was in Cameroun. Ten years later when I went back to N'Gaoundéré and slept in the dormitory block constructed of the very bricks I had made a decade before, I visited the mission hospital where I had seen my first ever Caesarian section. There I was disturbed to see the same loudspeakers throughout the hospital giving out Jesus messages in Hausa and Fulani, even though by then in this independent country proselytizing was illegal.

Another result of the religious views of my protestant colleagues was the banishment of Monica, a young American missionary teacher in the college. She fell in love with the local *garagiste*, a Frenchman called Jean-Pierre who was already my friend as he was one of the few expatriates who I could share a beer with. We also shared the pleasures of Gauloise and Bastos, the local tobacco equivalent, which were small dark cigarettes, so strong they made me cough and splutter.

First Hunting Expedition

Not only was Jean-Pierre an excellent chef, but he was a hunter, and it was this that forged my strong friendship with him. Once a month he would take me off for two days in his short wheel-base Land Rover, way up north towards the kingdom of Rey Bouba and the savannah plains where all manner of wild African animals roamed. We would stop at a village, make camp and after a decent meal, usually steak barbecued al fresco, Jean-Pierre would end up with a young nubile girl in his tent in those days before Monica arrived on the scene, and I would go to sleep under the brilliant African sky hoping a leopard or lion would not get too interested in me. Mohammed, Jean-Piérre's friend and tracker always kept watch by the fire and would tell me ancient stories of his heritage in Fulani until I passed into dreams.

We would rise as the sky was lightening and were marching through tall elephant grass and acacia as the sunrise exploded. One morning, having been walking an hour or so, Mohammed raised his hand and we stopped. He was examining a very large pile of fresh elephant dung, still steaming in the sun. Then he did an amazing thing. He introduced his index finger deep into this steaming pile, considered deeply for a few seconds then marched us on. "It's within 15 minutes of us", said Jean-Pierre, which livened up the stalking considerably, especially as I had only an ebony staff to protect me. Fortunately, we never found that elephant, nor did it find us. But Jean-Pierre did find and shoot a fine impala, though my own shot was through the view finder of my Voigtlander 35mm camera.

It was fascinating to watch the relationship of Monica and Jean-Pierre blossom, me being only 18 and inexperienced in these matters. The missionaries strongly disapproved of this relationship, and made that very clear, even to me, but such is the power of sexual attraction that even the thought of Jesus' retribution via the missionaries could do nothing to prevent this beautiful liason. So, one day there was a form of religious tribunal involving the whole mission, starting with the inevitable reading from the massive bible they used. The missionaries condemned Monica to eternal damnation and a life outside the mission. I was very shocked by this, but I was only young, and I knew little in those days about the perversities of religion or politics, or how high ideals can be blighted by bigotry.

Benefits of the old school tie

I was at work teaching class 3 one afternoon when a boy ran in to tell me there was a man who wanted to see me. This was a most unusual event in my life, and when I went outside, I was even more surprised to see a moustachioed chap with pith helmet and regulation below the knee white shorts, leaning on a Land Rover with a Union Jack flying bravely on its bonnet.

Thus, it was that I met Jack Warner, the British Ambassador to the Republic of Cameroun. He was out on a 'meet the Brits' mission, including the four of us VSO volunteers who were spread all over Cameroun. He had also come to advise me and Tak that the Director of VSO was coming out in two months' time to visit the first-time projects, of which mine was one. He was very British but also warm and friendly and he invited me to come and stay with him when in Yaoundé. He left the following day, leaving me feeling like Scott of the Antarctic, marooned in a far-off place, as I watched him and the Union Jack disappearing into the dust.

As a teacher of both English and Music I had a fair bit of latitude within the classroom, and a lot of fun with my students. For example, when we did a Nativity play that Christmas not only was there a real live baby in the arms of Elisabeth, one of my four female students, but there was a real live donkey on stage as well. I decided to put on a show for this coming British chief, so we started learning a few English songs. Well, if there was one thing these young people enjoyed more than dancing, it was singing. By the time that the Director entered the college hall he was greeted by a pretty acceptable version of 'God Save the Queen', followed by 'Jerusalem', and was visibly impressed.

Dick, for that was his name, had come out to assess the viability of new projects and spent two days with me. During these heady days at N'Gaoundéré I was still doing all I could to gain an entrance to medical school. I had even applied to schools in Canada and Australia, so motivated was I to become a doctor. However, my F grade in Physics 'A' level was a major stumbling block to my endeavours. Three 'A' levels were the minimum requirement for acceptance to any 2nd MB course, and I only possessed two. But once again, my karma continued good.

Dick asked about my further plans, and when I told him of my impossible problem with entry to medical school, he said he would see what he could do. One week later I received a telegram saying,

"Accepted Liverpool. Suggest reply immediate. Stop"

I spent the whole of my weekly allowance on that telegram reply, but it was worth every cent. When I finally arrived at Liverpool Medical School for my interview with the Dean some six months later, I found myself in front of a genial old doctor, Jack Leggate. He had passed much of his life as a missionary doctor in the tropics but had also gone to the same school as Dick, the Director of VSO.

In the end, it was that simple. The old boy network and the public school tie still did mean something in those days, and had it not been so I would never had become the doctor I did. My parents had struggled hard to find the means to send me to a public school, and I think they were well aware of the advantages it would bring in the future. Speaking the Queen's English and playing cricket and rugby – but never football, were just a few of the prerequisites for a privileged life which I learned at the King's School, Ely.

The Drums of Rey Bouba

There are, of course, other forms of privilege. One of the greatest privileges I ever had was to enter the world of Africa. Everything was new and wonderful to me, but of all the marvellous sights I saw in Africa in 1964, the Festival of the Drums in the kingdom of Rey Bouba in northern Cameroun was without doubt one of the most memorable.

Rey Bouba lies at the northern extreme of the Adamaoua plateau, 100 kms north of N´Gaoundere, and every five years its ruler, the Lamido, celebrated by throwing a massive party which lasted four days. Representatives of every local tribe attended whilst three huge drums, carried on the heads of the Lamido's household beat out their rhythm across the savannah plains.

These three drums were enormous, being about four feet in diameter and five feet long and were beautifully painted. They were carried horizontally on one person´s head, whilst being regularly beaten, and must have weighed a considerable amount.

Of all the sights I witnessed during this festival, that of these three great drums beating out their constant message is the one which struck me most.

The drums of Rey Bouba

The festival at Rey Bouba

I am still impressed when I look at my photos and see the finery of these rural Africans and the variety of the tribes and their dress and markings. The Lamido was carried by four men in a golden, silk-covered palenquin to his lavish throne, surrounded by courtiers and his women, as well as his guards on horseback. For four days the dancing and music went on and always in the background was the steady beat of the three huge drums.

Neither my written descriptions nor my slides can adequately portray the magnificence of this African fiesta. How can one describe the colours, the smells or the rhythms beating out across the savannah of Rey Bouba? Even a film would not do justice to this vibrant gathering of souls. The chevaliers of the Lamido's horse guard were dressed in chain mail which dated from the 15th century, some of which was Portugese, and their horses were caparisoned in chequered, multi-hued cloths dating from the Middle Ages. Even the metal helmets they wore dated back centuries. The world I found myself in was one of great richness and long history and of a diversity I had never imagined. At this time we missionaries were the only strangers at this great fiesta apart from a small Belgian film crew.

The Lamido had power over thousands of people from the north of Cameroun. As Rey Bouba was the seat of the most powerful authority in that area, the mission had decided some years before that it would be strategically wise to have a Christian presence there. Bud the engineer and Jeannie his nursing wife were the team who had been appointed. They were well-liked by the Lamido because he was very arthritic and the only relief he found from his pain was in a tablet of Aspirin 300mgm. which Jeannie provided from her clinic. Thus, relations between the evangelizing Christians and the Muslims were very cordial.

Bud was also a man of many talents, and like most of the mission mechanics and engineers I ever met, he was capable of solving almost any practical problem. I still have the photo of the ingenious bicycle water pump he designed and made to supply water to Jeannie's clinic.

It was the rear half of a crashed bike on which one sat on the saddle, but the pedals turned a small rotary water pump which raised the water from a 10 metre well which Bud and his assistants had dug by hand. To the local ladies it was a miracle. It was hilarious to see them queuing up for their turn on the saddle when, as soon as they heard the water splash into the bucket they would stop pedalling to look round in wonder – at which point the water fell back into the ground and they had to start pedalling again.

In the middle of the big rains during that winter of 1964 Jeannie developed abdominal pain. She had also missed a period, and it was she who made the diagnosis of a possible ectopic pregnancy. Bud sent a message to the director at mission HQ at N'Gaoundéré, but the rains kept falling and the roads remained impassable in spite of every effort made, and five days later Jeannie was dead.

In her last days she wrote a diary. After her body was brought back to be buried, I was able to read it in her original handwriting. It really made me sad, knowing that this brave nurse had died from an eminently treatable condition. The missionaries did make many sacrifices for their beliefs, including dying.

Hitch-hiking across West Africa – Cameroun to Ghana and Niger. 1965

Africa was a huge space in which to enjoy interesting adventures as well as experience every single form of nature amongst indigenous people of every shade and culture, and in those early days I could voyage freely without hindrance or fear. In March the College closed for a long vacation, and with it ended my first of many experiences as a teacher. Having two months of freedom before my next posting with VSO, I decided to go and see a bit more of Africa.

Just to be out of N'Gaoundéré and on the open road under a hot sun was a delight. I was carrying my guitar and a small ex-Army haversack furnished by Kjeld the Norwegian dentist. I also had 25 pounds sterling which I had saved from my meagre allowance, but nothing much else other than a goat skin *bota* full of water. Monica, who was now happily ensconced with Jean-Pierre, had given me a tin of German sausages – which I still had intact when I returned 10 weeks later. Jean-Pierre had given me a precious packet of Gauloises – always un-tipped, and an Opinel knife which I still have. I was well prepared for a few weeks on the road.

I began by hitching north and west towards the Faro River and a village called Tchamba up in the Atlantika mountains which border Nigeria, where Binjamin, one of my students lived amongst a tribe who specialised in a very unique form of drumming.

Everywhere I ever went in Africa there have been drums. From the small ceramic ones of Morocco to the djembes of Mali and Senegal and those huge drums of Rey Bouba, drums have beaten out the messages and formed the background to any celebration's singing and dancing. I still have the exquisitely made talking drum which the Emir gave me when I left N'Gaoundéré. I was eagerly anticipating this trek to Tchamba to learn more about African rhythms and drums. I was never much in sympathy with the plaintive mediaeval plainsong chants we used to sing in Latin in Ely cathedral, but the rhythms of Africa have always moved me, and still do through the music of Salif Keita, Ali Farkah Toure, Mory Kante, Fela Ransome-Kuti and many others.

It was yet another facet of the puritanical mission life that 'native' music was not allowed in the Mission Protestante, being considered heathen and ungodly, and even though I went to sleep most nights to the sound of drumming in the town of N'Gaoundéré, the drums were banned from the mission.

Once I left the dirt road leading to Garoua I was walking through wild country with no evidence of habitation, slowly ascending through open savannah dotted with acacia trees and into the foothills of the Atlantiki mountains. I spent one night sleeping in a small sort of tent made of rocks, cleverly balanced to make a shelter. It was only when I got over the border into Nigeria two days later that I was told this construction was in fact a leopard trap. At the apex of the roof was a keystone to which was tied a grass cord, normally attached to a lump of goat, the idea being that a tug on this from a carnivore would collapse the roof and trap the animal. Binyamin told me later that lions and panthers were a problem in these parts, which made me rather more thoughtful about where I would spend the next night.

The following day I arrived at Binjamin's village. No one in the village had ever seen a white man, neither had they yet come across clothing. The chief was the only person with any item of clothing, this being a pair of antique shorts. I was not used to the nakedness of people, and the missionaries certainly abhorred it, but I spent two days up in the hills with Binjamin´s tribe of innocent and naked natives who wore only a simple form of *chache-sex* made out of leaves. I suppose that these days the natives would get paid to 'get authentic' for the tourists but then I saw it as being a completely natural thing which accorded well with their way of life.

Binjamin´s family were very kind and made me welcome in spite of obviously being very poor. There was a big party to celebrate the arrival of the first *mzungu* into their isolated village and we all got drunk on their home-made maize beer. I went to sleep that night with a belly full of wild pig and the sound of native drumming in my ears. For the first time in my life I was alone amongst a tribe of Africans, but for some reason I felt no fear, and I slept very well.

The drummers woke me in the cold darkness of pre-dawn and showed me how they tuned the skins of their drums by placing hot coals from the fire onto the up-ended drum skin and beating it until the heat had dried the skin to the correct tension. They then turned the drum over and tuned the other end. Each drum was double-ended and about four foot long, hanging horizontally from a leather strap around the neck. They were hollowed out from hardwood tree trunks and each one was a work of art.

Then they used a small lump of soft beeswax to precisely tune the drum once the skin was dry and taut. This delicate tuning process took some time and the sun had risen by the time all six drums were in tune. Then they began to serenade me, and I was mesmerized. The drummers played these drums in a form of choir, with five or six drummers at a time playing different sizes of these hollowed-out tree trunks.

A primaeval thrill ran down me as the six drums played in chorus a complicated series of rhythms and scales to which the women gyrated. Sitting on top of that mountain in the wilds of Africa, listening to the sound of the drums as the sun rose in the clear blue sky over the endless plains below, etched a memory which I still treasure.

The next day Binjamin took me down the mountain and across the border into Nigeria. There was no border post or Customs, just a meandering river to cross, me holding onto a liana and praying that the crocodiles were otherwise engaged. There we parted company. I never saw Binjamin again, but I never forgot him and his family of drummers. It was a good and auspicious beginning to my voyage of discovery.

Across the mountains and into Nigeria

When I got to Yola late that afternoon after a gruelling hike of some 10 miles I was put up at the police post by a kindly sergeant and slept in a cell for the first time in my life. On this occasion the cell door was left open, and the constables cooked sweet potatoes and monkey for me that night and shared a rare bottle of Guinness. I was finding only kindness and generosity wherever I travelled, which had not always been the case back in England.

It is worth noting that Nigeria had only gained its independence from Britain four years before. It still retained very good relations with the British and enjoyed many of the attributes introduced by the Europeans, so my passage was relatively easy as the Nigerians were well-used to the British by this time. At the roadblocks I passed the police would make cars or the local taxis known as mammy wagons, stop and take me on board – for free. I was only grateful, but I was too naïve at that time to realize what a privilege that had been, for Nigeria is now a very different place, the legacy of the British being long forgotten.

Thanks to the discovery of oil in the Niger delta around this time Nigeria is now the richest as well as the most populated country in West Africa. Sadly, the indigenous inhabitants of the delta region have barely benefited from this huge wealth, mostly as a result of rampant corruption. Even their traditional livelihood of fishing has been ruined, as the petroleum industry has spread, poisoning the many waterways and destroying the fragile ecology of the delta.

I was aiming for Ibadan where the Deputy British High Commissioner was a friend of our family, being the father of my lodger friend, George, and there I was well received. After my life with the puritans at the Collège Protestante and my two week of rough travels, the luxury of the diplomatic life was a stark contrast. Butlers brought me gin and lime, servants served us all manner of rich foods and my hosts introduced me to the cultural life of the Yoruba who were the dominant and energetic tribe occupying the southwestern corner of Nigeria. Yoruba plays and poetry were famous. I was taken to a Yoruba play at the main theatre in Ibadan, which was a memorable experience after the simple life I had been living in Cameroun. It was excellent and brilliantly acted, even though I did not understand the Yoruba language, and it demonstrated what a vibrant and rich culture West Africa had to offer outside the mission compounds.

From Ganvie to Ghana

After two days of luxurious living I continued west to Cotonou in Dahomey, now re-named Benin, and it was there that I came across the unusual village of Ganvie. It was in the middle of a big inland lake and was built completely on stilts. All life took place on water. The lake was full of wooden *pirogues*, some fishing, some sailing and others carrying all kinds of fruit and vegetables, for even the daily market took place on the lake's surface. In the centre of this strange village was a large, palm-thatched building on stilts with a sign above reading, "Bar-Restaurante de Ganvie" which also turned out to be the chief's residence. The paraffin fridge within contained only luke-warm bottles of Fanta, but I made do, and even slept the night there after a very fine meal of local fish. All I had to do was play my guitar to the chief, and he charged me nothing for my food and lodging.

The Bar-Restaurant de Ganyie

All life took place on the water

From there I continued west along the Bight of Benin until I reached Lomé, the capital of Togoland. I stayed with the ambassador and his Spanish wife, again in great luxury. She had a collection of vinyl records amongst which was one by Trini Lopez, and it was then that I learned ´La Bamba´, a song which still gets my Spanish neighbours up and onto their feet when I play it at the Bar el Zahori.

My guitar was really becoming useful. Even though I was no way good, just the sight of a traveller with knapsack and guitar seemed to make a connection with people wherever I went. Sometimes I played at diplomatic gatherings, and sometimes in remote villages and very often under a tree by the roadside while waiting for a lift. It never failed to get me a meal and a roof for the night at the very least. This was much to do with the fact that I arrived back in N'Gaoundéré two months later still with 10 pounds left in my pocket of the 25 I had started with, having hitch-hiked around a good chunk of West Africa.

I got as far as Ghana before a minor border dispute put an end to my western trajectory. Dahomey was full of soldiers massing at the border, and I was lucky to hire a small pirogue and get paddled across the lagoon separating the two countries in the dead of night. I spent the journey holding my guitar over my head whilst praying that this sliver of tree trunk would not roll over and throw us into the water.

Thus, I arrived in Ghana, not by any legal means and without any stamps in my passport. So it was not a great surprise to be picked up by an armed patrol and spend my second night in a cell. But this time the door was locked, and I had nothing to eat. The soldiers took my guitar, and I went to sleep that night to the sound of Ghanaian rock played by one of the soldiers. He was good, and in the morning we had a jam session before they took me back to the border and pointed me east, with a warning that war was on the way so I had better keep heading east and not come back.

I was still young and naïve, even though I was really packing in the life experiences as I travelled around Africa, but the second night in a prison cell convinced me that Nigeria was a safer bet than Ghana. I very much wanted to go to the far north, so I hitched back to Lagos. Then I went north to Ije-Bode where Vicky, another VSO friend was teaching. I had met Vicki on the VSO training course in London, and we soon became good friends, so I was looking forward to seeing her again.

The Road to Agadez

Together we hitched up north to Ilorin and then to Jebba where the long road north to Kaduna crosses the Niger river, and from there we got a lift on a BP petrol tanker which drove us up onto the Jos Plateau which rises over 1000 metres and has a climate and people very similar to N'Gaoundéré in neighbouring Cameroun. The Hausas and Fulanis were still the predominant tribes there and everywhere were fat cattle grazing on the fertile land.

Because of its perfect climate Jos has always been a hill-station retreat since colonial times and there were certainly quite a few expatriates living and working in this pleasant area. Jos was a fascinating town and a centre for several industries, including leather tanning. From all manner of clothing and handbags to footwear and weapons, working leather was a major industry in these northern parts where the cattle herds of the MBororo roamed, and I still have some of that exquisite leather work some 50 years later.

I had no idea of what happens to a cow skin from the time it left the cow to the time it arrived in my pocket as a wallet, but here in Jos it was all laid out before us, and the stink was the most powerful memory. It beat anything John Davy had ever dreamed up in the Chemistry lab at Lewes Grammar.

The tanning vats were dark, evil-smelling pits full of skins being treated by a cohort of natives dressed in filthy rags. With the fires burning all around and the smoke and the smell it was not a place to linger. However, the end results of this toxic-looking industry were objects of extraordinary beauty made out of leather in a rainbow of colours.

Another big industry in this area revolved around cotton, which was one of the main crops in these latitudes of West Africa. At Jos were spinners and weavers and also the dyeing pits full of deep blue indigo which was used to colour the hand-woven sheets of cotton. I still have the thick cotton sheet I bought there, and it is still in perfect condition.

Hand spinning cotton

The woven cotton was dyed with indigo

The streets of Jos were full of tailors, almost all of them men, sitting in front of their Singer treadle machines clicking away, creating all manner of fine clothing, much of it embellished with delicate, stitched embroidery. It was obvious that in this rich and at that time peaceful corner of Nigeria the society was also rich in their culture and it showed. It was far from the humid coastal jungles, and a world I much preferred.

We continued further north to Sokoto where the savannah was turning into the southern fringes of the Sahara desert. The architecture of the towns was already different, being composed mainly of low mud-brick houses with very narrow streets filled with increasing numbers of Arabs, as well as donkeys and camels. From Sokoto we continued heading north and crossed the border into the République Niger at Burnin-Konnil, then hitched east to Maradi and on to the town of Zinder. I well remember the night we spent there, sleeping on a huge pyramid made up of sacks of peanuts.

I do not know what it is that draws people to the desert. Probably it is many things, but whatever that magic is it drew me. I had had a vision for a long time of one day being in the geographic centre of the Sahara Desert, which is a town called Agadez, some 300 kilometres north of Zinder.

From Zinder to Agadez was the only part of the two-month voyage that I ever had to pay for. Vicki and I paid 10 dollars each to board this derelict old Citroen lorry with bald tyres and a choking exhaust. We joined a jolly crowd of Africans up top sitting on huge sacks of peanuts and maize meal. It was a testing three-day voyage, full of breakdowns and punctures, freezing nights on the desert floor and the utter emptiness of miles and miles of sand. I heard it sing at night when the truck was silenced, the wind playing orchestral tunes in the dunes which surrounded us as I went to sleep wrapped in a blanket, watching the flames of the fire dance to the tunes of the desert.

The Oasis of Taghouaji

I had always imagined oases as magic gardens in the sand, and so it turned out to be. Vicky and I spent two days on camels heading east into the desert from Agadez with Ahmed, our guide and cook. I had wanted to visit an oasis ever since I read my first Beau Geste book in which, at the limits of his endurance when all is lost after his camel dies, his life is saved by the miraculous appearance of an oasis.

At the oasis of Taghouaji my dreams came true. It truly was a magic paradise in the middle of a million hectares of sand, with date palms shading beds of irises and all sorts of fruits. In the background was the Massif de Taghouaji, its summit stretching 1100 metres above the desert floor. It was in that cool oasis that Vicki and I later sat, eating a huge bowl of freshly picked strawberries, sitting under a palm tree listening to the water gushing from the artesian well which gave life to this tiny chink of desert. It was hard to believe that not 100 metres from where we were sitting in this verdant wonderland, the endless, desiccated desert which had taken us two days to cross, stretched as far as the eye could see.

Since then, I have travelled through many other deserts, and among my great heroes I include Wilfred Thesiger as well as Laurens van der Post, both of whom were truly great explorers and travellers of deserts, who also wrote the most erudite and fascinating accounts of their travels. Sadly, both have died in recent years, but their inspiration, courage and endeavour remain an example to follow. The Empty Quarter and the Kalahari Desert are both places I know something of, but these two chaps spent much of their lives enjoying the magic of these deserts, and their writings are what have since inspired me to see more of these empty spaces.

Vicki and I parted company after three hard but fascinating weeks on the road. She had been a great travelling companion and I was sorry to see her go. I headed back to Yaoundé, where Jack Warner the Ambassador informed me that he had just sent a telegram to my parents saying that I was lost and that a search party was being organized. When I thought about the vast space I had just spent 10 weeks exploring, I laughed. There was zero chance of anyone finding me in most of the remote places I had just been, but that night, after a most generous dose of British hospitality from Jack and his wife I did give sincere thanks to God for protecting me and getting me back safely from another voyage of discovery.

The next day I headed back to N´Gaoundere and said my farewells to the mission and my other friends outside, including the Emir and his household who had been so kind to me. Monica, Jean-Pierre and I finally finished off the tin of sausages which I had been carrying across Africa for 10 weeks. Then I returned to Yaoundé where the ambassador drove with me in the official Land Rover, still with its Union Jack fluttering, to Ebolowa, a town deep in the southern jungle. There I was to spend the rest of the year with an American Presbyterian medical mission whose chief surgeon was Jack Payne MD, the man who was to become my most influential surgical mentor.

3. JUNGLE DAYS IN CAMEROUN   1965

Into the Jungle – and the Hôpital Central, Ebolowa

The change from the open savannah of N'Gaoundéré to the southern rain forests of Cameroun was dramatic. Even as the Ambassador Jack and I left Yaoundé in the official Land Rover the jungle started encroaching, and after the recent rains the remains of the laterite road had turned into a series of massive potholes, some of them big enough to swallow a car.

Everything was green in the dense forests we passed through, only the dirt road carving a line through this otherwise impenetrable green screen. Now and then we passed villages by the side of the road, chickens and small black pigs wandering between the huts of mud and palm leaf roofs. These dwellings were very different from the magnificently decorated houses of the Adamoua Plateau, whose manicured reed and straw roofs and round walls of terracotta exquisitely painted in sunshine colours were far more decorative.

The people were also of another race. Down south they were dark Bantu negroes, whereas the indigenous tribes of N'Gaoundéré had been finely featured Nilo-Hamitic types, who, some said, were related to the Queen of Sheba. The great majority of these northern people had been Moslem, but south of Yaoundé was the territory of the Christians and animists. Christian missions had been established here for over a century.

The Presbyterian Mission Hôpital Central at Ebolowa is where His Excellency and I parted company. He had been a great Ambassador as far as I was concerned. He had looked after the four of us young VSO volunteers working in Cameroun like a locum father, and he and his wife were always pleased to see us. After my austere months with the Lutherans at N'Gaoundéré, being served large gin and limes by James, his ebony – skinned butler in his pristine white uniform, and going to bed in an air-conditioned room fairly drunk with a four – course meal inside me is one of the great memories I still have of my first year in Africa.

I was given into the care of Jack Payne, MD. and his wife Ruth. They were Presbyterian missionaries and were streets ahead of the puritanical Lutherans as far as normal living was concerned. There was also far less aggressive evangelizing of the locals. They didn't drink or smoke, but at least they accepted my own weaknesses without judgement, and for that I was grateful.

Jack became my surgical mentor and father figure. He had such an effect on me that 10 years later, after I had got my Diploma in Child Health in London, I went back to Ebolowa to spend another six months with him, just for fun and no pay. But also, to learn more and more about all aspects of tropical health care, surgery, and Africa itself.

"Well", he said in his Cinncinati drawl, "they tell me you are interested in surgery. Let's take a walk round the hospital and show you what we have."

The Hôpital Central at Ebolowa was considerably larger than the one at N'Gaoundéré. In the several wards there were sometimes two or more patients sharing one bed, their relatives sleeping underneath. The usual chickens scratched around the hospital grounds which were cut out of an acre of dense jungle.

Snakes were a serious menace in these parts. One of Jack's first warnings to me was never to go outside at night without a torch and shoes, rather than sandals. The very first night I arrived I was invited to dine with the head of the mission, Pastor Ben and his family. Leaving Jack and Ruth's house where I lodged, I was walking across the lush grass of the mission when I spotted a dark shadow just in front of me. I was terrified to miss treading on a four-foot puff adder by just a matter of inches.

There was a fine laboratory which had several trained technicians doing a wide variety of tests from biochemistry to parasitology and haematology. There was even an antique Xray machine. But it was the operating theatre (OT) which took my breath away.

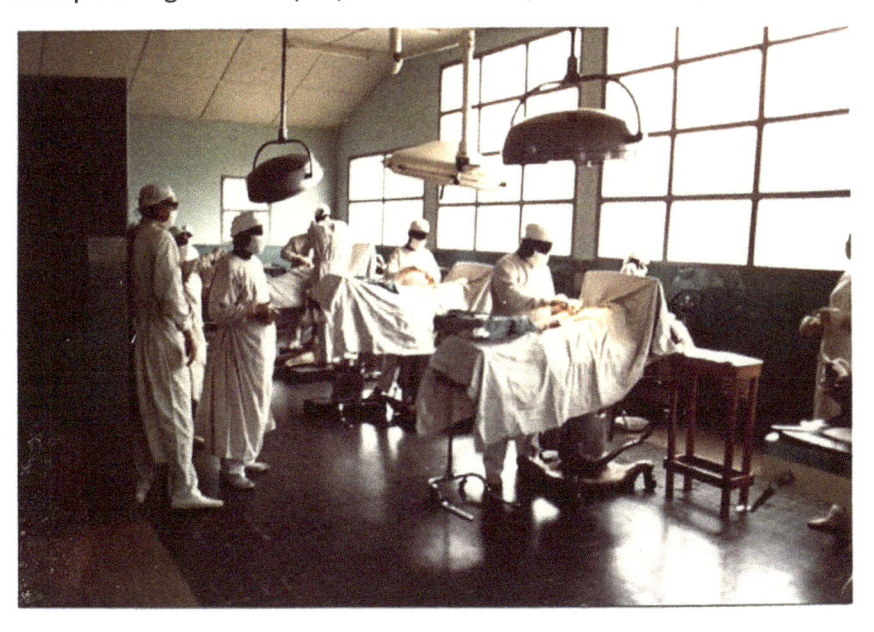

The operating theatre at Ebolowa took my breath away

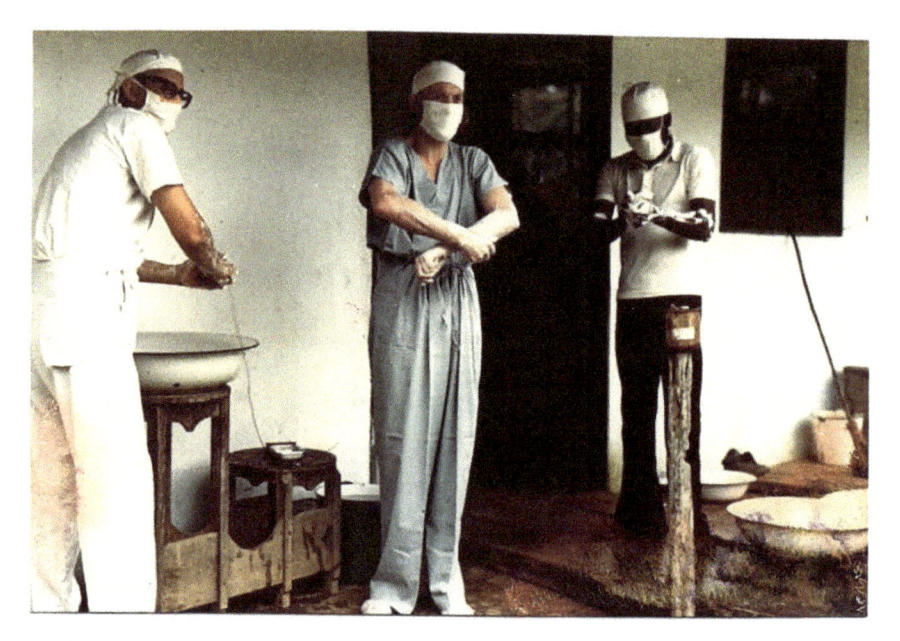

Ambam Leper Colony. Scrubbing up with Jack. No taps here!

Six Simultaneous Operations at a time

The OT at N'Gaoundéré had contained a single operating table as was the norm, but here in Ebolowa I walked into a veritable hall, along which were parked in neat order six operating tables. Six! I have never seen the like since. When all six were on the go with Jack or Dick, the other surgeon, keeping an eye on things it was an impressive sight.

Six surgeons operating simultaneously in the same room, yet hardly one was a qualified doctor, and there was no general anaesthetic machine. Almost all the operations were performed under local or spinal anaesthetic which I soon discovered was made up of a mixture of Lidocaine and Dextrose solution which was included to weight the liquid anaesthetic. This was then injected into the third lumbar intervertebral space…..if we were lucky, for it was a delicate procedure.

If a patient needed a general anaesthetic, ether was the drug of choice. This was dropped onto a cloth face-mask over the patient's face, until they became anaesthetised. It was a very primitive form of anaesthesia and required great skill to avoid accidentally killing the patient with an overdose. But these two surgeons still managed to do a wide variety of major operations, from mastectomies to thyroidectomies, where spinal anaesthetics were inappropriate.

The people operating were clinical assistants who had worked as nurses and then graduated to become surgical assistants. They had been trained by Jack and Dick to perform such operations as inguinal hernia repair, hydrocoeles and other minor and intermediate surgical procedures. It was an amazing achievement by Jack and Dick, but I could understand the need, for every day scores of patients presented with all manner of clinical problems and there was no way that two surgeons alone could cope with this volume of work.

Throughout my days in the tropics, it was clear that to me that the demands of the population invariably overwhelmed the resources of a single doctor. When I spent six months alone, deep in the Congo some years later, I was the only doctor for a population of about 250,000 jungle dwellers, and in Kenya my catchment population was over a million. Therefore, nurses and clinical assistants were expected to undertake clinical responsibilities which only a qualified doctor would normally perform in England. Anaesthesia was a case in point.

At the Hôpital Central there were only three doctors, so the bulk of the daily work was done by non-medically qualified staff, overseen by a stern American matron, known by us as The Queen.

The constant hospital activity and admissions of all types of emergencies was non-stop and for the first few days I just followed Jack around wherever he went. I had never seen anyone work so hard. He just never stopped, was always willing to go the extra mile, and was always kind to the natives who arrived by the score every day - and also during the night, when came the inevitable Caesarian sections. These were often conducted by the light of hurricane lanterns, for the hospital generator was ancient and access to fuel was a major problem, especially as the Yaoundé road was often washed out by the intense tropical rains.

I now found myself in one of the areas of highest annual rainfall in the world. We are not just talking of rainfall in inches here, but metres. The area around Mount Cameroun in the west of the country has over 1100 mms of rain a year. The southern Cameroun rainforests also have a very high annual rainfall. Wetness was the word, and dampness became a daily part of my existence in that pestilential and humid jungle. Ruth had a special cupboard, heated by a lightbulb, which was the only 'dry' area, where we were able to keep a few of our vestments from growing fungus within hours of being washed. Green mould grew on everything and nothing was ever really dry. It was not a pleasant way to live, but as with most things in life, in the end you get used to it, and take measures accordingly - the most important at Ebolowa being an umbrella.

There was a sister mission not far away which held the national record for the highest annual rainfall. Here there was a frequent change of missionaries, as some often went slightly mad after a few weeks of non-stop rain and wetness. Yet I was always impressed by the ways in which the indigenous inhabitants had adapted to this less-than-ideal climate in which they lived, in manners of which many of the better educated missionaries knew little.

Trainee Surgeon and Laboratory Assistant

After a week of very stimulating activity as I learned my way around the hospital, it was decided that I would do most of my daily work within the hospital laboratory. This appealed to me as I had enjoyed Biology and Chemistry above all at Lewes Grammar. A hospital laboratory is nothing if not a centre for the investigation and experimentation on every form of human tissue and effluent, with the chance to look down a microscope at the world unseen.

The last Biology practical I ever did at Lewes was to stain a section of frog's bladder (which was all that was left of the unfortunate amphibian we had dissected in the Biology lab of Sammy White, our unforgiving biology teacher and cricket coach). Looking down the monocular microscope at the result, I was amazed at the way that the Haematoxylin and Eosin stains had differentiated the tissues into a veritable work of art. I just loved histology and histopathology, so the laboratory became my second home, and the family of technicians within became my very good friends and teachers.

With my Laboratory team at l'Hôpital Central. Emmanuel to my right

Emmanuel was the head technician and spent hours patiently showing me how to do the relatively primitive biochemical and haematology tests. Of all the many tests he taught me, the erythrocyte sedimentation rate (ESR) has to be the best.

It was the simplest of all the tests to perform. Take a 20-cm hollow glass tube, seated vertically, coated inside with heparin, which is a blood anticoagulant. Inject 10 ccs of the patients blood into the lumen of the tube – and wait. As time passes the two main components of blood, the cells and the plasma, begin to separate leaving a red line of blood cells below and a clear line of plasma above. The proportional relationship of these two components, measured after a specific time, provided a good general assessment of a patient's health. In normal health the red cell level would be low, less than 20 % of the total, but in active disease this could increase to over 50%. So, it was a good indicator of general health, but could never provide a specific diagnosis of disease. Nevertheless, it was very useful in measuring the evolution of a disease such as tuberculosis. Even today, 55 years later, it is still in common use in cases of auto-immune disease.

The ESR must be one of the cheapest laboratory tests and one of the simplest to perform, and the fact that it has survived decades of scientific and technical advances says a lot for its validity.

Emmanuel was also an expert microscopist. He taught me to differentiate the four main forms of malaria, which was endemic throughout the equatorial rain forest. Tuberculosis was also very common in all ages, but diagnosis was often extremely difficult as the tubercule bacillus was very small and difficult to spot unless the microscope magnification was exceptionally high. Emmanuel told me that there was a very good microscope in a cupboard, but it was never used as the lenses had become fogged somehow. I asked him to show it to me. It was a magnificent Carl Zeiss binocular microscope which could magnify up to x 1,600, twice as much as the ones we were using.

That evening I began to strip the microscope. Never having done this sort of thing before, it was all a bit scary as tiny lenses rolled around and washers appeared from hidden places. All the screws were minute, and soon my corner of the lab was looking a bit like a jeweller's workshop.

I saw that the lenses were covered in an opaque film which would not rub off with a cloth. I turned to an ancient tome on Laboratory

Techniques, published in 1947 in which this problem was described, saying it was due to a fungus which thrived on glass in humid conditions. It added that this may be removed using a tar-based cleaning agent. By a huge stroke of fortune Jerry, our mission engineer, had some of this stinking black liquid. Using cotton wool I polished the lenses and slowly removed the cloudy film until all but one of the four objective lenses was perfectly clear. The low-power lens seemed permanently scarred by the action of this fungus, but it was the x 400 objective lens that I needed to be clear in order to improve our TB detection. It took several days to get the microscope back in one piece and functioning, but when I put a drop of oil between the high-power lens and the Falciparum malaria slide I had prepared as a test, I was astonished at the size and clarity of the parasites I was observing. This was very much better than what we had been used to, and certainly helped to improve our TB diagnoses.

The laboratory was full of all kinds of pathological samples, as may be expected, from urine to vomit and pus to faeces, most of it infested with various noxious tropical worms such as Ankylostoma, Ascaris and Trichurius. Tapeworms and even schistosomiasis as well as pathologic amoebae and flukes also lurked in the bowels of many African patients and occasionally the Europeans, and I soon learned to differentiate between the different species by their larvae and eggs.

One great advance in public health has been the banishment of parasitic infestations from the populations of most developed countries. But in the poorer nations, adequate sanitation, clean water supply and preventive measures such as impregnated mosquito nets had yet to arrive. The subsequent high prevalence of so many preventable diseases has had a major effect on nations' health and economy.

Louis – the strange case of the Calabar swellings

When I was not working, I used to spend a lot of time with Louis, a young missionary teacher. He and I used to play chess together, and one night as we were playing, I noticed the back of both his hands begin to visibly swell. Louis told me that this had been occurring occasionally in recent weeks. I knew that he had been under the weather for some time, but no diagnosis had been made. However, from my studies I knew that these swellings could be diagnostic of infection with the filaria worm, in which case they were known as Calabar swellings and were some sort of inflammatory response.

I invited Louis to the laboratory next day and took blood for an ESR and also thick and thin films to screen for parasites. And finally, a stool sample. The ESR was 48% - grossly abnormal. Microscopy of his thin blood film showed an eosinophilia of 75 % - again grossly abnormal, and indicative of significant infective pathology. The normal percentage of these white blood cells is less than 10%. In his thick blood film, I could see the sinuous movements of microfilaria, the juvenile forms of the adult filaria worm. And in his faeces I found the ova of both Ascaris, the roundworm and Ancylostoma, another intestinal parasite with a spine on the edge of the ovum which could penetrate the gut wall and cause anaemia – and indeed Louis was anaemic, with a haemoglobin of just 10,7g/l.

Even I was impressed by this mass of pathology in Louis. After several weeks of treatment, he was considerably restored. I never saw those Calabar swellings again – but I still have the photo I took. Infective parasites were another area in which I was becoming a minor expert, learning that they could exist within any part of the human body.

I was rendered sick and stupefied at the first vaginal delivery I attended at Ebolowa to see a stream of foot-long round worms sliding out of the mother´s anus as she strained every muscle in her abdomen to expel her foetus. These were Ascaris, as Jack casually remarked, so common a parasite in these parts that they had an almost symbiotic relation with their human hosts.

Defeated by a Holy stool sample

On only one occasion was I completely defeated. The offending excrement was holy, having been brought in by one of the priests from the Catholic mission nearby with a history of bowel dysfunction.

Well, the more I studied this light brown stool the less I understood what I was looking at. The only outstanding thing I could see in a sea of homogenous brown were fat droplets, whose significance I did not know, nor did Emmanuel when he had a squint. In the end I had to say I could find no eggs or larvae of any parasites, which was pretty unusual since many of the Europeans also suffered worm infestations from time to time.

Two days later Fr Emile came back for his results and smiled when I told him of my failure to find any pathogens.

"*Trés bien*", he said, "and here is the rest of my sample – producing a glass jar of the same specimen from beneath his cassock.

"Please, have a taste", and he proffered the jar as I retreated in some shock.

"*Non*?", he smiled, and took the top off the jar, offering it. "Trust me, *ayez confiance* – for I am a priest". I knew him for a bit of a joker, so took the jar and sniffed. It was peanut butter! I tasted it to confirm the diagnosis and watched Emile laughing his head off at his good joke. When I thought of the time I had spent trying to find some evidence of worms in this nutty paste I realized I had been well and truly had. But I was glad that I had been honest in my findings, even though the temptation to imagine some worm egg was always there. I had at least gained a good jar of peanut butter from Fr. Emile, which Jack, Ruth and I demolished with gusto.

On Venereal Disease in Africa – and a painful introduction to Bouginage

I was beginning to learn that a great deal of human pathology existed within the perineal region. From protozoans to spirochaetes and multitudes of bacteria, there was always a pathogen lurking.

Venereal disease was as common in Ebolowa as it ever has been throughout the world. It affected both men and women, but the outward signs were most visible in the men. Both syphilis and gonorrhoea were common, as well as such nasty conditions as soft chancre where large oozing ulcers would appear around the vulva or over the penis and in the groins. But the sight which remains with me to this day is that of the queue of men waiting outside the Bougie Clinic, feared by all, which I eventually added to my responsibilities.

As each patient entered the small wooden shed from which the clinic operated, he lifted up his robe to expose a rusty tin tied around the base of his penis, into which dripped his infected urine through a series of penile fistulas.

It the West we are fortunate today that most acute infections can be arrested at an early stage. But in 1965 within the sweaty primaeval rain forest in which we worked, such diseases as gonorrhoea became chronic because of the lack of access to the necessary antibiotics and primary health care. The disease then progressed to form scar tissue within the urethra which blocked any normal egress of urine. The result was often kidney failure through urine obstruction and the formation of fistulae from the urethra to the outside of the penis. It was through these minute channels that the urine constantly dripped into the rusty tins.

For these unfortunate patients, life was a daily misery. The bougie was their only hope of salvation. The bougie was developed in France during the 18th century, when gonorrhoea and its sequelae was also a common problem amongst the gentry. It is a long, curved steel instrument which is passed down the penis, in the hope of re-finding the proper urethral passage and dilating it. The Cluttons bougies came in 12 different diameters. I squirm as I write these words, for the first time I witnessed Jack performing bouginage on one of these unfortunates and witnessed the pain it caused, I went pale. It took great skill and patience as well as a soft touch to find the correct urethral passage, but in those days it was the only chance these patients had of ever passing urine normally again.

As far as the women were concerned venereal disease was a much more secret and dangerous enemy because the infections were more often deep-seated in the pelvis, affecting the cervix, the uterus, and Fallopian tubes as well as other pelvic tissues and organs. The pathological effects were therefore usually more advanced by the time they arrived for treatment.

The most common problem was infertility as a result of the Fallopian tubes becoming blocked with scar tissue, but acute abscesses of the pelvis and pelvic organs also commonly caused peritonitis. Another common sequel was ectopic pregnancy where the actual pregnancy took place outside the uterus, often in one of the tubes. As the size of the foetus increased the women began to experience low pelvic pain which could mimic appendicitis, especially if the affected Fallopian tube was on the right side, but the greatest danger to life was haemorrhage from rupture of a Fallopian tube.

At a certain point in the evolution of the ectopic pregnancy, the increasing size of the foetus causes the Fallopian tube to split, leading to pelvic bleeding from ruptured blood vessels, which in these isolated communities was often fatal.

It is a sobering thought that just the timely provision of simple antibiotics such as penicillin or tetracycline could have saved so much morbidity and premature death from venereal disease.

Apart from my hours in the laboratory there were also the daily ward rounds and my sessions in the operating theatre with Jack and Dick as well as the various clinics I attended, so I had very little free time.

On Missionary Recreations

In spite of the heavy clinical workload Jack always had time for fun and games. Recreation at the mission was daily and took the form of tennis at 1700h every day, rain permitting, with Jack, Dick and several African friends. As with everything he did, Jack took his tennis seriously and energetically. He is still playing in Cincinnati aged 84. I never heard a missionary swear, but Jack came close every time he mis-hit a ball or lost a careless point. The first time this happened and I heard his shout, "Oh, SHhh…..oooooooot !", I was almost astonished. But that was Jack. He was a man´s man and a wonderful, brave surgeon who really cared a lot for his patients as well as being an aggressive player of games.

The tennis court, like the rest of the hospital, was also carved out of the solid jungle. If a ball went over the boundary netting it would take ages to find amidst the dense foliage, and there was always a significant risk of meeting one of the many venomous snakes which lived there. Bites from these reptiles were very bad news, for even the anti-venom we used was sometimes fatal, as it was then made from horses' serum, to which some people were fatally allergic.

Jack also had another excellent recreation. Every Sunday noon he and I and Mark, his eight- year- old son, would head for a strange open space in the jungle about the size of a football field. There we would fly control-line model aeroplanes until they had all crashed into smithereens, usually in my inexpert hands, and would then spend the following evenings gluing them back together so we could destroy them again the next weekend. I still remember the day that we had just a single plane left fit to fly, two others having been wiped out in fatal crashes already. I could see that Jack really wanted to fly it, but he said,

"Go on then, do your best", as he handed the control line to me. Within five seconds I had put managed to guide the plane into a high-speed power dive and turn it into a bunch of matchsticks which even Jack's skilled hands could never repair.

"Well, I guess that's it folks", he said with just the trace of sadness on his face, as Mark and I started gathering small bits of balsa wood. He was a great man.

An investigation into gorilla faeces, pygmies, and my first dose of malaria.

One day a young post-graduate student from UCLA California arrived at the mission in an ancient Citroen 2CV. Becky was on her way back to her lonely outpost in the rainforest where she was living and working with the pygmies, doing research into gorillas. It sounded fascinating. When Jack allowed me to escape the mission for a week with Becky and the pygmies, I was off like a shot.

As religious as the worship of Jesus was the Sunday ritual we all performed at breakfast in Jack´s house, when Ruth handed out our weekly dose of the anti-malarials, chloroquine and paludrine. Malaria was rife in the jungle and a big cause of morbidity and mortality, especially in the children. All the missionaries suffered now and then, in spite of their preventive measures, but none had so far died of 'black-water fever', a dreaded complication caused by the parasites blocking the kidney tubules and leading to haemorrhage and renal failure. It was a very nasty fever to encounter, as I was about to find out.

After six hours driving with Becky through dense jungle, we arrived at the pygmy village where she was based. For the third time in a year I found myself in a totally different culture and race, all within the same country.

The pygmies were indeed small, and perfectly proportioned. They lived not just in, but with the forest. Every single thing in their lives came from the forest, from their housing, their hunting weapons and poisons and their food. They even knew where to catch fish in hidden rivers, but most of all they knew every plant and their uses.

Becky's work was marking 50 metre square tracts in the jungle, and then on hands and knees looking for and collecting any gorilla faeces. These were then bagged up and sent to the Pasteur Institute for analysis of the seeds passed in the faeces, in order to learn more about the diet of these primates.

For two days I had great fun, also on my hands and knees, racing Becky to fill my plastic bag with gorilla turds. It was heady stuff after the operating theatre at Ebolowa.

I was extremely impressed with the pygmies and how they had adapted to their very different jungle way of life. The children were great fun, never having seen a white man before, they could not stop studying me and touching me and my blond hair. The nearest school was six hours away at Ebolowa, but they were already learning survival techniques in the rain forest and did not really need a classroom. Theirs was all around them, lush and green and damp.

On the third morning I awoke with a blinding headache and then started vomiting and shivering with cold. I managed to work for an hour and then collapsed and Becky had to help me back to the tiny grass hut where we stayed. I felt like death, sick as a dog, blinded by the headache and shivering and sweating at the same time. Becky was really worried and went to find the headman. I woke up to find him leaning over me, feeling my pulse and mumbling. Then he produced some leaves and told Becky to make a boullion with them which I should then drink.

At first I kept vomiting, but slowly, a spoonful at a time with Becky's help I did manage to drink this herbal remedy. When I awoke the next day I knew I was better. I had no headache or fever even though I was still weak. It was miraculous, but I was just beginning to learn about the pygmies and their encyclopaedic knowledge of the plants around them.

Three times a year an old Citroen truck, driven by a Greek trader from Kribi on the coast, would appear. The pygmies would then fill it with gunny sacks of various leaves and plants which they had collected.

These were then shipped to Germany where the giant pharmaceutical company, Bayer, turned them into early cardiac glycosides and other therapies. From penicillin to aspirin, many of our life-saving therapies derive from plants.

The Origin of AIDS.

On the way back to Ebolowa we met a solitary bush-meat hunter with his haul. I still have the photo of the chimpanzee and two monkeys propped up on the bumper of Becky's 2 cv, all of them shot by his gun. There was a huge trade in bush meat in the jungle, much of which I had enjoyed at our local restaurant, 'Le Cabin Bambou' in Ebolowa. Whilst I was aghast to see this dead chimpanzee, I also realised that this was part of an indigenous way of life. The natives had used bows and poison-tipped arrows to hunt for food before the white men and their guns arrived. Wherever I went in Africa the natives hunted animals for food, just as generations before them had, but unlike the whites they did not hunt just for the fun of killing animals.

It was around this time, from this exact area of the southern Cameroun rain forest that the simian immune deficiency disease passed from monkeys into humans and became AIDS, almost certainly through the consumption of bush meat. This viral disease has now killed more than 30 million people worldwide and after 40 years there is still no vaccine available. Other major plagues since then such as SARS and MERS and avian flu have also evolved from the invasion of natural habitats by humans and their trade in bush meat, corona virus being only the latest and the deadliest of all.

Jack was happy to see me back in one piece, more or less, and was not surprised to hear of my miraculous cure by the pygmies. He had been their neighbour for years and knew much about them. For me the trip had been a revelation into another hidden aspect of human existence. It was one which engendered in me a love of plants and continuing interest in their protective and healing properties.

Performing my first operation – aged 19.

Twice a week I assisted Jack at his operations in the big theatre. He never stopped teaching, and I absorbed it all like a willing sponge. Soon he was letting me do small procedures as well as teaching me precisely how to perform an inguinal hernia repair.

"When you've done your first 25", he drawled, "then you might be getting to know where the hell you are in the inguinal canal!"

As usual, he was right. By the time I left Ebolowa at the age of 19, I had already performed five such hernia repairs by myself, with Jack as first assistant. That is how good a teacher he was. He spent hours with me over the operating table, teaching me a huge amount about the surgical anatomy and all the ways it could be deformed by pathology, and how to restore it.

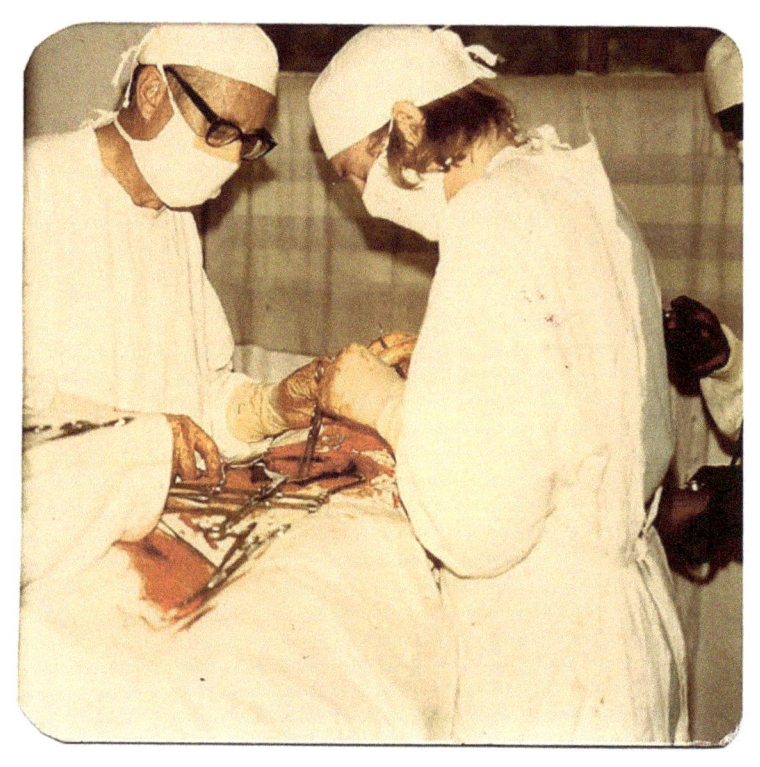

Jack was a wonderful, patient teacher and mentor

The nearest I had got to surgery before Ebolowa had been the unlucky rabbit I met in the Biology lab at Lewes County Grammar School for Boys. To allow a 19-year-old straight out of school to perform hernia operations on humans may seem strange to some today, but Jack knew what he was about. I think he saw in me something similar to himself.

I did love surgery and the whole of clinical tropical medicine, and seeing that, he responded like a true maestro. I was a fast learner and I think Jack realised that I could soon actually be of some practical help in the surgical team. When I look back on those early days I am indeed astounded at my good fortune. Jack was one of the cleverest and most caring surgeons I ever worked with. He always set the highest standards, not just in surgical techniques but also in his care and compassion for all the patients.

It took me a further eight years to complete the 25 hernia repairs required by Jack, and since then I must have done hundreds and also passed on Jack's wisdom to quite a few other young surgeons in training.

I guess that this is actually the sort of thing that Socrates and his colleagues must have been doing under those Greek olive trees two thousand years ago - passing on freely the fruits of their own knowledge and experience to those acolytes who wished to join their vocation.

Dinner with Dr Schweitzer

It was during my time at Ebolowa that I met Dr Albert Schweitzer down in Lambaréné, in Gabon. He had always been a hero to my parents, who loved listening to his organ playing, but to me he was a hero for his medical work in Africa, which had made him an international celebrity. He was the first famous person I ever met and was certainly the most daunting. It took a three- day trip through forest and down rivers in pencil-thin pirogues with my main man Mahimbu, and then an invisible border crossing from Cameroun into Gabon, before I finally stood before the great man.

He was impressive, standing over six feet tall and commanding the scene. He was an authoritative figure within the mission hospital and appeared to run it rather like a military camp. I do not doubt that he was a very clever man with Doctorates in everything from Music to Medicine, and I am sure that he did a lot of good for the people he worked with, but it was not the way I wanted to practice tropical medicine. After three sombre days at Lambaréné I was glad to get back to Jack and my friends at Ebolowa.

As I write I am listening to an old vinyl record of my mothers. It is Dr Schweitzer playing Bach - the Toccata and Fugue in D Minor. I am thinking of Lambaréné in 1965, shortly before he died, and the ancient harmonium he used to play for us after dinner at night. Sitting in the remote jungle with this strange but gifted man, devout follower of Jesus that he was, I wondered about the strange clash of his brilliance but his blindness to the other cultural needs of the Africans. He was another one who just knew he was right, because Jesus told him so.

On the way back I was walking through the jungle with Mahimbu, when we heard a loud crashing sound from not far away. We froze in the shadow of a huge tree trunk and within seconds three big elephants came trundling by, swinging their trunks as they passed us, disappearing into the gloom of the forest. This takes me back to the hunting habits of the missionaries…..

On Elephant Hunting

Now elephant hunting may not appear to be the most likely recreation for a Christian missionary, but it was at Ebolowa that I first saw a missionary dressed like a commando in camouflage fatigues, clutching a massive .475 Magnum rifle, on his way to slaughter a few of these fine animals. The first time I was invited along with Bud, the secondary school teacher and his son Spike and a couple of trackers, I went for the experience. It was such an experience that I never repeated it.

"Forrad Ho!", Bud was no longer the benign missionary, he was a re-incarnation of John Wayne, minus the horse. As I walked in file behind him and Spike I felt like an actor in a film. The set was the living jungle, full of the noises of parrots and monkeys as we stalked silently along the forest floor.

The primaeval rain forest of Southern Cameroun remains for me one of my most precious African memories. Today it is all but gone, and even in 1965 the logging companies were driving roads as straight as rulers through this pristine and previously untouched forest paradise.

Primary rain forest has no undergrowth because the forest canopy prevents the rays of the sun from ever reaching the forest floor. Only when man interferes with this natural umbrella does the sunlight fall and give life to the million seeds lying in wait. The result is secondary forest, which very soon becomes the impenetrable jungle we are so used to seeing in Hollywood films.

On my first and only elephant hunting expedition I had the singular experience of walking on the open floor of an untouched primary forest. The trunks of the hardwood trees were just massive and stretched upwards to the limit of my vision where the green umbrella of leaves completely blotted out the sun. As a result, we walked in a relative gloom, and it was only a warning whisper from Bud which alerted me to activity ahead.

Something was indeed moving ahead of us, but to me everything was a shade of grey and it was only when Bud grabbed his attack cannon to his shoulder that I knew we were in for some serious action.

"Get your head down", shouted Spike in excitement as a huge grey shape came for us. As I tried to melt into the adjacent tree trunk, hiding between its butterfly wing roots, there was a mighty explosion and then another. Then came a plaintive cry from Bud,

"Help, my ear….", but when I ran up to his bloody figure lying prostrate on the ground it soon became apparent that he no longer possessed his right ear. Instead, there was a bloody mess with spurts of blood gushing. I was carrying a First Aid kit and it did contain one Major Abdominal Pack. This was the size of a small mattress and had been purloined from ex-Vietnam stores by some friend of Bud. Applied to Buds wound it did staunch the flow of blood and allow us to hobble home. The elephant was long gone. Spike was full of remorse having just blown a large chunk of his fathers' head off, and I was determined never, ever to go elephant hunting again.

"Have a good time?", Jack asked laconically on my return, dishevelled, exhausted and mildly shocked by recent events in the jungle. He was a man who hated guns and all forms of hunting.

"I think I'll stick to crashing planes in future", I replied, as we both headed for the workshop where we had two more planes to restore before the weekend.

The resourcefulness of the missionaries deserves mention. They usually did four-year stints in those days and when they travelled from the USA they needed every single thing to survive for four years – Christmases, Easters, all the birthdays and other celebrations. They were quite extraordinary in their ingenuity and intelligence when it came to procuring what they needed, and the hunters were no exception.

"Bud", I said shortly after he re-appeared in the mission – sporting a pretty pink plastic prosthesis over his absent right pinna, "tell me, how on earth do you manage to bring those dirty great elephant-killing bullets into Cameroun?"

"Well," began Bud, "Ah gotta brudda in Wyoming. He gotta canning factory. He sends me cans of Green Giant, peaches, you know……fruits".

"Are you telling me that he cans bullets for you?", I enquired, slightly astonished at this revelation.

"Sure thing", replied Bud, ".380s, Magnums, .475s, you name it. Whatever we need for hunting some meat!"

There was no end to this resourcefulness, even if I did not entirely agree with canned bullets for elephants. It truly was a case of necessity becoming the mother of invention every day in these remote parts of Africa.

In those early post-colonial days in West Africa communications were very tenuous. The roads often disappeared with the rains, along with the postal deliveries and many supplies. Telephone lines were also subject to the weather and pulling fallen telegraph poles off the road was a fairly regular occurrence. Ordering something from Yaoundé and expecting it to arrive was always an adventure. Hence the need for innovation and ingenuity.

Of all the inventive mothers, Ruth was by far the greatest. Not only was she the patient and loving wife of a busy tropical surgeon, but she was also the mother of three young children as well as a stalwart part of the mission community at Ebolowa. She had taught Daniel, our excellent cook, all manner of great recipes, including several French delicacies, all manufactured from whatever happened to be around plus a few bits from the depths of her 40-gallon drum of HOME WARES! She taught me to make coffee cake, better known as cinnamon roll, a delicious form of cake consisting of a simple roll of cake pastry with a filling of brown sugar and crushed cinnamon. I still make it in Spain and one roll will last me a week. Sadly, Ruth died of cancer some years ago, but not before she and Jack and the kids had come to visit my own family at Deanlands Farm, Vines Cross.

I still have some great photos of that reunion in England, the first time for Jack and his family. He was one of the very few Americans I ever met who had a true sense of history. He and Ruth were lit up at the sights of the Norman country churches and other historical monuments around the farm where I grew up in East Sussex.

I was really sad when the day came to leave Jack and Ruth and everyone who had looked after me and taught me so much at the Hôpital Central, but Medical School was beckoning. I was on my way to Liverpool, a place I had never been to, somewhere up in the northern wastes of industrial Britain. It was a place that my parents spoke of in bated breath. It seemed a galaxy away from the romantic life which I had enjoyed at the expense of VSO for one glorious and momentous year of my young life in the Dark Continent, during which Africa had seeded itself into my system.

Amongst the items I packed in my old man's ex-RAF soft leather travelling bag for my return journey was an exquisite small clay pipe, given to me by one of my Bougie Clinic patients, which I still smoke. I was also carrying a perfectly matched pair of virgin ivory elephant tusks about a metre long.

These beautiful tusks were a gift from the father of a young boy with measles I had helped look after. During my time in Ebolowa I was given some amazing presents, including a dead baboon, slung from the handlebars of the hunter's bicycle, which tasted pretty good when skinned and roasted. I was also gifted one African Grey parrot called Jo-Jo who could swear in three languages, amongst many other treasured items. I had to get rid of those two ivory tusks the end. By 2004, just 40 years later, the world had changed, Wildlife Protection had entered the lingua franca and the ivory trade was now illegal.

The trip to Yaoundé with Jack was bad. Recent rains had completely destroyed the road out of Ebolowa, and even in the huge 4.7 litre Dodge pickup with 4-wheel drive we had to dig ourselves out of the mud at least four times in 200 kilometres. When Dr Jack Payne met Ambassador Jack Warner at the British Embassy in Yaoundé around midnight after an exhausting trip, I was ready for bed, but still managed to down an anaesthetic quantity of brandy. Meanwhile

Jack, my surgical mentor for the last six months, enjoyed his tea, which was all he ever drank. Then I collapsed into dreams.

A thousand memories of an unforgettable year were imprinted in my mind. There were lions and elephants, there were fantastically attired warriors on horseback as well as the Legionnaires at Fort Lamy, the brooding figure of Schweitzer as he read the bible before dinner, gin and lime served by James at the British Embassy in Yaoundé, and then there were the drums at dawn in Tchamba, being tuned with red-hot coals upon the skins……BoomBoom, BongDa…..BoomBoom, BongDa….

By the time I started at medical school I had already spent a year in Africa learning about every aspect of tropical medicine and surgery. This later proved a huge advantage in my studies, as well as igniting my love of medicine in a way which no academic course could ever have achieved.

4. FROM AFRICA TO LIVERPOOL   1965 – 74

Merseyside in the '60s

The view as I crossed the Runcorn bridge in early October 1965 was depressing.

I was on my way to Liverpool to begin my medical studies. In those days I knew nothing of the delights of Coronation Street, but the lines of Victorian terraces stretching into the distance as the train crossed the bridge became an icon during the next 10 years of my life. The sky was grey, the bridge was grey, and the Runcorn River was grey. And most of the factories were black. After the myriad colours of Africa, the drab greyness of northern England was hard to bear, and Runcorn epitomized it perfectly. I had crossed the Thames long ago and was now in the industrial heartland of the British Empire, heading west for Liverpool.

Even though I had just spent a year travelling and working all over West Africa, often by myself, my first experience in Liverpool was as challenging as anything I had experienced on the Dark Continent. When I boarded the red double-decker bus to take me to Sefton Park I found it impossible to comprehend the weird accent of the conductor who came to take my fare.

"Weer ya bun fah?", he said.

"Pardon me?", I replied, not understanding one word, but offering a ten-pound note, my sole wealth.

"Wa th fooks u wijya?", the conductor was beginning to look less than welcoming, and became even less so when it became apparent that he had no change for this note. By the time I escaped the bus outside Rathbone Hall of Residence I was shaken, after further unintelligible abuse from this foreign-speaking public servant.

That was my introduction to Scouse. Scouse humour, Scouse pie, the Kop and the thousands of Liverpudlians who became my neighbours, friends and some, my patients during the following 10 years in this great seaport.

There cannot have been a better time to experience Liverpool than 1965. The great trans-Atlantic liners were still arriving and filling the Adelphi hotel with rich Americans. The Mersey Beat led by the Beatles was bringing fame to the city. The port had yet to become containerized, an act which completely changed the economic outlook for the thousands of stevedores employed at that time.

Liverpool was still one of the major British seaports with a history going back to the beginning of the British Empire and the era of slavery, from which much of the city's wealth was derived. Much of the produce extracted from Britain's many colonies passed through this port as well as numerous immigrants from every corner of the globe. I became used to seeing Jamaicans, Somalis, Hindus and Chinese wherever I walked and also became familiar with their cultures, including their food.

The first dose of Liverpudlian humour I ever came across was, "What's a mile long, black at one end and yellow at the other?" The answer was Upper Parliament Street, which stretched from the Jamaican and Somali communities in the north, where we learned to enjoy fiery curries, to Chinatown at its southern terminus by the docks, where I first ate chicken chow mein. There were also the Liverpool night clubs to enjoy. It was a great contrast after the quiet, studious evenings at the Mission Protestante, N´Gaoundéré where the lights went out at 10 pm. My friends and I used to go to the Jacaranda club to listen to ska, inhaling the sweet fumes of ganja as the Rastas waved their dreadlocks and jived.

The Cavern Club in Matthew Street was not so well-known in those days, but Gerry and the Pacemakers, Freddy and the Dreamers and quite a few other up and coming Mersey groups came and played there, and in 1968 I also got a spot there. By then it was becoming the creative centre of the now famous Mersey sound.

From the outside of The Cavern, you would never have known it. Damp steps led down to a murky interior where everything was shabby, from the plastic-covered tables to the tiny stage where there was barely enough room for one, let alone four mop-haired musicians. Liverpool Council later 'restored' The Cavern once The Beatles became famous, but of course it was never the same.

First days as a Medical Student

My student residence was at Rathbone Hall, a most comfortable and civilized place to begin life as a university student. Opposite it was a street sign which has become iconic:Penny Lane. The song by that name, immortalized by the Beatles, became a big hit around 1966 and during my first year at Liverpool Medical School I saw that street sign every day from my bedroom window on the first floor of Rathbone Hall.

That famous sign disappeared within a few weeks, stolen as a souvenir by some fan, and then so did the replacement. When I re-visited that hallowed spot 10 years ago the sign had been replaced by a concrete brick, inscribed with those two famous words. It was now un-stealable, but was no longer a picturesque antique icon.

Rathbone Hall was relatively new and was divided into corridors of eight bedrooms with a communal kitchen and bathroom. Friendships made early in life are often long-standing, and it was on my corridor that I made my first medical friend, Ian, who is still my oldest and most constant friend from university days. He had a similar background to me, having spent his schooldays at Pocklington, a public school in the wilds of the Yorkshire moors.

Our characters were quite different. Ian took his studies more seriously than I did, though we both shared adventures and escapades in and around Merseyside. Exactly 10 years later we both celebrated gaining our Fellowships of the Royal College in London, me in General Surgery and Ian in Anaesthetics.

Ian and I both had public school accents, unusual amongst Liverpool's mostly northern student body. One of the other new friends on our corridor was Rod Andrew, a gifted young man from Morecombe Bay. When Rod's girlfriend Lisa knocked on my door by mistake, he later told me that she had said,

"'Ere, ooze that foony chap with the posh accent?", which made me laugh. Rod and I became close friends, much because of his exceptional skills as a guitar player. It was the first time I saw a guitar player with inch long fingernails on his right, playing hand, and I also learned to keep my right fingernails long rather than use the steel finger picks which some favour.

Going down to the refectory with Ian one night we passed Rod's door and I heard the most beautiful melody being played. The song was 'Angie', possibly one of the best known of all folk blues pieces, written by another genius of the blues guitar, Davy Graham. It was Rod who taught me 'Angie'. I was told some years later that you could not play guitar in Ronnie Scotts unless you had mastered Davy's 'Angie'.

Among Rod's gifts was the innate ability to listen to a tune once and then reproduce it perfectly on his guitar. He was a gifted maestro, and over a period of weeks he patiently taught me that complex syncopated rhythm and other finger-picking methods which have been the basis of all my guitar music ever since.

Rod was studying Electronic Engineering, but he hardly ever went to lectures, deeming them boring, and did not usually leave his bed in Rathbone until threatened with physical abuse by Doris, our cleaning lady.

I never knew where all his academic knowledge of electronics came from, for there was never a book in sight in his room. However, he still obtained one of the best First's in Electronics that Liverpool had seen, his only concession to academia being to lock himself in his room for the week prior to finals for, as he put it, "a bit of revision". He went to Belgium soon after with a professorship in Antwerp and I have never seen him since, but every time I play 'Angie' I remember my gifted friend.

On the corridor below was Long John, like Ian another second-year medical student. He was also some sort of genius, but a very different one, for not only did he put in the necessary 10,000 hours of study but he was the only one amongst 120 medical students studying for the 2nd MB (Bachelor of Medicine) exam who understood something of what went on inside the brain.

To most of us aspiring doctors anything above the shoulders was a mystery. Our lecturer in NeuroAnatomy, whilst being an international authority on the central nervous system, was incapable of transferring his boundless knowledge of the brain and neural system to us. But Long John had triumphed by learning and understanding Cunningham's Anatomy from cover to cover. He spent hours every night that first year studying this huge tome and deservedly won the gold medal in both his pre-clinical years. Understandably, after joining the Percy Street gang, (of which more later), his shining academic performances fell off as he was sucked into our less challenging approach towards medical studies.

Long John was also a real joker with a wicked sense of humour and managed to fit in most of our pranks as well as his academic studies. These eventually led him to some of the highest honours in the land as Professor of Gastro-Intestinal Medicine at the London Hammersmith Hospital.

Tragically, one year after taking up that position he was diagnosed with Glioblastoma Multiforma – the most malignant of any brain tumour. I came over from Spain to say hello/goodbye to this dear friend. As he lay on his deathbed he asked me,

"Do you think it's because I over-used my brain?".

"What brain?", I replied, and we both laughed, but inside I was crying, to see this wonderful, gifted friend for the last time.

Spending most hours of every day for a year together proved to be a great bonding experience. Long John, Ian and I were always close mates ever since those early days in Rathbone Hall, and we picked up a few more good friends during that first electric year.

An Early Tragedy

One of the first was Martin 'Curly' Clarfield who lived on another corridor in Rathbone. I met him in the bar the first night where our college Bursar was holding an introductory drinks session for freshers. Curly was the first Jew I ever met. He was the eldest son of a family of orthodox Jews in London who had made their fortune in bespoke tailoring.

After downing four double whiskies we staggered back to my room carrying a crate of Newcastle Brown, and all I can remember of that night is the sight of Curly vomiting down his bespoke, three-piece suit and crying.

When I awoke, with a massive headache, Curly was unconscious on the floor and there were eight empty bottles of Newcastle Brown scattered around the room and a terrible smell of stale vomit. Since that day I have never been able to face that ale.

We were so young and so naïve that the thought of taking the day off to recover never occurred to us. It was a jump of some 15 feet into a rosebush in order to catch the university bus to make the very first lecture on time. With a cranium mostly still full of alcohol I do not remember a single word of that lecture, and nor did Curly, but that toxic beginning to our career as medics was an event which bonded us like nothing else.

We also continued to get uproariously drunk more often than we should, in between getting intimate with as many of the delightful female students across the road in Darby Hall as time allowed. It was a beautiful time to be alive, care-free and young.

It says much for my friendship with Curly that I was the first goy ever to enter his parents luxurious flat in London. It was June 1967, and the whole of St Johns Wood was hung with Israeli flags whilst the Middle East exploded yet one more time.

In his second year Curly fell in love with Ena, an attractive Biochemistry student who did not have one drop of Jewish blood in her buxom body, and soon the pair were inseparable. Even our own macho union was disturbed. Then one day I came across Curly in unusually low spirits. It turned out that he had taken Ena down to London to meet his parents, who had rejected this goy lady and sent them both packing.

It seemed that the thought of any non-Jewish blood in the family was more than his parents could bear. It transpired that Curly's father had told him he would be disinherited from the family unless he parted company with Ena. I was appalled at this, for only the authoritarian Lutheran missionaries in Cameroun had ever behaved in a similar, inhumane fashion in my life before.

That summer, after successfully passing my 1st MB exams I set off on a 10-week voyage to Morocco, aiming for the Youth Hostel at Marrakech. After several weeks hitching around the foothills of the Atlas Mountains I bid a fond farewell to the green fields of Ouazazate, and the medinas of Fez and Rabat and returned to Liverpool in October, bronzed and thin, but fit as a fiddle.

I was greeted with the news that Curly had committed suicide during the vacation, having failed his 2nd MB exams, no doubt as a result of his emotional turmoil over Ena and his family's attitude towards her.

My view of religion as a malign force since my days in Cameroun was again reinforced.

He was the first of my friends to die, in such a manner, and for such a reason that I have never forgotten. We were all shocked at Curly's death. Our lives till then had been happy, and full of youth's illusions. This sad event was one more step in the rite of passage we were all making. It cast a pall, and I was left bereaved and wondering much about the madness of religion and race.

The First MB year

As a result of failing Physics at A-level at school I could not pass into the Medical 2nd MB course until I had achieved my 1st MB, which was basically a one-year course, taken in the university Faculty of Science, and was not very demanding. It also allowed a few who had done Arts at A-level and then changed their minds, to enter the medical course. We were only 10 such students, compared to the 100-odd in each of the other five years, and a jolly gang we were, who by virtue of our rather exclusive existence became very close friends, and still are.

Having a strong interest in the human mind I also enrolled in the BSc.(Hons) course in Psychology which was a part of the Arts Faculty. In that first year at university, I had the unusual privilege of being in 3 Faculties at the same time – Medicine, Science and Arts.

In those days about 30% of the intake of medical students was female and inevitably, lasting relationships were formed. I also had the great advantage of being in the Arts and Science faculties where the proportion of females was nearer 50/50. It was 1965. The contraceptive pill had just been invented and the Abortion Act was soon to become law. A social revolution was on the way, and I was right in the centre.

Let me tell you about MSS, the Liverpool Medical Students Society, which was the vital hub of the medical school in those days. There were about 700 members, and several thousand previous members, many of whom had become well-known and famous. At the weekly Thursday evening meetings, we saw them begin to unfold and evolve into debaters, leaders, orators, jokers and every other representation of the creative spirit. There were sub-societies, the medical student magazine Sphincter, of which I became the editor in 1968, sports, music and brewery trips. We even had a small chamber orchestra. And then there was the Medic Smoking Concert, more commonly known as the Medics Smoker.

Every December each of the five clinical and pre-clinical years put on a half-hour review composed usually of the most disgusting rhyming couplets circling around the pelvic organs and mammary glands, taking the piss out of our teachers, the Pope and any other figure of authority, including the Dean, Jack Leggate.

In 1965 there was a sixth entry into the Smoker competition, the class of us 10 brave warriors from 1st MB. It was not a large number of would-be actors and singers, but we were nothing if not enterprising. One of our number, Myron was from north Wales and spoke with that lilting accent I got to know so well. A prankster who became one of my closest friends, it was in his company that one winters day in 1965 we found ourselves on Denbigh Moor outside a stone farmhouse, standing in the middle of a large flock of sheep.

Miss Charity joins the medics

We were about to enjoy another interesting escapade, which later resulted in my premature exit from Rathbone Hall of Residence and may have been related to Myron's later exit from medical school having twice failed his 2nd MB exams.

"Faith! Hope! Charity!", cried out Mrs Bliss, the 60-year-old farmer who farmed these wild and windswept moors. And astonishingly, we saw three of this big flock detach themselves and head for this strapping lady who gave them each a carrot and then asked us, "And which one would best suit your need?"

We settled for Charity, who was the most beautiful. Minutes later, having traded my valueless Students Union card for one mature lady sheep, we managed to wedge Charity onto the lap of Myron, who occupied the passenger seat of AKA, my 1935 Morris 8 Sports Tourer.

Our problems with Charity began as we exited the Mersey Tunnel at St George's Place in the centre of downtown Liverpool. During our return from the bleak Welsh moors Charity had relieved herself, mostly down Myron's trouser legs, but she showed no shame. At the traffic lights at the tunnel exit, always alert and interested, she poked her furry head out of the side window for a better view of Lime Street.

"Wa tha foox tha'?" said the first pedestrian about to cross, staring unbelievingly at our new companion.

"Issa phookin ship!!" said his mate, and soon there was a small crowd of Scousers enjoying the sight of Myron sitting rather embarrassed, with a full-grown sheep on his lap. Then the police arrived.

We were lucky to make the Anatomy Department in the Victoria Building without being arrested, but we did. We then wondered what to do with Charity until the concert began some hours later. Once again, it was not what you know, but who you know that matters in these cases.

Joe was the senior technician in the Anatomy department, and was a good friend of mine, as I had instinctively fallen in love with anatomy and the human body and spent hours in the dissecting room and Joe's specimen preparation room. I often visited him in the animal house which was like a miniature zoo, containing everything from rats to monkeys and other primates which we studied.

He was impressed when I introduced him to Charity, and agreed to house her until the concert began, and when Myron and I left her, she was having a friendly chat with a Macaque monkey in the cage next door.

Charity proved to be a winner for us, her crowning moment being when she defaecated and urinated on the stage floor as she made her entry, so our footwork for the rest of the show was both smelly as well as dangerous.

After the riotous concert finished, not only did we have a special prize, in the form of a firkin of Tetleys Best, but a still very much alive and frisky sheep to care for. Not one of us was sober, and it says much for those glorious days that we thought nothing of tipping Charity into AKA before driving back to Rathbone Hall. Then we encouraged a suspicious Charity up the stairs to my corridor and into the bathroom. We thought she would be safe enough with a bowl of water and a cabbage.

It was a shock to awaken a few hours later to the sound of a broom handle being battered against my door by our outraged cleaner, Doris.

"Wa´ the hellza ship doin' in my bathroom?", she was shouting through the bedroom door, whilst I was trying to connect ship and bathroom as well as cope with an almighty headache. "This ain't a zoo, y'know". She stood like an angry spectre in front of me brandishing her broom furiously. Someone had passed a bowl of cold porridge under the bathroom door, which a bleating Charity was presently using as a foot balm.

Then the Warden arrived. Dr Woods was normally found floating somewhere in the higher realms of academia, but today he was obviously back on Planet Earth, flanked by a phalanx of angry cleaners in their blue dustcoats, each waving a broom in protest. It was a memorable early-morning experience and cost me another five pounds in fines as well as the news that I would be looking for alternative accommodation at the end of the academic year – if I was still at Liverpool Medical School.

My first car, AKA, 1934 Morris 8 Sports Tourer

On Life in Liverpool 8

That was how I found myself at No 9, Percy Street, Toxteth, Liverpool 8, for the next five years, in the company of seven other medics who became my friends, mentors and drinking companions in a fellowship known throughout the medical fraternity as 'The Percy Street Gang'. I was the youngest member and learnt an enormous amount from my housemates. Most were now in final year and were regarded with awe by me for their seniority and experience. Under their careful tutelage I matured into a genuine medical student, streetwise and lecture-shy, while absorbing the urban culture of Liverpool during those glorious years of the 1960s.

Whilst a hall of residence was a comfortable and cushioned start to university life there was nothing to beat the streets of Liverpool, and Liverpool 8 in those halcyon days of the '60s was just the place to get the real flavour of this great city.

The following year Ian, Long John and Tony moved in, then Sandy and Jean and JS, as the more senior members graduated and went on to their house jobs in the hospitals around Merseyside. Ian and I had the two garret rooms at the top of this classic Georgian terraced house overlooking the Anglican cathedral, in those days still under construction.

Liverpool had many positive attributes, and one of them must be the existence of two huge cathedrals, one classic Anglican Gothic and the other a futuristic Catholic rocket with wonderful stained-glass windows. During my 10 years in Liverpool, they both remained icons for the continuously warring Irish Catholics and the Proddie Dogs as they were known.

It was only when the Pope came to bless the new Catholic cathedral in 1967 that I realized the full force of the Roman Catholic community in Liverpool, maintained in large part by a likeable and garrulous Irish immigrant population. Indeed, I always thought that the Scouse dialect had a bit of the Irish brogue in it.

Liverpool really did have a long, sea-faring history. The greatest monuments to it were the many Victorian buildings which filled the city centre, of which the Philharmonic Hall, a most wonderfully embellished concert hall, is arguably one of the most famous. Just opposite is the Philharmonic pub – known by everyone as 'The Phil'. This edifice is possibly even more famous, for the astounding men's toilets. Every surface within is composed of dark green striated marble, including the cubicles. The plumbing is all copper, polished to perfection, and the combination is both unique and outstanding. This temple of refreshment has recently been made a listed building, and I am honoured to have spent so much time within.

Every autumn term the city went wild with Panto. This was the annual opportunity for every student in the university to spend a week patrolling the streets of Liverpool, dressed in all manner of outrageous clothing, collecting money for charity. It was a great chance to see more of the city and its people, and I was sorry when our clinical responsibilities prevented us from taking part during our 2nd three years of study.

Panto Week, 1967

It was inside The Phil that we of the Percy Street gang used to pass many frigid winter evenings, drinking copious Tetley's Best to ward off the cold. Then, in various states of drunkenness we would go to the Somali restaurant off Catherine Street for one of their rat curries, as we called the fiery Madras curry of indefinable origin, which they provided for just five shillings. Occasionally our drinking habits got us into trouble, and it was at this same establishment that we had our only serious fracas with the local fraternity.

As usual we were all in joyous and biblious humour as we entered, singing ' Dinah, Dinah show us your leg, a yard above your knee' in great voice. We ordered the usual Rat Madras and were into the final chorus when a female voice piped up,

"Why the phook doan yer shurrup!"

JS, normally one of the most respectful and sober of our company and a GP all his life, was sitting nearest to her and riposted, drunkenly, "Shut up yourself!", possibly unwisely, for the next moment this lady lashes out at JS who grabs her handbag and gives it to her in the face.

There were about ten plates of curry and beer glasses on our table when this lady´s male companion jumped up, gave JS an almighty kick in the balls which laid him horizontal and speechless and then up-ended our table at which point I received a blow on my jaw which also felled me.

My outstanding memory of this great evening as I collapsed into an anaesthetic coma was the unusual experience of seeing most of our meal disappearing through the window and onto the street below to the orchestral sounds of smashing crockery, the tympany of the cutlery, and the sibilant siren of a fast-approaching squad car.

By the time the boys in blue arrived we were breathless and bruised, but safe back in No 9. The saddest bit of the whole jape was that the following day I was due to start a three-week locum with Dr Baker-Bates at the Providence Hospital at St Helens.

This was a Catholic institution run by Irish nuns, famous throughout the whole medical school for the terrific cuisine offered to the young doctors who came to cover the wards, as well as the opportunity to play tennis with the nuns. These locums for B-B were fought over for that sole reason, but when I awoke the following morning, I didn't just have my usual throbbing headache. This had been eclipsed by the acute pain from my right jaw which was considerably swollen and impossible to open more than half an inch. So, for the first week at the Providence I suffered greatly as I watched full English breakfasts, pork chops for lunch and steak for dinner being enjoyed by Thomas, my fellow junior house officer, whilst I dwelt briefly on the dangers of alcohol in all its forms, and occasionally rued my moral turpitude.

This event did little to change my social habits, as a result of which, during my Final Year I found myself passing a less than pleasant night inside the main Liverpool jail – the Bridewell, as it was infamously known amongst the lesser mortals of Merseyside.

An Unpleasant visit to the Bridewell

The night began as usual with the cry "Drinkies!" bellowed up the stairs of No 9 by JS. It says much for the character of Long John that he rarely missed these alcoholic excursions, despite being the outstanding Gold Medal student of our year of 118 medical students.

Our jolly quorum of eight set out once more for the foggy backstreets of Liverpool 8, ending up once again at a curry house in Docklands. It was on the way back that the Black Maria stopped us, just as we were passing St Luke's bombed out church, always creepy at the dead of night.

In those days even the cops in Liverpool were still fairly polite. They certainly did not cruise the streets in expensive BMWs and Volvos painted in such fluorescent colours as to pose a substantial risk to any epileptics, as they do today.

"You boys all right?", enquired the constable of our inebriated group.

"Oh, absholutely offisher", replied someone, still able to vocalize as we leaned against each other in the cold night air. As usual, it was my big mouth that caused upset to this officer of the law, and before I knew what was happening, I was flying horizontally into the back of the black van, propelled quite sharpish by a large black boot. Sadly, I still cannot remember what I said that so provoked this officer of the law.

The last I heard was Ian crying out in desperation to the constable something to the effect, "Good sir, I pray thee release this innocent for he is destined to become a doctor", to which came the laconic reply, "Over my phookin dead body", which, as my medical career evolved, was more than possible.

I cannot recommend too highly to my readers that they avoid at all costs taking shelter in any of HMP' s various facilities. The main Bridewell was not even Dickensian, it was positively Tolstoian in its filth and misery. Furthermore, the presence of a ragged, stinking down-and-out by the name of Dave sharing my lodging for the night reduced my spirits even further as he greeted my entrance with a copious vomit onto my feet.

Even though Dave and I may have been far apart socially, for our mutual sins that night we were indeed brothers-in-arms.

In my personal annals of medical science this nocturnal experience has yet to be surpassed for sheer unpleasantness, and it was almost a relief the following morning to present myself, not looking at my best, in front of a finely attired gentleman sitting in a court room. The only thing missing was his black hat, and when he sentenced me for Drunk and Disorderly Behaviour, despite the accompanying five pound fine, I felt relieved that I was not on my way to the Antipodes on a prison transport.

Sitting in front of me in my moment of shame were the remnants of my surgical firm, and it was they who clubbed together to pay my fine, for as they said, it was rich entertainment seeing such a look of contrition on my face for this brief instant, and in such regal surroundings.

The interview I had with the Dean later that day was considerably less pleasant. In spite of being a kindly old buffer, he did not take well to the lowering of 'The Standards' of the Medical School.

"Are you quite sure that you really do want to become a doctor?", he asked. "You do realize that within six months you may actually become a junior houseman, and this is not the sort of behaviour which we expect from our medical students, particularly so senior". Suddenly I was aware. I was aware that there was never going to be anything else I wanted to do more at this time in my life, and the thought that this dream might now evaporate was scaring.

"Of course, I want to be a doctor", I responded earnestly. "I'm going to be a surgeon......."

"Maybe, one day, if and when you grow up", said this old man with his years of wisdom. "Remember, your patients will always look up to you, so you must never let them down. That is your duty as their doctor. Now go and get on with passing Finals", and with this I exited his study, moderately chastened and thoughtful.

Half a century later when I look back, I am horrified by the way we students behaved from time to time. Few of us were immune from occasionally getting drunk and behaving abominably. No wonder that students often get a bad press. However, I do believe that such anti-social behaviour is for many young people, not just students, an inevitable and important part of exploring moral boundaries and growing into a responsible adult.

Each one of us was free to choose their own path. I, along with many others had pitfalls, but, with luck on my side, I did always manage to extricate myself. Some were not so lucky. Jeremy, a student in the year above got hooked on gambling and having lost all his student grant in one night, blew his head off with a shotgun. He was just 23 years old. So, the liberated life we led was not all just fun and games.

We all had to work very hard at our pre-clinical medical studies as well as find time for the important social events in our formation as medical practitioners. During my second year we had to undergo viva voce examinations on the human body every week, and if you failed them you had to re-sit the viva, which was a big pain. And if the failures continued you were usually invited to retire to a less taxing discipline than Medicine.

If I did have one good skill at medical school it was the ability to achieve 49% in an exam, and thus pass by the skin of my teeth. I never got any gold medals, but I never failed an exam. It was dangerous to cut things so fine, because another problem with having to do re-sits was the Summer Holiday. This could extend to as much as 10 glorious weeks of freedom, but the September re-sits killed any chance of that. So, I avoided them.

Sommelier to Charlie Chaplin

I had decided at the start of my studies to get a paying job during the Christmas and Easter breaks, in order to finance long summer vacations to far-off places. I knew that if one needs money then go to where the money is, and the four-star Grand Hotel in Eastbourne was just such a place.

I began as a humble commis waiter and was later promoted to station waiter where I joined a small fraternity of foreign waiters, including the oldest of us all, Jean the Belgian, who must have been 70 years old and did not actually walk but slowly shuffled. He was known by us all as 'lead-boots', but never to his face, for he was someone who demanded respect.

In 1966 I was further promoted to the post of sommelier, after a one-week course in Bordeaux during which I learnt a huge amount about wine. The head sommelier at the Grand Hotel was a humorous Irishman called Bob Loney, and he became my friend and guru in all matters concerning alcohol. He taught me how to wash and polish a wine glass, correctly pour from a wine bottle, and how to de-cork a bottle of champagne silently, amongst many other skills. This was a great advance on my previous experiences with alcohol in the pubs and bars of Liverpool.

The summer of 1966 was truly memorable. England was going mad with World Cup fever, and when they beat Germany in the final the whole country went wild. It was a good moment to be alive. During this fevered period, Bob Loney approached me one day and said, "We are expecting an honoured guest next week, and I am putting him on your station". Thus, it was that I got to know Charlie Chaplin and his family.

My station was at the far end of the big restaurant and when I got my first glimpse of Charlie Chaplin as he entered, I was surprised, for he looked nothing like the images we were all used to from his many films. He looked impressive in his white linen suit, but of course, he was now in his '70s. His hair was white, and he was now portly, but he had great presence, and all heads in the restaurant turned towards him as he slowly walked with Oonagh, his wife towards my station.

Then, as he approached me an astonishing thing happened. He spotted 'lead-boots' Jean in his black morning suit and bow tie, and both old men walked towards each other in the middle of the restaurant, one in white and the other in black, and then embraced. I could see tears in Jean's eyes, and Charlie was also looking emotional as well when he sat down at the table. I was mystified at this strange encounter.

In all the family numbered seven, including a nanny and the four youngest children of whom Geraldine was the eldest. They were with me for two weeks during which time I got to know them well, and eventually I plucked up courage to ask Charlie about his relationship with Jean. It turned out that during the Second World War Charlie was on the continent giving morale-boosting concerts to the allied troops and was in Belgium when the Germans invaded. Jean was the Belgian taxi driver who helped Charlie escape from the Germans, driving him into France, and Charlie had never forgotten. He had been amazed to recognise Jean in the Grand Hotel restaurant after so many years.

The weather that year was typical of a British summer, being often wet and damp, and I could see Charlie's children fretting as they were confined inside the hotel. I asked Oonagh if they would enjoy a trip out to my parent's farm to break the monotony. She was delighted, and so were the kids, so I rang my mother and said, "Would it be possible for Charlie Chaplin to pop over for afternoon tea one day with his children?", to which my mother replied, "Of course!"

On the appointed day I completed my cleaning up operations in the restaurant after lunch and exited the Grand Hotel to find a massive black Austin Princess limo waiting for me. Inside this huge limousine was a small gang of excited children playing with the in-car valve radio – a revolution in those days.

To get into the farmyard at Deanlands the chauffeur had to do a three-point turn, whereupon a glorious sight met my eyes. My father was semi-naked on top of the dung-heap in his ex-RAF shorts and wellington boots, forking manure into a wheelbarrow. But as he saw the huge black limo entering the yard, I saw his eyes start bulging as he stepped backwards, arse-over-tit into the middle of the dung heap. Then he took off in his green wellies and we never saw him again that afternoon.

It turned out that my mother had forgotten to mention to my father that Charlie Chaplin was paying a visit.

There was mutual sorrow when the time came for Charlie and his family to return to Switzerland. He shook my hand and gave me a small visiting card. "Come and see us in Montreux sometime", he said. I have very few regrets, but one is that I somehow never made it over to visit Charlie and his great family in Switzerland. But I still have his visiting card.

Learning to love Anatomy

Going back to my studies after that glorious summer was hard. The standard of our teaching was very high, and so were the demands placed on us by our tutors. We all spent hours and hours every week with our heads buried in books. There was no time to daydream of sun-kissed beaches anymore.

My account of medical school days should not exclude a taste of the great Victorian lecture theatres where we were taught every day, which had already been in constant use for over a century. There were multiple ranks of benches on which we sat. They were of oak, darkened by a hundred years of use and endless polishing. The small stage below was where operations were performed for student surgeons in earlier days, and it was in one of these fine theatres that we also held our weekly sessions of MSS every Thursday night. There could not have been a better arena for our Society to flourish.

There were also the sights and sounds of the Dissecting Room, including the unforgettable smell of formaldehyde which preserved the bodies, and also got into our very pores. Most of us 2nd MB students carried wafts of this evil stink about us for weeks on end, and it was not so great for making up to the girls.

Much of the work in the first year of 2nd MB was the dissection of a human body, and so a second cohort of life-long friends was established as groups of eight of us, alphabetically selected, dissected our way through a corpse over the course of an academic year. There were some faint hearts who swooned to the floor on meeting their particular corpse for the year, and others who rarely if ever visited the dissections.

Alex was such a student, who introduced himself to our group saying, "Greetings comrades, I'm Alex!", and that was about it for him and the anatomy course. He did go on to qualify, but he disliked the manner of teaching on the course so much that he took an extra year before he could bring himself to do his compulsory house-jobs. Ever since, has been a Public Health specialist, where, as he once put it, one can enjoy the pure air of academia without the bothersome presence of patients.

But for me, anatomy was something I really enjoyed. To finely dissect away fat and connective tissues with a razor-sharp scalpel and to expose a neurovascular bundle, or a lymph node lying so beautifully in a chain along the thorax, or even the spaghetti junction of the neck with all its major nerves and blood vessels was a beautiful revelation. However, after my months of surgery with Jack Payne at Ebolowa I knew that the living anatomy of a human was far more beautiful than that of a cold cadaver.

By the time final 2nd MB came round there was no corner of the human body I was not familiar with, but even so, I was still considerably relieved to see my name on the pass list at the end of June.

In spite of the many pressures, those pre-clinical years were the greatest fun, even idyllic compared to what was soon to follow.

5.   TO WAR IN BIAFRA   1968

Back to Africa

By my third year of medical school as the final 2nd MB exam approached, I started thinking about a summer sojourn in Africa.

I was keen to revisit West Africa having hitched across it in '65 and found it much to my liking for its vibrancy and colour.

Nigeria was then a focus of international news. The Ibos were the dominant tribe in the south-east, which they now called Biafra. This just happened to be where a very large pool of oil had been found. The Ibos were trying to part company from the rest of Nigeria and a civil war had resulted, but I was still keen to revisit.

Money was a big problem. It would cost an arm and a leg to get there and back, and sustenance would also be required for several months. I mooted my ideas over several pints of Tetleys at the Grapes in Edgerton Street with the rest of the Percy Street gang. Following the advice of Chris Hunt, who was by then the president of the Students Union, and at the cost of one bottle of half-decent whiskey, I came into possession of the list of every scholarship and award open to students at the university.

This file was a goldmine for any impecunious student with the wit to find it, so I retired to 9 Percy Street and buried myself in the list. It was a stupendous document. Some of the scholarships were for small fortunes, and not all seemed to demand a lifetime of sacrifice. Within these precious sheets of paper lay the potential for a great summer holiday, all expenses paid. Little did I realise what was in store for me.

I lay on my bed up in the freezing garret where Ian and I survived and read every page. Then I went out to the Grapes and leant on the public bar clutching a pint of Tetleys whilst I hatched my plan.

The following day I leapt into action and paid a visit to an old friend who lived in a malaria-infested laboratory in the depths of the School of Tropical Medicine and explained my proposal.

Buzz was one of my early teachers of tropical medicine. He had dedicated his life to the study of insect-borne diseases and thought little of shooting himself up with evil concoctions of macerated mosquitoes. He loved nothing better than reminiscing about his early years in Africa, and in me he had an eager audience.

"So, you see", I said, squinting down the objective of Buzz's binocular Leitz at a beautifully stained trophozoite of Pl. Falciparum, "I just need some sort of project for a few months, and I don't mind at all what it is as long as it's in Nigeria."

"I'll have a word in the department," he replied. "I'm sure we can find you something to do", and he did. I was to become a family planning specialist in Lagos.

I then decided to call every listed donor in alphabetical order and was impressed to receive an invitation to discuss matters further after only my third call, from the Bibby family. They were a historic part of Liverpool and its seafaring past, running a shipping line and a huge cattle-feeding operation as well as being influential Liberal politicians. I arranged to visit them and a week later I was sitting in the opulent surroundings of the Bibby mansion on the Wirral, making my case.

My good friend John Adamson had lent me his decaying Ford Popular for this excursion, and I remember driving up the long, tree-lined avenue to find an elegant country mansion in front of me, in the forecourt of which a sculpted fountain was playing. By the side of this work of art was standing a highly polished Austin-Siddely Sapphire limousine. I was so embarrassed that I reversed my rusting jalopy and hid it behind a big rhododendron bush.

But the Bibby's would not have minded. They were genial hosts, and eager to hear my plan.

"It will involve a three-month follow-up of women attending Family Planning Clinics in the poorer areas of Lagos," I explained. "My role will be to find out how acceptable the various methods of contraception are, and how efficacious".

"Well," said Bibby senior, "it sounds a splendid idea, and probably not before time. I'm sure you can count on our help."

He was as good as his word, and barely ten days later I was with the Percy Street gang in the Grapes, celebrating the deposit of £500 into my account at Martins Bank.

Whilst my companions were all planning their summer holiday jobs in sweet factories and bars, I was filling my ex-army haversack with everything I would need for a three-month sojourn in Nigeria. Little did I realise then that this holiday in the sun would end up shaking me to my very core, introducing me to all the horrors of war as well as several near-death experiences.

Back to Nigeria

Shortly afterwards, having cheated the examiners yet again, I found myself with guitar and haversack sitting in a plane with two delightfully pretty and well-educated Nigerian schoolgirls. They were on their way home to Lagos for the summer vacation.

"You must come and stay with us", said Layla, the elder sister, who at 18 years of age was in full bloom. "We have a big house and a big family, and you would be very welcome", said her younger sister, Grace, "and besides, we can show you lots of interesting things."

I needed no further bidding, and once again landed on my feet in a strange country, this time within the mansion of one of the most powerful and wealthy families in Nigeria at that time.

Layla and Grace's father was a High Court Judge, and his brother, Professor Ransome-Kuti was the Director of Community Health at Surulere, Lagos University Medical School. He was thus going to be my most immediate boss in Nigeria.

The most interesting and influential of all that great Nigerian family was Fela, a cousin and close friend of the girls. He was one of life´s true eccentrics, a revolutionary figure and a gifted musician, already becoming known in England for his "high-life" jazz. He ran an exotic music club called the Pink Parrot in Surulere and lived in a compound together with a large harem of female followers.

Within a few days of my arrival, I was already part of a lively student scene, enjoying a style of life which made the greyness of Liverpool seem a very long way away. But soon it was time to present myself at the Family Planning HQ at Ikeja, a rich suburb of Lagos.

"Oh boy! Are we glad to see you", exclaimed the matron who ran the clinic with enormous enthusiasm and energy. "You know, we just can't keep up with demand", she said. "I don't know what all these young ladies comin' here must be up to, I'm sure!" After my recent tour of interesting parts of Lagos with Layla and Grace, including a dreadfully toxic night at the Pink Parrot, I had a very clear idea of what they were up to.

A Brief Introduction to Family Planning

The Pill and the intra-uterine contraceptive device (IUCD) had revolutionised social life in Nigeria as they had in England in recent years. Even in the Catholic diocese of Liverpool it was now possible to be prescribed the Pill by some brave doctors, and a sexual revolution was under way.

Nigeria's birth rate was astronomical, which, some cynics believed, was why good Christians in the USA gave millions of dollars to an outfit called the IPPF or International Planned Parent Federation in order to do all possible to stem this advancing tide of black humanity. Hence the shiploads of condoms, known by everyone as *'rubbaz'*, which I was now helping to handout to the locals and the IUCDs I was learning to insert.

After a month of toil in the hot and humid clinics of Lagos I realised that my present cause was hopeless. The women loved babies. They loved shagging as well. The IPPF was clearly on a losing wicket but did not appear to realise it.

The day a patient presented to me in my clinic with her recently inserted Lippes loop prettily rearranged on a silver chain around her neck, I decided I had done enough family planning. I easily convinced myself that there would always be something else more exciting and fulfilling in my life.

So, I bade farewell to matron at the clinic and to Layla and Grace. Then I packed up my haversack and guitar and started hitching up north of Lagos towards Ije-Bode and Ibadan and beyond. I wanted to see some more of Nigeria even if there was a war going on, though you would hardly have known it in the peaceful suburbs of Lagos.

North of Surulere I got a lift from a jovial Yoruba merchant in a beaten-up van, heading for Ibadan. When he heard of my plans for adventure, he became quite excited.

"You must come and stay at my place. We like the British. I have a sister an' she will like to see you an' talk about the Queen!"

Well, I didn't know a whole lot about the Queen, but I had done enough hitch-hiking by now to recognise a good offer. Hercules, my new chauffeur had also warned me that there were a lot of armed soldiers about.

"Hercules, I'd be delighted to see your place. Now, how old might your sister be?"

"Old enough," he replied. And so it proved. Mary, for that was her name, did not appear to be so interested in learning about the Royal Family as showing me a good time. She took me to a high-life club just to limber me up and when I was starting to feel a bit weak from drinking and dancing, she took me home and taught me some more interesting things.

I limped out of Ibadan the next morning feeling depleted but impressed with life. If this was what Nigeria had in store I was already looking forward to the next adventure, and it wasn't long in coming.

I was now heading for Ilorin, an important town which sat across the Benué River where it fused to form the Niger River and effectively divided the Muslim north from the Christian south. The bridge at Ilorin was the only remaining intact bridge over which the government could supply the north. Food, fuel and other essential supplies had to be supplied during this civil war if the loyalty of the northern Muslims was to be maintained by the government.

In order to protect this strategic bridge, there were frequent roadblocks. I headed north in a BP petrol tanker driven by an educated Hausa called Ibrahim from Sokoto, the town in the extreme north which I was trying to get to.

"Oh yes, man, we sure got big problems up here," he said. "If the Ibos blow the bridge, how are we goin' to get this juice up to Kaduna?" This was the seat of government in the north and the biggest town.

But it was Mother Nature which caused the flooding which took out the main pillars of the bridge that day, not the Ibos. Only when we hit the back of a huge queue of piled up traffic just south of Ilorin did we realise we would not get across that night. I jumped down with my guitar and haversack, thanking Ibrahim for the ride.

"I may be able to get a boat across, anyhow I'll give it a try," I said as I turned towards the bridge. But the African darkness fell like a stone as I walked towards the river and feeling fatigued, I thought "what the hell", and laid down under a large mango tree, tying the guitar to my haversack and rolling out my sleeping bag. It never bothered me to crash out wherever I happened to be in Africa. Until that night my worst fears had been hungry carnivores, but tonight was to prove different.

Another near-death experience

A ferocious dog barking in my face was immediately followed by the feeling of cold steel at my throat.

"Git up! Git up, man!" someone was shouting at me, and a torch was blinding my eyes. Then I was kicked till I rolled out of the sleeping bag, still in a dream.

"Git your han's up", came the voice behind the machine gun which I now saw wavering a foot in front of me. My hands shot vertically up like rockets. I now knew this was not a dream any longer and started shaking with fearful anticipation. This type of nocturnal thrill had not yet been covered in my medical curriculum, but I could recognise a gun and the drunken soldiers.

"Where did you steal this", asked the soldier in charge, hooking up my haversack with his gun.

"I bought it in Liverpool", I replied, which was the truth. I had paid £5 in Millets, Lime Street for this immaculate example of 1940s British Army hardware. That was now the problem. There was no doubt it was an army haversack, and I suddenly began to see the soldier's point of view and trembled even more inside.

"You are a SPY! We shall shoot you! We shoot all spies". The soldier spat his alcoholic fumes into my face and then forced me up against the tree at gunpoint, the muzzle resting heavily on my larynx. The soldiers seemed uninterested in knowing anything else now they had the proof of my guilt and forbade me to speak.

I have an indelible memory of the terrifying moment when one of the soldiers going through the contents of my Millets haversack spied my tube of toothpaste, and in drunken rage stamped on it. By strange accident a great snake of pink paste shot out and hit him square in the eyes.

Only God could have ordained this timely petard. It was hilarious to witness, but at the same time I was quaking with terror. Too many people had warned me about the dangerous antics of the drunken soldiers of the Nigerian Army. And so it turned out.

The blow in my kidneys from the butt of his rifle floored me completely and left me gasping for breath. Then he kicked me until I was once again standing against the tree, with the cold steel of his Kalashnikov pressed so hard underneath my jaw that I could barely breathe.

I stood at gunpoint from two in the morning until seven when the soldiers were relieved. Feeling considerably bruised and beaten I was wondering what was going to happen to me. I really was in bandit country now, with the army taking me for a spy – of which there were many during this war, both black and white. And there was no one around to help me.

The sky was now lightening, the military curfew was over and from the long line of accumulated traffic in front of me I saw a white man leave his car and approach.

"Excuse me sir", he addressed the soldier in charge. "Can I be of any help?"

My spirits lifted.

"This man is a spy, and we are going to shoot him", replied the soldier. "No, no, you can't be right", said the stranger, "for I am in charge of the mission where he is working", he never having set eyes on me before.

"Let me see your papers", demanded the soldier, and perused the proffered documents. "Ah, so you are from Ilesha -- that is my place, and I know you from the hospital there".

"I am the senior doctor in charge", replied the stranger, whom I was warming to in a big way. "I would be grateful if you would let my friend go. There must be same mistake I'm afraid ".

The soldiers were at first confused, but finally with the help of a few gifts of potency pills, which all the missionaries carried for this sort of emergency, they were convinced. Still giving me suspicious looks, they gave me into the care of this stranger, whose timely arrival had miraculously delivered me from a nasty fate.

Out of the frying pan ……..

Once inside his car he introduced himself to me. I was still shaking with relief. He was called Peter and was indeed a missionary doctor from Ilesha, a town west of Ibadan.

"I'm in charge of Maternity", he told me, "at the moment I'm submerged in a research project as well as all my clinical work". When I had explained who I was and how I came to be in Nigeria Peter laughed.

"I work on the principle that if I do ever bother to do something altruistic -- you know, go the extra mile, I invariably get the benefit. Somehow when I saw you standing there with all the guns pointing at you I just felt I ought to do something. And what I need more than anything at the moment is an out-of-work medical student!"

Thus, it was that I came to meet one of the great pioneers of paediatric tropical medicine, Dr David Morley. He was Peter's medical colleague at the Wesley Guild Mission and was currently engaged in a detailed survey of a village called Esem-ile, in order to scientifically evaluate the true state of health of the children. The great value of this work would later become recognised globally and lead him to a brilliant career in Child Health in London.

Nearly 20 years later I was to meet David whilst doing my Master's in Public Health at the London School of Hygiene and Tropical Medicine (LSHTM) in Malet Street. He was just around the corner in Guildford Street at the Institute of International Child Health, but this time he was Professor D. Morley. His ground-breaking work at Ilesha in Child Health will always be epic and original, and also the true basis of all Primary Care in Undeveloped Countries which is commonplace today. His book, ´Practising Health for All´, which he signed for me and in which he wrote kind words, is one of my treasured volumes.

Helping with their medical research work is how I came to learn the intricacies of punch card filing systems at the Wesley Guild mission hospital, and to relate the various complications of Caesarian sections to such things as size and weight of a patient, or their nutritional state or other associated conditions, including their access to Ante-Natal care.

Dr Peter offered me a deal which would provide me with not just shelter and food, but the chance to experience some more quality tropical medicine and surgery. Through his connections he also fixed for me to attend the Accident and Emergency room at University College Hospital, UCH Ibadan for two days each week.

After my recent experiences at Ilorin bridge, I was very happy to enjoy the security of the mission, and I found them a good lot on the whole, a far cry from the puritanical Lutherans in Cameroun.

On Gas Gangrene – the spoils of war

Every Thursday I hitch-hiked from the hospital to Ibadan where I spent hours in the Emergency rooms at UCH learning about war surgery. The wards were full and overflowing with all manner of wounded soldiers from the battlefront which was then over 100 kilometres east, separated by blown bridges and dirt roads as well as a shortage of transport. Many soldiers died unnecessarily and many more suffered greatly increased morbidity as a result of delayed and inadequate care. It was a powerful learning experience for me, a pre-clinical third year medical student.

Whilst in Ibadan I always stayed with the medical students, and a lively lot they all were. We had a whale of a time as well as working like dogs in A+E. It was they who taught me the delights of kuku pili-pili – for breakfast! I used to have it, for it was the norm for these hardy souls, but red-hot chilli chicken at 0730 hrs was a novelty for me. The sauce which accompanied this fiery chicken was made with pili-pili, peanuts and peanut oil, and was delicious.

Many Nigerian medical students were already involved in this emergency care, and even though I had yet to start any formal clinical attachment back at medical school, my previous experiences in Cameroun had well prepared me for much of what I was now involved in.

In the Trauma theatre I saw many limbs amputated because of gas gangrene, even though they should have been salvageable. Unknown today in England, here it was endemic. The Clostridium bacillus thrived in battle conditions, where nearly every wound was contaminated by filth and dirt and any form of first aid was often hours away. As the tissues necrosed and the gangrene spread its blue-black shadows over the bodies of the injured, the sweet but sickly smell which marked this dreaded complication would fill the air of the wards. It was a smell I would never forget.

Rocking and Rolling with Sir Victor

One day I was hitching on the muddy road to Ibadan when a white Transit van skidded to a halt and a voice rang out,

"Jump in the back, brother". Whereupon I found myself crushed in a mix of musical instruments and the human elements of a rock band.

"Sir Victor Uwaifo and his brothers, at your service", sang out one, and that was how I met one of the best bands in Nigeria.

"So, where you headin' for", they asked. "Show us your guitar!" I explained my situation, played a couple of riffs as the van bounced crazily over innumerable potholes, and was then co-opted to become a temporary group member.

"You come and play with us tonight", said Sir Victor, a big and brightly clothed Yoruba whose idea of a good time was to get a load of alcohol on board, smoke a bundle of weed and then play music till he and the others collapsed from exhaustion. "We're at the President tonight -- start any time from 9, so you come by an' we'll have us some fun!"

As an antidote to the wards full of wounded soldiers, Sir Victor was unbeatable, and he introduced me to a way of life which I had never imagined, as well as to scores of his 'sisters'. From Friday afternoon till Sunday when I left Ibadan to hitch back to Ilesha I led a pretty debauched existence, but I had loads of fun and also made some money playing my music on stage in between Sir Victor's sets.

Back at the Wesley Guild on the Monday morning ward round Dr. Peter fastened his gaze on the dark circles below my eyes

"I hope they are not overworking you at UCH", he remarked.

"Well, it does get pretty busy there", I replied, not wishing to give too much away about my Jekyll and Hyde existence, which was quite a few degrees off these Christians' chosen way of life.

"Do you want to take a few days off?" Peter was a truly kind man.

"No, no", I replied, "I'm fine, and I enjoy the change from the big city".

In fact, I needed the tranquillity of the mission to recover from my weekend excesses with Sir Victor and the band.

The Real Horrors of War

The following Thursday, instead of heading west for my usual stint at UCH Ibadan, by dint of much wangling I hitched a lift east to Onitsha and the battlefront in one of the returning Army trucks. I must have been mad. At a time when I would normally be whooping it up with Sir Victor and his friends, I found myself in a tented Army hospital, stinking of putrefaction, surrounded by the cries and moans of wounded soldiers. It was a world of confusion, pain, death, and a perpetual feeling of inadequacy in the face of so much lethal trauma.

"Give me a hand doc", yet again, from one of the orderlies. I was lifting one corpse from a stretcher and filling it immediately with a very young boy who was legless and bleeding profusely from both shattered stumps.

"Bring me dressing packs", I cried, but then I realised there were none. I had used the last one about two hours earlier on another dying patient.

"Doc, you must use this", said the orderly, tearing off his stained shirt and throwing it at me. "I'll go get haemostats", and disappeared, semi-naked into the further dark depths of the First Aid tent.

"That's all I could find", he said on his return, thrusting two rusty clips at me, who by now was getting used to the various inadequacies of the acute surgical services the Nigerian armed forces provided for their soldiers.

"How old are you?", I asked the near-comatose young boy as I lifted the torn muscles of his left thigh, looking for the femoral vessels.

"I am from Warri and I have 15 years", replied the boy, very faintly. "What is your name", I asked as I clamped the right femoral artery and vein.

"I am Samuel, from Warri and my father is the chief", in a voice that whispered.

I tore the belt from my Levis and with all my might tightened it around the right upper thigh, so mangled that there was little chance here of finding any vessels to clamp.

"And what do you want to do when you leave school?", I asked, but there was no reply. Only the vacant gaze into the dark abyss far beyond the eyes of the boy from Warri.

"Samuel, did you hear me?" I was looking at the face of the young boy, pleading and hoping.

"He is gone", the orderly said quietly. "War is too bad".

The civil war had wreaked havoc throughout the land and food shortage was now a big problem, leading to famine. I began seeing children with extreme malnutrition suffering from marasmus and kwashiorkor admitted to the field hospital, as well as all the trauma cases.

I cannot forget grasping the withered arm of a child as I inserted yet one more intravenous line. It was just like a dried stick, with no subcutaneous tissue or muscle mass. I had rarely seen the like before and it was all distressing. I quickly became competent in resuscitating these poor children, even though some eventually did die from a combination of malnutrition, malaria and their injuries.

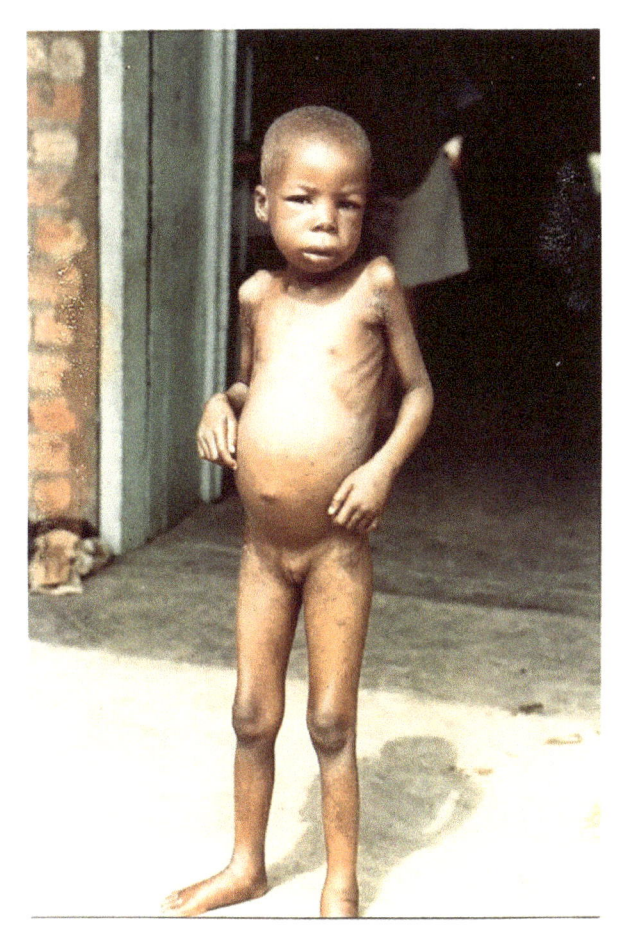

The collateral damage of war. Kwashiorkor

I had only just fallen into exhausted sleep on the second night when I was awakened by Mambo, the senior surgical nurse. I was wanted in the operating theatre urgently. Oh God! I thought, what now?

Inside the OT there was blood everywhere, a body on the floor and the remains of one on the operating table. A mortar shell had fallen on an army truck and this soldier was the only survivor – what was left of him, for both hands had been blown off at the wrists, which were bleeding like fountains. Shrapnel had completely destroyed his face and eyes and his scalp was shredded and bleeding furiously.

Akimbo, the senior surgeon was already at work tying second-hand urinary catheters around the upper arms. These were our only tourniquets. Then he and I started to clip the severed arteries and veins whilst Mambo covered the scalp in a filthy towel and leant on it to staunch the blood flow from the scalp. Speed was the essential for this patient was bleeding to death in front of us and we had not one pint of blood to offer him. It took two hours to patch the soldier up and dawn was breaking as I went outside, considerably shaken by what I had just been involved in.

Two Mig jets flew low overhead making a deafening noise which scared me even more. I knew I would not be going back to sleep, so I joined Akimbo on his morning ward round. It was worse than the Emergency Room at UCH Ibadan where at least there were more facilities. Here we had practically nothing to offer our patients other than our own skills.

We had no antibiotics, very little intravenous fluid and there were no dressings or bandages. Even a bit of rag was a blessing. I was horrified to see the human destruction and degradation around me. By the time we had finished the round there were four more wounded patients to operate on. I continued at Akimbo's side for the rest of yet one more exhausting day on the battle front, performing four more amputations and more surgical debridements for shrapnel wounds and gangrene. Truly it was a vision of hell on earth, and I had had enough.

The next day, feeling shell-shocked after this inferno I had just been so closely involved in, I took the next west-bound truck back to Ilesha. There I said my farewells to Peter, David and the other good folk at the mission and hitched down to Lagos.

Back to Civilisation

Layla and Grace looked after me in their comfortable family mansion whilst I recovered from the horrors I had just seen. The contrast with the luxury all around me was enormous. These people in Lagos knew little of the reality of what was going on in Biafra, but I had just seen it all, and wondered at the two different worlds of Nigeria.

This cruel war was about wealth and greed and corruption. The newly discovered oil fields in the south-east were the main cause of the Ibos desire to separate from the rest of Nigeria. Having seen the terrible human destruction which resulted, I was left with very mixed feelings about my experiences in Nigeria.

The collateral damage of the civil war was not the sort of thing I felt I could comfortably discuss with Layla and Grace, but they did enjoy hearing about my escapades with Sir Victor and his entourage of brothers and sisters.

I was very saddened to hear a short time later that Sir Victor had been killed in a road accident. He and Fela Ransome Kuti were the first black musicians I ever became friends with, and I probably learned more about Nigeria and the Africans from them than anyone else during my months in West Africa in 1968.

The night before I was due to leave Nigeria the two girls dragged me out for another night in town. I was going to miss them, as well as Nigeria, in spite of the horrors of the civil war. The girls were going back to Roedean but I was Liverpool-bound, late as usual, for the beginning of my first year of clinical studies.

A Painful Return to Reality

"Where the hell have you been?"

Ian, my garret-sharing gang member at No. 9 Percy Street was concerned.

"Well, actually Ian", I replied, "I've been to war in Biafra, and found it most stimulating!"

"Prof. Heath told us you have got to re-sit Pathology. And he said he wants to see you the moment you decide to re-join the university!"

Suddenly the ogre of medical academia was in my face once again. The bloody operating theatres I had been working in just a week before now seemed many miles away, even though my memories were still crystal clear. After my various Nigerian adventures, it was going to be very difficult to adapt once again to the hard discipline of academia and the high expectations of our clinical teachers.

My experiences with Layla and Grace and Fela, and Sir Victor Uwaifo and Drs Peter and David at Ilesha, as well as the Trauma Unit at UCH Ibadan had all had a profound affect on me, though how they were going to contribute towards my Pathology finals in nine months time, I was not yet sure. However, I had a confident feeling that all would be well. And so it proved.

The last thing I did before I went to bed that day was to sit at my small desk in the garret and write a lengthy letter of thanks to the Bibby family, including a detailed report of all my medical activities during the previous 10 weeks in Nigeria. A copy of this report may still be lurking in the archives of Liverpool Medical Students Society.

I told them of my time at the Surulere family planning clinic, suggesting that strong local cultural influences had a large part to play in the booming population statistics, which overseas agencies may have failed to take into account. I wrote about some of the less gory details of my war surgery experiences and also of the primary health care research I had been involved with at Ilesha. But not one word did I write of the many riotous and bibulous times I had shared with my musical African friends.

It was those electric memories with which I went to sleep that night.

6. CLINICAL YEARS TO FINALS 1968 – 71

First Days on the Wards

As soon as I returned from Nigeria, I began the first of three years clinical studies in all the major medical disciplines. Everyone was excited at being allowed onto the wards where we could actually talk to and touch real live patients. I had the advantage over my fellow students after my months in Cameroun and my recent Biafran adventures and was already familiar with clinical work both on the wards and in theatre. However, the spotless wards of the Liverpool Royal Infirmary were a far cry from the pitiful conditions I had just experienced on the Biafran battlefront.

I never tired of seeing the enormous range of pathological conditions on the wards and tying them in with my academic pre-clinical studies. But there was more than a mountain to learn in the three years to come, as well as enjoying the many social diversions with my medic friends in No 9 Percy Street.

'Uncle' Gordon, Chris Hunt and John Ballance were the most senior medics in No 9 at this time, being in final year, and Chris was also the President of MSS. He was the son of a Sheffield bricklayer and was already a fervent left-wing politician. He followed his presidency of MSS by being elected president of the Students Union at Liverpool the following year. We could all see that he was heading for great things, for he was not only a gifted speaker with a razor- sharp wit, but seemed capable of anything and was indeed some sort of hero to us younger members of the No 9 gang.

The following year he went off to Africa to do voluntary work, so it was a numbing experience to return from the States in the fall of

1974 to be told that Chris had been killed in a road crash in Zambia. It was to be the first of five tragic and premature deaths of our compatriots at No 9.

More than half of us young students living at No 9 Percy Street would have untimely deaths. Malcolm had already had a large pituitary tumour removed from his brain when I first arrived at No 9 in 1966. When he greeted me, he had a shaven head and a livid scar which spanned his skull from ear to ear, reminding me of someone from a Hammer horror film. But he was a lovely chap and had also been a gold medal winner in Biochemistry before he got his tumour. He was never the same after this heroic surgery and died a few years later from a stroke.

Andy was probably our most brilliant member. Shortly after being appointed consultant in anaesthetics, he never awoke after a heavy night out, probably dying from aspiration of stomach contents. His wife Annie found him dead beside her the morning after.

Sandy died from cancer of the colon, after a life with ulcerative colitis. By then he was a consultant surgeon in his early 50s and was my closest surgical friend. When he came out to see me in Spain in 2005, his body was already riddled with metastases, and we both knew the inevitable outcome. It was the very first occasion I had spent time with a dear friend whose days were numbered, and for that it was a poignant moment. Nevertheless, we did have a load of fun, just as we had done when we were students together all those years ago. His last project was to bolt my heavy steel vice securely onto the workbench inside my workshop, something which was right up Sandy's street. I use that vice often, and every time I touch it, I am reminded of a very precious friendship.

Most shocking of all, within a year of being appointed to a professorship at the London Hammersmith hospital, Long John died of a glioblastoma, the most fatal of all brain tumours. Ian and I went to see him whilst he was still undergoing radiotherapy, even though we all knew it would not effect a cure. It was a very sad time for us.

As I write, there are just four of us who remain alive out of the original eight students who qualified in 1971.

Prof Cyril Clarke was one of those charged with preparing us for Finals. He was not only the internationally respected Professor of Medicine whom we all loved and feared in equal amounts for his piercing intellect, but a man with a dry sense of humour who did not take gladly to fools.

A clinical teaching round with Prof Clarke was always stimulating, as we students were easy game for him. When he invited Holy Joe to present the clinical history and examination findings of the patient in front of us on another tense morning at the Royal Infirmary, we were all expectant, Joe being a rare, religious member of our clinical firm. He did not disappoint. Holy Joe surpassed himself on this occasion with his own novel diagnosis, which had even the registrars sniggering behind Prof Clarke´s back.

"This patient is suffering as a result of distancing himself from God, and as a result has developed obstructive airway disease".

With a poker face Prof Clarke then enquired of Holy Joe, "And what was the serum righteousness?", at which everyone started falling around. What the patient thought of this exhibition I never knew, but I give thanks to Prof Cyril and the many others who did their best to disabuse us of our ignorance in medical matters and better prepare us for the Final MB.ChB exams.

Locum Adventures in the Isle of Man

One thing which assisted my studies greatly was doing locums. Today, the idea of letting a medical student loose on the public is unthinkable, but in 1969 it was *de rigeur,* and nobody thought twice. Covering a houseman´s holiday could net us students 15 pounds a week, as well as giving us some front-line experience which was often terrifying, but great preparation for Finals.

Thus, it was on a bleak winter's night in 1969 that I found myself on the packet steamer from Liverpool, heading across the freezing Irish Sea to Douglas in the Isle of Man, and Noble's Hospital.

Amongst this hospital's attractions was not just the annual TT racing, which was great experience for aspiring orthopaedic surgeons, but the hospital's proximity to the Manx Brewery, which, in the spirit of social cohesion provided one bottle of good beer every day for each of the eight junior doctors. When I entered the doctors mess the first day, I was stunned to find a backlog of about 100 bottles of beer waiting to be drunk.

Four of the eight doctors were females and didn't drink beer and the four males were usually too tired to drink much. I therefore set to with abandon and also called the gang in Percy Street to come and share this bonanza, for I now had two weeks of free beer to enjoy at Noble's.

Things got even better at Noble's when one of the young female medics, a beautiful Asian girl called Narita took a shine to me and invited me to her bed. It was only a frantic phone call from JS in Percy Street which persuaded me onto the steamer back to Liverpool. Apparently, Professor Heath, head of Pathology, was going to castrate or excommunicate me if I failed to be in his office next Monday to explain my recent absence from his tutorials.

By that time, I had already survived several terrifying experiences, including my first insertion of a urinary catheter in an NHS hospital. Since that day at Noble's I must have inserted thousands of catheters, but on this very first occasion I can still remember the clutch of fear when I was called to an old man in urinary retention who needed catheterising.

During the six months I had spent at the Hôpital Central at Ebolowa in 1965, Jack Payne had taught me this simple procedure, but that now seemed a long time ago. Suddenly I was conscious that I was just a third-year medical student and had never touched a live NHS patient until now, so it was a bit of an electric moment for me. Thank goodness the nursing staff were excellent. I think they knew how naïve I was in these matters, for they had seen student locums before. The nurses laughed when they saw the look of triumph on my face as the urine flowed out of the catheter, but my hands were sweating inside my sterile gloves.

My first student locum had proved a very valuable learning experience in several ways, and I did go back and do other locums at Noble´s when the TT races were on, for I just loved anything to do with motors and the smell of Castrol-R.

The unmined potential of the NHS ……… "Crabs in my Autoclave!"

It was during this first locum in the Isle of Man that I became a friend of Dave the theatre technician-cum porter, who was actually a Manx fisherman, doing part-time work for the National Health Service. He was a splendid chap to have around the operating theatre, always full of amusing stories and well-loved by the nurses who enjoyed mothering him.

Dave's sad demise came suddenly one night when a rare event occurred – two mothers needing Caesarian Section at the same time. So, most unusually the second autoclave was brought into action, at which point the night sister was heard to scream quite loudly, "Crabs! in my autoclave!", which brought me running to the sterilizing room along with a nurse or two to witness the impressive sight of Dave's last catch of crustaceans sitting pretty, well-cooked and dead in the instrument tray, ready for consumption.

It was an epic moment, and possibly my first example of alternative uses of NHS resources. The theatre sister was apoplectic and purple with rage, but by the grace of God the second patient was delivered successfully by forceps and a potential catastrophe was avoided. But I never did see Dave's smiling face again at Noble´s.

I was once again in trouble when I got back to Liverpool, and after a tense meeting with Prof Heath ended up doing hours of extra pathology to pay for my pleasures in the Isle of Man, but I reckoned it was a fair trade-off, for I not only had 30 quid in my pocket but the memories of my first intimate encounter with a lovely Asian lady.

Although they would never be sanctioned today, I do believe that the pre-clinical student locums I did contributed greatly towards my success in Finals and my development as a doctor.

The Final Exams

As 1970 passed into 1971 we realised that our student days were soon ending, and that if all went well, we would soon be having to earn our living. But before that day arrived, we were going to enjoy Finals.

Finals was a period which struck terror into the hearts of the bravest and reduced some lesser mortals to tears. All those hours spent drinking at the Grapes in Egerton Street and most of the other pubs in Liverpool over six years suddenly became moments of regret. The nights spent partying and the weekends in the arms of some soft, sweet lady faded into distant memories as the dark cloud of Finals marched relentlessly towards us.

After over five years at medical school, I entered the Cohen Library in May 1971 for the first time and was stunned to see the endless shelves of medical volumes before me. There seemed little hope of assimilating the acres of knowledge which would be required for a pass, and there was no chance of catching up just two months before Finals. I was going to have to make do with a mixture of native wit, Lady Luck, and what I had osmosed during three years of clinical teaching on the wards.

Fortunately, the months I had spent in Africa had already taught me a great deal of clinical medicine. My natural interest in Anatomy,

Physiology and Pathology also provided a good foundation. But now at this critical moment I had to just sit and imbibe academic knowledge from a tome, which I always found daunting.

The partying declined, and the nocturnal sorties ground to a halt apart from the obligatory attendance every night at The Grapes. Up in the garret which Ian and I shared at No 9 it was sometimes even possible to hear our brains working, such was the intensity of our studies.

On the Quality of Teaching

The academic side of medical life was continuously demanding, but I really enjoyed the clinical attachments on the wards. It was a continuous wonder to see the enormous range of pathology which the human body can experience, and also to have such fine clinical teaching. Just being on the wards in our pristine white coats was a thrill.

Every teaching hospital consultant spent hours along with their registrars, implanting knowledge into our receptive brains, often on the wards, sometimes in their outpatient clinics and also at weekly tutorials. Some of them were truly outstanding, such as Dr Baker-Bates, known by all as ´BB´, a consultant physician and teacher to us all. He seemed to love us students and was always inviting groups to eat with him in his terraced house in Rodney Street. He was a master of the aphorism and I can still remember several, for example, 'Fat mothers have fat children', or ¨Choose your parents wisely!" It says something for B-B that whenever we of the class of ´71 meet up, our conversations are still embellished with many of those unforgettable aphorisms.

Every Friday there was The Circus. This was an aptly named drama lasting an hour or so, conducted by Black Jack Robinson, consultant in Medicine at the Liverpool Royal Infirmary. This took place in the teaching theatre and involved the participation of up to five unwilling medical students. These unfortunates were presented with some usually rare and unfathomable morsel of human pathology from Black Jacks extensive wards and then subjected to a period of humiliation before the rest of the students. As eager as we all were to see the downfall of each Friday's victim, each one of us knew that our own time was soon coming.

Black Jack even reduced some of the brightest to a paralysed silence, as happened to Angela, another gold medal student during a discourse on diabetes. She was the star of the Circus that Friday, and Black Jack was holding a small glass of yellow liquid. "In ancient times the diagnosis of diabetes was made by tasting the urine thus", he said, introducing his finger into the liquid and then sucking on it.

"Indeed", he said, smacking his lips, "there is sugar within. Now, you do the same", offering Angela the glass. We were all transfixed by this gripping charade. Would she, or would she not be brave enough?

Shaking like a leaf, Angela declined his offer, at which point Black Jack took the glass and swigged the contents down his throat, which stunned us all. Until we spotted the joke. "I prefer my tea without sugar", he said to Angela, who was still speechless and shaking on the stage. No-one had noticed the change of Black Jack's finger from the index finger introduced into the glass, to the middle finger inserted into his mouth.

This demonstration actually had little to do with diabetes, but very much to do with observation, such an important part of our clinical training and of our later clinical practice. Inspection, palpation, percussion and auscultation with a stethoscope formed the basis of all clinical examination and diagnosis in those days, and we spent hours perfecting this art.

Much of our clinical pathology teaching was based on a few of the most significant diseases of the day, including tuberculosis, syphilis, polio and rheumatic heart disease, all of which were caused by infective organisms. Penicillin had only been around for 20 years and there were still only a limited number of these 'magic bullets' to treat these conditions. Conventional treatment usually involved simple measures such as impeccable hygiene, postural drainage of pulmonary abscesses and the use of digitalis and simple diuretics for heart failure.

In the 50 years which have since passed, both the incidence and the management of these diseases have changed enormously. The advent of newer antibiotics gave rise to a general, but mis-guided optimism that science could now solve all our major infective health problems during the '70s and '80s. The preventive power of childhood immunizations had also reduced child mortality and morbidity by a huge degree in the post-war years. We were conquering infections, and mistakenly thought that soon infectious disease would be a thing of the past.

The diet I was brought up on in the post-war years was austere and food was still rationed, but we children still all got free milk, orange juice, cod liver oil and molasses. In those days junk food did not exist, and obesity was virtually unknown. The idea of performing barometric surgery for obesity would have been laughable back then, but today it has become a norm.

It is a salutary lesson to us humans that today, some 50 years later drug-resistant tuberculosis has now become a global problem. Syphilis and gonorrhoea are also very much on the increase once again, partly due to increasing antibiotic resistance, but also because of high-risk human behaviour. Since the mid-80s AIDS has also intervened in a most malignant manner, mainly because of high-risk human behaviour. Other new and untreatable viruses are also on the move. Nature is always one step ahead of us humans.

Drug resistance and a decline in general standards of hygiene care by both doctors and nurses over these years in England have led to a catastrophic increase in hospital-acquired infections which now directly cause the deaths of thousands of patients every year, but these problems were unknown to us clinical medical students then.

The Problem with Sex

There are some areas of medicine which never change, and of these the process of childbirth remains one of the most important and, for me the most terrifying. I can still remember Sammy White in the Biology lab at Lewes Grammar using a piston and cylinder to demonstrate the process of evacuating a human foetus from the uterus.

With a couple of finely honed pieces of metal and not a blood vessel in sight he made obstetrics look easy. But after the very first of 20 human deliveries I was obliged to assist with during my clinical Obstetrics term at Mill Road Maternity hospital I had another perspective. There were enough screams and mess and blood to put me off obstetrics forever. Even contraception was a nightmare.

The Student Health Clinic was run by Roman Catholics, and as a result even though The Pill had just become available and was indeed a big part of the major ongoing social revolution, getting hold of it from those doctors was almost impossible.

The barber at the students Union always had boxes of Durex sitting on the side of his sink, as did all the men's hairdressers in those days, so most of us had to make do with them and all their attendant problems. These included immediate flaccidity at the sight of one to the embarrassment of losing one somewhere within the dark recesses of the cervix. Then there was the rather scary wait until the next period which, for quite a few unfortunate young ladies, never did appear, and then led to the awkward process of abortion and all its attendant problems.

The part of Finals I was dreading most was Obstetrics and Gynaecology. Professor TNA Jeffcoate was not only the feared boss of the Obs/Gynae department, but he was also a world authority on woman's anatomy, and had written a huge volume on gynaecology, which only such stars as Long John had the strength to open. When my turn came to be examined by him, he was standing by the shaking figure of John Tappin, the captain of the medics rugby team.

Tappin was a pretty strong chap under normal circumstances, which these were obviously not, for he was as pale as death and sweating. Prof Jeffcoate was in the process of handing him a rubber glove, saying,

"I prefer to use one of these when I examine a patient!" It was typical of the sort of catastrophe which so easily happened in Finals when the heat was on and the fear of failure uppermost in most of us students´ minds.

It turned out that Tappin, in a moment of mindlessness in this most stressful of situations, when asked by the Prof to perform a vaginal examination on this patient, had simply stepped forward and inserted his naked fingers.

All very well in a social situation, as the great man said, but never in any professional encounter.

When I finally exited the Victoria Building after a bruising 15-minute encounter with Professor Jeffcoate, I felt badly in need of some form of pick-me-up. As I headed for the 'Augustus John' I passed the student travel shop, in the window of which was a large poster of a seagull flying over some Arabian coastline with the legend, 'Fly to Egypt'. This immediately caught my attention. I needed a diversion, and a journey was always something I looked forward to.

By the time I was sitting in front of my pint of Tetleys in the Augustus John, I had a ticket to Cairo in my pocket. I had yet to thwart the examiners in Clinical Surgical Pathology before the agonizing wait for the Pass List, but I now had something to look forward to.

Surgical Pathology - The Final Hurdle

When Professor Heath faced me across the mortuary table, I was already expecting the worst. After my various journeys to the Isle of

Man, and absences from his scintillating tutorials, I felt that he had actually come to hate me. My heart sank as he passed over a pathological specimen for me to identify.

My interest in Anatomy usually made this sort of guessing game easy for me, but this lump of tissue had no real form, it was just a dark red, bi-lobed, tumour-like swelling. It was not like any normal organ I had ever seen. It could have been a lymph node, but it could also have been some gland, so indefinite was its shape. Then, as had happened before in my career, I had a moment of pure inspiration. From where it came, I still have no idea.

"It is a thyroid gland", I said with full confidence, which was half the battle. If you were going for a guess, you may as well speak as though you believe it, and I always worked on the assumption that 50% of my guesses would be correct. In this moment I hit the jackpot and had the pleasure of seeing Prof Heath choke slightly at this true shot in the dark.

"Describe the common tumours of this gland", he then followed up, still looking for blood. Amazingly, thyroid tumours was one esoteric corner of pathology about which I had some knowledge, and when I exited the Victoria Building shortly after, I had a small smile on my face as I headed for 'The Royal' where the rest of the gang were already sinking yards of ale.

Three days later the results were posted. There was a scene of grand emotion with much weeping and wailing amongst the louder cries from the joyful, which latter included me. As soon as I had recovered from two days of solid celebration, I went to see Mr Green. He was the manager of Martins Bank, the nearest source of money to the Student Union bar. He was known by all of us at No 9 as Mr Yes, as he never did say no to our requests for extended credit.

"I was wondering if, on the strength of my incoming fortune from the National Health Service, I may be granted a couple of hundred to see me across Arabia", I began, having offered him a Strand, to which he was partial.

"Couldn't you perhaps sell one of your cars?", Mr Green began, "as you do seem to be a bit overdrawn".

He was not a terrific negotiator for Martins Bank, as after a couple of nights out with the Percy Street gang during our clinical years, not only had he become a good friend, but he found it harder and harder to say no to us.

So it was that I left him with the promise to sell one of my three cars, and enough loot to see me on my way to the Middle East. It says much for the way things were in those good days that Mr Green came to the door of the bank to shake my hand and wish me well. By the time that I had finished my intern year, Martins Bank had been swallowed by Barclays, and we never saw our personal bank manager again.

Final Year. Medical Dinner

A Farewell Party to Remember

We were all now on a new trajectory, which would take us away from our roosts in Liverpool 8. Leaving the homely surroundings of No 9 Percy Street after five years was an occasion for yet one more party, and it was such a one that it has never been forgotten.

We had decided as a *tour de force* to blow up the redundant outside toilet in the back garden at midnight. It was a frigid little shed with no light, not much roof left and a china pan which I discovered would hold a one-gallon petrol can perfectly. There had never been any door since Chris Hunt had torn it off its hinges and converted it to firewood, so we all had a good view from the big kitchen window.

I had only done a petrol can bomb once before, but the effect was spectacular. The bomb itself was very simple indeed. Into an empty petrol can you pour an inch or two of water and then an inch or so of petrol. Screw the lid on tightly, light fire underneath and wait till the water boils, when the can starts to swell and slowly becomes more and more globular until there is an almighty flash and bang at the moment the water and petrol vapour escape the tin as it explodes.

In this case we made the fire within the china toilet pan which had never held water for years, and after placing the can inside we went back inside to enjoy the coming spectacle. Those of us who were still sober enough to focus were impressed as the tin slowly swelled and then came a fantastic explosion and a huge flame shot into the black sky between Catherine Street and Percy Street, blinding us all by its intensity.

Something solid and massive came straight through the kitchen window just missing Sandy and then everything went dark as a huge cloud of ash rose into the air and windows started opening in Back Catherine St. Shouts and cries of fear were still echoing as the first fire engine arrived, followed by the police. But by the time they were making enquiries in our residence I was away through the garret window and onto the roof. Two garrets away at No 7 lived Rita, a very close friend of mine, and I spent the night fearfully awake in her warm bed, realizing that once again I had over-cooked the goose.

The next day when I crept into No 9, the back garden looked rather like a war zone, with bits of shattered toilet spread amongst a thick carpet of black ash. The top half of the kitchen window was no more, and inside the kitchen was a large chunk of china cistern with a bit of melted lead pipe hanging forlornly from it. Once again, fortunately for us no arrests were made, but a further Police complaint was issued to the Deans office regarding the behaviour of certain medical students. By that time we were all far from Merseyside, and I was on my way to Arabia.

7.   EAST TO ARABIA   1971

When I walked out of the Student Travel shop 32 pounds poorer, but with a one-way ticket to Cairo, I was already dreaming of minarets and *felafels*. After six torrid years of study, I couldn't wait to get out of Liverpool, even if I knew I was returning in three months' time to start my surgical houseman year at Broadgreen General. The fact that the police were possibly on the hunt for me again after our explosive farewell party was another incentive to head east.

I had decided to explore the eastern end of the Mediterranean. Somewhere around there was one of the crucibles of civilization. After my early experiences in Morocco and Libya I was entranced by Arabia, and I wanted to know more about these biblical lands. My intention was to pass two weeks each in Egypt, Cyprus, Israel and Turkey, but I also inadvertently included Lebanon in this itinerary.

As the Middle East Airlines plane took off from Gatwick, I was already preparing myself for some unintelligible Arabic script. When we landed in the heat of the eastern Mediterranean I saw the big Arabic sign over the front of the airport, which I assumed said "Welcome to Cairo" and disembarked with the other passengers.

An unexpected diversion to Lebanon

We marched through Immigration and Customs, a strange and exotic mixture of blue jeans and turbans. It was only when I exited the airport that I was stunned to be made aware by an exasperated taxi driver that I was not in Cairo at all. I was in Beirut! What? How could this be? It appeared that I had joined the transit passengers by mistake, and there was no way I was going to catch that Cairo-bound plane now. Then I felt the weight of my guitar case in my left hand, and immediately felt reassured, for with it I could always earn a roof and a crust of bread, no matter where I was.

One thing I had learned during my formative years at Liverpool when in pursuit of loot, was always to go to where the money was. Thus, during my student days as a waiter I only ever worked in four- or five-star hotels, where the tips were always more generous. In Tangier in 1967 I quit the drug-filled roof-top I was occupying in the medina with fellow hippies and travellers and entered the most expensive nightclub in that cosmopolitan city on the south shore of the Mediterranean together with my guitar. I was well-received as well as being richly paid, enough to get me comfortably to Marrakesch and the Atlas Mountains.

So, as I watched my flight to Cairo take off, I turned to Abdullah, my voluble taxi driver, and asked him to take me to the best night club in Beirut, ending up outside the front door of the Café de Paris, an elegant building, flanked by a row of Rolls-Royces and Cadillacs. A huge poster outside announced the arrival of Tom Jones the week before. It looked just the job, so paying off Abdullah I entered the luxurious reception area and asked to speak to the manager.

I guess that my appearance alone was enough to surprise the receptionist, with my long blonde hair and denim jeans. The sight of my guitar case and haversack must have caused him some doubts, but soon enough the owner himself arrived, and when he understood that I was an English doctor (even if only by a week or two) he became quite animated, and insisted on taking me to see his brother, who was very ill. Even though I was mildly concerned about where I would lay my head that night, I trusted this affable gentleman and followed him outside to his Mercedes saloon.

On Stage at the Café de Paris, Beirut.

We wound our way up into the cedar-covered hills above the city, climbing through groves of fruit trees and olives. The vista below of the floodlit corniche and the port of Beirut was impressive. Passing increasingly rich villas we entered a small forest of cedar trees and stopped in front of a regal mansion.

As soon as I saw the sick brother, I knew he was doomed, for he was cachectic as well as being semi-comatose. Mohammed, my Lebanese benefactor had told me his brother had cancer of the rectum and had been ill for more than a year. He was desperate to send his brother to London, but I had to say that I thought there was little hope of any cure. He seemed to accept that but was happy I had come with him. Most important of all, gave me a three-night spot in his magnificent night club, paying me 25 Lebanese pounds a night as well as putting me up in his mansion.

It was an amazing stroke of luck, after my initial mishap, but a great introduction to the Middle East. Mohammed was not only very rich but had a heart of gold. He gave me his car and chauffeur to explore Beirut for two days, and in the evenings I sang and played guitar in the opulent, carpet-hung nightclub. I was following in Tom Jones' footsteps, and the whole floor show was of the highest quality cabaret. During my time there one of my fellow performers was a stark naked, fantastically beautiful Arab girl painted all over in gold who performed a stimulating bondage scene on the stage in a take-off of the James Bond film, 'Goldfinger', which got the chaps in the front seats all salivating.

There was still a lot of French influence in Beirut in 1971. From the croissants I used to 'ptrompe' in my *café crème* in one of the bar-restaurants which lined the corniche to the ubiquitous smell of garlic and Gauloises. I spent much time in these cafes just enjoying the buzz of human energy around me and speaking French again.

I found the cosmopolitan meld of peoples most interesting of all. In this ancient city there was still a real mix of cultures and civilisations. French was the lingua franca, but most people were speaking Arabic, and quite a few Lebanese spoke English. They were the same traders I had known during my Cameroun days and probably still had links to the Phoenicians. I could see that Beirut was a true multi-cultural city and appeared to be a very liberal Muslim state. Many of the women did not even wear the hijab. The impression I took away with me was of a city rich in its heritage and welcoming to the world.

Liverpool was far away, and after such a fun time I was sad to leave Beirut and Mohammed, but Cairo beckoned.

To Egypt and the Pharoahs

The city of Cairo was totally mad. I had done a fair bit of travelling by then but had never been in such a huge, disorganised place. Trying to get on a bus with my haversack and guitar was almost impossible, and once I arrived in Tahiri Square I decided to quit the crazy buses, so full that there were passengers hanging off every corner.

The streets were also dangerous to navigate on foot as there was a state of near-total anarchy on the roads. They were choked with all manner of transport, from the donkeys laden with massive sacks of millet, lentils and corn to bicycles, cars, and crippled beggars in small carts which they propelled by hand through the hordes of people thronging the streets.

At a major intersection near Garden City, I spotted an elderly woman dressed in black attempting to cross the street, and without thinking much, I went to her assistance. We managed to reach the other side of the road after several near-fatal collisions with traffic, where she thanked me and invited me for a cup of tea. And that was how I came to spend three days being shown the sights of Cairo by her granddaughter, one of the most beautiful ladies I ever had seen.

Aisha was a final year student in the Egyptian National School of

Ballet, and she set my heart on fire with her long black hair, olive skin and bright, shining eyes. She arranged to meet me at the nearby Youth Hostel in Garden City next morning, and I went to sleep that night after an excellent meal of shish kebab and felafels washed down with mint tea, full of romantic dreams. I now had my Egyptian Youth Hostel Association card, written and stamped in fluent Arabic which I could not decipher. But I was beginning to learn a few words of this poetic language.

Aisha proved to be a patient teacher as she showed me the wonders of this ancient city. She took me into the Grand Souk where we lost ourselves for a whole morning amongst the extraordinary commerce which went on inside. From gold merchants and carpet sellers to the tiny chai shops where I could sit and smoke a hookah with rose-water-flavoured tobacco and a glass of mint tea, sitting amongst Egyptians in their flowing robes, I was mesmerised.

We went to the Cairo Museum where I marvelled at the history of the Egyptian people, their kings and queens and gods going back more than seven millennia.

From the Sphinx at Midnight ………

Aisha also knew much about the current art scene in Cairo and told me the national orchestra would be playing at the Giza pyramids the next night, so off we went.

There was a huge desert moon shining over the pyramid of Cheops. A broken-nosed Sphinx stared at us as we enjoyed the Cairo Philharmonic and a son et lumière performance with the lights of Cairo glinting just behind us. It was one thing to visit these huge pyramids during the heat of a Cairo day, being trampled on by the hordes of tourists and camels, but during the dark of night with only the desert stretching to infinity and the pyramids silhouetted by the moon, the music of the orchestra provided a magic moment.

……… to the Valley of the Kings

I really enjoyed Cairo in spite of the chaos, and when Aisha put me on the train to Luxor I was sad to leave her. But I was soon entranced by the sight of feluccas plying the Nile as we headed south at a slow and civilized pace which allowed a good view of rural life along the banks of this iconic river.

My next stop, Karnak was awe-inspiring. Most of the city was in ruins but the size of the original construction was incredible, on a scale I had only ever seen before in books. I spent two days wandering about these remains, trying to understand a little more of the many regal hierarchies which had existed millennia before.

The whole foundation of regal Egypt was based around the Nile Delta, or Lower Egypt as it was then known. From the Ethiopian Highlands to Memphis, the river Nile has governed life for centuries in a land that is otherwise desert.

When the warrior kings of the 19th Dynasty established their seat at Thebes, known as Karnak today, they also controlled from Syria to Palestine and had found rich sources of gold as well as other treasures which sustained their empire.

Still dazzled by the wonders of Luxor, I crossed the Nile on a felucca and hired a bike for a day to explore the Valley of the Queens and all the tombs and temples, many half-buried in the sand. That night I slept inside a tomb whose roof was painted with a galaxy of stars against an indigo sky. My silent companions that desert night were bats.

I decided to hitch back to Cairo, but it was a slow trip down the Nile valley. The Egyptians were not much in tune with hitch-hiking, and the best lift I got turned out to be on the back of a bullock cart doing about two mph. As I lay on sheaves of corn, just cut and smelling so sweet, I was able to see the passing rural life in detail. Saidi, the farmer who was my driver, invited me to stay on his farm with his wife and seven children. She was a wonderful mother and not only managed her swarm of kids but cooked a memorable cous-cous with apricots, almonds and figs, as well as some succulent lamb. After this feast Saidi insisted on teaching me backgammon, which was played at crazy speeds in every chai house along the route, where I often stopped for some thirst-quenching tea between lifts.

Hitchhiking to Cairo. Saidi's family

Soraya, age 10. Bearer of water

I was sorry to bid this family farewell the following morning, but I still had miles to go to reach Cairo. They and other Egyptians had been kind to me, a stranger amongst them, and had fed me and given me shelter when I needed it. Would that everyone was like that, I thought as I hit the highway north.

In Cairo I took a train to Alexandria on the northern coast where I hoped to find a boat for Cyprus. I was two weeks into my adventure and had already had a good time in Lebanon and Egypt. Now I was on my way to one of the few remaining outposts of the British Empire, Cyprus. One of the ancient gateways to the Middle East, even today the British have a small army there and listening posts sponsored by the Americans to spy on events in that biblical melting pot, the Middle East, which was never far from war.

My father had spent time there during the war and was in Jordan at the time of Israel's creation. His generation were still of a colonial mindset, and his attitude to the Egyptians was that of the British Raj. In Alexandria he had played squash for the Royal Air Force at the famous club known as Sporting Alex, and it was to this that I made my way, interested to see this part of my father's former life.

Alexandria had a long history, the most recent being the arrival of the old trams from Blackpool. It was a memorable experience to be drawn along the long corniche by these gaily coloured trams, now full of richly attired Egyptians on holiday.

Alex, as my father always called this city, was the Egyptian equivalent of Brighton. It had always been a seaside retreat for the gentry of Cairo, just as it was for my father and all the other allied forces in the Middle East during the 1940s. Today I could see the long beach was a mass of olive-skinned bodies and black chadours. The summer heat was oppressive, and the beach was not for me. I got off the tram at Sporting Alex and found the squash courts where I sat and watched two young Egyptians bashing the ball around. Then, one of them looked up and saw me.

"Please sir, come and play", he entreated, so I did, and got well thrashed by both. What really got me was the way they so politely apologised each time they scored a point. By strange coincidence Ali and Abdi were both medical students at the university and spoke fluent English, as did many of the Egyptians I met. They were splendid fellows, and I spent the rest of the day in their good company.

On Belly dancing with Fairuz

As the afternoon faded, they said they were off to a wedding of one of their fellow medics. Would I like to come along? Unreal! Five minutes later we were in a donkey cart bouncing along the corniche to Al Azahar, a very prestigious Alexandrian restaurant. Inside were a couple of hundred wedding guests, all having a good time, and soon I was seated at a table full of medical students. The food was good and rich, and it kept coming. Then there were toasts to bride and bridegroom. These relaxed Muslims had a rich supply of drinks, from Krug to the finest clarets, and of course Egyptian brandy.

When Fairuz, a famous Alexandrian belly-dancer appeared on the table in front of me, I was impressed by her serpentine movements and the chinking jewels hanging off every protruding part of her anatomy. Then, she beckoned to me, and all my new medic friends forced me out of my seat and up onto the table with her.

I have never fancied myself as a dancer, but whether it was the generous toasts I had slid down, or the magic of the moment, suddenly I was gyrating on the table with a hundred guests applauding. The black and white photos which Ali took and kindly sent to me in England are a warm reminder of a memorable night in Alexandria.

Belly dancing. Alexandria.1971

Belly dancing. Brighton.   1996. My 50th birthday

Mixing it with the Russians

The following morning, I could remember little of the night before, nor where I was, only that my jeans were still on and that my head was exploding. After adequate resuscitation my two new friends took me to the port where I found a Russian boat leaving for Limassol that very night. I bade them a very fond farewell, bought a one-way ticket to Limassol for a few pounds and spent the hours of dusk lying on the deck playing my guitar, totally at peace with the world.

My tranquility was interrupted by a voice with a thick Russian accent coming out of a loudspeaker requesting the assistance of any medical person. I realized that now included me, so I packed my guitar and headed for the purser's office. There I met a huge Russian lady who shook my hand and took me off to the restaurant where an Arab lady was lying on the floor having an epileptic fit. They produced a medical kit, all in Russian, but I recognized the small vial of diazepam, 10 milligrams, and slowly injected five ccs intravenously while several other big Russian ladies pinned the patient to the floor. Within a few seconds all was peaceful again. I sat with the lady and her husband until her breathing was regular and then left her in the coma position while I went on deck to recover.

It was the very first time I ever was called on in an emergency medical situation whilst travelling, but it has happened many times since then, mostly with positive results for the patient. On this occasion the Russians proved very generous with their thanks for my intervention, and I was invited to the captain's table that night. I ate an enormous meal and drank far too much vodka and good red wine from the Carpathians before collapsing in my spotless cabin. I was impressed by the ship's cleanliness. Russian ladies were cleaning non-stop, and they then appeared behind the bar in a different uniform a few hours later to serve drinks and a good meal before returning to their cleaning. It was a good voyage for me and an interesting introduction to things Russian.

Cyprus

I escaped the port of Limassol quickly and headed north towards Nicosia, the Cypriot capital. The war between the Greek and Turkish islanders, which had continued in various forms for centuries made Cyprus a sad island in many ways. There was a lot of fear and hate. The Turks inhabited the northern half and in 1971 it was still possible to traverse Nicosia, but it had been scarred by years of conflict. The barriers of barbed wire and soldiers everywhere were enough to keep me heading north to Kyrenia, another ancient port, with an architecture dating from before the Phoenecians. There I spent several days, playing guitar in the port-side cafes and bars which were full of British armed forces enjoying some time off. The Brits were very much in evidence in Cyprus, too much for my liking, with their expatriate way of life, their clubs and pubs and golf courses and their complete lack of interest in the local people or their culture. In that regard it was much as I remembered Gibraltar, another British colonial outpost.

The Turks and the Greeks were equally hospitable, and from Kyrenia to Paphos on the southwest coast I found only good food and wine and friendly locals. From Kyrenia I hitched west along the wild north coast until I came to Myrtou where I turned south across the fertile Mesaoria plain until I hit the foothills of the Trodos mountains. The tallest summit was that of Mount Olympus, home of the ancient gods. I wanted to climb to the summit which at just under 2,000 metres gave a terrific vista of Cyprus over the huge pine forest guarding this holy mountain.

That night I stayed in the youth hostel, halfway up the mountain. It was a wooden shack with bunks and a big communal kitchen with a wood burning cooker which threw out clouds of sparks from the pine logs burning inside. I was inadequately dressed for the freezing temperatures at that altitude at night and after an excellent *stifado*, soon made my way to my sleeping bag, exhausted after the long climb up the mountain.

The journey down to Paphos was a wonder. Descending through the dense pine forest I entered vineyards and pastures of sheep. Olive trees and holm oaks began to appear. That evening I ate red mullet in the port of Paphos under a brilliant Mediterranean moon. I stayed at the campsite, under the stars in my sleeping bag enjoying the balmy night air after the frigid heights of Mount Olympus the night before. Unfortunately, Paphos was already going the way of so much of the Mediterranean coast, with concrete hotels, bars and flats spreading in ugly fashion from the picturesque and ancient harbour, so I left next morning.

I was really enjoying travelling around. Every aspect of the trip was good, even the long waits between lifts. As long as I had my guitar and a tree for shelter, I never minded these enforced waits. They gave me a good chance to check out the local scenery, the fields of beans and peppers, orchards of citrus and olive groves with trees that were so gnarled they must have been centuries old. Everywhere I travelled there was architectural evidence from the Greeks and the Romans to the Byzantine empire, much of it on a monolithic scale.

The name Cyprus derives from copper which abounded in the island and was one reason apart from its strategic position why the island has been colonized by so many tribes over the centuries, from the Assyrians, Egyptians and Persians to the Ptolomaic empire. Then during the mediaeval period came the Byzantines, Arabs, Franks and the Venetians until 1571 when it was conquered by the Turks. I knew little of this history, but simply seeing what had been so long ago and which had lasted for so many centuries motivated me to learn about this ancient civilization, a quest which still continues as I write this on the banks of the Mediterranean.

It was in Paphos that I was amazed to see an old chap on a moped come by – and sitting so prettily on the back seat was a pelican. I was astonished, and asked about this at the restaurant that evening, and was told that this was Georgio, a local fisherman who used his pet pelican to assist him in his work. He was a well-known sight around

Paphos, but to me it was yet another wonder as I hitched around the eastern Mediterranean. There was so much to see in this world, and the more I saw the more I wanted.

I returned to Limassol where I took a ferry on a Thursday night for the port of Haifa, my first stop in Israel. I was looking forward to visiting this biblical melting pot of religions, but it was there that the first clouds on my sunny holiday appeared.

Israel and Palestine. Starving on the Shabath.

The boat arrived in the port of Haifa the following day, a Friday, and I had hardly disembarked when my problems began. At Immigration I was greeted by a smiling Israeli as I handed my passport to him. I told him in answer to his enquiry that I had just come from Cyprus. His expression changed considerably as he pointed to my Lebanese and Egyptian visas, and soon I was in the interrogation room while they tried to establish what an English doctor was doing going to Arab countries. They made me take all the strings off my guitar so they could search it inside. Then they found the Septrin tablets in my washbag and got really excited, accusing me of importing illicit drugs, and made me wait hours while they had them analysed.

All the while I received nothing to eat or drink, in spite of asking, for they told me it was the Shabbat, whatever that was. To me it meant that there was no food or drink available for some religious reason, something which even the strict Lutherans in Cameroun had never sunk to. I was eventually released from my incarceration in Haifa late that afternoon, well-pissed off, and hungry as well as very thirsty.

My mood was not improved by finding out that every single shop was closed, because of this religious holiday, and when I went to sleep that night, my stomach was crying with hunger. All I had eaten that day had been half a watermelon, kindly given to me by a young Arab boy. It had certainly been a rude arrival to Israel, and as I went to sleep, I was wondering what other adventures might befall me in this explosive country.

Shaving in Lake Galilee

I was bound for Lake Galilee to fulfil a strange desire which I had held for some time. This was to swim and shave in that biblical patch of water, and maybe even catch a few fish. I don't know if it is related to my Piscean horoscope sign, but I have always gravitated towards water, possibly because where there is water there is always life. I still had the image of another long-haired chap going round the lake, 2000 years before, persuading the fishermen to leave their livelihood and follow his revolutionary cause, so there was also a historic reason for going to Galilee.

I had had to make a practical decision before I left Haifa regarding my mode of travel in Israel. The national bus company, Egged, offered a two-week student ticket, valid all over Israel but it cost the equivalent of my two weeks daily allowance, and Israel was markedly more expensive than either Lebanon, Egypt or Cyprus. Therefore, I decided to save the bus fare for food and shelter, and continue hitch-hiking, which had served me well so far.

By the time I left Israel I was well wised up to the hitching lore in that small country, for there was a strict hierarchy. First came the Israeli Army, and the country was full of young men and women in army uniform wherever I went, Israel being in a constant state of subliminal war. Then came any females and lastly came any blond-haired hippy, which was approximately me. So, my progress was slow as I headed out of Haifa, but by the following evening I was inside the campsite at Galilee and in the midst of a very global mix of young people, most of them Jews from all corners of the earth.

I checked in and then headed straight for the lakeside. It was a beautiful expanse of water, and there were fishermen in small, gaily coloured rowing boats throwing out nets hopefully, just like the pictures I had seen in my paternal grandfather's bible. There were also several long-haired guys like me around the shores, but none of us was on a mission, and most of them had a lissom girl hanging on their arm. Nevertheless, my dream was fulfilled, and I did shave in the Sea of Galilee as well as making my first friends in Israel.

The following day I was washing my clothes when I heard a shout from outside the perimeter of the campsite and saw a young couple approaching me. "Hey man, can you get this if I throw it over", he said, showing me his haversack, and I was soon in charge of two haversacks while their owners, Dave and Barb skated round to the campsite entrance and walked in.

In those days of economical travel there were all sorts of dodges to maintain budget levels, from rolling up to supermarkets just before closing time for some cheap food, to staying for free in campsites, which was Dave and Barb's wheeze. They were two American students from Queens in New York, and we soon became friends. Barb had an aunt in Jerusalem, and she gave me her address, saying that I would be welcome in case I needed a roof. We arranged to meet up there in a few days' time.

Israel has always been a magnet for the Jewish diaspora, as was Mecca in Saudi Arabia to the Muslims, and both came to congregate with the Christians in Jerusalem and pray to their respective gods in that old city, the Jews at the Wailing Wall, the Muslims at the Golden Mosque of Al Aqsa and the Christians in their churches. You could not move a metre in Israel without religion becoming an issue, whether it was stocking up on Thursday in order to survive the Shabatt or the sight of poor Arab families being molested by Israeli soldiers at the countless roadblocks on every road.

The roadblocks were a pain, and very different indeed from the freedom I had enjoyed exploring Egypt and Lebanon. I suppose I was in some way fortunate, since it was only those who looked liked Arabs who got a hard time from the Israeli soldiers. Nevertheless, I was very surprised and disappointed to see the manner in which the

Arabs were treated by the Israelis. They were obviously second-class citizens in Israel.

Palestine. This young boy gave me a comfortable lift

Palestinian boys going to market

I left Galilee and headed south towards Jericho. I had to see the place where Joshua played his horn, but when I got there, I found only a few crumbling bits of masonry on the banks of the river Jordan, for the walls had indeed come a-tumbling down. But the river itself was a wonder as it wound its way from the heights above Mount Lebanon to the south as it divided Jordan from Israel. In a land of desert this river gave life to all, Arabs and Jews alike, and the Golan Heights in the northeast controlled all access to this life-giving water. Since 1967 these strategic hills had been in the hands of the Israelis, and it was no longer an area to go hitch-hiking.

Jerusalem.

Having sated my wish to experience the history of Jericho I headed for Jerusalem. Of all the Near and Middle East cities I visited that summer, Jerusalem was the most complex and had the most violent history, being the religious capital of the Christians, the Jews and the Muslims. It was small wonder that there were pock-marked buildings and battalions of soldiers everywhere, amongst a million tourists that summer who filled the narrow streets and every hotel bed.

I was forced to call Barb's aunt and was very happy to be met by Barb and her cousin, Rafaela who was 22 years old and looked exactly like Aisha, whom I had recently left in Cairo. It was quite uncanny. Within two weeks I was looking at two girls, one Arab and the other Jewish, in two different countries separated by much more than distance, both of whom were not just adorably beautiful, but were also both ballet dancers with their national ballet company. I couldn't decide if I was lucky or just destined to remain frustrated as I dreamed romantic dreams with Rafaela sitting so close beside me. After my days with Aisha in Cairo it was very strange to meet her doppelganger in Jerusalem.

Barb's aunt was a regular Jewish momma and was a champion kosher cook. She could not have been more welcoming and for three days I was mothered and smothered in good food and shown the sights of Jerusalem by Rafaela. She had lived all her life in that city and was sympathetic towards the Arab population.

She and her mother taught me a great deal of the tumultuous history of Israel as well as much about their religion. They were not an orthodox family even though they followed many rituals from the daily kosher cuisine to the keeping of the Friday Shabatt . Rafaela took me to the Wailing Wall where we watched hundreds of black-robed Jews standing before it with holy books in their hand, their heads nodding up and down as they offered their prayers. The ancient blocks of stone were separated by a million tiny pieces of paper, each one with a prayer on it, stuffed into the cracks by these fervently religious people.

It was only when I entered the barrio of Mea Sharim and the world of the ultra-Orthodox Jews that I became slightly apprehensive, as these were a violent breed who thought nothing of stoning any visitors they didn't like the look of or who were not dressed correctly. They were also committed to the greater Zion and had no wish to have anything to do with the Arabs, except treat them like serfs. It was all a bit too extreme for me and made me fear for any possible future integration of these two warring peoples.

Israel was a country full of paradox. I went to see the Hadassah university and was impressed by the campus and the architecture but found the many carved dedications to the American Jewish benefactors outside every building a bit much. The holocaust memorial, Yad Veshem was also a beautiful and very expensive building, overflowing with every gory detail of the Jews hard times, but less about all the gypsies, homosexuals and disabled who were also butchered. It was clear to me that the Israeli Jews had no intention of ever forgetting the traumas they had suffered over the years and moving on.

The United States connections with Israel were evident everywhere, from the millions spent on the university, to the army which they heavily sponsored. The army was everywhere and constantly threatening to me as I hitched around. I had never seen so many soldiers or so much military hardware, and I realized by the time I left that Israel really was a country in a state of constant but suppressed war.

There was conscription for all, and guns were worn like jewellery. The atmosphere was so oppressive, in spite of Jerusalem being a very tourist-orientated place, that I was happy to hit the road again, heading south towards the Dead Sea – another biblical patch of water which I intended to visit.

To the Dead Sea – and another dangerous moment in Israel

That afternoon I found myself on the northern outskirts of Hebron, an Arab town, and from where I was dropped off, I could see an Israeli army outpost on a hill about a kilometre away. The last words from Barb and Rafaela to me had been to beware of being alone in Arab places, for they had the same sense of insecurity and fear of the Arabs that I had found all over Israel. It was only four years since their last major confrontation, and it looked to me as if the whole country was just waiting for the next. Nevertheless, I had found the Arabs I met to be generally friendly but cowed by the huge Israeli military presence and the colonial attitude of so many Israelis.

As the light began to fade and I was still without a lift I spotted a group of young Arab men carrying sticks and staves coming slowly towards me, and I began to become a bit apprehensive. Were they friend or foe I wondered, and looked at the army outpost, unable to decide what to do, when the situation was saved by the arrival of a cranky old Dodge pickup.

"You wan' leeft?", a genial Arab face leaned out of the driver´s window. I didn't wait a second, and soon found myself in the back with six children and a dog called Fou-Fou. Mohammed was a Palestinian Arab from Tel Aviv, taking his family for a weekend at Ein Gedi, a place I had heard of on the banks of the Dead Sea. It was not far from Sodom and Gomorrah, both places I also wanted to visit. So it was that I passed two delightful days living with this warm and generous family. All I had to do was play songs to the kids and swim in the crystal lakes of Ein Gedi which descended in a swirl of freezing water under a blue sky, hazed by the heat of August. I still have some black and white photos of that weekend, which was the best part of the two weeks I spent in Israel.

A weekend with Mohammed and his family at Ein Gedi

Mohammed was a teacher, and from him I learned much of the Arab view of Israel and the Israeli Jews. There was no doubt that the Arabs were a subjected people today, ruled in a fairly heartless fashion by their recent conquerors, with many restrictions on every aspect of their lives from jobs and schooling to healthcare and travel. It was also strange to pass in one day from most excellent kosher cuisine of Barb's mum to the equally good Arab cuisine prepared for us by

Fatima, an earth-mother wife who had a heart of gold. We ate late and I played guitar under a shining moon as the kids fell asleep on the ground around me. We cooked shishkebabs over the red coals of the open fire still glowing in the dark. I could not have been happier.

We went down to the Dead Sea whose water is so salty it renders the body buoyant enough to lie in the water whilst reading a book. The salt-saturated water felt soapy and under the terrific heat it dried to form an irritating and unpleasant crust on the skin. Thank God for the cold clear water of the showers bordering the waterside. It was a great experience, and even the drive down to the Dead Sea was a rare treat, as we descended to one of the lowest points on earth. The heat increased with every metre we travelled until it was almost unbearable at the water's edge, being over 45 C. At this point, 400 metres below sea level I was standing on the lowest point on earth. It was an epic moment to share with Mohammed and his family.

I was sad to bid them farewell, especially the children who had been my amusing companions and willing audience for two memorable days, but I wanted to spend a night on the heights of Masada and see the sun rise over the Jordan valley. It was there that I had one more scary moment in Israel.

Another rude awakening

I had seen an Israel Youth Hostel on the way to the summit of Masada, but apart from the cost, which was a dollar a night, I wanted to sleep out in the wild just to complete the natural experience of this sunrise, so I made my bed in a patch of sand, tied my guitar to my haversack and was soon asleep.

The cold steel muzzle of an Uzi submachine gun in my neck was my first waking experience. There were two armed soldiers standing over me, and it was not a dream. They were pretty brutal, even after seeing my British passport and hearing my explanation of why I was there. To these young men I appeared to be some form of terrorist.

"You are forbidden to sleep outside!", they stated. "You must go to the hostel", brooking no argument as they propelled me the kilometre to the hostel, locked and dark at this hour of night. But that did not faze these guardians of freedom, and soon I was before the hostel manager, furious when he saw my Egyptian Youth Hostel Association card, all scrolled in fluent Arabic. It was amazing to me how emotional these people got at any form of alliance with the Arabs, even from me, a simple tourist.

I did not sleep the rest of the night, and as a protest I sat outside in the compound just waiting for dawn. I could not wait to get out of that hostel and the unpleasant memories of my rude awakening by the soldiers. My reward was a vision I have never forgotten as the huge red sun slowly poked itself over the far horizon on the east side of the Jordan valley. No wonder so many people came to witness this singular natural phenomenon. But this morning I was alone on the mountain top and for a moment I felt as though I was the only man on earth, under the power of the rising sun.

A tourist guide to Israel's nuclear facility

I never did find Sodom, but I passed through Gomorrah, not a place I would recommend, on my meandering way through the Negev desert to Eilat at the head of the Red Sea.

It was whilst walking in the heat of the day east of BeerSheva, near the town of Dimona, my view just a shimmering sheet of sand, that I came across an endless fence of razor wire stretching across the desert, enclosing strange silver domes which I could just make out in the distance. Hanging on the fence were signs in Hebrew, Arabic and English warning of the lethal consequences of crossing this barrier. I did not know it at the time, but this was the Israeli's secret nuclear bomb facility, never publicly acknowledged but, with much American help there it was – just in case things got really awkward in the Middle East. It was a frightening thought.

Eilat was the only place I have ever been in over 60 years of travel that I had had to pay for drinking water out of a tap. Also, the sand on the beach where I slept that night was so hot by 0730h that it was impossible to stand on in bare feet. So, I left Eilat fast, not liking that tourist haven at all, and headed south into the Sinai peninsula, to Sharm el Sheikh and the Arabian Gulf, where the tourists did not venture.

How to strip an Uzi machine gun in two minutes

It was a very hard trip in the ferocious heat, and not much to see of interest along the way, but I was fortunate to hook up with a young Israeli soldier, Esther, sweet as could be, in spite of carrying a lethal amount of arms on her slight body. I was fascinated by the Uzi machine gun she carried and while we waited for our next lift, she showed me how to strip it in about a minute and then reassemble it. She told me that by the time they were 21 every Israeli youth was familiar with the guts of this killing machine. Well, it wasn't the sort of thing we were taught at Lewes County Grammar School for Boys. Nonetheless it was an impressive performance and the 9mm bullet which Esther gave me as a token of our meeting was the only souvenir I took out of Israel three days later, having seen a decent chunk of Israel during two weeks of hitch hiking.

The contrast with Lebanon and Egypt could not have been greater. I could see that the Israelis were a proud and powerful people, but every Israeli seemed to be on the defensive and slightly fearful of their Arab neighbours. Under the benevolent American umbrella, and after quarter of a century of continuous warfare, from the Brits to the Arabs, they had managed to develop all manner of counter-terrorist warmongery, a people's army on constant watch as well as an effective air force and the secretive, dark Mossad security apparatus. But I did not believe it was a just way to run a civilised country.

Whilst trekking in the Negev desert an old Arab shepherd had shown me an enormous subterranean stone cistern buried in the sand. He told me it was hundreds of years old and had been built by a previous generation of Palestinian Arabs, when they had been the masters of the Middle East. But today it was in the hands of the Israelis, so history was just repeating itself as it had done for centuries.

From Anatolia to Alexandria, I was in a most fascinating corner of the world, far removed from England in every sense, and with a long history whose evidence lay around every step of the way.

To Istanbul and the Sultan´s Harem

The final country on my itinerary was Turkey. I arrived in Istanbul, relieved to be out of the restrictive and violent Israel, to be met by JS, Long John and Ian, the stalwarts of No 9, Percy Street, Liverpool 8. Together we had a great week in Istanbul, that cosmopolitan melting pot which separates Arabia from Europe.

We found a cheap hostel in SultanHama, not far from the Grand Bazaar, full of penniless travellers like ourselves and where, in a moment of mindlessness I put my guitar under my bed – and was saddened to find it gone when we returned later. Another bitter lesson learned, especially after the great service my guitar had provided during eight weeks across the Near and Middle East. I spent 120 pounds on a new John Pierce Aria from the music shop in Grove Road, Eastbourne when I got back to England, and that same guitar is at my elbow as I write. I could not say which I would rather lose today – my left leg or my acoustic-electric guitar, which has become a living extension of my body during the 41 years we have been together.

My most vivid memory of Istanbul is the crunching sound as I walked the streets in my flip-flops, crushing the shells of pistaccio nuts and sunflower seeds which covered every square centimeter of pathway. Half the population were chewing seeds and spitting husks and shells like bullets as they strolled along, as eclectic a mixture of humanity as I ever saw. There were loads of young tourists like us, for Istanbul has been a magnet to voyagers for centuries and we were no different in wanting a taste of East meets West.

There were Turks in traditional Arabian attire, but many others dressed in conventional western fashion, and many women who did not wear a hijab. Turkey was still a pretty secular country in those days in spite of having a strong Muslim presence, and everyone seemed to get on well, as I had found in Beirut, another extraordinary city where two major cultures met and drank strong coffee or shared a bottle of good wine from the Bekaa valley.

The food we ate in Istanbul was good and cheap, similar to Greek and some Persian cuisine, and vastly superior to what we had been used to in Liverpool during our student days. I loved every single thing I ate during those eight weeks, and I had also learned a lot about Middle Eastern cuisine by then.

In Cairo I had learned the receipe for falafel from Aisha's grandmother. In Jerusalem, Lilli, Barb's aunt taught me a simple kosher fish dish. I learned about the different kebabs in Beirut and in Istanbul. And in Istanbul, Layla, the owner of a tiny restaurant in the centre of SultanHama, just round the corner from the hostel, was happy to teach me how to stuff and cook a capsicum. Half a century later I am still enjoying these excellent recipes.

We took a boat to see the Golden Horn, that small gulf which has always been so much more than a slight geographical separation, and laughed as we compared this ferry trip with the one we so often used to take across the grey Mersey to Birkenhead. Today we were under a brilliant Mediterranean sun and the sea was an azure blue. The banks were full of fishermen, a sight which gladdened my heart, and the waters of the Bosphorus were jam packed with all manner of boats, many of them fine sailing craft, close-hauled in the stiff westerly which whistled under the famous bridge which unites Europe and Arabia.

I wanted to see the Mosque of Suleiman the Magnificent which dates from the early days of the Ottoman empire in the mid-15th. Century. This magnificent edifice overlooks Istanbul, its massive cupola and tall minarets dominating the skyline. It was even more mighty than Ely cathedral, which has dominated the Fens of East Anglia since the 14th century, but that holy place unfortunately lacks a harem, whereas Suleiman possessed the biggest harem in Arabia, which was one of the many internal assets of this ancient palace of the Ottoman kings.

The gardens were magnificent, redolent with palms and aloes and every sub-tropical plant imaginable, and everywhere the sweet scent of jasmine and the brilliance of bougainvillea in the bright sun. I found it hard to imagine old Suleiman and his harem of 800 ladies in this oriental chateau on the banks of the Bosphorus, but by the accounts in the book I had, there was a complete community within these walls with all means to survive a siege as well as serving the needs of Suleiman's harem. Those were the days.

Before we knew it we were once again heading back to England on a DanAir flight, popular with budget travellers. I had little time to dwell on my recent Middle Eastern adventures as within a week we newly qualified doctors were all lost in a mist of insomnia, near-catastrophes, leaking catheters and blocked intravenous drips as we began our career in medicine.

As the grey days of winter in Liverpool approached, my thoughts turned to that brilliant Mediterranean sky and all the history of mankind which had evolved in that crucible of civilisation. The plants and flowers so brilliant, the sea itself a carpet of azure blue and such a mix of humanity it was hard to imagine. But overall, I found the state of Israel worrying, even though I had met some very fine people there from both sides of the religious divide.

I had never yet travelled in a country where one part of the population was so obviously subjugated, but I saw the evidence every day I was in Israel. My heart went out to the Arab population who had seen their farms appropriated by the victorious Israelis so recently. Their ancient olive and citrus groves had been bulldozed, their water rights taken from them, and their livelihoods had been destroyed, rendering them beggars. Even their land was now being seized illegally by the Israelis and used to build settlements for the Zionists.

I do not know the national health statistics for the Palestinian and Jewish populations of Israel, but I am betting that the future lot of the Arabs there will only worsen, and the effects will be reflected within the published World Health Organisation data sheets in 10 or 20 years' time, particularly in the younger age groups.

Remembering the bible which our family used on a regular basis during my own childhood, the stories of the Old and New Testaments tell a fantastic tale of a land in turmoil and of the peoples who then inhabited the Near and Middle East. It was a place which I now also had some personal experience of.

This particular trip was to be just the beginning of a series of similar voyages over the following years, each one of which opened my eyes wider and wider to a world that was full of wonder as well as people who were essentially good and who shared a common humanity, whatever its shape or form or colour. However, my journey was also teaching me that there was also injustice and inhumane treatment of people everywhere one looked, and in the Middle East I had just tasted both sides of this humanity.

After 10 weeks travelling around the Mediterranean, the main thought I took back to Liverpool with me was that some countries were just a bit more civilised than others, and it had not much to do with wealth or power necessarily. It was more to do with the customs and culture of centuries, and a sense of social justice. I had already seen many examples of this during my voyage through five countries, travelling widely and recording everything of interest I saw, both in writing and on 35mm slides. It is these records which I have just referred to.

Post Script. I must have been lucky to visit Israel when I did, and shave in the Sea of Galilee, for today just 50 years later the fishermen in their gaily painted boats are no more, for the fish have disappeared. That great sea is now a shallow pond full of poisonous algae. Likewise, the Jordan river barely exists, being reduced to a rancid stream devoid of life. Even its source in the Golan heights is drying up.

The Israelis may be clever farmers, developing viable systems of farming the desert, but not only have they denied traditional sources of water to the Palestinian Arabs for decades, but they have also now depleted their own water sources, and even the subterranean aquifers are drying up.

8. DOCTOR AT LARGE - THE HOUSEMAN YEARS 1971 – 74

Our first six months as junior doctors were a nightmare. Broadgreen General was a very busy teaching hospital on the periphery of Liverpool. There were no specially trained junior doctors to run Accident and Emergency (A+E) in those days, so we surgeons in training had the added burden of treating every patient admitted to A+E as well as those in the general surgical wards.

First near-death experience – of a patient

I had been a working doctor just one week when I was called to A+E to sort out a patient with a locked knee. I drew up 10mgm of Diazepam and injected it intravenously – too quickly and was suddenly looking at a patient in respiratory arrest.

God Almighty! One week on the wards, and I had already killed my first patient. Fortunately, Sister Thomson who ran this urban battlefield, was used to the likes of us ignorant new-comers and did the needful – leaning on the Cardiac Arrest alarm quite heavily, and the situation was saved. That was just how scary life was at the beginning my career. Thank God for those magnificent nurses.

Just a few weeks later I was doing a weekend locum for my friend Ian, lately of the garret at No 9 Percy Street. The Northern Hospital was a grim Victorian monolith on Dock Road, surrounded by the lodgings of seamen from every corner of the world. They had just opened up their first Intensive Care Unit and there was a great sense of expectation waiting for the first patient, when I was called to see a middle-aged man with chest pain in A+E.

Second near-death experience – of a patient

I have always had a slight mental block about anything cardiac, including the ECG – ElectroCardioGram, to those in the know, which was a relatively recent innovation. You connect eight chest leads and four limb leads to the patient, switch the huge machine on and if you and the patient are lucky, a jagged line appears on the paper strip. At least the patient's heart was still beating – though the finer interpretation of this jagged line has remained a mystery all my life.

I regarded the straight, black line which appeared from the mouth of the Machine with interest. This was not what I had been expecting. There must be a problem with this new machine, so I checked the leads and the mains connection, forgetting to observe the patient, who was by now in a state of cardiac arrest.

The straight black line was in fact diagnostic of asystole – total lack of heartbeat. My diagnosis finally confirmed, I hit the Emergency button and started cardiac compressions whilst the resuscitation team arrived and saved the day. Our lucky patient became the first visitor to the new ITU, and after our mutual near-death experience, he left in one piece.

That was my first Saturday locum as a qualified doctor at the Northern.

The following Sunday morning at 0730h my crash bleep went off again. When I phoned A+E the sister just said, "we've got another axing. Better come quick, he's bleeding a lot".

There was blood all over the emergency room floor – always a bad sign. The patient, an Irish dockworker had been drinking with his son, who drunkenly struck him with the family axe. This blow had completely removed the left pinna and a good chunk of the scalp, and the temporal artery was gushing blood. There was a small Irish war going on in Docklands, and this was the third axing within a month. Such was life on Dock Road back in those days.

We virgin doctors arrived on the wards in our new white coats, knowing nothing much about the practical side of how to manage surgical wards or the Emergency Department after our six years of hard study. As medical students we had not been allowed to do much on the wards, so most of our knowledge was theoretical.

After my first six months as a houseman at Broadgreen I had learned a lot, including how to work solidly for days on end with barely any sleep. It's not to say we did not make mistakes whilst half-asleep, for we did, through both ignorance and fatigue. Watchful nursing staff became among our best daily teachers and helped much to avoid disasters.

I can see how valuable those busy days and nights were in my later formation as a doctor. It is impossible to become a good doctor without great experience. In those days we were able to acquire a lot of experience in a relatively short time, and I would continue working those long hours until I retired.

From the very first weeks, the demanding regime at Broadgreen hospital produced a good spirit of *camaraderie* among the doctors and nurses, with parties and surgical firm outings as well as a shared sense of vocation which carried us through the inevitable hard times.

The Irish nurses at Broadgreen were a scream, and Ginger Bob, my general surgical registrar was a thoroughly good fellow who often came with us on our ward outings. Another valued colleague on our surgical firm was Averil, our senior registrar.

In those days female surgeons were rare, for surgery was a very male-dominated discipline. But Averil was no ordinary woman. She was a dedicated vascular surgeon who later rose to become the first female professor of surgery in England and later the Vice-President of the Royal College of Surgeons in London and was later honoured by the Queen. Since then, an increasing number of women have chosen to specialise in surgery, which has greatly benefited our profession. I shall always remember Averil as a courageous pioneer who continues this day to inspire many of the next generation of surgeons.

Long John, Averil Mansfield, me, Joyce, Ann and Ian. Averil became my first post-graduate mentor in surgery, and we are still close friends

We all need professional mentors, no matter how senior or junior we are, and I was very fortunate, for Averil became my mentor. There never was a kinder or more cheerful person, nor a more generous teacher. She was also a wonderful surgeon whom I was always eager to assist at operations and learn her delicate skills. Her mentor in turn, was Edgar Parry, a very kind Welshman and dedicated vascular surgeon who was one of my two consultants.

The other consultant on our firm was Shep, a bluff old Scot who was quite different from Edgar. It was Shep who did most of the general surgery, from breasts to bums and a lot in between, which was where I wanted to be.

Vascular operations could often take up to 12 hours, which I found both boring and exhausting. Lord knows how Averil managed to survive, and always with her sweet smile. After spending 13 hours on Christmas Day 1971 in the operating theatre with her doing venous thrombectomies instead of partying, I knew I would never be a vascular surgeon.

There is now a law which forbids people working more than 55 hours a week. This is far less than the 90 hours a week which was our norm in 1971, and I must assume that new doctors and consultants must know less and have less experience than we did, which, from talking to professional colleagues I know to be true.

Lessons in Communication

I also learned to never be rude to anyone over the phone. Such modern gadgets as bleepers were barely invented then, and telephones were vital for all aspects of hospital work. This meant that the telephone operators were important people. One night when I was on call, having just got to sleep I was woken by the phone and rudely cursed the lady who called me. The following day every telephone call I made went astray for some reason. I even began receiving calls from people I had nothing to do with, and my life rapidly became a misery. So, I went to Sister Sean who was Irish and brilliant and had run ward 17 with military precision for years.

"It sounds as though you have upset Mrs Green, she being the queen of the telephonists in these parts", she told me. "And that is going to be a bit of a problem if you have been rude to one of her girls". My heart sank at the thought of more days of impossible communications.

"However," continued Sister Sean, "it is a strange coincidence that Mrs Green is presently in a private room recovering from a minor procedure. Possibly you may think of something…….?"

Once I had finished my night rounds, I then passed every bed again, taking one flower from each bedside vase and by the time I shyly entered Mrs Greens private room I was hidden behind a massive bunch of free blooms.

"So sorry to hear of your illness", I began manfully but sincerely, "I thought a few flowers may help the pain". I dumped the flowers into her small hand basin, but they spilled onto the floor in profusion, embarrassing me further. "Oh, and I'm sorry if I happened to upset anyone in Switch (as this hospital nerve centre was known), but I've been a bit tired recently".

"And that's no excuse for being rude to my ladies", riposted Mrs. Green from her hospital bed. "Let's see how things go. We all have to learn lessons, you know", she added sagely, as I removed my crestfallen body from her room, relieved that I had actually had the courage to face her.

It says something of the recent changes in the National Health Service that last year an edict was passed forbidding flowers on the wards, thus removing another small piece of humanity from patient care. Apparently, they can cause infections.

Since that day I have never stopped listening to women. From my mother and my sisters to the nurses who daily surround me, they have a view of life which most men know little of, to their detriment.

All the social and spiritual needs of the patients were cared for by our female nurses as a rule. We doctors, who were mostly male, tended to became more distanced from the daily needs of the patients as we became more senior. But as a houseman I was in constant contact with the nurses and my ward of patients every day, and thus came to learn a great deal about the social care of patients, as well as the ways of women.

From House-surgeon to House-physician, and a moment of Fame.

After my six months of surgical internship at Broadgreen I obtained a medical post across the Wirral at Clatterbridge, another major regional centre. This general hospital was in rural surroundings and had a more relaxed atmosphere than the central teaching hospitals, and also had a doctor's residence to match.

Two more members of the Percy Street gang, JS and Sandy had already done six months surgery there. They both knew the ropes, so they met me on my arrival and took me to the bar. This was as usual the centre of all activity and well stocked with beer at highly subsidised prices as well as a fair gathering of pretty nurses and physios. Then JS took me outside to see the swimming pool which was completely covered in mist, rendering it almost invisible, when a young, female voice called out from the steaming water,

"Hey, can you throw me my bra top?"

"No way baby", says JS, always a gentleman, "let's have a look", and as I picked up the flimsy garment and threw it into the pool a vision somewhere between Excalibur and a mermaid rose out of the mist and did indeed show us her anatomy.

"Crikey!", I exclaimed as we went back to the bar, "is it always like this here?"

"Most of us are getting sex insomnia," said JS. "And there's no let up! Just hope that things continue quiet on the wards", which they mostly were. It was a far cry from the mad rush of surgery at Broadgreen with all its acute trauma, strangulated hernias and haemorrhoids, all of which required a lot of fast work. General Medicine at Clatterbridge was an altogether more civilized existence and it was rare to be called out at night once we had tucked up our patients.

There were two wards, male and female, which JS and I cared for under the watchful eye of Sister Bennett, and Dr Woods our medical consultant. He was very much from the old school and drove around in a maroon Rolls-Royce with his initials monogrammed in gold on the front doors.

He was a fine gentleman, who dressed accordingly. He always wore a 3-piece suit, a club tie and leather brogues from Jermyn Street. He must have been about 60 years old, and always spoke in a quiet voice.

Woody's ward rounds were always civilised affairs, beginning and ending with tea and biscuits in Sister Bennet's office, and a gentle review of the round we had just done. He commanded respect, as did most of my clinical teachers and consultants during my formative years as a general surgeon.

Back in 1972 Bob the Butcher was the sole surviving transplant patient on Merseyside, and Clatterbridge was his local hospital.

Every Tuesday night Bob showed his gratitude by arriving in his butcher's van laden with sausages, pies and every savoury meat product imaginable. They were his gift to the staff who had cared for him, and once Sister Bennett had exited the ward, we began the makings for a ward party.

1972. The Tuesday night ward parties at Clatterbridge were legendary

The parties we held every Tuesday on the Medical wards at Clatterbridge became legendary. The male ward was responsible for preparing Bob the Butcher's offerings, while the female patients who were not bedridden prepared the gateaux and sweets they had been busy constructing in the ward kitchen after lights out. When I look back on those crazy days and nights, playing guitar to these patients and eating a monstrous buffet with Bob serving and JS passing the drinks, it was something like the old television show M.A.S.H. But the strange thing was that during all those six months we never had a single catastrophe with any patient, in fact they seemed to get better more quickly.

A Sideways Shift to Showbiz.

It was during these heady days that I started my second career as a musician and professional nightclub entertainer, beginning one evening in the doctor's bar after a few beers with Sandy and JS. I had always played my guitar and harmonica, emulating my heroes, Bob Dylan and Donovan and I wasn't scared of singing in public after my five years as a choral scholar at Ely Cathedral.

As usual we were in good voice and singing away the night when I had the thought that it must be possible to earn some decent money from making music. I broached this idea to the others who laughed in my face, so I rashly extended myself.

"I bet you five quid I can earn more in a week playing guitar than being a medic!", I blurted out – and that bet was immediately accepted by JS and Sandy, who imagined I was just having one of my regular ego boosts.

Each one of us earned the sum of 18 pounds for a 90-hour week on the wards, which was never enough for our needs, so any small bonuses were very welcome. The Swinging Sixties had just given way to the even more Swinging Seventies and Liverpool was now a world centre for all kinds of music from ska to rock and roll, thanks to the Beatles.

I had already played once in the Cavern Club as well as quite a few other Liverpool clubs, and during the summer of '67 instead of learning Pharmacology I was playing with a group of Liverpool poets including Roger McGough and Mike McCartney, Paul's brother, in an outfit called The Scaffold, which was a vibrant part of The Liverpool Scene. Another member of The Scaffold was Andy Roberts, a gifted guitar player of folk-blues and he taught me some useful riffs. So, I did have some form.

JS agreed to cover my male ward from 8pm to midnight if I ever got a spot, and I would then cover his ward during the dark hours from midnight to 0800h, so all was set and I just needed a connection to a night club. Amazingly, I did have one.

That connection was Ben the Bouncer, a 22-stone giant and one of my first ever surgical patients at Broadgreen, from whom I had excised some benign abdominal tumours. I had really liked him from the first day we ever met in the outpatient clinic. He was a typical Scouser and a fantastic source of amusing tales. He had told me he worked at a nightclub called the Wookey Hollow and the following night I was there renewing our acquaintance.

"Greetings Ben", I said, "I've just popped by to check on your post-operative situation".

"Phoogh me doc, that's mighty kind of you", replied Ben, impressed no doubt by the reach of the NHS, and proceeded to lift his cummerbund and dress shirt to expose the acre of wobbling flesh I remembered so well. "You done a great job", he exclaimed, pointing out the two healed scars. I was relieved to see my minor surgical success and moved in for the kill.

"Er, Ben, I was just wondering if there's any chance of getting a spot here?", "I play guitar and mouthorgan, and I've played the Jacaranda and the Cavern". Which was only half true. That is how I won my bet with JS and Sandy. But in doing so I nearly ended my career as a surgeon before it had begun.

After a brief audition I was signed up by Big Bill, the maestro of this nightclub, who was even larger than Ben and an equally good fellow. He was tickled by the idea of a doctor playing in the club.

I was to start the show, six nights a week playing 30 minutes for 10 quid a night, and when Bill stuffed 60 pounds into my hand after the first week I was as stunned as JS and Sandy were. When I returned to Clatterbridge ready to take over from JS´s shift I bought everybody in the bar drinks with my newly earned income.

The Wookey Hollow was an up-and-coming club. Shirley Bassey had just done a week there, and I was to lead in Bob Monkhouse the following week. I suddenly found myself in the Land of ShowBiz and very interesting it was. I clearly remember meeting Bob Monkhouse. He was standing in front of a mirror preparing himself, but his face was covered in sweat. "It´s just nerves", he said to me, "I always get them". And he was not alone.

I was terrified those first nights, playing on a revolving disco stage of transparent plastic squares lit from below – which was a revolution in nightclub style. I found it amusing once I had got over my fear, playing Dylan at one revolution a minute before the serried ranks of Liverpudlians, out for a good night´s entertainment.

In those days there were thousands of hippies going around with guitars, but there were not so many who were true clones of Dylan and Donovan who also played harmonica, but I was one. Even if my guitar technique was basic and my voice just adequate, a blast and a wail on the gob-iron always improved a song.

From Disaster to Triumph : a magic moment

One of the common effects of fear is dryness of the mouth, and the second night I played I still had beginner´s nerves, my mouth was dry and at the end of a riff I suddenly found the mouthorgan had become stuck to my lips. So, I played the chorus again. At the end I still found the mouthorgan stuck to my mouth and began to panic. In desperation I tore my mouth away from the mouthorgan, at which point it jumped out of the bent coat-hanger I used around my neck to hold it and fell onto the stage floor.

It looked like the end of my career as a solo artist, even before it had really started. Sweating with terror now in front of a bemused audience I bent down to pick up the mouthorgan, at which point one end of the coat-hanger went straight up my left nostril, causing considerable shock and pain.

"Jesus Christ!", I shouted in pain, at which point the whole audience burst into laughter. What they were suddenly enjoying was a brilliant, spontaneous moment of comedy, and their laughter and cheering went on for ages – long enough for me to replace the harmonica and become completely free of fear. That five-second catastrophe-into-triumph moment freed me from ever having stage fright again.

I had a knack for composing rhyming couplets and had had considerable practice writing the annual medic smoker scripts with the rest of the No.9 Percy Street gang. An idea came to me during the first week. On the Saturday night I launched into one of my own songs, relating to life in Liverpool in 1971. I do remember that both Harold Wilson and Princess Anne featured in this number, and it seemed to go down well, so well in fact that the next Monday Big Bill came up to me after my spot and told me that Radio Mersey wanted me to stop by and do a recording of it for them. No problem, I said, and just before midnight found myself singing the song inside a recording studio in central Liverpool. Then it was a race back through the Mersey Tunnel in my newly constructed electric blue beach-buggy (of which more later) to the medical wards, with prayers for a quiet night.

Imagine my shock the following morning, halfway through Woodie's twice-weekly ward round to hear a patient shout out in fluent Scouse,

"'Ere doch, they're playing your song!". And she proceeded to fill the ward with the sound from her antiquated radio, Woodie and Sister Bennett looking on bemused at this novel interjection. There it was. "Homage to Liverpool", the song I had been singing in Radio Mersey only hours before.

Well, that was just the beginning of three days of utter mayhem as the press and media arrived faster than vultures to a carcass with their interviews and cameras. Then Granada TV rang up wanting me to go to Manchester and the final straw was the call that came from the producer of a TV show in London called "Doctor in the House" asking me to come for an audition. It was at this point that Dr Wood took me on one side and asked,

"Are you going to be a popstar or a doctor. You can't be both!" And of course, he was right. I could not possibly do both.

Even though my big ego was drawing me towards the lights of showbiz, I remained a surgeon at heart, so my chance of stardom faded as rapidly as it started, and I went back to being just another junior houseman on the wards. But hanging in my stable in Spain is a big black and white photo of me in my white coat and stethoscope, wearing my green 20-inch bell-bottom Levi jeans whilst playing guitar and mouthorgan to the ladies of ward 15. It was sent to me by the Daily Mail reporter and remains one of the treasured memories of my houseman days at Clatterbridge hospital.

Motor Mechanics in A+E : the creation of Beautiful Blue

Sandy and I had always shared an interest in motors as well as surgery. Having some sort of motor was a great advantage in the endless hunt for girlfriends. My first car was AKA, a 1934 Morris 8 Sports Tourer which I had rebuilt on the farm. I later became the only student in Liverpool University to own a Jaguar, which was terrific for attracting the ladies. When I qualified, I was the proud owner of a

Triumph TR3, my first car which could exceed 100 mph.

During my six months at Clatterbridge, Sandy and I embarked upon our biggest project yet. It was one which later caused a serious rift in my relationship with Jane, Sandy's girlfriend. We decided to build a beach buggy during our on-call hours, mainly because I had come across the corpse of a GP buggy on top of a car park in downtown Liverpool. Every time I passed by it there were a few more bits missing, until only the engine and fiberglass body were left.

We had a good mate Rob, who ran a shady backstreet garage down in docklands and who agreed, for a small favour to tow us through the Mersey Tunnel in his 7-litre Dodge towing truck, a massive red beast with an exhaust stack the size of a factory chimney and a sound like a Spitfire taking off.

It was a trip to remember. Technically we were stealing a vehicle, or what was left of it, for this GP buggy carcass lacked even brakes. We borrowed the four wheels off Roger Chitty's orange VW beetle and after a terrifying trip through the tunnel, arrived outside the Accident and Emergency Department at Clatterbridge. Immediately adjacent to the A+E entrance there just happened to be a carport, a perfect refuge to use as the garage for our project.

Two days later two police officers entered the ward, to speak to me about a stolen vehicle. I could not believe our bad luck. It turned out that the owner of this purloined buggy was the boyfriend of one of the Histology technicians at Clatters, and it was she who had spotted the buggy in the Casualty department.

Sandy and I were about to get busted for theft. It was only a 50 quid cash donation to the owner of this wreck that persuaded the police to leave and the ward round to continue. That's how it was in those days, a riot of fun mixed with a lot of serious hard work, and I think we were all the better for it.

It took us four months to complete the transformation of the beach buggy.

The creation of Beautiful Blue

We cut 16 inches out of the floor-pan of a crashed 1967 beetle and spent hours re-aligning the gear-shaft and re-setting the rear axle torsion bars, but finally the Beautiful Blue Beach Buggy was ready for the road. By then our mate Rob had sprayed the bodyshell a brilliant electric blue. Everything was psychedelic in those days, and we did not intend to be left out.

We had also made good use of the available NHS resources, using cast-off XRay plates to act as formers for the bodywork and discarded rolls of bandage and cotton wool to create a decent roll-over bar. The final result was impressive. With her big Jaguar tyres and white exhaust this was a car to drive and be seen in.

Sandy and I were proud of our new creation

I spent five years with Beautiful Blue. However, the whole buggy project had caused frictions with Jane, so reluctantly Sandy handed it over into my care.

On Becoming a Qualified Surgeon

By the time I had finished my houseman year I was certain I was going to be a surgeon, and nothing else. This was a serious decision as it would involve a minimum of six years of very hard work and two exams for the Fellowship of the Royal College of Surgeons. These were famous for having a pass rate of barely 30% as well as being expensive to sit – and to re-sit, for many.

Primary Fellowship covered the whole of pre-clinical studies, from Anatomy, Physiology and Pathology to newer sciences such as Immunology, still in its infancy at that time. One way of getting a head start was to spend a year on a small stipend as a Senior Demonstrator in Anatomy to the incoming 2nd MB year students. And that is what Sandy and I ended up doing.

By good fortune we both had a friend and mentor in Colonel Eric Parry, lately of the Indian Medical Service. He was our highly respected Senior Lecturer in Anatomy. I never met anyone who knew more anatomy than he did, and he was one of the very best of my many good teachers. He also became a good friend with whom I later stayed in later years on my infrequent returns to Liverpool.

The Colonel also used to teach anatomy at a college in Wales, and one dark and miserable winter's evening he was driving across Denbigh moors towards Mold when he was stopped by police patrol. He told us next morning at tea-time that when they looked into his Mini Traveler and found a corpse – or rather, half a corpse in the passenger seat, he had the devil of a job convincing them that these human remains were actually his next anatomy lesson, and not his recently deceased wife.

The Colonel had been a surgeon all his life, most of it in the Indian Medical Service during the colonial days, and his tales of the Raj and of pig-sticking, tiger-shooting and amputating blown up limbs were music to my ears, even though he was talking of a long-forgotten colonial past. Then he was asked to set up the national health service in Kuwait where he passed his middle years until his fingers stiffened with osteoarthritis. He subsequently returned to his home country to teach human anatomy, to the great benefit of hundreds of students.

The other Senior Lecturer was Daddy Mac, never without his soft Highland burr and cherrywood pipe. Whilst the Colonel taught every aspect of anatomy, Daddy Mac had spent most of his professional life studying the blood supply of the human testis. There was even a massive picture of a testicle on his study wall, looking like the Missouri River in full flood, with every rivulet of blood vessel coloured bright red or blue.

It may have been a true work of art, but after 50 years I have to say that the blood supply of the testis has never been a problem I needed to know about. If one needs to do an orchidectomy then one grabs the cord in the inguinal canal, and ligates the testicular vessels. Whatever they are called, blood vessels all still bleed the same. So, some of our teaching, though very good, was not so relevant to our later clinical work.

In the Anatomy Department, "Tea-time" was a religious moment at 1100 h every day when Betty advanced with her tea trolley and its massive, chipped enamel kettle. That was when the Colonel recounted his latest adventure and had us all falling off our chairs at the thought, for the Colonel was an extremely respectable and respected doctor. Unfriendly nocturnal interactions with the police on a lonely Welsh moor were not at all his usual style.

The Tearoom was a sacred place. It was meant to be a library, but there were more dead bones than tomes on the shelves, and it was full of comfortable chairs. There was even a pipe rack for Daddy Mac.

It was one summer's day in 1972 that we all had tea with Tutankhamen, in a manner of speaking. Bob Johnson, our Human Biology lecturer had persuaded the Cairo Museum that we had the expertise within the Liverpool Anatomy Department to make some more sense of this ancient Egyptian mummy. The desiccated regal mummy duly arrived in the laboratory next to the tea-room, and we were all silent in wonder as we gazed upon that young man's beautifully preserved body, now over 3,000 years old. That was when I learned about the embalming properties of myrrh, which the Egyptians had become expert in all those years ago. The aroma of myrrh alone was a vast improvement on the more modern formaldehyde, now in use universally as a tissue preservative.

We were all used to seeing cadavers of recent vintage, preserved with formalin and smelling poisonous, but in spite of its great age, the shrunken and desiccated body in front of us was perfectly preserved and was virtually free of any odour. The Egyptians had developed the use of myrrh for embalming and were masters of this art, but it was something none of us had ever seen before. I still have the photo I took of the X-ray of Tutankamen's body, a strange memento of times past.

The amount of biological matter that came through the doors of the Animal House and into the Dissecting Room was incredible. Not just human remains but a complete zoo of live and dead animals, for our department had some sort of 'arrangement' with Chester Zoo. It was no great surprise when one day the Colonel asked me to start dissecting the body of a male orang-outan weighing over 200 kilos.

For one month I was immersed in this huge primate's body, as well as teaching regular human anatomy to my tutorial class. It was a brilliant practical lesson in Comparative Anatomy, a subject which has always lit me up.

The Museum of Comparative Anatomy in Paris, which I first visited many years ago, is near the Tuileries Gardens and the scope of its anatomical specimens is enormous. From the anatomy of ants to humans, I recommend it to any student of anatomy. As I walked round the exhibits, I passed from the invertebrates to vertebrates, and finally to the primates and Homo Sapiens. The pièce de resistance was a life-sized sagittal section through a heavily pregnant woman, including the foetus, an astonishing sight to me. This unique exhibit was in fact a real human body – deceased in the 1800s, then embalmed and bisected. It was not the sort of thing which would be allowed today. But it was a wonderful educational exhibit, for all the blood vessels had been injected red and blue and the whole anatomy of the gravid uterus and pelvis was clear to see, from a most unusual aspect.

My elevation to Moral Tutor

During my year of post-graduate study and teaching I was also fortunate to obtain a post as Moral Tutor in the mixed student residence of Derby Hall. This sinecure came with a small but very adequate flat and the pastoral care of eight delightful students. They kept me in touch with life both inside and outside the Faculty of Medicine and were excellent company on our frequent social outings. Amongst this jolly group were two Hong Kong Chinese brothers, Xi and Yang. They were the first foreign medical students I had so far ever seen, and it was through my friendship with them that I came to appreciate the huge history of China and the myriad talents of the Chinese people. Both were well educated and were very able students, on a par with the best of the English. Yet they were always up for a prank or a night out, and soon we became very close friends. Fortunately, I had no desire for any of the many beautiful young ladies who now surrounded me, for I was in a steady relationship with Mo, a teacher trainer student and a natural hippy like myself. It was she who introduced me to patchouli oil.

The year passed very pleasantly until the black cloud of the Primary Fellowship exam began looming ever closer. On a freezing February day Sandy and I headed for the foggy streets of Glasgow, along with Chris and a few others. The train ride to Scotland was as grim as the grey and rain-swept streets of Glasgow. Our hearts were as heavy as the books that each of us was carrying, as we attempted some last-minute cramming. My own particular novel of the day was 'Human Pathology', of which I had no knowledge of about half – which was the section on Neoplastic Disease, or cancer.

Flipping through the 700-page tome with little hope of learning much more at this late stage I happened to see a picture of a beautiful germ I had never heard of. It was called Nocardia and was a rare fungus that occasionally attacked people and was virtually incurable. It sounded interesting, so I forgot about all the Path I didn't know and read the whole gory life story of Nocardia.

Five days later, walking down the many steps of the Royal College of Surgeons, Glasgow for the final time with Chris, another of our gallant gang, both of us with a Pass certificate in hand, I remarked on how amazingly lucky I had been in the final testing Surgical Pathology viva when the evil-looking examiner in front of me had demanded, "Tell me all you know about Nocardia !"

"What on earth is Nocardia?", asked Chris, in complete ignorance of this rare germ, so I told him of my fortunate reading on that northbound train.

Things did not improve greatly when the cadaverous companion of my examiner produced a radius and asked me to define every bony point on it, something I was well able to do.

"And this is the dorsal radial tubercule", I said confidently, pointing to the small bony protuberance on the dorsal and distal end of the forearm bone.

"Ay", he said in his thick Glaswegian accent, "maybe in yurr Liverpool it is called rradial, but in Glass-gow we know it as Listerr's tubercule!", pointing his arm sideways. And indeed, there on the wall was a huge, sombre oil painting of the father of antisepsis.

"Well, what did they quiz you on?", I asked Chris.

"Oh, I was so lucky – it was all about carcinoma of the pancreas", replied Chris, a disease of which I knew nothing.

That is just how lucky we both were with the questions we were asked. There is no way that any normal human being can know all that is necessary for a pass in Primary Fellowship. I have found throughout my life that a good dose of luck and a positive karma are essential ingredients for success in most matters, including stiff exams.

Sadly, Sandy did not pass, and the train ride back was a muted affair, but it did not stop us getting drunk that evening. The following morning a policeman found me asleep in Sefton Park. I was led home nursing an almighty hangover, but still carrying my precious pass certificate.

Kids, and Initiation into the Art of Plastic Surgery

I was bound next for Alder Hey as senior house officer (SHO) in General, Plastic and Reconstructive surgery. This was the main Liverpool children's hospital where I would spend six months as senior house officer on the paediatric burns unit, as well as performing much general surgery. Once again I was on call every other night, working a one-in-two rota on a very busy children's ward run by Sister Dot and her four sisters. They were highly skilled nurses and they loved their work, which also included teaching me many useful things about childcare and children, from neonates to teenagers.

We had the whole of Merseyside paediatric pathology to care for, from traffic accidents to congenital defects and many more. One day sitting in Dot's office writing notes, I saw a boy passing by on a stretcher with what looked like a dart sticking out of his head, which indeed it was. It was buried to the hilt in his skull and presumably tickling his brain.

Amazingly the 15 year old boy was perfectly conscious and not obviously suffering very much. He had been walking back from school when he felt a blow to his head and now looked like some strange species of Indian. In Africa, all I would have been able to do would just been to have pulled it out and prayed. But in Alder Hey we got him to main theatre and removed it with the whole neurosurgery team on hand ready to crack his skull in case there was any intra-cerebral bleeding. Luck was on our side, and he was discharged the next day, but this event reminded me how far away this English teaching hospital was from the Hôpital Central in Ebolowa, West Africa.

Children behave in very different ways to adults and constitute a whole separate medical discipline, which demands particular knowledge. Yet there was no obligation for trainee general surgeons to study post-graduate paediatrics, as I had chosen to do. However, in almost every discipline of medicine we are bound to come across children as patients. In the developing countries where I have practiced over 10 years, children represented a major part of any hospital intake, so a good knowledge of children and their care should be an important part of every doctors' training.

It was the nurses who were the greatest experts, and of them all Sister Dot was the real queen. Not only was she a kind and gentle person but she had eyes sharper than an eagle's and she could smell a sick child from yards away. I will always remember the time when, having completed a quick tour of her charges she said to me,

"Don't you think that child in cot seven is a bit jaundiced?", and sure enough, on my closer examination the child did look a little on the yellow side. How Dot spotted the icterus from yards away as she walked the ward I can only put down to years of looking into infants faces to measure their health.

In order to be a good diagnostician, it is important to be very observant. This skill has to be learned over years of training, and my nurse companions, who were almost all female in those days, were always my best tutors on the wards

In my last post in the NHS, I was used to seeing some consultants pass from bed to bed without ever washing their hands between patients. This was at a time when the dreaded infection MRSA (methicillin-resistant staphylococcus aureus) was already killing hundreds of patients. I am thankful that I was taught simple hygiene and principles of cleanliness by these nurses at a very early stage, at a time when there was far less reliance on the power of antibiotics – and the drug companies.

As well as such simple matters as basic hygiene there were also larger issues to contend with, such as morals and ethics as they related to the care of children.

On Insoluble Moral Problems

The thalidomide disaster was still current news. Another difficult moral problem at that time was the management of babies born with congenital spinal cord defects such as syringomyelia and spina bifida. Almost inevitably hydrocephalus would subsequently develop. This turned the head of the poor child into a huge deformed balloon, and was a visible horror to any parent. The technology to repair the spinal defect (but not the vital nerves) and to drain the excess spinal fluid from the brain had just become available, and Peter Paul Rickham was the lead neo-natal surgeon at that time in Alder Hey.

It was considered a big advance that the lives of these children could now be saved, but it has led to enormous problems over the years as to how best to help these children, most of whom are paralysed forever and also have other severe defects of kidney and heart, even if their intellect was usually unaffected.

In earlier days these unfortunate children would all have died, but the evolution of surgical and anaesthetic techniques now meant that many could survive but were left with severe physical defects. This would become a heavy burden for the parents to shoulder, as well as them being forced to spend much of their time in hospital.

Like much of surgery, once the technique had been learnt it was fairly easy to perform. However, the tiny tubes which drained spinal fluid from the deep ventricles of the brain often became blocked, and we began to see more and more of these babies coming time and time again for revisions. It was a heart-breaking process for the parents, and there would never be an end to their suffering until their child eventually died, which they often did from infective disease as a result of their immobility. I found this corner of neo-natal surgery depressing, and I could never quite convince myself that PP Rickham's work was where I wanted to be.

Later in Kenya I was faced with the very same paediatric problem. Even though I was well capable of repairing the anatomical defect of spina bifida, I decided I would not operate on these unfortunate cases, because of the lifetime costs to the parents and the minimal chance of any success. The child would be forever paralysed, and therefore become a dreadful burden to an already impoverished family. It was always very hard to tell the parents there was nothing I could do, but I still believe it was the correct decision, even though the temptation to operate was always there.

Once again, the important question of prevention, as opposed to cure becomes most relevant, for there has never been a cure as such for spina bifida, only the basic surgical repair of the anatomical defect. Fortunately, there are now tests available to detect this congenital defect at an early stage. More recently, a simple blood test has become available which will allow the detection and early abortion of such defective foetuses without the current risks that amniocentesis carries.

These recent scientific developments have led to a huge decrease in the number of births of children with congenital malformations and the need for surgery. Direct medical interventions during pregnancy such as the addition of daily folic acid 5mgm have also greatly reduced the incidence of foetal malformations.

This type of focused intervention is particularly important in the prevention of Down's syndrome, as one of the main risk factors for impaired cognitive development in the new-born is the age of the mother at conception. Today more and more mothers are delaying getting pregnant for social and economic factors, so the incidence of Down's syndrome is actually increasing in the UK population.

By the time I left Alder Hey I had learned a lot about childcare as well as paediatric surgery. I had also found my metier in plastic surgery, which still remains my favourite part of all general surgery and which became extremely important during my years of surgery in Africa and with Médecins Sans Frontières, MSF, where burns were so common.

On manipulating children

My consultant, Roger 'Cuddles' Cudmore, was a genial chap who was wonderful with children. He was rare, in that he never wore a flash three-piece suit like most consultants, but a tweed jacket that always smelt of pipe smoke. The kids all thought he was Father Christmas and never knew a thing about the bits he chopped out of them in his quiet and skilled manner. He used to sit on their beds and make puppets out of the sheets, and then he would teach the kids how to make them. It is called 'distraction' and was the most valuable lesson I learned from him.

Fear is a killer. It drives us crazy and blocks all normal pathways, so examining a child or adult in pain can be incredibly difficult. However, children with their insatiable curiosity and innocence can be kindly manipulated in all sorts of ways, and Cuddles' approach was impeccable. He could create a toy out of rubbish, and he knew how to get down to a child´s level. This was rare for any consultant, most of whom rode about in extra-terrestrial orbit.

Over the years I have improved my own distraction techniques. In the right- hand pocket of my old white coat, today hanging unused in my stable, there is a small clockwork doll in a car which has never ever failed to stop a child crying, it does such amazing things. I also have a clockwork kangaroo which does loop-the-loops, and even a child of two can wind it up. And of course, a bunch of keys. These remained essential diagnostic tools for me during all my years working with children, equally as valuable as my stethoscope and patella hammer.

Qualifying in Child Health

I had to decide whether I could afford to take the Diploma in Child Health exam or not. Aside from the cost, it was a serious intellectual test which required a very good knowledge of paediatric medicine, as well as surgery. I went to see the Colonel, as I always did when I had a significant problem.

"Of course, you have to take it!", he exclaimed. "Why not! You will always work with children, and you will never have a better opportunity than now". And that is how I found myself once again in front of the examiners of a Royal College, this time in Queens Square in central London. This time it was the more kindly but equally demanding examiners of the Royal College of Physicians who were putting me through the hoops.

I did gain that diploma and I was proud of my efforts. In the end it is no use to just profess competence in any discipline. The scrutineers will always be looking for the proof of attainment from a Royal College, in this case the DCH – Diploma in Child Health, Royal College of Physicians, London.

My mind was now focused on a return visit to Cameroun, West Africa. Jack was still the head surgeon at Ebolowa and he had written, inviting me to come over and 'give a hand' for a month or two.

A month later, instead of doing an orthopaedic SHO job somewhere in the UK, I found myself inside the bar of the Guinness factory in Douala, West Cameroun, in front of a bottle of freshly brewed Guinness.

9.   FROM CAMEROUN TO THE CONGO 1974 – 5

Back to West Africa.   Overdosing at the Guinness Factory.

One of my patients at Alder Hey had been a close relation of the manager of the Guinness factory at Douala, the major seaport of Cameroun. This explains my arrival at this impressive brewery in April 1974, still with my haversack and guitar, ready for a dose of tropical medicine and surgery at Ebolowa once again.

Ten years had passed since I was in Ebolowa as a 19-year-old. Now, I had not only my MB.ChB. medical degree, but I had also just acquired the Diploma in Child Health. After 10 years in Liverpool, I was on my way back to the mission at Ebolowa to spend six months with Jack.

Mike, who was the general manager of this brewery (which also dabbled in Fanta and other toxic non-alcoholic beverages) had been three years in Douala and was a most excellent fellow. He was Irish, with a great sense of humour as well as generosity – so generous in fact that by the time we arrived back at his house where I was to stay the night, when his wife Helen greeted me all I could do was collapse speechless on the floor. It was not one of my great moments, but Mike and Helen were kindred spirits, and when I finally regained consciousness later the next day it was to be greeted with a huge bowl of papaya, mango and pineapple.

"You get your English mouth around this, and you'll be feelin' fine agin!", announced Helen as she breezed into my room.

Such was their friendship and hospitality that I found myself reluctant to depart on the train for Yaoundé, and thence to Ebolowa where I would be enjoying some months of religious abstinence in the jungle. After two days of enjoyment with Mike and Helen, I finally winched myself off the beach and onto the train for Yaoundé. Clinking like a small orchestra in my haversack were six precious bottles of that magic black beer.

On African Train Journeys

I love to travel by train and an African train journey was always stimulating, as much for the life that went on inside the train as for that which passed outside, and this train was no exception. The countryside was mostly jungle with the occasional village cut out of it. The huts were mud-walled with palm or banana leaf roofs. Children played amongst pigs and goats while women in bright cotton wraps were beating manioc in great wooden mortars. It was all much as I remembered.

Among my fellow passengers there were six chickens looking down on me from the luggage rack. There was also a big cardboard box with some hidden beast inside giving out plaintive wails, and a small monkey which was jumping around acrobatically, swinging from the luggage rack and entertaining us all. I was the only European on the train and the rest of the passengers were a jolly mix, the women brightly clothed and garrulous. Many of them spoke pidgin English which is a strange but most musical form of the language, dating from a time when the first European slavers and traders appeared in the Bight of Benin.

After a while the women started opening their food rations and we all shared what we had, including the Guinness, two precious bottles of which I opened for us. The monkey was very curious and suddenly made a grab for one bottle and swung with it up into the luggage rack and started to drink it with obvious pleasure. It was a highly amusing sight, and we were well entertained until in a fit of drunken pique the monkey threw the bottle from the rack above where it shattered on the floor, then stood and urinated onto my head before launching himself onto the face of the lady opposite me, attaching his teeth to her left ear.

The monkey had now become a malignant devil. The woman was screaming blue murder and starting to leak blood. The other passengers grabbed their stuff and exited, leaving me and the monkey's owner with six terrified chickens in the rack above. It was like a scene from a madhouse. We finally got the monkey into a sack, and I did a makeshift dressing for what was left of the lady's ear, by which time the rusting suburbs of Yaoundé were approaching. It had already been a most interesting trip and I was barely halfway to Ebolowa.

Once again, the British Embassy kindly put me up for the night, even though Jack Warner had long since departed, and the following morning I made my way to the bus station and bought a one-way ticket to Ebolowa.

The antique charabanc which bore me from Yaoundé was driven by a maniac. The rain was sheeting down onto the road, but our driver was undeterred, and within two hours we were axle-deep in a muddy pit, which had been previously the main road to the coast at Kribi. There we passed two completely miserable days, hungry and cold and without any help. The whole road south of Yaoundé had become impassable and it was only on the third day a Mercedes lorry came by and offered me a lift out of this hellhole of mud. It was a long way from Lime Street.

Back to the Hôpital Central, Ebolowa, and my introduction to witchcraft.

There was a joyous reunion when I finally arrived at the Hôpital Central in Ebolowa, three days later than planned. Jack and Ruth were on fine form, and now there were four children.

The story of Jack and Ruth's children is very unusual. They tried for some years after their marriage to have a child, but failed, so they adopted Mark, following which Ruth almost immediately fell pregnant with Julie in the depths of the Cameroun jungle, which was where Jack was forced to perform the first Caesarian section on his wife. Then there was another fallow period, so they adopted Maureen, following which Ruth immediately became pregnant again in the depths of the rain forest. Jack was once again forced to perform an emergency C-section on Ruth, "but this time", he drawled, "I tied her tubes!"

I was delighted to be back in his family's company again. I noticed that Daniel, their faithful retainer and cook was no longer with them. It transpired that he was in his village in a moribund state as the result of a spell which had been cast on him. This was my personal introduction into the powers of witchcraft. I have seen it many times subsequently in Africa, enough times to know that it is real and that it exists and that it really can cause peoples' deaths.

Jack had visited Daniel every week but could find nothing to explain his gradual collapse. Even this Christian doctor had to accept that this was something beyond the normal, and eventually he decided to go and negotiate with the witch doctor himself. The upshot was that a price was agreed for the lifting of the spell, which turned out to be a pig. Not just any old pig but a champion breeding boar. This is how Jack and I found ourselves' in the big Ford estate bumping down a narrow jungle track to the farm where this animal was kept, in the middle of a teeming downpour which turned the track into a morass.

I had forgotten about the power of the equatorial rain. It fell in sheets which defeated the windscreen wipers and even obliterated any sight of the forest. It rapidly created muddy lakes of unknown depth, which could completely consume any ordinary car. Sometimes it would rain like this for 24 hours or more which made life miserable.

After twice digging ourselves out of the African mud, we arrived at an isolated breeding farm where the owner proudly showed us his prize boar. which looked more like a hairy hippopotamus it was so massive. It was covered in long dark bristles, two huge tusks protruded from his mouth and his scrotum was bigger than a football. The animal was more of a wild forest hog than a prize pig and getting it into the car was going to be interesting.

Jack really was courageous, not just as a surgeon but in every aspect of his life, as this moment demonstrated. I was keeping very much in his shadow as I saw the malevolent look in this pig's red eyes as he and the owner advanced on it. Jack was holding a length of rope in his hand, looking determined and business-like. That was, until the boar charged him, knocking him flat into the brown mud. The rain continued falling incessantly. Jack had now lost some of his composure as well as his glasses and when he got to his feet he looked as though he had fallen into a vat of melted chocolate. But he was not to be defeated.

He just got more angry and muddy, and so did I. It took the three of us an hour to wrestle this monster to the ground and eventually hog-tie it, by which time we were unrecognizable as humans and had lost any trace of good humour. It took two more locals to help us lift the huge pig into the back of the Ford where it ripped the back out of the rear seat with one angry swipe of its tusks before we slammed the tailgate on it. The whole car was rocking with porcine fury as Jack paid off the farmer, and I could see this was going to be an interesting return trip. There was no way to remove the cake of mud covering us before we drove off other than stand in the rain getting even wetter and more miserable. We were a sad and bedraggled sight when we eventually arrived back at the mission long after dark, having delivered the pig.

It had been a heroic day, not one to be repeated too often, but it had certainly been stimulating. We were all agog to see what effect our efforts would have on Daniel and were well rewarded a week later to see him walk through the front door looking healthy. Daniel explained how a debt he had owed had led to his near-death as a result of the witch doctors spell, but there was no rational explanation for what had happened to him.

During his 17 years in the jungle Jack had seen all sorts of unorthodox medicine practiced, and witchcraft was no exception. But even he could not explain the power of the witch doctors spell, although he accepted that it was some element of a common spirituality and belief amongst the Africans which allowed this phenomenon.

Such experiences left an indelible impression on me. At the same time as I was performing regular, orthodox surgery and medicine I was learning about other important components of health, such as the beliefs, rituals and taboos which governed the lives of the society in which I was then living.

The role of the local medicine men and witch doctors was always important and was often to the disadvantage of the patients, but it was one of the things we had to live with. When a young girl was admitted with abdominal pain one day, a diagnosis of intestinal worms was made initially, so she was dosed with vermifuge and allowed home. Three days later she was re-admitted, this time with a large second-degree burn over the abdomen where the local medicine man had poured boiling water over the painful area, and she then spent a further 10 days in hospital while the burn healed.

These sorts of events made Jack furious, but they were part of my work as a tropical surgeon for more than 10 years, and I learned to accept that not all patients are prepared to accept our Western approach to their problems. It is also true that a large proportion of all patients seek help from outside the orthodox in every society, and our own society is no exception.

Head of Paediatrics and a measles epidemic.

I had no time to relax when I arrived at the mission, for we were in the middle of a measles epidemic. My own children have known nothing of measles, thanks to Mr Jenner and his vaccinations, but I did suffer measles as a child and my ears have never been right ever since. There were no mass vaccination campaigns in Africa such as exist today, and periodically a wave of infection would spread across West Africa, killing thousands of babies and young children and leaving thousands of others incapacitated.

"Since you just got your paediatric diploma, I am putting you in charge of Paediatrics", said Jack, and took me to the children's ward. There were 40 beds and cots, but about 100 patients and 10 intravenous lines hanging suspended from the ceiling like a trail of spaghetti and mothers either asleep under the beds or breast-feeding. Near the nursing station were the sickest children, and I could see three at least that looked as though they were not long for this world.

Measles is a very serious illness with many sequelae. Diarrhoea, dehydration, pneumonia, meningitis leading to blindness and deafness were all common complications. Worst of all was septicaemia, when bits of the body became gangrenous and black, leading to amputations if the child was lucky but more often to death. This became my daily diet for six months, as well as a host of other tropical paediatric problems from malnutrition to multiple trauma, worms to polio and so many other diseases unknown in western Europe.

Jack was always around to support and advise, so I learned an enormous amount in a relatively short time, but it was very hard work being constantly on call for the masses of sick children who came every day and night. I became expert at inserting intravenous lines, even in the tiniest babies. We had none of the more sophisticated devices that exist today, just re-useable gold needles and a length of very small diameter tubing. It was very delicate work and time-consuming, but it was also lifesaving to many children suffering dehydration and malnutrition.

Malaria parasitology at the Pasteur Institute

After three months I was offered the chance to study malaria parasitology at the Pasteur Tropical Institute in Yaoundé. With Jack's blessing I set off for an intensive week of microscopy, staining procedures and diagnostics under the tutelage of Jules, the senior malaria technician. He was one of the few Camerounians I met who had been to France to study. He was an exacting master and an excellent teacher and became a very good friend. He had spent 10 years looking down microscopes and was happy to share his addiction with me.

I never got tired of seeing that microscopic world at the end of the steel tube. The view of the parasites was never the same. Sometimes what you saw was quite beautiful in its colours, stained from pink to purple with Giemsa or Leishman's stains. At the same time, these parasites could also be deadly, like the Plasmodium falciparum gametes which floated around the blood of patients with malaria and caused all sorts of nasty and often fatal problems. I also learnt much about the pink, Gram-negative intra-cellular diplococci of gonorrhoea and countless other parasites and bacteria.

By the time I left the Pasteur Institute I could recognize all four forms of the malaria parasite in the blood and had also improved my microscopy technique considerably. I had also enjoyed a break from the routine of mission life.

How to Roast a Crocodile

When I got back to Ebolowa I found the whole mission in action, preparing for the formal opening of the Nurses Training School which had been under construction for the past year. The Minister of Health was to be the guest of honour, so there was an air of frenetic activity from all the mission mothers as they dug into their 40-gallon drums of supplies and started preparing delicacies and delights for the many guests. The pièce de resistance was the main course, supplied by our local restaurant, Le Cabin Bambou. It was to be a whole crocodile, buried in a five- metre-long trench on a bed of hot coals, then covered with banana leaves and cooked for two days. I watched this process with great interest, and on the great day I was pleasantly surprised by how delicious the light coloured meat was, considering that the reptile lived on a diet of rotting flesh.

Le Cabin Bambou was the only form of restaurant at that time in the town of Ebolowa and its menu was the most unusual of any restaurant I ever ate in. Outside there was always a red light glowing, which made it look like a brothel. Below this was a blackboard on which was chalked the *menu du jour* – which depended entirely on what particular species of meat the local hunters had brought in. During my six months at Ebolowa, amongst other delights I ate python, baboon and monkey, parrot and even once a pangolin. All I can say is that it all tasted good, and I was never ill following one of their organic dishes from the forest.

I continued to enjoy the paediatrics and surgery, all of it at an intense pressure. But with the good tutelage of Jack and Dick, his fellow-surgeon, I expanded my skills in surgery considerably and was soon invited to share the night calls. Whilst this was a privilege it also meant a night of disturbed sleep, as well as a scary walk across a snake-infested lawn in the dead of night. Not the sort of thing for faint hearts.

The snakes in this jungle were really nasty. From the black and green mambas whose neurotoxin killed you in seconds, to the Gaboon viper which killed you with haemotoxins slowly, in days. There were a good number of snakes around, and we had a fair few patients as a result. Some of them required amputation of a limb in order to save their life, and several died, in spite of the horse serum anti-venom we had then.

I saw such a range of human pathology as would never have been possible in England. During those months Jack also put more responsibilities on me, some of which were really testing.

When he casually said to me one day, "How do you fancy going to the Congo?" I was immediately interested. The Southern Presbyterian Church of Carolina had a mission in Kasai Province, deep in the Zaire jungle at Kananga, and even deeper in that jungle was the village of Mushenge, the seat of the King of the Bakuba, one of the last great Central African kingdoms. There was a vacancy for a single-handed surgeon at this isolated mission hospital for a six-month period.

Jack, being Jack would not have asked me if he had not felt I could cope. He had also been my master, mentor and teacher for the last six months, so he knew what I was capable of, and he had taught me well. Instead of going back to the UK, clerking patients and excising lipomas, I ended up becoming personal physician to the King of the Bakuba, Kasai province in The Congo, or Zaire as it was called during the era of president Mobutu Sesse Seko.

On becoming a Royal Physician Zaire 1975

To fully appreciate The Congo, or Zaire as the country was originally called in the 15th century, one needs to look at a map of Africa. The Congo stands out by its central enormity, just as the Amazon basin does in South America. It is not just the size of the country itself, but the Congo River, which is one of the most mighty in the world, and when I saw it first just south of Matadi at Banane where it flows into the Atlantic Ocean, it took my breath away.

The Congo basin drains an area which is 10% of the whole area of Africa and extends into five other countries including Cameroun, Central African Republic, Tanzania, Zambia and Malawi, where the river rises in the highlands 1,700 metres above sea level. It then travels 4,700 kilometres north and west to its mouth on the west coast, at which point the river is 10 kilometres wide. The Congo River is the longest in Africa after the Nile, and the ninth longest in the world. It is the second largest in the world after the Amazon in terms of its outflow to the sea. At some points it is over 200 metres deep, but the series of 32 cataracts between Kinshasa the capital and its estuary at Banane prevent any major river transport from the port. The Malebu Pool at Kinshasa is the point from where all upstream river transport begins.

The jungle stretches east from the coast, as huge and dark and impenetrable as when Joseph Conrad described it in 'Darkness at Noon' in 1902. Thousands of square miles of green canopy and the life that went on a hundred feet below still remain unexplored. It is home to flocks of brilliantly coloured birds and butterflies, lethal forest hogs and even panthers, though I only ever once saw one. This was going to be my home for the next six months.

David, the head of mission met me at Kinshasa airport and took me off to the mission HQ via a tour of the capital. Superficially it all looked civilized, but as David told me, there were a lot of problems going on below the surface, of which one of the worst was endemic corruption. The whole history of the Congo from the Arab slavers to the Belgians and now the neo-colonialists has been one of greed and rape and pillage. But the corner where I was to spend the next six months remained tranquil under the reign of King Munanga of the Kuba tribe.

Mushenge and the Kingdom of the Bakuba

Looking back on those Congo days in the heart of the ancient Kuba kingdom, I know I was particularly privileged. The mission hospital at Mushenge had always bonded the king and his family to these Christian foreigners with whom I now worked, and as a result I was given every access to him and his court, and it was quite wonderful to behold.

Within a kilometre of the king's court the Belgians had built a fine government hospital only a few years before, but as I had seen before in other places in Africa, this was now empty and dilapidated, everyone preferring the services provided at the mission hospital that I was now in charge of.

In those days the king still wielded complete authority over his many people, but the government of Mobutu was encroaching, and the king had been ordained some form of government administrator, for which his reward had been the gift of a bright yellow VW Passat saloon. The fact that there was a bare kilometre of driveable track through this vast jungle seemed irrelevant as it stood so proudly outside the king's palace with just 11 kilometres on the clock. It was his incongruous badge of office from Kinshasa, and an object of great wonder to his thousands of followers, most of whom knew nothing of the ways of the outside world.

The Kuba kingdom had existed for over 4 centuries, covering a large part of central Africa, extending in the east as far as the Kasai River and including several tribes and dialects, Tchiluba being the one used around Mushenge.

What was most astounding about these people was their art and sculpture. It had been famous for centuries already, and when I first arrived I was amazed at how sophisticated and beautiful so many daily items of their lives were. The Bakuba were famous for the fabrics which they created out of palm raffia and the geometric designs woven into them which are unique in the world, each one of which represented the dreams of the king.

All the weaving was done by men, and they also made the ochre-coloured skirts which the men all wore. Cowrie shells were used to decorate many of the fabrics and the small caps which the men wore.

Even the long cane baskets in which the women carried the manioc back from the fields were exquisite, being decorated with woven palm fibres of different colours.

Just on the outside of the village was the Art College, run by two kindly old missionaries, one from Holland and the other from Belgium. They had been at Mushenge for many years and spent their lives helping the young Bakuba to develop their craft skills. Some of the carvings were test pieces produced by students, and I have never seen any finer carving anywhere in Africa. It was clear that this was a powerful, rich and stable society, which was still able to produce and develop art and sculpture which stand amongst the very best in the world.

In this hidden corner of the rain forest even money hardly existed. Payments were often made with cowrie shells or antique Venetian glass beads. The mission hospital was a private concern, desperate for income. I had been posted there as a surgeon to help the hospital's income generation through my operations. For example, a hernia repair cost five Zaires, and a hysterectomy or other major operation cost 10 Zaires. But as the patients rarely had any cash they would pay me with their artwork, which I bought off them for cash, which then went to the hospital. Thus it was, that when I left Mushengue I took with me a 40-gallon drum full of exquisite pieces of art, from finely carved ebony and ivory to raffia mats and pottery, most of which I still enjoy today.

The dances and rituals of the Bakuba people were also very sophisticated and were an important visible part of their daily lives. Even though the missionaries had made a few converts over the last century, it was apparent that the influence of the outside world on this vibrant African community was not much.

Munanga was such a great king that he had over 60,000 people within his domain, and when his eldest son sadly died of burns during my tenure the whole hospital become devoid of staff for three days as every staff member went to the funeral, and I suddenly found myself looking after every need of the hospital more or less by myself.

There was a 200-patient TB camp adjacent to the hospital to take care of as well, which I did by the expedient of getting the fittest and most able of the patients to be responsible for all treatment with the help of one auxiliary nurse. I had another 75 patients to take care of in the hospital, to say nothing of the wild pig woundings, Caesarian sections and other crises which were a daily part of my medical diet out there.

Burns were also a daily occurrence. A combination of epilepsy and open cooking fires was lethal wherever I went in Africa. But so was the misuse of fuel, and this was how the king's son died.

In 1975 the idea of switching on an electric refrigerator was unheard of at Mushengue. All the fridges ran on paraffin, and that was often hard to come by in the depths of the Congo jungle. Not knowing any better, if there was no paraffin the natives would use petrol, with often fatal results.

The king's son was admitted with 95 % burns, most of them 3rd degree, and there was no chance that he could live. I knew I would have to go to the king and tell him that his eldest son was going to die, and there was nothing I could do that could save him.

So, with Emmanuel I walked over to the king's palace and broke the bad news. The king took it well, even though I felt very anxious, being new to this jungle kingdom and I still had a lot to learn.

It was a wonderful six months for a 28- year- old to experience, in spite of the nerve-wracking moments. I also had two good friends, Becky and Peggy, who were young American teachers at the mission school. They taught me how to make ice-cream and also how to play Yahtzee, a crazy American game. To entertain us we also had Polly, a verbose African grey parrot and a baby gorilla called Jane who later went to SanDiego zoo.

Apart from the heavy responsibility thrust on me and some dire moments it was yet another long period in another part of Africa to enjoy.

It was one Sunday morning at the mission that I was first introduced to marihuana. Usually, once I had done the morning rounds the day was relatively quiet and I was sitting outside my round hut reading 'Of Mice and Men' when a youthful American voice greeted me.

"Hi!", said this tall blonde figure, "I'm Brad, from the mission at Mbuiji-Maya. We just came over for the day", and that was how I made a new friend, smoked dope and fell unconscious all in the space of an hour. When Becky and Peggy came upon me, they thought I had had a stroke or something similar, so paralysed was I.

"I think it may be a touch of ague", I said feebly, whilst enjoying the weird feeling of gently spinning inside my own body. I was relieved to awake two hours later feeling perfectly normal. Brad left a whole pillow-case full of weed for me and it became my sweet-scented pillow for the rest of my time there, and when I left, I also left my marijuana pillow on the bed, wondering from time to time what the next mission surgeon would make of it.

On the Perils of Working in Isolation

Even though the jungle was much the same as it had been in Ebolowa, here in Mushenge I was far more isolated, and we relied for almost everything on the brave pilots of Mission Aviation Fellowship. This is a Christian charity that flies small planes into impossible places in some of the worlds wildest and poorest regions. Every two weeks, the tiny runway carved out of solid jungle had to be cleared of goats and pigs as soon as we heard the welcome sound of the single-engine Cessna.

We all looked forward to the Mission Aviation Fellowship plane every two weeks

The pilots always did two sweeps of the runway before landing and the plane had never halted before it was surrounded by a crowd of excited Africans. There were supplies to be off-loaded and sometimes patients to be transferred, but it was the arrival of mail which excited us most for it was our only contact with the outside world back then. It says much for our meagre existence at Mushengue that Coca-Cola, without which the Americans cannot comfortably exist, was almost invisible. Only twice during the six months did I drink a bottle, and then it was after another killing bout of malaria, from which we all suffered now and then. It was a salutary reminder of how things were, that my house was next to the small mission cemetery, where over half of the graves were for children and there were 11 graves spanning a 70 year period.

It was during my time at Mushenge that I performed my first solo hysterectomy for ruptured uterus. I had always been used to the advice from Jack or Dick, or of my seniors back in England, but here I was utterly isolated. When this poor lady came in, at deaths door with a obstructed labour of two days duration, she was in total shock with an unrecordable blood pressure and a dead baby inside her. Her haemaglobin was just 3.5 % and her blood so thin it was actually pink. So I was forced into action.

The patient was so far gone that I was able to open her abdomen using only intravenous diazepam and local anaesthetic. The trauma inside the abdomen from the rupture of the uterus and the bleeding vessels made any normal anatomy invisible. President Mobutu's army had chosen to block all signals from the mission's single-sideband radios whenever they felt like it, so there was no chance of any verbal advice from mission HQ. I really was on my own.

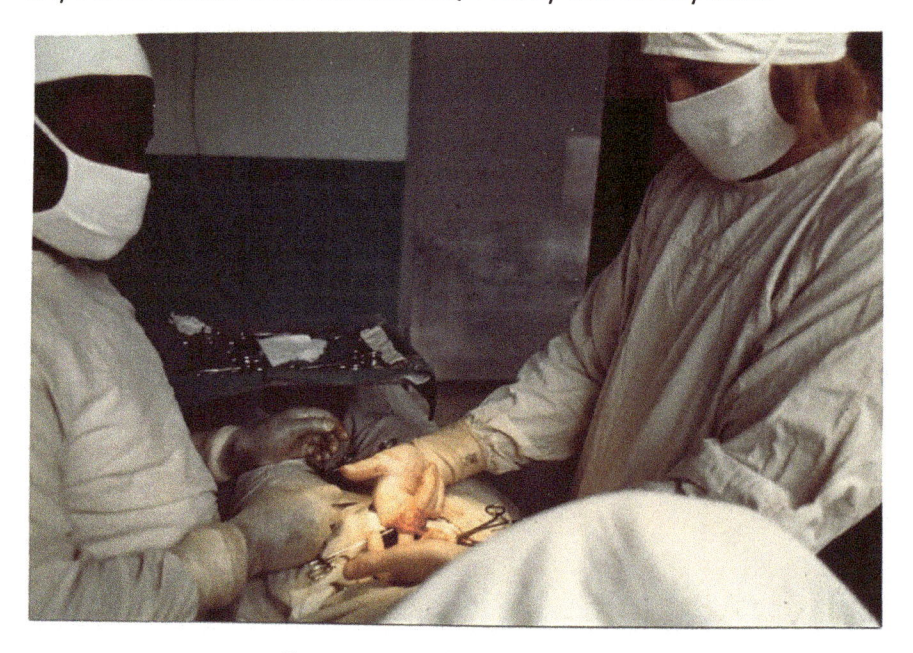

Now I really was a single-handed bush surgeon

It took me two hours to finish the operation and I was shaking and sweating at the end. But the mother's life was saved and she eventually left us two weeks later.

Obstetric and gynaecological problems occasionally reduced me to terror. I had not had any formal training in these disciplines, so I was really learning on the hoof. I was also responsible for the anaesthetic side of things, another discipline I had only a shaky knowledge of, except for spinals.

I was competent at doing spinal anaesthetics by now and used it for most major operations. It was relatively safe and usually worked well, but there was one serious danger.

If the local anaesthetic ascended the spinal canal too far the respiratory muscles became paralysed, and the patient stopped breathing. This is exactly what happened one day when a lady in obstructed labour came in needing a Caesarian section.

I gave her the spinal and laid her back down for 10 minutes with the bed head slightly elevated – but obviously not quite enough, for as I was incising the uterus the nurse at the head of the table said in French, which was our common language, "this patient is not breathing!". When I looked up I could see that she was correct. God Almighty! Don´t Panic! Suddenly I was in battle mode once again.

I was never far from my Ambu bag and a 7,5 endotracheal (ET) tube, and could slip a tube in easily under normal circumstances. The big problem was the foot-wide incision in the anterior uterine wall of this paralysed patient, bleeding copiously from the lateral margins, and the compromised infant inside.

I quickly slammed on two Duval forceps at the angles of the incision, told my assistant Moses to exert pressure on the wound and then shot to the head of the table. I then grabbed the Mackintosh laryngoscope and ET tube which I rapidly inserted into the trachea, connected the Ambu bag and started pumping.

Adina was my good theatre nurse, and it was she who kept pumping the Ambu bag for another 20 minutes until I had a screeching baby delivered and the horizontal skin incision sewn up. Once again, I was sweating with fear, but the outcome was reassuringly good. The patient walked out three days later apparently none the worse for her anoxic moment, with a big and bouncy baby boy.

My nurses were all well-trained and beautiful

Accidental surgical adventures like this took years off my life, but in the process they did give me that breadth of experience which no book can give. I got used to being the only surgeon around, with nobody to consult or assist me, and in the end it probably made me a better doctor. I suppose one could count every moment of such surgical terror as a step along the winding road of experience. In such a desperate situation, even with very limited resources, a surgeon has to do something.

I had also seen both Jack and Dick tackle some very major tricky cases at Ebolowa, mostly, but not always with success but always with much courage, so I had some fine examples to follow. After six months running a bush hospital solo, I felt much more at ease with the daily input of patients, or so I thought until the day the hospital drains got blocked.

More Black Magic

It was one of those things that just happens, even in the best regulated institutions, which Mushenge was not. When the charge nurse called me down one Sunday morning, I was expecting to be dealing with a patient rather than a flood of sewage which was occupying quite a large part of the compound by the time I arrived.

"Emmanuel", I said to the senior nurse, "why am I here?"

"No-one will go near this", he answered, "they all know it is poisonous, and they are frightened". And that was how I came to spend a disgusting two hours doing what someone else should have done and getting covered in faeces for my pains. But I was in Africa, and normal rules did not ever apply. Once I had recovered my composure I went back to Emmanuel and asked him to explain exactly why everyone was so scared of this human excrement.

"It is because they know they will die if they touch it", he said, "but they know that you will not".

"What do you mean", I asked, a bit confused, "why won't I die as well?"

"Ah, doctor", replied Emmanuel, "it is because you are a white man, and the white man is protected from poison!" And he meant it, in spite of having worked as a nurse with American missionaries for years.

There were some fundamental beliefs that all the Africans seemed to have about the white men they knew, from David Livingstone to the Greek and Lebanese traders and the American missionaries. To me at that time it often seemed irrational, but I found this deep belief in the magic of the white man to be the case in all the wilder parts of Africa I worked in.

Apart from having to come to terms with such alien ways of thinking I was also having to become ever more resourceful as I learned more and more of the essential requirements for becoming a single-handed surgeon in the depths of the African jungle, including water and waste management. I didn't suppose it was going to earn me any plaudits from the Royal College of Surgeons, but it was absolutely where I seemed to feel most comfortable.

I didn't give a thought for England as I hurtled down the narrow forest track on my 49cc Peugot moped, scattering a huge cloud of swallowtail butterflies on their annual migration through the evergreen jungle.

One Sunday afternoon I was called to the hospital to find a family of 8, each one of them, including the six children totally blind having drunk home-made beer. This was my first encounter with the lethal effects of methyl alcohol.

All medical students know much about the toxic effects of ethyl alcohol. Even the missionaries could not stop the Africans from making alcohol, and I have found alcohol wherever I have travelled in the world, made from everything from maize and manioc to pineapples. The Russians make theirs from potatoes. The problem with any home-made alcohol is the generation of methyl alcohol if the chemical process is not carried out correctly, and methyl alcohol is far more lethal to humans. If it does not kill them outright, it makes them blind, and such was the case on this sad day. There was nothing I could do to help this blinded family.

When I left this jungle kingdom after six months there was a massive party. The missionaries and the Africans, the medical staff and even the TB patients put on a magnificent performance. The drumming and the dancing are in my blood, even as I write these words on the banks of the Mediterranean.

My leaving party was full of drums……

….. and the marrimba

I have only ever worked in the remotest regions of Africa. It is in these parts where the reach of the white men is less evident that I have been able to see and experience an Africa not so different from that which David Livingstone must have seen a century before.

Since that more innocent time, the need for raw materials to feed the western industrial revolution and the economic motives of the neo-colonialists have decimated the rain forests. The search for petroleum, uranium and diamonds have turned much of Africa today into a war zone. Corruption and the inexorable spread of AIDS now also contribute to this process of degradation. But back in 1975 I was in a different world, where life had gone on uninterrupted for centuries, and it was a way of life which much appealed to me.

10. WEST TO AMERICA   1973

Getting the B.T.A.

Once Primary FRCS was completed successfully there were four years of post-graduate surgery training before attempting the Final Fellowship exam, an essential requirement for progress towards a consultancy in General Surgery. There was one important pre-requisite, which was the BTA, the 'Been To America' ticket.

The United States was a world centre for all areas of science, medicine and surgery, and a period of training in the USA was considered a big advantage in the ascent of the career ladder. I obtained a teaching fellowship in Surgical Anatomy at the Medical School of the University of Texas at Houston (which also paid a lot more than our paltry NHS salary).

In June 1973 I took a plane to New York to pass four months in the humid plains of Texas. It was a singular voyage of discovery, in the company of a fellow medic from Liverpool, but one who was as different from me as chalk from cheese.

Jim was a political animal, albeit a surgeon in training like me. In our final year he had been the president of Medical Students Society, and was aiming for higher political station, whereas I spent most of my free time chasing girls and repairing the sports cars in which I chased them. We were to be companions for the next four months.

Don't ever think it was easy getting into the USA, even in those days. It was not. It was necessary to provide a detailed life-history, including any sexually transmitted disease such as gonorrhoea or syphilis, any criminal convictions or other shortcomings of body or character. It was a far cry from popping over to France on the Newhaven-Dieppe ferry for the weekend. The inquisition continued when we arrived at JFK airport, when a large and intimidating customs officer took umbrage at my guitar and mouth organs.

"Ya'll hafta pay dooty on them", stated this portly officer, which began a lengthy and painful discussion. It was not a very warm welcome to the United States, but the trauma of New York Customs was offset by the welcome from Barb Habif, my friend from Middle East days in Jerusalem and her extensive family.

Barb lived in Queens and the next day took Jim and I on a grand tour of New York. To me it was just a mass of concrete, unending traffic and neon signs, but Central Park was wonderful and huge.

I wanted to see Harlem, so reluctantly Barb agreed to take us, saying that it was dangerous and a place to be avoided. Passing from Times Square to the Bronx and into Harlem was a real eye-opener. Although I was used to the poverty of certain corners of Liverpool and London, the scale of Harlem and the poor who sat on every stoep casting malevolent glances our way was daunting. We were glad to exit safely and stop at an ice-cream parlour in Queens, which is where I got my first taste of American life.

On Ice-Cream in the Big Apple - More is Better, and the Origins of Obesity

Behind the chrome steel bar of this establishment was a board advertising the delicious wares on offer. Barb ordered a small milk shake, and so did we, but when this arrived, Jim and I were amazed to see a glass bigger than a pint appear before us, full of white stuff. Neither of us could finish this mass of ice-cream, cream and God knows what else. It was simply too much.

"How big is the large one?", I asked Barb, who pointed out the 1 litre vases which quite a few New Yorkers had their faces stuck in. "I can't believe people can eat so much!" I said in some horror, and as I looked around it was apparent that a goodly proportion of the people around me were rather porky, if not obese. It was my entrée to the American way of life.

Exploring the Southern States – and a taste of modern slavery

Jim and I had decided to explore some of America on our way to Texas, so we bid our farewells to Barb and her generous family and flew to Atlanta where we hired a car with the aim of driving across the southern states to Texas. The recent release of the films 'Cool Hand Luke' and 'Deliverance' had lit up something in me which I wanted to explore further, and I was not disappointed.

Our problems began at the Hertz car rental when we were introduced to the monster of a car we had hired, a Ford GT. Neither Jim nor I had ever driven an automatic, let alone this huge Ford Gran Turismo sedan, so we tossed a coin and Jim got the honour of steering us out of Atlanta city and onto the open road, heading south and west towards Alabama.

It was hot and it was humid and there was not much of interest to note as we crossed the State line into Alabama, but I was happy playing with the in-car air-conditioner, something neither of us had come across before, but which greatly improved our comfort. There was also a jazzy hi-fi system which occupied quite a chunk of the front fascia. As we crossed the state line we were listening to Merle Haggard singing 'Okie from Muskogee', a song which I thought summed up a lot about rural America.

George Orwell wrote brilliantly about the social deprivation in England during the `30's, but it was John Steinbeck's book, 'The Grapes of Wrath' which awoke the world to the poverty and sufferings of the poor whites in the Mid-West during the days of the

Great Depression and the Dust Bowl. They fled west towards California, to be despised and discriminated against by their richer cousins and were known by all as 'Okies' from Oklahoma, from where most of them emigrated. Today 'Okie' is now a commonly used epithet. But for the black descendants of the slaves who inhabited the southern states, there was far worse.

Jim and I had agreed that we would each choose our accommodation for the night on alternate days. Jim, with his big green suitcase and conservative outlook always wanted to stay in Holiday Inns, the bland and franchised formlessness of which I hated. I, with my haversack and guitar preferred to sleep out, which Jim utterly refused, or at least to pass the night in some more homely dwelling. It was my turn to choose where we stayed that night, as dusk fell on the second day of our trans-America tour, when we arrived in the outskirts of Eutaw Town, Alabama, and the first of several near-death experiences which I enjoyed during four months in the USA.

As we entered this small town it became apparent that we were not on the main tourist track. It was abject in its decay and depressing to see the telegraph wires strung across Main Street like wilting black lianas in the jungle of fast-food stores, ice-cream parlours and booze shops which seemed to constitute the main drag of most towns we passed through. The Americans seemed to delight in the very things which always terrified me, such as shopping malls, endless avenues of suburbia without even a shadow of public transport and supermarkets which were so over-loaded with food that I knew there was a serious problem with the spirit of the American people. It was simply not possible to eat so much food without killing yourself, sooner or later.

As we slowly drove along the main street, I spotted a sign in red neon announcing a hotel which, as we approached it looked to be straight out of the set of 'Psycho'.

"Let's give it a try", I said as Jim pulled the car over, "but keep the motor running!"   I was slightly paranoid about the crime rate down these parts, and we never quite knew what to expect in this rather strange, English-speaking country, so I was continually looking out for rapid escape exits, just in case.

The entrance lobby was in darkness, and there was no one at the reception desk, but there was a line of light coming from beneath a doorway leading off the lobby, so I pushed the door open to reveal a small bar in which were about 10 good ole Alabama boys downing beers and shots.

"Excuse me," I said in my best Queen's English, "would you by any chance have a room for the night?"

"Ah guess so", came the laconic reply from the man behind the bar. I returned to the car, we grabbed our luggage and walked into the bar. We ordered a beer each while we took stock of our surroundings, and pretty grim they were. The hotel was indeed reminiscent of the one in 'Psycho', being quite old and built mainly of wood. The bar was basic, as were the white yokels who sat around talking some almost unintelligible form of English.

"Wheah yew boars from?", asked one.

"We are from Liverpool in England", Jim replied, always the politician, wanting to connect. "We are doctors on the way to teach at Houston, but we are driving so we can see some of your country on the way".

"Kin you play that geetar?", asked another, indicating my guitar case on the floor.

"Indeed, I can", I replied, "and for the price of two beers I'll sing you a Liverpool song, if you like", and that is how our night in Eutaw Town evolved into a seriously drunken escapade which scared both of us to our boots. The damage began when Ike, the portly barman pushed a shot glass full of clear liquid down the bar to us.

"You boars ever drink tequila?", he enquired. "Er, I don't think so", I replied.

"Well, get it down", he said as he slid another shot glass towards Jim, who proceeded to sip it like a gin and tonic, which was obviously not the way. Ike gave us a fast demo from his perch at the bar, putting salt on his left hand, biting into a lime, and then slugging the tequila down his throat.

"Doan teach you boars much in Liverpool", he said, eyeing us disapprovingly.

"Here boar, you better get some practice 'fore you sing us a song", sliding down another two glasses of this 40% liquor as I started unpacking my guitar. It looked to be an interesting night and playing in a small bar or club was the sort of scene I enjoyed much more than the big stage.

Nevertheless, my audience this night was not the cognoscenti I was used to playing before in Liverpool. The white farmers sitting in the bar were all rednecks, in a town in Alabama which had just elected its first black mayor barely one week ago, and these white locals were not happy.

To me it was reminiscent of the election of the first Asian mayor in Bradford, West Yorkshire, where some white Brits perceived themselves under threat from within. Here in downtown Alabama we were actually living it, and the murderous talk and intent of these white locals against their black neighbours was frightening to hear.

Jim and I were surrounded by a room full of ardent racists who made Mayor Daley look liberal. After 'In the Heat of the Night', 'Easy Rider' and 'Deliverance' we all knew something of what to expect in the USA and it looked like it was happening around us in this grimy little bar, where Jim quite obviously did not want to be. But it was late, and we were tired as well as hungry, so we stayed, and Ike continued slamming shots of tequila westwards down the bar.

It was pretty much a shot of tequila for every song I sang, and when I saw Jim fall off his bar stool, I was also thinking it was time to retire.

Suddenly the door of the bar burst open and a man, dripping blood staggered in.

On the conflicting role of Inebriation in First Aid

"That bastard Jake jus' shot me!", he cried as he collapsed in a chair. He got a shot of medicinal tequila from Ike. It turned out he had gone to visit a friend nearby who mistook him for some alien being, and then shot him. That was America, land of the free, where the law allowed all card-carrying white men to carry a gun.

Having already wiped out most of the indigenous tribes of America and slaughtered the bison into near extinction, the recently evolved Pilgrim Fathers were now setting on themselves. Of all the many paradoxes I came across in America this gun-toting, gun-worshipping mentality was the most frightening. Even in Houston on Friday nights the cowpokes would drive in from the ranches in their big 4x4 HiLux pickups, all of which had a gun rack behind the front seats with one or two rifles. What they thought they were going to shoot was anyone's guess, but it wasn't the sort of thing Jim and I were used to on a night out in Liverpool.

Jim and I did our doctor bit for the wounded warrior, binding the bullet wound of his left arm with one of the bar towels, so steeped in alcohol that there was no chance of that wound ever getting infected, and then his mates carted him off to the local hospital. At this point Jim and I staggered off to bed having just treated a patient in the most drunken state we were ever likely to be in, one certainly not recommended by the General Medical Council.

After that night I have never been able to face tequila again. The following day we were both nursing sore heads as we jumped into the Gran Turismo tank. We were grateful for having survived the night and after a FAB (Full American Breakfast) in this creaky old hotel, we headed west for Mississippi and the town of Jackson.

´Cool Hand Luke´ and the Chain Gangs of Mississippi

As Jim and I entered the swamplands of Louisiana life got visibly poorer. We had already seen a chain gang by the side of road in Mississippi and Jim nearly had a heart attack when he saw me leaning out of the window to get a photo.

"For God's sake", he cried, "put the bloody camera away. You want to get us shot!"

It was just like a scene from 'Cool Hand Luke', with gun-toting guards all wearing RayBan Aviators and a line of shackled prisoners cutting the grass, most of them black. After our experiences in Alabama, we were less surprised at life in the south, but I still have that photo, just to remind me of the sort of thing that goes on in some parts of the United States.

This was only 10 years after Rosa Parks and Martin Luther King made the running for the blacks of north America and for the past several days we had been driving through the bedrock of that huge social revolution. But today there was little to see except rural poverty. The cotton and tobacco plantations were still all around, and it was the blacks who were still doing the harvesting.

My favourite image of that trip we made through the southern states is of an old black man rocking gently in a wooden chair on the stoep of his small wooden shack deep in the Louisiana swamps. He looked at peace with the world, even in the midst of so much poverty.

One thing we didn't see down there was much obesity. How anyone could make a living in these humid bogs was a mystery, and as far as we knew they were also full of copperheads, rattlesnakes and alligators which made any form of aquaculture rather dangerous.

From the Nodding Donkeys of Texas to Space Control

Even when we got to Texas there was not much of beauty to see, just miles and miles of endless, arid prairie until we reached Houston. That desiccated landscape and the nodding donkeys which inhabited it. Hundreds and thousands of them marring the barren land as they sucked up the black mineral which kept the American Dream alive.

The price of petrol, or gasoline as the Americans called it was 19 cents a gallon in Houston that summer of 1973, and when there was talk of raising the price by two cents there were riots. After the relative privation of Liverpool, the waste and over-consumption of the Americans was mind-blowing to Jim and me.

At Houston we were barely an hour's drive from Space Control. The was the state of the art nerve-centre which, in those early days of space exploration drove supra-terrestrial vehicles beyond the limits of our normal human existence, and lit up the world with the romance and danger of extra-terrestrial voyages, Yet, in what was possibly the greatest paradox of many which I encountered during my four months in the USA in 1973, the disparity between the lives of the poor blacks and the aspiring whites in that *soi-disant* country of the free was a revolution to my naïve British eyes.

When we arrived at the Medical School campus at the Texas Medical Centre we were welcomed by our hosts and found ourselves in the company of four other young British surgeons in training, all from London medical schools. We were to teach a group of 60 medical students the anatomy of the human body in a bare three months.

Most of our students seemed very centred on the money they expected to make from their medical careers. There was not much altruism amongst this lot of doctors-to-be. It says much about the new students we had acquired that two of them, both females, used to arrive at the medical school in Rolls-Royces.

The first evening we were invited to a barbeque given by the Professor of Anatomy, where we were able to meet many of the faculty members, who were generally a good bunch and very keen to make our acquaintance.

It was our first introduction to a Texas steak. We were astounded at the size of the massive slabs of meat sizzling on the barbecue. Each one was about a pound in weight and would have filled a grown man twice over. There were also equally giant hamburgers, frankfurters a foot long, and great chunks of pork belly. We were simply not used to seeing consumption on such a gross scale. Their ethos seemed to be Bigger is Better, and More of Everything is Good.

In those days Texas was indeed still a rich state, providing a significant proportion of the USA's insatiable demand for oil. Although the massive consumption of these white people did give the impression of great wealth, wherever we went there were always the crowds of poor blacks subsisting on a lot less.

The second day we were taken on a tour of the medical campus, including the Ben Taub Trauma Centre, where I spent many interesting hours learning about the various types of wounds which bullets can cause. We also explored the Cardiac Unit where, from a glazed gallery above the operating theatre we were privileged to watch Dr DeBakey doing one of the early heart transplants. It was only a few years since Christian Barnard had performed the first human heart transplant in South Africa and this radical surgery was still in its infancy, so this was an exciting moment for us young surgeons.

There was no doubt that America could do some things very well, and this tour demonstrated that. We were all impressed but wondered about the almost total absence of black patients.

"Where are all your black patients?", asked Thomas, one of our bolder members, of the surgeon who was taking us round.

"Ahem, er...well I guess they go downtown to the community hospital", he declared, a little embarrassed.

"Is this because of segregation?", Thomas continued, bluntly but politely.

"No, no, that's all finished with", exclaimed the surgeon, "it's just that they can't pay. Most can't afford any health insurance".

Which is how we came to better understand the complex and unfair nature of healthcare in the United States. If you could pay it was great, but if you were poor, it was quite another situation, and as often as not you were out in the cold. It was another perplexing paradox after the imperfect but more equable service which we were used to in our own NHS.

There was something about the Americans which made many of them seem to yearn for the antiquity of Britain, and while they revered such British heroes as Churchill, they tended to live in a vacuum as far as the rest of the world was concerned. It was quite amazing how ignorant many of them were about anywhere outside Texas.

I hooked up with a young Houston dentist, and passed pleasant times with her and her friends, but when she said in her southern drawl, "Ah think that Houston is the most bootiful city in the world!", I practically choked. To us six Brits Houston was a 40 square mile block of concrete with no public transport system and nothing of a cultural nature to commend it to us other than the free weekly concerts given on The Mound, a tranquil park near the university campus.

"Where else have you ever been in the world?", I asked her.

"Nowhere!", she answered, and that was just how we found most of the Texans.

As a result of the non-existent public transport, we decided to hire two cars for the duration. Between the six of us it cost just a few dollars and it gave us some freedom to explore this sprawling city. We took it in turns to use the cars, and there were evenings during my brief romance when I had no wheels. So, I took to hitching, as had always been my habit. But the three near-death experiences I enjoyed whilst hitching in Houston town put me off ever sticking my thumb out again in the USA.

On The Road – but Dangerously

The first fright occurred just after I left my dentist friend´s house after a fine meal with her and her parents – both of whom were enormously rich private dentists in Houston. I started hitching as soon as I hit the road and was happy when a sedan stopped with two young men inside. As soon as I was in the car, they started verbally abusing me for no good reason. They were obviously crazy on some drug, and could not even speak coherently, let alone drive.

When the elder of the two produced a massive shooter and said they were going to kill me for fun, I got really scared for the first time in ages. This was serious, for we all knew about guns in America. The only thing which saved my life that night was the set of traffic lights on red. I was out of the car and running like a hare before I knew it. Back at our flat, I unwound to Jim and the others, but they just laughed. No way any of them were going to brave the streets of Houston at night.

The second time I got picked up by an aggressive gay man, who was masturbating as we drove the highway, and trying to touch me up as well as drive. Another set of lights on red saved me, but by now I was getting paranoid about life on the Houston streets.

The third and final fright came after another evening at TikTock's bar on the campus. A guy in a green Mustang picked me up. He was gulping coloured pills and washing them down with a half-bottle of whiskey. I was wondering how to cope with this new threat to existence when he swerved into a garage, ripped a shooter out of the glove compartment, robbed the till and then drove off – with me in the passenger seat, and this time there were no red lights.

Every light at every intersection was green, and not a police car in sight. If something dodgy happened, I was going to get busted for armed robbery, and this maniac next to me was doing up to 100 mph through downtown Houston, still swigging his pills and booze. I took a huge risk as he slowed behind a truck, opened the passenger door and was rolling fast onto tarmac in a second. Thank God there were no kerb-stones. I came to rest in a ditch of stinking ordure, paralysed by shock.

America – I really hated that place by now. It appeared to be populated by three types of people. Rich whites, of whom about 50% were certifiable. The poor blacks, looking on at the antics of the whites, and a small minority of really excellent people, black and white.

After 10 years of hitching across Africa, and never a problem, my experiences in Houston left me traumatised, and forever vehemently against the Americans and their ´culture´.

There were brighter moments. Every Wednesday, a free day for us, we used to drive out to Galveston, on the coast, and took up dinghy sailing, which was glorious fun in the warm waters of the Gulf of Mexico.

One long weekend we took off for Mexico and had a wild time amongst the narco-traffickers, colourful street walkers and fast-food enchilada and taco parlours of Nuevo Laredo. We did enjoy one memorable Mexican meal at a good restaurant, where were serenaded by a group of *mariarchi* for the first time. It certainly helped the digestion, and it was the first time I had seen any living culture since my arrival in the USA.

Mexico was full of music and colour and life, even if it was visibly poorer than the USA. I vowed to return in order to explore it more if I could before I went back to England. I was also interested in following the route of the pre-Columbian Indians who had begun the whole process of agriculture as we know it today up in Mesa Verde in Colorado where they tamed wild grasses and turned them into flour. The cliff-face caves in which they lived were a geological marvel which I also intended to visit.

On Anatomic Anomalies

Back in Houston teaching was rewarding and fun. Our Professor of Anatomy was not only a committed alcoholic, but was presently on his fifth wife, one of his ex-students.

As far as any assessments were concerned at Houston, we were in No Mans territory that first week. The prof wanted us to continue our English teaching method of weekly viva voce examinations. Because we really knew little about our students' proficiencies, at the end of the first weeks teaching we agreed to give everyone a 'B', and the best and worst a B+ and B- respectively. So, we were somewhat put out to be dragged to the prof's office the day after posting the first week's results, to be told in no uncertain terms that his students only got Grade A's! Any semblance of honest assessment was already out of the window, and every time I now hear of someone getting 'Straight A's', I smile a wry smile.

The corpses we were dissecting were not what we had been used to back in Liverpool. Quite a few were derelicts whose bodies had been claimed by the Anatomy department and some of these had evidence of rampant tuberculosis.

Another body posed an interesting but different problem. A group of students were dissecting the inner ear but had come across something that was not included in God's inventory when this embryo was formed, which they could not identify. I went to the body in question and was astonished to pull out a very bent .38 bullet from the petrous temporal bone. No wonder the students were having a problem defining the normal anatomy of the ear. It turned out that criminals were also included in the corpses dissected by the

Houston Anatomy department, and the risks of infection from this unhealthy gathering of corpses was considerable. From then on, the six of us took great care to always wear gloves and a mask when we approached the dissecting room.

Sometimes, during that long, humid summer it was easy to forget that we were inside the richest and most powerful country in the world.

West to the Rocky Mountains

At the end of September came the final exam for our students, and then the post-exam piss-up at Tic-Toc's Bar which was always full of medics, nurses and students. The thin beer it provided was poured into litre glasses kept in a freezer, whose only benefit appeared to be disguising the taste of the pale Budweiser which none of us Brits thought much of.

The others had all planned to visit Las Vegas on their way back, but I could not imagine anywhere I wanted less to visit. Casinos, gambling and all their trappings were all anathema to me, and I was planning on taking a trans-America drive during the last week of our car-hire. I could not believe that Texas was all there was to the USA. There must be somewhere attractive in that massive country, so I had decided to head west towards Colorado and the Rocky Mountains. However, I was keen to find a travel companion if possible. So, in the middle of this noisy, crowded bar I stood up on a table and shouted out,

"Anyone female, young and pretty fancy taking a trip with me?", and was pleasantly surprised to be approached by Julie, a very pretty blonde paediatric nurse, whom I had never met before, but was definitely up for a voyage of discovery. We arranged to meet the next morning and set off early with the car boot full of beer and provisions in a big cooler box.

My only proviso to Julie was that I wanted to try and sleep beside running water every night, and I also wanted to try to reach Mesa Verde and the Rockies, where I was hoping to find some countryside more stimulating than the endless plains of Texas.

That was not a problem to this engaging young nurse, so we headed north and west, passing Dallas at speed, only stopping to fill the tank of this gas-guzzling monster every 200 miles. In the middle of nowhere up near the Oklahoma border we stopped for more fuel at an outpost with just a shack and two pumps and a chalkboard with the message,

'No beggars, No dirty Hippies, No vagabonds!'

A fierce-looking old guy came out, took one look at me in my bare feet, cut-off Levis, tank top and long hair and said, "Ain't servin' you!', and disappeared into his crumbling shack. That's how things were in the States sometimes – unbelievable prejudice and ignorance.

We slept the first night in Oklahoma, after an epic drive of about 1000 miles, and collapsed around midnight by the side of a waterfall, to be awoken in the morning by a child crying out to her mother,

"Momma, come and see, there are hippies here!"

I shot up like a jack rabbit, expecting to see a rifle pointing at us, but in fact it was a kindly lady and her two children out gathering flowers, who was amused to find Julie and me sharing a blanket on the banks of the river.

From Oklahoma we crossed into Colorado and entered a countryside which was beautiful, fertile and covered with trees, something I had missed in Texas. Ahead of us rose the peaks of the Rocky Mountains where we made camp that night, again on the banks of an isolated river running through a valley flanked by aspen and willow. Now I was beginning to see the parts of the USA which I had so far missed, and even Julie delighted in this new and verdant countryside, so very different from Texas.

We headed south towards the point where four states meet – Utah,

Colorado, Arizona and New Mexico. In Monument Valley we were in John Wayne country, with massive mesas and buttes rising from the desert floor and the first of the tall cactuses, so iconic in these parts. There was no doubt, the natural beauty of the mountains and the desert was spectacular. However, wherever we went in these parts we began to see the degradation of the indigenous Indian tribes, reduced to living in penury in fenced off reservations. Many of them had become alcoholics, and at every petrol station there were Indians begging us to buy them some whiskey, which they were forbidden to do. Ragged mothers with infants on their backs approached us with their hands outstretched, begging for some food. Even Julie was horrified to see their destitution in the midst of all the wealth around them.

It was Charlie Chaplin who had told me about the Indians´ part in the development of Manhattan and New York back in the 1930´s when the skyscrapers were taking off and he was making his first classic films. The indigenous Indians were the only people who seemed unfazed at walking along foot-wide steel girders 200 metres up in the sky, and in those days they could earn good money. But now all their mineral-rich lands had been stolen by the whites and their hunting grounds destroyed, and they had nothing.

I had already seen how the black people were treated during our drive through the southern states, but it was more shocking to see the plight of the indigenous Indian tribes in the mid-West. I knew I could never live in this strange country, nor did I ever want to visit it again. There was something malign about the subjection of the other races by the whites in the USA, and 50 years later little has changed.

Sunrise over the Grand Canyon

We arrived fairly late at night at the Grand Canyon, driving past miles of huge campervans, all with barbecues flaming and televisions blaring. It was not the authentic experience I had been hoping for, so I just kept driving on until we arrived at the very edge of the canyon at a place called Desert View, where we suddenly found ourselves completely alone, possibly as the signpost indicated, because this was a restricted site. But this did not concern us, so we made a comfortable camp on the cliff edge, looking down on a fall of several hundred metres to the floor of the canyon.

We stayed awake, smoking joints and drinking beer until dawn, when we were gifted to experience the breaking of a new day over this vast natural wonder of the world.

It was strikingly beautiful to watch the changing pastel colours of dawn merge into golden sunlight, which at first lit up the far rim of the canyon, and then as the sun rose in the sky lit up more and more of the wall of the canyon until it reached the floor, almost a mile below and turned the whole valley into glistening green, flanked by the massif of the canyon walls. In my experience it only compared to watching the sun come up over the Jordan valley at Masada.

At 0900h a park warden came by and moved us on, but by then we had shared one of the most moving natural phenomena I had so far ever experienced.

From there we turned east towards Phoenix, which I found hot and ugly, and then to El Paso on the Mexican border. We followed the Santa Fe Express train as it travelled west at 70 mph. I toot-tooted the horn as we drove parallel to the train and was well rewarded by a great blast of horn. This continued for miles as we headed for San Antonio and the Alamo.

All students of American history know of their disastrous defeat by the Mexicans at the Alamo. To me it was like a combination of Rorke's Drift, the Second Afghan war, Gordon of Khartoum and other great British defeats. With every great military disaster there always has to be a losing hero, and Davy Crockett was the Alamo's.

Today there is a museum to celebrate this early American disaster, which even includes Davy Crockett's spoon as well as his coon-skin hat and other possessions, worshipped religiously by the Americans.

Within the museum everything was peaceful until we suddenly heard a loud Bang ! At which point visitors started hitting the deck and reaching for their own personal artillery. Julie and I just stood, bemused at this charade, particularly when a small boy proudly displayed the paper bag he had just burst. I have never forgotten that instinctive reaction of all the visitors to this child's antics. It was a vivid reflection of the paranoia and fear which was an inevitable part of the ubiquitous gun culture in America.

Another near-death experience – but the venison was free

On the way back to Houston, late at night, we were doing 80mph along an empty road when I saw a pair of animal eyes reflecting in the headlights, and as I approached at speed a suicidal deer jumped into my path. There was no avoiding it. I was terrified but kept driving in a straight line to avoid any skid, reckoning that the weight of this Buick sedan was more than enough to counteract any high-speed impact with a deer. It was, but only just. The cloud of stinking brown, eviscerated venison which impacted on the windscreen was more than the wipers could cope with, and for a hundred metres or more I drove completely blind, and once again gave thanks to Allah that there was no oncoming traffic.

The smell of the deer's intestinal contents spread across the car's windscreen was pungent enough, but where was the rest of the animal? It took us a good five minutes to find the completely eviscerated corpse, which had been blasted about 50 metres into a field. The car didn't look too healthy either, with a massive bit missing from the off-side wing and the bonnet looking a bit like a moonscape. Julie was pretty cool considering this sudden nocturnal attack, and as I was stuffing bits of freshly killed venison into the boot she said, *en passant*,

"I hope you realize that you get five years in Texas for killing deer out of season!" She was knowledgeable about these sorts of things, but I thought, "Bugger that!" after the minor cardiac arrest I had just suffered at this deer's expense. I had some medic friends back in Houston who would only thank me for this fresh and free roadkill. I have to admit that the rest of the journey back was somewhat qualified by a seriously bent front suspension and the intoxicating smell of maturing venison.

I was relieved that my insurance covered all the extensive damage to the car. I said goodbye to dear Julie, then took a plane to Mexico City and continued my peregrinations through Mexico as far as Guatemala. She had been a most excellent travelling companion, but I never saw her again. It was only in her company that I saw any beauty in the States, and to see it in the company of such a fine person was a privilege.

I left Houston knowing that I would never return to the Land of the Free.

11. TO KENYA WITH THE FLYING DOCTORS 1975

From the Jungle to Savannah, and a Land of Milk and Honey

Once my six months in the Congo at Mushenge was up I had a choice. Either to return to England by going west down the river Congo – following in the footsteps of Livingstone and Speke, or to go east via the Ruwenzori Mountains of Ruwanda and on to Kenya, which is what I eventually decided to do.

I took a plane to Kigali, the capital of Ruwanda, for I had a strong urge to visit the Ruwenzori mountains, even if I did not spot any gorillas. The Ruwenzori is one of the great African mountain chains, dividing the Congo from Uganda in the east and rising up to over 5,000 metres. I spent two days in the foothills of the extravagant rain forest which covered the slopes, spending freezing nights in a ranger's hut whilst keeping a lookout for gorillas during the damp grey days. It was a pleasant diversion, but I found it rather too damp and cold for my liking, so I took a plane to Nairobi.

In this wondrous city the jacaranda was in purple blossom all the way down Kenyatta Avenue. There was fresh milk everywhere, bacon and even fine sausages in abundance and loads of good restaurants to eat at. Many of them were Asian, as there was a large Asian presence all over East Africa. Hindus, Sikhs and Muslims all seemed to coexist peaceably amongst the Africans.

After the steaming jungles of West Africa, the Congo and the Ruwenzori, it was a magical delight to witness the open savannah again and fresh dry highland air, but this time not in the Adamaoua plateau of northern Cameroun, but the Athi plains of Kenya just south of Nairobi.

And then there was Tusker. Wherever you were in Kenya in those days you were never far from a bottle of this life-giving liquor. It was probably the very best thing that the British colonialists ever did for East Africa. Even Guinness was available, and also bottles of wine of dubious provenance, but drinkable to a desperate man. I had never seen the like of all this munificence before in Africa.

East Africa was a jewel to all the colonialists, from the Arabs in the Middle Ages to the Germans at the turn of the last century, and then to the Brits, who had left, but continued to leave a large imprint on this fabled land, so full of milk and honey.

I spent a month travelling all over Kenya, from Mount Elgon to Lamu Island, and I loved every bit. I was particularly taken by the elegant Swahilis of the eastern coast and their exquisite culture and cuisine. The taste of the tiger fish cooked in coconut milk which I enjoyed at a small beach bar at Watamu Beach still lingers.

Swahili dhow, Lamu Island

There were so many different peoples, from the reigning Kikuyu tribe of Kenyatta who had most of the good land around Nairobi, to the tall and beautiful Masai in the Ngong hills where, in the verdant suburb of Karen, Issac Dinessen had lived and written her masterpiece, "Out of Africa ".

There were also the Mkamba round Machakos who were the great honey-gatherers, the Kalenjin and Samburu from up around Isiolo, and the Turkana around Lodwar. Around Lake Victoria lived the Kisii and the Luo tribes. I once read in an authoritative tome on East Africa that there were 72 different tribes and languages within Kenya.

The Dangerous Roads

I was mostly hitch-hiking around Kenya at this time, which was both exciting and extremely dangerous. The standard of driving generally was appalling, and the roads left much to be desired, many with lethal potholes which were the cause of a lot of fatal accidents. The cheapest, but by far the most dangerous way of seeing Kenya was by *matatu* – micro-buses or Hilux wagons, crammed to suffocation with jolly Africans. These were often driven by drunken drivers who seemed to have little knowledge of the fatal consequences of their wild driving.

I was twice involved in accidents, fortunately with no serious sequelae, but enough to convince me never to use that mode of transport again. The death rates from road traffic accidents in Kenya at that time were stratospheric – and still are today.

After a stimulating month in Kenya I hitched into Tanzania and spent two days camping at N´Gorongoro crater. I was struck by the natural beauty of this Masai homeland, so full of wild animals, plants and birds of every brilliant hue. I knew I was going to come back here to work, even before I got on the plane back to England and a job as

Senior house officer in General Surgery at Frimley Park hospital in the stock-broker belt of south London.

But how? That was the burning question. As has happened so often in my life, serendipity played a part…….

Resignation – and the Realisation of a Dream

As was normal in those days, all of us middle-grade surgeons in formal training were working at least 90 hours a week, being on-call every other night and weekend. This was always exhausting even at the best of times. Even though my advertised job and pay was for a senior house officer, I found myself working a one-in-two rota – but as a Registrar, with all the extra responsibilities. My partner was Bannerjee, a jovial Hindi and a demon in the kitchen, but after my own experience at his hands I had some doubts about his clinical practice.

I have always suffered with periodontal disease, and once again I could feel an abscess building up in my lower left jaw as I did the morning ward round. I was also on-call, and by 2200h that night had already done two acute appendicectomies and was facing a woman with a thrombosis of her femoral vein, as well as having an almighty toothache, such that I could no longer focus properly. The swelling on my jaw was growing bigger by the hour, as was the pain. So, I called Bannerjee, and along he came.

"Ah!", he exclaimed on examining my aching jaw. "No problem! I can fix that in a second", and before I could stop him, had plunged a No.15 Swann and Morton into the heart of the abscess.

"Jesus Christ", I shouted in shock. But the agonising pain of incision had already passed, and then came the blessed relief as the laudable pus exploded into my mouth. By the time I had washed my mouth and re-composed myself, Bannerjee had evaporated, and I was left to do a laparotomy on an old man with intestinal obstruction whilst the woman with the thrombosis went to sleep with an armful of heparin, and a prayer from me. Such was life at the sharp end at Frimley Park DGH in 1975.

I complained to the two consultants I worked for about my unfair situation. Roger was a good general surgeon and Mike was mainly a vascular surgeon – which always made me wonder as he sat through his Vascular Outpatients chain smoking Players untipped.

Neither of them seemed able to help me for some reason, so the next Wednesday at 1400hrs I presented myself as usual at Mike's Vascular clinic and said, "I´m sorry, but I´m off. I´ve had enough of doing registrar work for houseman's pay", and I left Mike open-mouthed whilst I headed for the doctors' mess where there was solitude, and a chance to think on what I had just done. To resign is never a good thing as a rule, and within the surgical hierarchy it was a definite No!

But it was not the first time I had stuck two fingers up at the medical establishment. Even though I knew it would tell against me some day, I could not tolerate unfairness or abuse in any form, especially if it involved me directly. We were all working extremely hard and had little or no social life. That was the price we paid for the privilege of becoming a fully trained general surgeon back in the 1970s.

Thinking deeply my hand fell onto a copy of The Lancet, that most revered of medical journals – and one which I had rarely touched before, as I found much of the analytical science within unintelligible. The BMJ was more my style, but my touch this day was truly fortuitous, for as I opened the Jobs Vacant section, I immediately saw an advert which sparked me into Instant Total Awareness.

"General Surgeon required, Flying Doctor Service of East Africa".

If ever a chap had a dream, mine was to be a flying surgeon – and here, right out of the blue, and at a bit of a blue period in my own life

– the Flying Docs had come to my rescue. The East African Flying Doctor Service later evolved in AMREF, the African Medical and Research Foundation. I just knew I was going to get that job – and I did. Over some stiff competition, but my months with Jack and Dick in the dark jungles of Cameroun and my six months alone in Congo counted a great deal.

Two weeks later, with help from the beautiful Nicola who ran the Flying Docs office in Devonshire St. WC1, I was leaning over a pint of Tusker at the Muthaiga Club in Nairobi. I was wondering why there was still a Men Only bar there, why blacks and Asians were effectively black-balled, and why croquet on a Sunday afternoon, with Pimm's and cucumber sandwiches was still *de rigeur*.

On Becoming a Flying Surgeon

I spent the afternoon after my arrival at Nairobi being given a thorough briefing about my responsibilities by the director of the Flying Docs, Mike Wood. He was the bush-surgeon who started the whole flying doctor business in East Africa. In fact, he was really a genetically modified bush-pilot with a single-engine Cessna, who happened to enjoy flying solo all over Africa, as well as performing all forms of surgery, especially plastic and reconstructive. He was later knighted by the Queen for his humanitarian services to Kenya and the Africans – and he well-deserved the honour, for he was a brave and gifted surgeon.

He introduced me to my other surgical colleague, Don Gilchrist, a very experienced bush surgeon, who was to become a life-long friend and colleague. During my months in Kenya Don taught me a great number of valuable surgical techniques.

Mike had decided to take us to a Japanese restaurant, where I had the unusual delight of being served a purple sea-weed soup by an ebony-skinned young man from Nyeri, just north of Nairobi. After my thin months in the Congo, to be in a Japanese restaurant just down the road, as it were, from Kinshasa was a surprise, but the meal was wonderful.

Don was a very spiritual man, a Scottish Catholic, and one of the kindest and most modest men I ever met, as well as being a real artist of a surgeon. No detail was too much for Don. He taught me that valuable lesson, amongst many others.

The operation I remember him most for was one to correct prolapse of the uterus, the so-called womb-sling operation. Prolapse of the uterus is a common condition affecting post-menopausal women all over the world. Especially those who have borne the most children – which includes a lot of the world's poorest populations. The problem is that the prolapse also causes other serious clinical problems such as urinary infections and incontinence, and if left untreated the cervix becomes infected and ulcerated as it protrudes from the vagina.

Don's solution was really simple, very fast to perform, and could be done under local anaesthetic with Diazepam sedation, and it went like this ....

Make a small incision in the mid-lower abdomen, through the rectus muscle and peritoneum. Grab the fundus of the uterus with a Duval forcep, put a No 2 non-absorbable suture twice through the muscle of the fundus, and bring both ends back through the skin. Haul tight on both ends of the suture, the fundus is brought up to the anterior abdominal wall. Bazooka! No more prolapse.

I note with amusement now, some 40 years later, that several of the operations which Don Gilchrist taught me during those heady months of 1975 are now considered either not *á la mode*, or else downright dangerous. But needs must, and Don was a master of many tricky surgical situations after his 30 years in Kenya and Tanzania.

Within three days of arriving in Kenya, I was off on my first mission with the Flying Doctors. Now I really was a flying surgeon, and a very proud one at that.

1975. Flying surgeon with the Flying Docs. First emergency medical evacuation

Resting between missions

Back to the Desert

That was how far Don and I were from any form of academia. We were at the front line, and there was no back-up of any kind. Thus, I honed my clinical and surgical skills, under the blazing sun of Northern Frontier District.

During six glorious months I had the time of my life – first at Garissa as Provincial Surgeon for Northern Frontier District – one of the wildest place on earth – bordered by Somalia to the east and Ethiopia to the north. These two countries never stopped warring, so Mandera, where Kenya, Somalia and Ethiopia meet, was a dangerous place to be at the best of times.

I had to go to Mandera every two weeks to do two days surgery on the locals, about half of which was war wounds of various sorts, from spear wounds through the chest to bullet and grenade wounds.

Back at Provincial HQ at Garissa the hospital was full of Somalis, Boran and others all needing surgery, a lot of which was from animal woundings, for we were in the middle of wild Africa and there were deadly animals all around, from the Echis or saw-scale viper – 24 inches of deadly venom, to rhinos and elephants in profusion, and also crocodiles.

But my first patient at Garissa presented with a very common surgical problem, an acute anal haematoma. Straining at stool can cause these and they are very painful, even though innocuous enough. The patient was Colonel Joseph, commandant of the army camp at Garissa, a very important local official, who later became a good friend.

A swift incision with a No.15 Swan and Morton caused the colonel to twitch in pain, but released a black clot of blood and brought instant relief and a smile to his face. I told him we were a bit short of local anaesthetic, and hoped he didn't mind too much, but he wanted to embrace me.

Joseph was not only the army commandant, but he also held the key to the NAAFI store in Garissa. The Navy, Army and Air Force Institution was one of the great triumphs of the British army, now also adopted by the Kenyan army. It was the duty-free store where all good British things were available at much reduced cost, including booze, bacon, sausages and Huntley and Palmer biscuits. In this desert outpost these were great luxuries, but from now on thanks to Joseph's generosity I also had access to this treasure- trove.

On Managing Wild Animal Woundings
i) The Rhino

It was a very hot and humid afternoon when they brought in what was left of Hamid, a Somali herder who had been attacked two days earlier by a rhino whilst guarding his flock of sheep and goats. How he had struggled across the burning desert with no water, no food and no functioning legs was a miracle in itself, for the injuries he had were huge and serious.

The rhino's horn had penetrated the anus, fractured the right ischial bone and pulled out the left sciatic nerve by the roots, leaving a massive open wound of his buttocks. This really was major trauma, and it took Samson, my faithful surgical nurse and I, two hours to do just the primary surgical toilet required for this complex wound. Subsequently I did seven more operations on Hamid, but in the end he did walk out, with just a straight leg splint to his paralysed left leg and a camel-skin boot attached. In these God-forsaken areas the loss of any limb was a fatal catastrophe for any native. They were inevitably reduced to beggary as they could no longer work as herders, so Hamid was well-pleased as he walked off into the desert again, and as with most of my patients in this far-off desert, I never saw him again.

ii)   On Anaesthetising Crocodiles

It was at Garissa that I operated for the first time on a crocodile. I was already used to spaying the odd cat or dog, and I had done a fair amount of dentistry as well, in the absence of any vet or dentist in these parts, but a crocodile was a new challenge.

Early one Wednesday morning Father Luigi arrived from the mission next door with a large melon box, asking for help. I was shocked when I opened the lid to find a three-foot long crocodile looking at me. Sticking out of its mouth was a big fishing hook with the remains of an iguana on it. The crowd of patients enjoying this theatre then all disappeared at speed.

I had already operated on several natives with crocodile bites. As a result of the crocodile's rancid diet most of these wounds became badly infected, and I could see a major challenge in the offing as the croc flashed its razor-sharp teeth at me.

Just to complicate matters I was in the middle of a list of 10 circumcisions which I did every week for the Somali orphans in the mission, and Samson, my trusty theatre nurse had also evaporated on seeing the crocodile. The Flying Doc's plane was also imminently due, to take me on my two-weekly surgical safari to Wajir and Mandera.

How to anaesthetise this animal? That was the question, and all I had available was ketamine. But how much does one give a young crocodile? In the end I gave it a dog-sized dose, which I injected into the croc's abdomen with great difficulty whilst Father Luigi held its head down with a broom. Then I went and performed the next two circumcisions, by which time the crocodile appeared inert enough to operate on.

Using my longest abdominal needle-holder I grabbed the hook in the throat and extracted it. Triumph! and I still had all my fingers.

I heard the plane arrive as I finished the last circumcision, grabbed my emergency bag and headed for the landing strip where Hugh was waiting for me inside the Cessna 402. He laughed his head off when I told him of my latest heroic surgery as we flew north to Wajir.

Three days later I was back at Garissa and suddenly remembered the crocodile, so after my morning round I went to the mission to enquire.

"Ah, zee crocodile, 'e jus wake up!", said Father Luigi, taking me to the small waterhole in the mission compound, and sure enough the croc was alive, still looking malevolently at me. Apparently, the croc had not moved for three days, and they were about to bury it thinking it dead. Now they were about to return it to the Tana River where no doubt it would catch and eat an unwary African fisherman at some time in the future.

Samson took two photos of me on the OT steps clutching a heavily anaesthetised crocodile in one hand and the forceps and hook in the other. Nobody would have believed me otherwise. I have yet to find any reference to anaesthetising crocodiles with ketamine, but I think between 5 – 10 mgs a kilo should do the trick, as it did for me.

From a fast inguinal hernia repair to sleeping with lions

Ken Smith was the Chief Game Warden of Tana River District. He had spent most of his life in East Africa and there was not much he did not know about life in the bush. When his long-wheel base Toyota Land Cruiser appeared one Friday outside the hospital at Garissa, I was looking forward to another night down at Elephant Camp on the banks of the Tana River with Douglas Collins. He was another old Kenya adventurer and a great friend of mine, who ran this ramshackle safari camp. I had passed many happy evenings with Dougie watching the huge variety of animals coming to have their sundowners. But today it was not to be, for Ken had a problem. His driver, Mohammed had developed a large inguinal hernia and was finding driving a problem. Could I help?

Within two hours Mohammed had enjoyed one of my Bassini hernia repairs done under local anaesthetic, jumped off the OT table, shaken my hand and disappeared back to the Land Cruiser.

The recuperative powers of the Africans were phenomenal. They were more able to cope with the effects of my surgery than the Brits I had left behind in UK. They were generally much fitter, and obesity was unknown except for the rich chiefs, and their expectations were very different.

Ken was on a mission to see our neighbour, George Adamson, another of my Giants of Men. He and his wife Joy were the couple who brought Elsa the Lioness to fame in the 1950's. He now lived with his lions in Kora, the game park which he and his brother Terence had constructed out of the wild African bush, and which had just been recognised as a national park by the Kenyan Government.

In an inspired moment I asked Ken if there was any chance of a lift to visit George with him, to which he readily agreed. Having arranged for some clinical cover from Peter, my counterpart at the hospital, I grabbed a couple of bottles of gin from the NAAFI, then we were off, heading east along the south bank of the Tana River in Ken's heavily loaded wagon. Inside it was like an armed version of Milletts, being full of every conceivable thing one would need for survival in the jungle, including several dangerous looking rifles and elephant guns.

There was no road at all, just endless savannah scrub, acacia trees and masses of animals to which the Tana River gave life. It was a rich hunting ground and Ken was its protector, as was George Adamson. He and his wife Joy had devoted their lives to the wildlife of East Africa, especially lions, and found global fame through the book and later the film 'Born Free'.

That Saturday night Ken, George and I were sitting with our gin and tonics about two metres from eight wild lions – separated by a chicken wire fence two metres high on which a bush baby was dancing. That was all that protected me, and I did drink quite a bit that starry night in order to render me more anaesthetic if and when a lion grabbed me.

A nervous night with the lions of George Adamson. I did not need to use my telephoto lens.

The night was enlivened by the remarkable stories of these two old African travellers, and when I finally went to 'bed'- my sleeping bag on the dusty ground, so close to this pack of wild lions that it was their gentle respirations which lulled me to sleep, my brain was full of tales of derring-do in the huge wilderness of Africa.

The next morning, we slaughtered and then butchered a camel. It was feeding time for George's lions, and it was me in the back of a short-wheel base Mark 1 Land Rover with half a butchered camel to throw out to the waiting lions. I found the experience of feeding hungry, wild lions by hand highly stressful and would not recommend it to anyone with cardiac insufficiency.

I have been very privileged to spend time with those I call Giants of Men. Ken and George and Douglas were such. So was Wilfred Thesiger, whose travel books I had read previously. We met up in Samburu country when I was with Douglas at Isiolo. Wilfred was very tall, an ascetic man who had done more desert travelling than anyone on earth. He lived in a Samburu encampment nearby and was coming in for his weekly shower. Just to share a few words with him was a privilege.

There are few such intrepid voyagers, and I never stop revering the courage and intelligence which allowed these special friends of mine to live such outstanding lives and die of old age.

In the footsteps of ancient man. To Lodwar.

After three months at Garissa the Flying Docs asked me to go to Lodwar in Turkana District, way out in the north-western reaches of the Lokodi desert. This was a desert outpost in the shadow of Lake Rudolph, which had been discovered by Count Teliki a century before. It was the place where Kenyatta was interned during the Mau-Mau years of the '50s. During the 1950's, Louis Leakey had found some of his most impressive fossils of early man in the wastes of this volcanic desert in which I now found myself.

Lodwar. The prison where Jomo Kenyatta was interned by the British. Now a national memorial.

I stepped out of the Cessna 420 in which Hugh had flown me up to Lodwar to see a rather straggly-looking person in ex - army shorts approach the plane.

"An' who the phourgh may you be?", were the words he uttered to me as I stepped out onto the black, larval ground of which this desert was mostly composed.

So, it was I came to know Father Joe Moran, the head of the Catholic Mission at Lodwar. He was an exceptional leader and through his ingenuity and energy he kept this remote mission functioning. A purloiner of all things edible and drinkable, he was also responsible for all the fragile flights landing at Lodwar – 500 miles north of Nairobi and bordering on the even wilder Karamoja country. He had a harem of five trusty Irish nuns under his wings, of whom Sister Brise was the Queen.

"I wonder, do you have anything for me", she innocently enquired of me, all covered in her habit in a torrid and debilitating heat which, after the glorious coolness of Nairobi nights was a serious thermometric shock to me.

"Do you mean 50 bottles of Tusker and four bottles of gin plus two of cognac", I responded, and she gratefully held out her hands. Then she took me to her remarkable chest freezer which ran on paraffin and was filled with lines of chilled Tusker beer. It was enough to turn me religious.

My Pilot is a Nun

Later that evening at the congenial communal meal I came to meet my pilot for the next several weeks and months. Sister Shaun was Canadian, aged 26 years, and extremely beautiful. She had her own plane, a Cessna 205 which had been bought by her home church back in Canada. She used to get up every day at 0500h and say her prayers, and by 0630h we were airborne, heading once again for a clinic at another un-mapped outpost in the larva-filled desert, full of ancient volcanoes.

To be flying over this endless desert at the side of a beautiful 26-year-old nun was a new experience of which I never tired. Sometimes I would be dreaming that I was on the way to Nirvana, and Sister Shaun was my pilot.

Clinics in Turkana District with Sister Sean

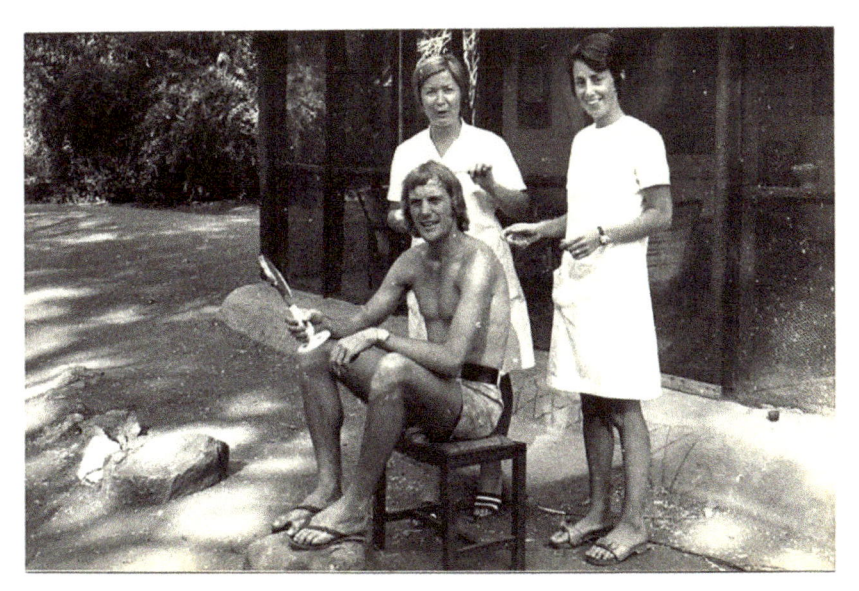

Being shorn by Sister Sean

The rustic clinics I attended with her were always interesting for the range of pathology I saw. At the general surgery clinics I used to do in England I always had a rough idea of the range of diseases I would meet, and had the facilities to investigate them. But in these remote desert areas a clinic would cover every known aspect of human pathology, and several more unknown. From pregnant women to a child with pneumonia, or an obstructed hernia, to a herder chewed by a lion I never knew what to expect. In these isolated clinics there were no resources to aid me apart from my stethoscope and my own knowledge and skills.

It was a hard way of learning, being alone with such responsibility, but it did improve my clinical diagnostic skills enormously within a short space of time.

The Loose Ladies of Lodwar

All in all, my days at Lodwar were delightful, if not unusual. For one thing, the District Commissioner proudly announced that I was also to be responsible for the health and well-being of the local prostitutes. This led to a monthly visit from a varying number of destitute women, all with children and no man to support them, who had no other recourse but to sell their bodies. I have seen it so very many times during my voyages. Men can be real, selfish bastards when it comes to women and sex.

In spite of their privations, the loose ladies of Lodwar were a jolly bunch. Lodwar had just two bars in its dust-blown Main Street, and I often used to meet them in one of the bars when work had finished and share a Tusker with them. They all told similar stories. Many of them were from other tribes, brought north by their husbands and later abandoned. They seemed to exist on fresh air, and there was certainly no obesity in that community.

I was able to help these women more by arranging supplementary food for them and their children from the World Food Programme

(WFP). This was a life-saving organisation in these famine-stricken parts of northern Kenya, for these poor women were the most under-privileged of all and had no resources to fall back on apart from their bodies.

Surgery at Lodwar

This was always an adventure – mostly because the only operating theatre had a four-inch wide, bottomless crack across the floor, the result of some past earthquake, of which there were many in that region. Every patient for surgery had to be carried over this dangerous gap before I had even touched them.

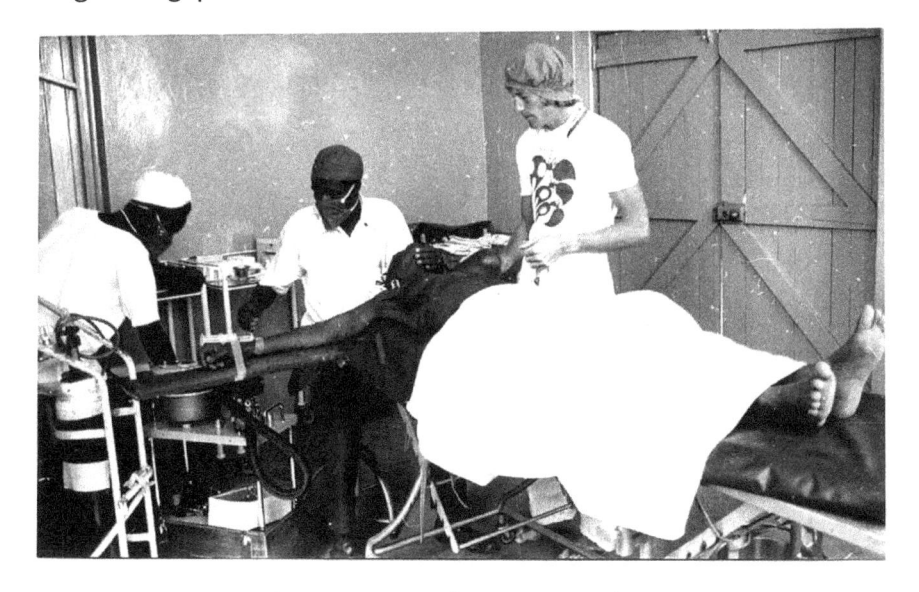

The operating theatre at Lodwar

Then there was Albert the alcoholic anaesthetist. He was from the Kamba tribe, way down south of Nairobi. He had fallen on hard times up in Turkana district and had turned to drink. The result was a persistent tremor of his hands, and days when he simply did not appear. To watch him put in an intravenous line was a nerve-wracking business as his shaking fingers searched for a vein. I was always fearful when he started up the ancient EMO anaesthetic machine, as it ran on ether – one of the most highly explosive of gases, and Albert was a serious smoker.

In spite of these hazards, we did a lot of good work, including dozens of laparotomies for hydatid disease to remove the mesenteric cysts which so commonly occurred. My record, never beaten, was six laparotomies in one day.

On Hydatid disease and the cyst with a thousand daughters

This nasty disease, transmitted through dog excrement, leads to cysts in every part of the body, some of them of enormous size, and the great danger was this   every cyst was filled with innumerable daughter cysts, so if one cyst burst the body became riddled with hydatid cysts – from the orbit of the eye to the vagina, and the liver, these cysts were a devil to deal with – and Turkana had one of the highest incidences of this disease in the world, for which at that time there was no treatment other than surgery.

Just as I was about to leave Lodwar, a scientific team from the World Health Organisatio (WHO) arrived. They were about to start Phase 3 trials of Thiabendezole, a completely new anti-parasitic – and it was a startling success. Along with Albendazole and other anti-helminth drugs it has almost completely removed the need for the surgery of hydatid disease. As I like to say to my patients, "Just try to live long enough, and a cure is sure to arrive!"

Swimming with the nuns – and the crocodiles of Lake Turkana

My work at Lodwar was considerably enhanced by Father Joe's Irish nuns. They were good nurses as well as being amusing companions, who loved nothing better than loading up the creaky old mission Land Rover with booze and food and heading for Eliye Springs. This was a tiny outpost on the banks of Lake Turkana where there was a small and primitive tourist hostel.

Rendille boys on the banks of Lake Turkana

The lake was a huge expanse of green water, full of enormous Nile perch, some weighing over 200 kilos, and also many hungry crocodiles. One month before, the upper torso of a young American had been extracted from the stomach of one of these monsters of the deep. It was enough to keep me in the safer shallows, but not the nuns, who loved playing a version of aqua-volleyball.

It was whilst enjoying the sight of four Irish nuns in black habits floundering around in the shallows of that glittering green lake that I suddenly saw the snout of a crocodile appear just between me and the playful nuns.

"Croc!", I shouted in horror, as metres of reptile slid past my eyes. The nuns were paralysed with fear and started mouthing Gaelic prayers. Obviously, God was listening out for us, and we were a happy and complete band of pilgrims who sang ourselves back to Lodwar.

December came, and I took a fond farewell of Lodwar, its dusty streets, Turkana warriors and their camels. My contract with the Flying Doctors was ending and so I headed back to Nairobi. My favourite bush pilot, Hugh and his wife Annie had invited me to have Christmas with them in Tanzania at a mission hospital in the shadow of Olduvai Gorge, where Louis Leakey found some of the earliest hominid remains during the '50s.

Boxing Day 1975.   Olduvai Gorge.

We flew down in a Gypsy Moth, the same type of plane in which Sir Francis Chichester flew half-way round the world. Its máximum speed was 80 knots, and I had the bizarre experience of watching the traffic overtake us as we took off from Wilson Airport on the outskirts of Nairobi.

Flying with Hugh was always interesting, and as we skated over the Athi plains at a gentle 60 knots we had a royal rooftop view of the myriads of animals we passed. Of all that wildlife it was the beautiful rhythmic motions of the giraffes as they ran away which most delighted me. They do not run like a horse, for their legs move differently. This results in a smooth, flowing run as they move from side to side with each pace, almost poetic in its motion, which can best be appreciated from above.

We landed on a dirt strip, having done the usual two passes to clear it of the goats and chickens, and were greeted by a crowd of young Masai warriors and Herb Watschinger, the Austrian doctor who had ministered to these handsome people for decades. He was one of the few *wazungu* I ever met who spoke Masai fluently. He and his group of elderly nuns were old friends of Hugh and Annie, and I was warmly welcomed.

Herb invited us into his ramshackle office and sat us down. Then he got Hugh to pass over a crate of intravenous fluids in glass, half-litre bottles. He then proceeded to take a bottle of 0,9% Saline, open the top and pour it into four shot glasses.

"Prost!" he exclaimed, smacking his lips. Hugh and Annie followed suite, and then I took a whiff – and it was the heady vapour of schnapps which delighted my nostrils!

Herb, like all the missionaries I ever met, was a most resourceful person. One had to be in these far-out parts of Africa. He had a brother in Vienna who was a pharmacist, and every year he sent Herb a crate of various home-made schnapps disguised in intravenous fluid bottles, to keep him going, whilst avoiding any awkward customs tax.

It reminded me of Jack and the jolly elephant hunters in Cameroun whose brother had a canning factory and sent this violent gang of missionaries .375 Magnum bullets sealed in tins of Jolly Green Giant corn. There was no end to the tricks these religious chaps got up to – and I learned a great deal from them about comfortable survival in difficult circumstances.

The Lady with Five Breasts

Herb invited me for a ward round, something I always enjoyed, for there was always a bountiful mass of human pathology on every ward, but this time I was more than surprised. For Herb had got me down to his remote bush hospital for a particular reason.

On a bed on the female ward was a tall Masai lady with five breasts. Not just five breasts, but two of them with tumours, one of which was cancerous, and the other turned out to be tuberculosis, that most insidious and ubiquitous of diseases. Furthermore, this lady was eight months pregnant, and of the other three breasts only one had a functioning nipple.

So it was that on Boxing Day 1975, feeling a mite jaded after Herb and the nuns outstanding Christmas Day barbecue overlooking Olduvai Gorge, I was to be found performing two mastectomies – still leaving three breasts on that same patient. Never before, and never again.

Don came down a month post-partum and took the other two non-functioning breasts off. The two black and white photos I possess of this patient, pre- and post-op, remain a heart-warming memory of those African years. It was not just the good success of Don and I, but the enormous smile cracking the face of this young mother with her one-month-old baby, swaddled under a tropical sun.

Hitching across the Nubian Desert

Six months had gone in a flash. I had never had such fun nor seen so much of life, but it was time to return to England. I was sad to leave all my friends at the Flying Doctors, but I knew I would be going back one day.

I had decided to cash in my return ticket and hitchhike back to Cairo from Nairobi. Having read Churchill's "The River Wars", I wanted to see the Sudan and experience a bit of this recent British colonial history for myself, as well as explore some of the river Nile.

My first lift was from Hugh, who had been asked to ferry a twin-engine Piper Aztec to Khartoum, which is how we ended up at the Khartoum Club, drinking pink gins with the stewardesses of Sudan Air, one of whom, Jenny, I would meet again a month later in Cairo. My father was posted to Sudan during the war, and also drank pink gins at the Khartoum Club, which was then another British expatriate oasis. But today you will not find alcohol on sale anywhere in Khartoum.

As we approached the confluence of the Blue and White Niles just south of Khartoum, we could see below us the vast plain between the two rivers which the Saudis were investing heavily in, creating what they called 'the breadbasket of Arabia', using sophisticated and extensive irrigation systems. After the miles of featureless desert we had been flying over for five hours, the geometric patterns of the green fields below us was remarkable.

After two fun days together in Khartoum, Hugh flew back to Nairobi and I continued hitching out of Khartoum to Omdurman. The battle of Omdurman marked the beginning of the end of British colonialism in north-east Africa, and Churchill wrote brilliantly about it and the part he played in his book,´The River Wars´. At that time the Mahdi's troops were fighting against the first British Maxim machine guns on horseback with spears and a few rifles. There was even a museum at Omdurman to celebrate this British victory in 1898 over the Mahdi's successor, the Khalifa, but when I entered it I found it dusty and un-cared for.

However, inside was one of the most extraordinary machines I have ever seen. It was the first desert armoured car, a very ancient Rolls-Royce, dating from 1914. It was a monster with six wheels, armour-plated and with gun mounts. It had seen better days, but still looked a fearsome weapon.

Omdurman has always had a famous silver market which I visited and was amazed to see the skills of the silversmiths, using primitive means to make the finest filigree jewellery. Much of the silver they used came from smelted Maria Teresa dollars.

The Road to Meröwe

Then it was out into the heat of the Nubian desert. In mid-August the heat was truly oppressive. As usual I was carrying my guitar and knapsack. My only sustenance was half a melon, a bottle of Egyptian brandy and my one-litre leather bota of water.

I wanted to get to Meröwe and see its pyramids. They were far off the tourist track and unheard of by most people. The pyramids of

Meröwe were part of another ancient middle eastern civilisation which I was most keen to learn more about. The road north from Omdurman was hard, hot and dusty and lifts were few and far between. There were no trees to shelter under, so in between lifts I just gently fried in the sun. It was not pleasant.

My best lift was on a lorry full of sacks of peanuts, maize and humanity. There must have been 10 other humans on top of the hessian sacks, half of them women, several with tubercular coughs expectorating regularly, much of which blew over me, mixed with desert sand and dust. So, I was not looking my best when the truck dropped me at Meröwe as dusk fell.

The mysterious pyramids of which I had read years before were silhouetted against the setting sun and having nowhere else to sleep I ended up on top of one of them, whose stone apex had collapsed leaving a flat but rocky floor. I was hungry and had already shared the melon with my fellow travellers on the truck. I had only my bottle of brandy for company. I went to sleep that night with my stomach rattling, the sky a galaxy of brilliant stars, and just the utter silence which enveloped me and the empty desert.

The mysterious pyramids of Merowe

Meröwe has long fascinated archaeologists for its antiquity and its origins. The hieroglyphics which cover the tombs have only recently been de-ciphered, and they represent a civilisation which existed over 3000 years ago.

The following day I met the eccentric English professor who was running the archaeological dig at Meröwe with a group of Canadian students. They had just discovered a skeleton at the fifth level of excavation, and when he found I was a doctor, he insisted on showing me this collection of ancient bones. All I could tell him was that it was almost certainly a male, and bore no signs of injury or disease. It was an interesting diversion on my trip across the desert.

That night together with the students we had a party on top of another, larger pyramid and easily drained the remains of my brandy. Going to sleep fairly drunk on top of a pyramid in the middle of the Nubian desert remains a crystal memory from this voyage.

Wadi Halfa to Aswan and the Temples of Abu Simnel.

From Atbara I took the train to Wadi Halfa. It was a capitulation in some ways, but hitchhiking across a desert is not only draining but dangerous, and after two weeks I needed a rest.

My father had been stationed at Wadi Halfa for a period during the war, as it was then a strategic outpost between The Sudan and Egypt, but when I arrived I found only a scabby collection of shacks selling lentils and bread. There was nothing else except the ferry which traversed Lake Nasser to Aswan and Egypt, on which I booked a ride. I then lived on water and lentil soup for three days, along with a jolly gang of Arabs who only wanted me to play my guitar as we chugged north under a stifling sun.

We passed Abu Simnel at dawn on the second day, and I marvelled at the work which had been carried out in order to rescue the massive stone statues from the waters of the Aswan dam.

Everywhere we passed there was now more evidence of a great previous civilisation, and Aswan was the entry gate to even more riches along the Nile valley leading to Cairo.

Aswan was magical after my desiccated days in the Nubian desert. I drank litres of freshly squeezed orange juice from the many stalls and filled myself on falafel and lamb kebabs and slept in a decent hostel for just eight Egyptian pounds, including a breakfast of yoghurt and honey with pistachio nuts. Paradise!

Then I continued north to Luxor where I spent two days studying and admiring the architecture. How did the kings and emperors manage to construct these massive edifices?

On the Dangers of Sleeping with Bats, and Histoplasmosis.

Once again, I crossed the Nile in a felucca, just as I had done in 1971 on my way to the Valley of the Queens. I spent the night in a deserted tomb, where my only neighbours were a thousand bats.

My progress was slow from Karnack as the Egyptians were not tuned in to hitchhiking. Then I started to develop a cough, and by the time I reached Cairo I was coughing up blood as well as sputum, and also had a bad fever. I found a cheap hotel in Tahiri Square and collapsed under four blankets, sweating like a fountain.

I was even sicker the next morning, still feverish and coughing up blood, but I had a Sudan Air flight to catch back to England, so I spent a fortune on a taxi, feeling far too feeble to contemplate an Egyptian bus ride.

Imagine my joy to be welcomed on board the plane by Jenny from the Khartoum Club, which now seemed a century ago. She was the first-class hostess on this flight, and she brought me endless glasses of champagne, which assuaged the symptoms of the pneumonia, to such an extent that by the time we arrived at Heathrow I could barely speak to my father, who had come to pick me up.

He dropped me at my cottage in Cowbeech where I continued weak and ill, still coughing up blood, which worried me considerably. I went to my GP and was investigated, had a chest X-ray, saw a specialist in chest disease, but no diagnosis emerged.

By now I was really worried about my health and was suffering greatly, but I had an important date to keep with some old friends in Liverpool, which is where, miraculously, I found the diagnosis and the cure for my serious problem.

"It´s batshit", said the Colonel.

I went up to Liverpool for the reunion at the Anatomy Department still feeling unwell. I arrived at 1100hrs one morning – just in time for tea with the anatomy team. I related my latest adventures in Africa to acclaim, including the mystery of my recent, persistent pneumonia.

"Batshit!", spoke Colonel Parry, definitively. "Batshit!" "Excuse me sir," I said, "why batshit?"

"You slept with the bats", he replied. "It's histoplasmosis, or I'm a dodo!"

Histoplasmosis was a disease I had never heard of until then and is one of several zoonotic diseases which bats carry. There are two varieties – the regular, and the pneumonic which like the Black Death, destroys the lungs in a day and you die from the asphyxia of flooded lungs in 100% of cases. I must have had the other variety.

Still coughing blood, I returned to Sussex and saw my GP with my new diagnosis. He gave me a course of erythromycin, and within a week I was cured. Subsequently I wrote a letter to the Colonel, thanking him for his great diagnosis and confirming that he most certainly was not a dodo.

God bless the Colonel and his knowledge of tropical diseases, for even the specialist at Eastbourne hospital had missed the diagnosis, and this disease could easily have killed me. After four weeks of atypical pneumonia it was a pleasure to feel alive again, and I gave thanks to all medical practitioners.

I recently heard on BBC R4 that 68% of the British are working in a job they do not like, and would have changed had they known better. I think that is a very sad thing indeed, and very bad for them and their country.

I have been fortunate to do a job for 50 years which I not only enjoy, but love!

12. BRIGHTON: THE LONG HOT SUMMER OF 1976

After my recent stimulating months in East Africa, the time had come to start studying again if I was to have any chance of being taken seriously as a general surgeon. There was one essential hurdle to surmount - the Final Fellowship exam of the Royal College of Surgeons in General Surgery. I began looking for a suitable middle-grade registrar job in general surgery which could sustain me while I was studying.

On the advice of my old Percy Street mate Ian, who was then anaesthetic registrar at St Thomas´ in London, I applied for a registrar job there in general surgery. The old boy network was very much in operation all over Britain but was especially strong in London – seen as the seat of all learning. Anyone who wanted a consultant´s job in the Sussex area usually graduated from one of the London medical schools. But coming from Liverpool I had none of those advantages.

On the appointed day I sat with six other hopeful candidates all chatting about their London lives, whilst I admired my favourite blue flower-power tie which I had chosen for this august occasion.

The sight as I entered the vast interview room was reminiscent of the Nuremburg trials, and about as amusing. Seven very serious general surgeons faced me, asking awkward questions about my adventures in Africa as well as the latest surgical research. It was no great surprise to be rejected. It appeared that club ties or equivalent were *de rigeur* at these formal professional interviews. Also, a short back and sides, whilst my luxuriant growth was falling around my ears and neck.

Later, as I was gathering up my damaged ego, one of the interviewing surgeons came up to me and said,

"How can you expect to get a job with a tie like that?", gesticulating at my near-fluorescent tie. And that is how I met Tony Lane-Roberts (LR), a consultant general surgeon in Brighton, and became his surgical registrar at the Royal Sussex County hospital. It was known by everyone as 'The County' and was the referral centre for the district, which included four other local hospitals, Bevendean, Brighton General, Hove General and the Women's hospital.

When Brighton went Mediterranean

I knew I was not destined for the heady heights of London. I was already warming to Brighton beach, the seafront with all its amusements, the two piers and the busy streets of Kemptown with a pub every 50 yards and scantily dressed maidens wherever one looked.

Nobody of my generation will forget the long hot summer of 1976. There was even a newly appointed Minister for Drought, Dennis Healy, sitting in Whitehall, and Brighton became positively Mediterranean. I was enjoying patrolling the seafront in my beach-buggy, Beautiful Blue, the same one which Sandy and I had built four years earlier. It was a great babe-magnet. Sadly, I sold her the following year, but consoled myself with a BMW 2002 Sports sedan as a replacement.

My contract in Brighton was as a middle-grade registrar in general surgery for two years, divided into four rotating six-month firms. Each surgical firm was led by two consultant general surgeons who each had their own particular speciality. There was one senior registrar who stood in for consultants and covered all the firms. Each firm also had a middle-grade registrar, of whom I was one, and then there were four newly qualified junior housemen who were responsible for the routine clerking and admission of patients and the daily running of the ward.

During the following two years it was in these tight-knit teams that I also learnt more about vascular, breast surgery, endocrinology and urology as well as the wider scope of general surgery.

My first day on-call at the Royal Sussex County hospital was a harbinger of things to come. My bleep went off barely an hour after I had put on my white coat and clogs. It was A+E calling me for a penetrating chest wound. Scary!

An 18-year-old girl lay on the gurney, having been shot in the chest with a gun. She was alive, and did not appear to be in shock, so we did the usual assessments and booked theatre while I wondered what the hell I was going to do. It was my first day at the County, I had never opened a chest in anger yet, and I knew no one who could help me.

So, I rang the on-call consultant, Keith Powell, known to everyone as Father. Better safe than sorry, and it was my very first day in a new hospital.

I had the wound over the heart opened and was looking at a silver bullet bouncing on and off the left ventricle through a small perforation in the pericardium when a small fierce man in theatre greens appeared at my side saying, "Just take the bloody thing out!" Which I did, with a pair of long forceps. I was sweating profusely, but as I closed up I was thinking this was really how wide-ranging general surgery is. You never knew what you were going to face, yet the problem always had to be dealt with one way or another. Therefore, referral for a senior's advice was a vital part of our training and protection.

Keith Powell appeared a to be a fearsome figure, even though he was not physically big. He had a snappy voice which often sounded angry, but it was just his way of speaking. In fact he was not just very kind, but an innovative and intrepid surgeon as I learnt during the second six month rotation when I joined his firm.

Amongst other surgical gems, he gave me a copy of a paper he had written in the 1950's concerning his innovative, trans-nasal approach to remove a pituitary tumour. Just the thought of ever doing brain surgery terrified me, even though as a general surgeon I would need to learn to be prepared for neurosurgical trauma cases.

The Day the Doctors went on Strike

By strange coincidence, the day after I started work was the very day that all the junior medical staff at the County hospital went on strike for UMTs – Units of Medical Time. For the first time we were about to be financially rewarded for all our extra hours of duty, which were considerable. I was supposed to be assisting my other new consultant with his surgical outpatient clinic at Brighton General, when I found myself in a very difficult dilemma. I had to show solidarity with all my new colleagues, but I also had my clinical duties to perform, and I was just beginning an important new job.

I went to Brighton General and introduced myself to this consultant, Bob Gumpert, saying, "I'm dreadfully sorry sir, but I am officially on strike, and feel I have to join the protest".

It says a lot for Bob Gumpert, whose specialities were breast, thyroid and vascular surgery, that he allowed me to go and join the march along the seafront, even though he now had 37 patients to see by himself. I still feel a twitch of guilt about that.

Doctors were not known for making noisy protests in those days. The photo from the Guardian newspaper of us all in our white coats, and me in my Swedish clogs striding from the Marina to the Palace Pier, banners raised aloft, was posted in the Doctors Mess the next day. It was an epic moment, but that is how we were then, fighting for our rights and taking to the streets for the first time ever.

On the Finer Art of Surgery

Bobby G became my mentor for six months and is still a valued friend. He was a meticulous surgeon, much of whose work was dealing with breast cancer as well as vascular and endocrine surgery, so I learned a great deal, for he was an excellent teacher as well as surgeon.

When you are performing surgery on recurrent varicose veins the sapheno-femoral junction in the groin turns into what surgeons call 'tiger country'. The veins have become huge and thin-walled, the normal anatomy is distorted and you are less than a millimetre away from disaster as you incise the fibrous adventitial layer over the femoral vein. It is then that you need nerves of steel and a steady hand.

It was equally nerve-wracking operating in the neck when performing a thyroidectomy. The thyroid gland is very well supplied with blood vessels, so haemorrhage is a constant risk, but there is also the recurrent laryngeal nerve to find and isolate - and never to inadvertently bisect, for that is what drives the vocal cords.

I must have done scores of these operations with Bob and learned a huge amount about delicate surgery in dangerous areas from him, and we never had a serious problem. His bedside manner was also impeccable, and he was respected by all the staff. He was one of relatively few surgeons who could communicate meaningfully with the patients. It was often left to me, the registrar, to translate for the patient the unintelligible diagnosis and prognosis the consultant had given as he passed from bed to bed.

Academic Surgery : preparing for Final Fellowship

I had signed up to take the Final Fellowship exam in General Surgery in London later in the summer of 1976, and for the first time in my life I really hit the library. I became great friends with Judy Lehman, the excellent chief librarian, who was later justly honoured by the Queen for her services to medical librarianship.

In those days the Post-Graduate centre was at Brighton General hospital, another Victorian monolith at the top of Elm Grove. Judy had started the library practically from scratch and had worked marvels.

For the first time in years, I was highly motivated to study. Judy was the one who helped me most to learn the art of intellectual study, for she also knew about pedagogy. She showed me how to use the Journal rack, research relevant articles and generally get my mind into gear for the big exam. This was all new to me, as till then I had been some sort of 'jobbing surgeon' with little interest in academia.

I was beginning to realise that I had a great deal to learn about the whole field of surgery, including research, and not much time in which to study once the clinical work was taken care of.

I was fortunate at the County to work with good doctors of all descriptions, and some excellent nurses led by the Matron, Sister Eaves, who was so authoritative that all the consultants were rather scared of her. She took no nonsense from anyone and was respected by all. She could spot a cobweb from 20 metres, and if the beds did not all have 'hospital corners' correctly aligned when they were made up, we all knew about that too.

We four surgical registrars were all good friends, and we covered for each other on occasion. The whole surgical department had a clinical academic meeting every Friday – the Mortality and Morbidity Meeting where we each had to present a clinical case in turn. It was a good preparation for the clinical surgical *viva voces* coming up fast on the horizon as Final FRCS beckoned.

We used to be on-call from Samson's burger bar in Kemptown, their Jamaican chili burger being for me the peak of burger perfection. It was there that Rick, an anaesthetic SHO, who was my neighbour in the Nurses Home, met Gillian, an architecture student who served us our burgers, and they are still happily married some 43 years later. Alastair, their eldest child and I still share a passion for Biggles.

The Social Side of Surgery

There was a highly developed social scene at the hospital, dealing with everything from our regular trips to Young´s Brewery in South London, to fishing on the high seas, and much more.

Roy was head porter at Brighton General and the team leader of what was then known as the Social and Recreational Club – which mainly involved the infamous Anaesthetic parties where everybody got a sniff of Nitrous Oxide from the blue cylinder at the entrance to the rave. There were also regular outings to pubs and other refreshment centres – and the SS ´Enterprise´.

The 'Enterprise´ was a 17- foot, half-decked fishing boat, bobbing gently on the waters of Newhaven harbour. Roy was our Captain, and once saved my life by very quick thinking when I drunkenly fell overboard about eight miles off Brighton.

 The current swept me away so swiftly from the boat that it became almost invisible in the waves. The long-length safety buoy which Roy chucked with all his strength, whilst my nine other medic companions were enjoying their beers, is what saved my life that day. It landed a foot away from me, but a God-given wave washed it into my aching arms, and I was saved.

"You stoopid runt", or some similar expletive came from Roy as we headed back to Newhaven and ´The Hope´ for even more beer while my sodden clothes dried out. And I was second ´on-call´ again from 2000 hrs. Oh Gosh! Life can be so cruel.

Every Tuesday afternoon during that hot summer of ´76 we doctors used to fill Beautiful Blue with beer and drive to Newhaven where 10 of us medical practitioners used to spend a glorious afternoon hauling in mackerel and getting drunk.

I have some great Super-8 cine film of Jace, another SHO anaesthetist, hauling in a line with 12 mackerel on 12 hooks. Awesome stuff on the high seas under a boiling sun. That was how it was in the summer of ´76.

However, at the same time as we were all having such fun on board 'The Enterprise', I should have been running an Out-Patient Urology clinic at Hove General hospital.

A Tricky Moment with Sir Henry

Henry Clarke was a very fine urologist who had an extensive private practice, and who spent most of Tuesday with his private patients, leaving me to manage his afternoon clinic alone, which I felt was unfair.

He was the last real gentleman surgeon I ever worked with. He always wore wing collars, and a black, formal 3-piece suit, with highly polished shoes from Jermyn Street. He had a regal, but quiet presence, and the patients were in awe of him. Even the sisters all deferred to Sir Henry, as we used to call him. I remain grateful for all that he and Neville Harrison and Mike Royle, the other two urology consultants taught me of urological surgery during my time at Hove General. It became a large component of my general surgical work during my years in Africa.

After a few weeks of frustrating absence from the good ship 'Enterprise' I decided to take action, and left a message for Sir Henry saying that I would be unavailable the next Tuesday afternoon – and I went fishing every subsequent Tuesday, until one day Henry said, "I understood that you were to assist me in my Tuesday clinic, but I have not seen you for some time"

"It's because I go fishing sir", I replied glibly, which caused Henry to wobble his eyes and struggle to speak. This sort of renegade behaviour was outside his orbit, and within the medical profession was tantamount to mutiny.

Then I explained to him about his habit of arriving for the 1400h clinic at around 1700h, when he had finished with his private patients, and I still had another 20 patients to see. He got my point.

He made a deal with me – I could go fishing alternate Tuesdays and do his clinic on the other, which seemed to me very fair, but it was yet one more nail in the coffin of my surgical career in England.

On Acute Trauma - Locking Apophyses.

The long hot summer continued most agreeably until the morning I awoke in the Nurses Home, stretched my length in the bed to welcome a new day, and then screeched in pain as something went ´click´ in my spine and I became effectively paralysed.

It took me half an hour to get out of bed and into my clothes, and every second I was in excruciating pain. Something serious had suddenly gone wrong in my body and I was now a bundle of pain as I headed for Hove General and a morning of trans-urethral prostatectomies with Mike Royle.

A trans-urethral prostatectomy is no easy task at the best of times, working down a 6-inch tunnel with a tiny diathermy cutter and blood vessels everywhere. After the first procedure I knew I could do no more. I was sweating with pain and even the nurses looked concerned at my obvious collapse.

Mike told me to go off, which though a great relief left me feeling guilty at the other six pending cases. I drove back to the County wondering what on earth to do. I was in extreme agony with every movement and knew I had done something to my spine, for around the mid-lumbar region was the focus of this pain, but I did not know why. I only knew that I needed to get it sorted out most urgently.

I went to the hospital bar for a beer and a think, for suddenly and unexpectedly I had become seriously incapacitated and incapable of work. Sitting at the bar I was delighted to see Jane, one of my favourite physios, enjoying a quiet moment.

I have always had great respect for physios as well as nurses. They were constantly on our wards caring for post-op patients and were a jolly gang, good-looking as well as being very capable. I put my acute problem to Jane.

"Oh, you need to see Julie", she said. "She's the manipulator!"

And within five minutes I was explaining my acutely painful problem to Julie in the Physio Department.

Julie told me to lie on her couch and then gave me a good examination, pressing all the way down my spine till the mid-lumbar region, when I nearly jumped off the couch with pain.

"You've locked your apophyses", she announced, and then told me what she intended to do. She made me lie prone on a hard wooden bench. Then pressing her locked hands down on my spine as I lay face-down, she said that when she got to the site of the problem, she would give a hard push and then, if I was lucky, I may hear a click in my head.

And that is exactly what happened. At the critical point she leaned her weight down, something went 'crack' and I felt the base of my skull rattle most strangely. Suddenly the acute, agonising pain had gone.

I still had soreness around the lumbar area, but now I could move normally again. It was miraculous, and I gave Julie a big smacker which made her laugh. It was barely 11 o'clock, just three hours after my disastrous start to the day, and I had already been diagnosed and cured – and not a doctor in sight.

I returned to the doctor's bar and cogitated. The apophyses are minute bony appendages on the vertebrae which inter-articulate as the spine moves. In stretching that morning, I had obviously overdone the twisting and forced the apophyses out of position. I myself could not have made that correct diagnosis of locked apophyses, nor could I have solved the problem. Only someone with great knowledge and skill could have managed it, and in meeting Julie I had been very lucky.

If I had been just a regular patient, I would still be waiting, in pain, to call my GP for an appointment. Then there would be the wait for an Orthopaedic outpatient appointment, which would be at least two months, by which time the damage would have been done and I would be left suffering chronic back-ache, as so many people do.

I considered that I had been incredibly fortunate. Firstly, in the good friends I had amongst the medical fraternity at the County, and then to have found Julie the Manipulator. I got out of my seat and walked down into St George's Street where there was a flower shop and spent £6 on a big chrysanthemum plant which I took to Julie.

"Gosh!", she said, "you didn't have to do this. I've never had a present before".

"What!", I exclaimed, shocked. "It's the very least I could do after your good work". And I walked out thinking how her department ought to be full of flowers of gratitude. I was still sore and stiff the next day but well enough to face my patients and their blood-filled urine bags at Hove General, impressing Sister Gloria and the other nurses with the story of my dramatic cure.

Of all the unpleasant things in life, I hate and fear pain the most. Pain is a daily part of our doctors' lives, but to feel it from the patient's side of the bed gives a very different view.

Final FRCS

The day of the written FRCS exam arrived. We were all stressed after months of hard study on top of all our clinical work, averaging about 90 hours a week, something which would not be tolerated in today's NHS.

But all those long clinical hours also added to our experience and expertise. The exams were still scary, as high-level professional exams always are, for they are designed to be a severe test of general surgical competence, but I would never be better prepared. The papers took three days to complete, and then came the clinical exams.

Once again, I was on my way to the exam halls. Passing The Queen's Head on the corner of Queen Square, it was too much of a temptation on this sunny afternoon, when I could have been hauling in mackerel instead of sweating fear.

I sat outside the pub with a pint of IPA enjoying the summer scene when suddenly above me a window opened and a huge shower of water deluged me and my Burtons suit – for I was on my way to the Surgical Pathology viva, the most feared of all the tests and the final hurdle.

"Jesus Christ!", I shouted in shock, and looked up to see a woman watering the geranium boxes above. Then a very big and muscular bloke exited the pub, saying to me, "Don't you talk to my missus like that! What's your problem?"

I took this as a seriously negative omen, and hurried on my way thinking dark thoughts, until I came upon 'The Little Dorrit', a quaint old pub which I just seemed to magnetically enter. Before I knew it another pint of life-saving London Pride brew was in my hand.

I was feeling somewhat relaxed as I waited in the queue of hopefuls about to enter the Pathology library to be examined, but the diuretic effects of alcohol soon became apparent, and by the time it was my turn for the inquisition I could hardly speak for the rising fundus of my bladder.

"Please may I go to the toilet", was my greeting to these two fierce men in white coats waiting to grill me. Not an auspicious start, but when I returned, able to think straight once again, I just sailed through their barrage of questions and formalin-filled glass pots of dead specimens. For some reason I felt no fear, in fact I felt almost confident.

As a *coup de grâce*, the more intimidating examiner, who bore a striking resemblance to a mortician I once knew, handed me a jar with what looked like a squashed kidney in it. Just a blob of protoplasm with no real form.

"Tell me about this", he said, staring at me through his pince-nez.

In a moment of true inspiration – I have no idea how I found it – I said with total confidence, "It's an adrenal gland", which rendered him mildly surprised, and looking into his eyes, I just knew I was right.

I was sailing on a sea of good fortune, assisted by two pints of London Pride.

That night my name appeared on the list at the top of the stairs in the Department of Pathology, and I was now F.R.C.S. – one of the fellowship of surgeons, despite my unconventional approach to life and surgery.

The strangest thing is that my lucky guess in that surgical pathology viva was an almost exact repetition of my final undergraduate pathology viva with Professor Heath in Liverpool five years earlier. In both cases I had been presented with a specimen I could only guess at, and both times I had guessed correctly. I cannot explain this good fortune, except by knowing that Lady Luck plays her cards, and if she smiles on you then you get lucky. People talk about being born under a lucky star, and I think that I was one.

That night Ian and I got really drunk. He had also just passed his Anaesthetic Fellowship and went on to become a very well-known and respected anaesthetist in London. One of my favourite memories of that glorious summer is the photo of Ian and I with our parents sitting outside The Queen's Head having a celebratory drink after the degree ceremony, and Ian remains one of my oldest medical friends.

One of the things that these middle-grade years of training did establish was a life-long group of friends and professional acquaintances. A large part of this was related to the enormous number of hours we all had to work, reducing any social life to a bare minimum.

In those days we were never restricted in the hours we worked. It was understood that we registrars always did a one-in-two rota on call. There was always a consultant not too far away in case things got tricky. The senior registrar had always done at least four years as a middle-grade registrar and was only a step away from becoming a consultant. Both of them during my years at Brighton were very fine fellows and were an asset on our brewery and pub outings.

On Going Home by Ambulance

It was at The Racehorse roadhouse in Pyecombe one summer's evening, celebrating the 25th birthday of Tom, my surgical houseman at that time, that I was privileged to witness the resourcefulness of Stuart, our current senior registrar. By the time 'last orders' came, all 12 of us were well into our cups, with no hope of driving home safely. Stuart went to the public phone and called the County, asking to speak to Eddy, who ran the ambulance service from Brighton General.

Within 10 minutes an ambulance made a very brief stop outside the pub, and 12 doctors were soon travelling fast towards the County, Tom on the gurney in alcoholic stupor, vomiting gently. Tony, our chauffeur for the evening, put the blue lights and siren on as we hit the Steine and we made it up Edward Street past the Law Courts at speed and into the safety of the A+E department, where Tony threw us out.

We later clubbed together and bought a bottle of Johnny Walker for the ambulance staff – really great guys they were. Female paramedics had yet to make their mark.

Tom was my surgical house officer for the first six months. He was a very funny chap, and a great companion on the wards. He was also very responsible and caring, so my time with him was a real pleasure, and we also had some fun. Like me he always enjoyed a laugh at the expense of someone else, and as his registrar in general surgery I suffered my share, which included one of my more serious mistakes.

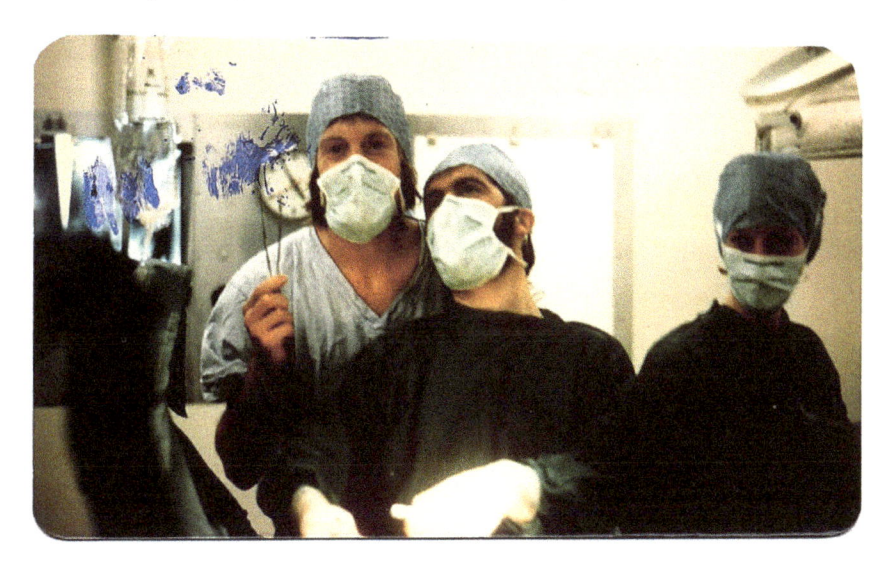

SHO Tom and me. 0455h. Another appendicectomy

An Embarrassing Disaster

I had considerable direct responsibility for major elective operations on the weekly lists, one of which was cholecystectomy – the removal of the gall-bladder plus stones. Cholecystitis was a very common affliction in those days, affecting both men and women, and often leading to the inevitable laparotomy, exploration of the liver and bile-ducts for stones, and their removal.

There were many big blood vessels knocking around these deep abdominal parts, including the Vena Cava, which was never, ever filled with cava, just gallons of dark red blood.

All us surgeons needed at least one assistant to heave on the retractors whilst we hunted for stones, and then did the obligatory post-cholecystectomy XRay of the main bile duct – just to confirm that there were no stones left. If there were, it usually meant a further laparotomy and exploration, which was not good news for the patient, so this intra-operative XRay was very important.

On this particular day, I checked the still-dripping XRay film brought into theatre by the radiographer, saw it to be clear of stones, and started to close the peritoneum. Most of these patients were obese, which made the whole operation much more difficult, especially the closure, and these patients wounds often became infected due to the impossibility of completely sealing every tiny blood vessel hidden within the disgusting rolls of grease.

Three days later, just before the consultant ward round, in came Tom, his usual smiling self, with an XRay report and the films of this particular patient´s gallbladder system.

I checked the films on the ward XRay screen, and said to Tom, "I think there is an air-bubble in the main duct".

"Er, ahem, sir" When Tom got like this, I knew there was bad news in the offing.

"That is not what the Radiologist says! It appears that there is a large stone still left in the main duct!", he said, smiling.

My short, sharp expletive awoke the comatose patient in the next bed, and before I knew it Father Powell had appeared at the ward entrance, flanked by Stuart, the senior registrar as well as a visiting medical student. Oh God! It was a real pants-down situation.

The case-history and operative results were given by Tom, as usual, and then came my report. Well, it was not one of my greatest moments, explaining my surgical incompetence to this eager crowd.

Father Powell explained in detail to this luscious young student from Guys, the potentially fatal consequences of retained bile-duct stones, as I looked on, considerably shamed. Tom, hiding behind Sister James´s pinafore, with his cheesy grin spread all over his face.

It cost me a pint in the doctor's bar later that day, and I had still not quite recovered my usual poise and elegance.

One day, months later, whilst working as the district surgeon at Voi in the shadow of the Taita Hills in Kenya, ten thousand miles away from Brighton, a letter arrived.

It was a very rare event in those days and was from Keith Powell. He had also enclosed the three-month follow-up radiology report on this patient, confirming that the inconvenient bile stone had passed spontaneously, and that the duct system was now clear and normal. That was how caring my surgical mentors were.

On Hospital Style in the '70s

I was pleasantly surprised to see how outrageous the clothing styles of my fellow medics at the County were, having just spent several months as a flying surgeon in Kenya, dressed only in a tie-dyed tank-top and cut-off jeans.

Only the consultants and senior registrars went about in 3-piece suits. The rest of us looked a real shower. I was an outstanding example in my jeans and Swedish clogs, an amusing variety of pin-badges adorning my white coat, such as, "Help the Aged" and an image of Che Guevara. Of us all, it was Steve, another SHO anaesthetist I often worked with, who was the most outstanding.

His hair was black and reached to his shoulders, and he also had an impressively long black beard. So, it was not a huge surprise when Sister Vernon and I, sharing a post-op pot of tea in the surgeon's room, both heard a loud cry of "Jesus Christ be praised!", coming from the female patient Steve was in the process of re-awakening after the latest of my emergency surgical interventions.

On returning to consciousness, the first thing this patient had set eyes on was the smiling face fungus of Steve and realised she had finally achieved Celestial Orbit. No big surprise that Steve was forever afterwards known as JC.

Rick was not much better. He was another SHO in anaesthetics, and was my neighbour in the Nurses Home where we resided. He styled himself on Groucho Marx, and had the moustache, as well as a long fuzzy mop of sticking-up hair. He also had a Lancia saloon with an elegant display of rust, in which we used to visit country drinking houses. He was a Mod and used to have a Vespa with about 20 mirrors, but he knew I was a born Rocker, and that I had always had a proper motorbike since the age of 14. We were also both avid push bikers and used to bike all over the Downs and Brighton's hilly streets in the summer evenings.

Rick and I biking The Sussex Downs

He later became a GP-anaesthetist in Lewes, and during my final 10 years in the NHS as resident surgeon at the Victoria Hospital, he and I must have done hundreds of operations with never any catastrophe. He also became my excellent GP, and certainly saved my life on at least one occasion. We are still the best of friends, even though he did not always appreciate my sense of humour.

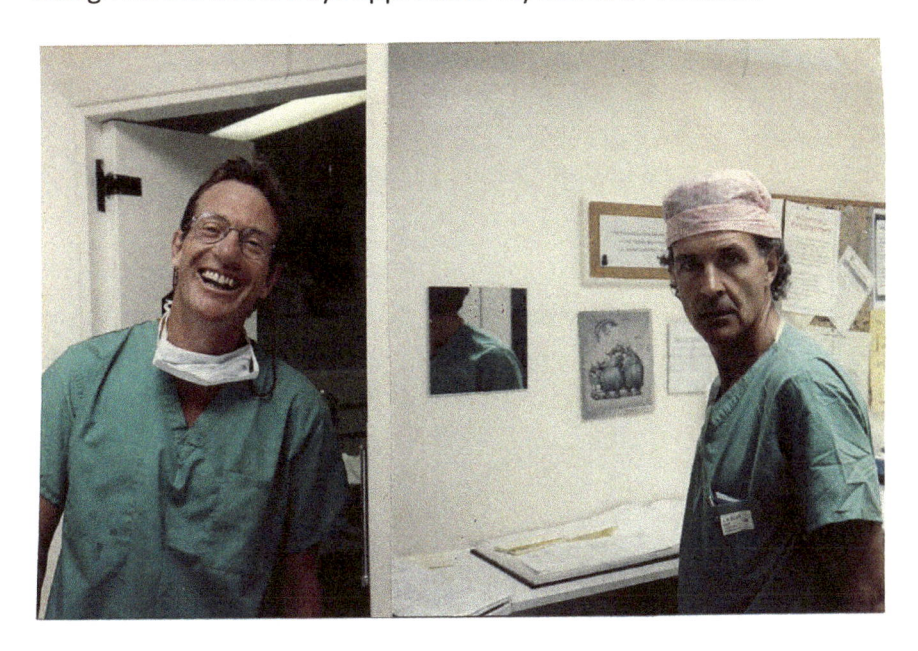

He didn't always get my sense of humour

It was biking with Rick one day in 1977 that I first spotted the old, terraced house in Arundel Street which was to become my British base for the next 30 years. It was just 10 minutes' walk from the County, bang in the middle of Kemptown with its brewery, laundry, pottery and carpenters workshops, bordering on Whitehawk where all *los pobres* lived.

It was also just 100 metres from Marine Parade which ran for seven miles east to Shoreham along the sea-front, which was in later years to become my roller-blading track.

Another of my surgical registrar colleagues was Jim, an Australian with the driest sense of humour I ever heard. The nearest he ever came to formal dress was his well-worn Australian bush jacket. He was a fecund Antipodean with a large family of kids who all fitted into his orange VW campervan, along with a big hairy dog called Vince. This genial dog used to enjoy wandering around the wards whilst we sat drinking beers and burning burgers on the big grassy slope below the nurses' home.

Jim was a master of the Australian aphorism. He used to say interesting things to patients, such as, to those with intestinal obstruction, "Well, me ole dear, les just open you up and see if we can find that nasty wombat", reducing more than a few to a state of frank terror.

It was easy to tell that Jim had spent a few years as a surgeon with the Australian Flying Doctor Service, and for that we were blood brothers. During my two years in Brighton, he taught me a lot of slightly more refined bush surgery than I had been used to in Kenya, and I was very sorry when we parted company in 1978.

The Halcyon Days of Summer 1976

The sloping lawn below the Nurses Home had one of the best views in Brighton, looking south to Marine Parade and the beach, which was becoming more topless by the day. The nurses we were feasting with were also skimpily clad as well, thus considerably assisting our morale. Truly, those were halcyon days.

Every summer there was the Consultants v Juniors cricket match, in the hospital grounds at Bevendean, just a stone's throw from the conveniently sited local graveyard.

We all wore whites, but the head-gear was impressively outrageous. Most of us doctors were ex-public school, so cricket was already instilled in us, though at school I never took it too seriously myself, preferring always to sit in the scoring box smoking a fag.

The photo of us all from June 1977 is a classic. Jace won the hat competition that year, rocking up in a heavily stained pith-helmet. Bobby G, my consultant at that time, and an avid cricketer, even had knife-sharp creases in his impeccable white trousers. There was no doubt, the consultants always put us juniors to shame in the outfitting department, but they didn't always win the match.

1977. Consultants v Juniors Annual Cricket match-(The Juniors)

David Bowden also played for the consultants, even though he had no medical degree. In fact, he was the senior hospital administrator at the County, well-known and respected by us all. His inclusion epitomised the relations we clinicians had with our administrators at the County back then. He was actually a close friend of the consultants, and playing a game of cricket together helped solve many of the hospital's daily problems.

Doreen and her kitchen staff made the cakes and sandwiches which we had at half-time, and for this auspicious occasion they even had their corners cut off. All in all, it was a most civilised moment for all of us. Bob and I still laugh about those memorable golden days in Brighton on my rare visits to the old country. I was never quite sure who was looking after the patients during the annual cricket match, but Tom, who was my main man on the wards and was fielding at square leg, assured me that the patients were still breathing.

In the mid-'70s the morale generated by these jolly capers was responsible in part for the good care which most patients then received.

The evenings when we were not either working, drinking or romancing girls, we used to go round to the big flat Jace shared in Sussex Square and spend the night playing with the 4-track Scalextric set, which was always in motion. I do faintly remember that there was also a 3-dimensional chess set in the flat, and my hilarious efforts to play whilst under the influence.

Sometimes during those two glorious years, I used to think about the unfortunate registrar who got the job at St Thomas' instead of me. To exchange the wonderful atmosphere in Brighton during that long hot summer for the brick and concrete and pollution of London streets, was unthinkable for me. Rather him than me, I thought, for the temperature in London hovered around 30 C for weeks at a time that summer, making the city a very unhospitable place to be. Quite apart from the hypoxic atmosphere of medical academia at a London teaching hospital.

After six months Tom left our general surgical firm to start his GP training, and along came Ashley, another very cool cat, to spend six months with me.

Ashley and the Grizzly Bear

Ashley came from landed gentry and spoke like it. Apart from a flourishing ginger beard, he also had a real bird-puller in the form of a canary-yellow Lotus Elan convertible. I was doing all right in that department as I had a BMW 2002 Sports sedan – a fast and different car in those days, but on my registrar pay and my free lodging in the Nurses Home, I could afford to run it.

It did need regular servicing, so it was as I entered the main BMW agents in Preston Park for the first time that I spotted the huge, stuffed grizzly bear standing amongst the shiny new BMW models in the show room. I was astonished, for it was not the sort of decoration usually found in car show rooms.

Suffice to say, 50 quid rapidly changed hands, my BMW was in their garage in bits, and five minutes later I now had a six- foot -tall grizzly bear to care for, and no transport.

It was time to call Ashley, my reasonably faithful SHO in general surgery, even though one could not easily call this awkward moment a surgical emergency.

Nevertheless, within 30 minutes Ashley, myself and one stuffed grizzly bear were travelling uncomfortably down London Road and into the Steine in this miniscule but speedy sports car. Which is where the police stopped us.

Suddenly, in an instant I was back at the Lime Street exit of the Mersey Tunnel. It was December 1965, when Myron and I were returning from our sheep-rustling action on the Denbigh Moors.

After a brief, gentlemanly discussion we were once again allowed to proceed, this time to the County hospital, followed by a curious police car.

The photo I have of Ashley and me in the main entrance to the County, grizzly bear rising out of the Elans passenger seat, was taken by one of the cops, shaking with laughter, and is another fine memory of those golden days.

SHO Ashley and me, plus the grizzly bear

All the junior housemen were extremely well trained and willing workers, so our ward routines were generally fairly stress-free, apart from the inevitable emergencies, which were always interesting. They ranged from the blindingly obvious, such as acute appendicitis to the totally unknown, but they all had to be managed competently.

The Roots of General Surgery - the ´acute abdomen´

There was always something magical about establishing a clinical diagnosis in an acutely ill patient, using all our hours and years of training to make that critical decision, and then deciding the definitive management.

Although much of my routine work was dealing with non-urgent, so-called 'elective' cases, it was the emergencies which provided the greater challenges. A common emergency in general surgery was abdominal pain, causing an 'acute abdomen'. This could be caused by a host of different conditions from appendicitis to volvulus, when the bowel twists on itself and becomes obstructed. And there were many other possible causes.

It was up to us registrars to make the diagnosis from the case-history and our examinations and investigations, and then proceed. In those days body scans had yet to be invented, and automated blood testing was in its infancy, so the clinical examination was critical.

Occasionally the cause was so rare and so obscure that the diagnosis was not made until the abdomen had been opened by laparotomy. These cases were often presented at our Friday surgical meetings, and even published in surgical journals. They were always memorable, one in particular.

The Case of the Obstructing Orange

Sister T oversaw the operating theatres at the County. She was a wonderful nurse, and a great human being, who ran her ship like a battle squadron. I only ever once saw her lose her cool during the two years of our life together in Brighton and predictably, I was the cause.

It was a lazy Sunday afternoon, and we were all on the grass slope outside the Nurses Home, where Rick and I lodged. The smell of burning meat filled the air, cans of booze were being cracked, and in the distant south there was a yacht regatta going on beyond the new Marina. It was as near paradise as one could get in those lazy, hazy days in Brighton town. Then my bleep went off.

An hour later I was with Sister T and her emergency gang of three in the OT, opening the abdomen of an 82-year-old lady with no teeth, who lived alone and had presented with an acute abdomen and intestinal obstruction.

This was the meat of my work as a general surgeon. You had to be able to do a laparotomy, and then cope with whatever pathology lay inside those writhing guts. Elective laparotomies for such problems as gallstones and gastric ulcers were predictable. But emergency intestinal obstruction could be anywhere from the oesophagus to the anus.

Today it was the duodenal sphincter which was obstructed, by a very strange, completely round object. Most mysterious. It was not a tumour, but something loose inside the distal stomach.

Then came the Magic Moment – when I incised the anterior stomach wall, and out popped an orange, minus its skin.

"It's a Jaffa!" I shouted in triumph, as the yellow ball fell into my eager hands.

We were all amazed at this easy bounty, which I cast into the air in triumph, crying "Catch!". Fortunately, it was caught by a staff nurse and disposed of, but Sister T was not amused and accused me of being unprofessional. I agreed, but said as it was Sunday, why didn't we just close up and get back to the party. And that's what we did. But Sister T was giving me dark looks for a couple of days.

We surgeons were so dependent on the nursing staff who were always at our side. The success of the operation depended on them just as much as the surgeon. The discipline within the operating theatre, so essential to maintaining high standards of care, was mainly the responsibility of the theatre superintendent, in this case Sister T, and she was treated with high regard by all the surgeons.

I was living my dream of becoming a general surgeon and could cope with a wide variety of general surgical problems by now, thanks to the excellent teaching I had always been so lucky to receive, and practical skills which were never forgotten.

Our surgical patients, from those in whom a diagnosis was difficult or impossible to those who presented with an obvious diagnosis, such as trauma cases, were a large part of our emergency work. Even if the diagnosis was apparent, the management was often complicated, and I relate such a case.

The Case of the Headless Prisoner

The call from A+E came at 1800hrs. A blue-light ambulance was on the way from HMP Lewes, bearing a decapitated prisoner.

"Er, Sister Vernon", I enquired hopefully, "isn't the mortuary more appropriate?"

"Apparently he's still alive", she replied. Surprising news to me.

So, I skidded down to A+E in time to see a turban-headed patient entering the resuscitation room. The loaded gurney was followed by a prison officer carrying a large, blood-stained bowl containing some sort of wig.

It turned out that this young prisoner, Tim by name, had been working on a lathe in the carpenter's workshop at the prison. His shoulder-length hair, unwrapped in any hat, had become entangled in the chuck of the lathe, and more than half his scalp had been torn off. This was the wiggish-looking thing I had seen passing by in a bowl.

His left temporal artery was pumping out masses of bright red blood, so after clipping the visible end, and after some necessary resuscitation we got the patient to theatre where I spent two hours putting his head back together.

The problem this time had never been the diagnosis. But the management of this wound was complex, because in effect I was applying a thick, free graft to the skull, with no primary arterial feed. This graft was unlikely to take without a direct vascular connection to nourish the tissues. The other end of the temporal artery had retracted into the scalp tissue and was impossible to find.

By the end of the operation, I had placed well over 100 sutures around his skull, and we all agreed that he was now the spitting image of Frankenstein, minus the bolt. We were all hugely impressed at the final result, especially the fantastic dressing which my nursing sisters had created around the head, complete with two vacuum drains poking out through the bandages, making this young chap look like a cross between a Martian and a zombie.

In the end about half of my graft took, the other part becoming like desiccated old leather, making Tim look even more ghoulish as he patrolled the ward with his tame prison officer.

He took a very healthy interest in his dressing changes, as we all watched the line of viability developing day by day. Tim insisted on a mirror so he could enjoy this gory, daily ritual, which amused the nurses greatly. He later went to the Victoria hospital, East Grinstead where the plastic surgeons completed my work.

From abdominal and vascular surgery via urology to cardiology.

During the first six-month rotation when I was on L R´s firm I was also the general surgical and urological registrar at Hove General hospital, a comfortable Victorian edifice where all sorts of major urology was carried out. It was just down the road from the Goldstone football ground, home to the Brighton Seagulls, who were having a great season in the First Division. This was the hospital where I also did my Tuesday afternoon clinics with Henry Clarke, previously referred to. There were two other urology consultants, Mike and Neville, with both of whom I got on well.

There was so much urological work to do that Mike R, the consultant and I sometimes used to run two operations simultaneously, with just one anaesthetist – a practice that would have us both condemned by the GMC today.

Another Genius Joke

I had just completed a prostatectomy in the main theatre and Mike Royle was in the anaesthetic room doing another with Dr. F, the consultant anaesthetist, a rather humourless chap. As I entered the surgeon´s room to write up the notes I saw a Post Office technician replacing the old Bakelite phone with a new plastic one.

"Are you going to bin that?", I asked. "If you want it doc, it's yours", he said, offering me a kilo of Bakelite phone with a metre of sectioned woven cable attached.

And then I had another of my genius ideas for a joke ……

I knocked on the door of the anaesthetic room, phone in hand, and said, "there's a call for you, Dr.F", at which a manicured hand appeared and grasped the handpiece.

"Hello, Mike here", he said, and then repeated it. Hearing no response, he then came into the main theatre where Sister Gloria and her team were cleaning the floor prior to the next case.

Then we all saw Dr F begin tapping the Bakelite bar on top of the phone, saying, "Hello, Mike here….. hello? hello?" Only when he looked down and saw the severed cable did his face change colour as he shouted at me, "You bastard!" before retreating to the anaesthetic room, whilst I and the nurses wet ourselves at this hilarious moment. 40 years later, Rick and I still laugh at this escapade, which was after all, just another nail in the coffin of my career.

The Hypoxic Realms of Cardiology

When my six months of urology finished, I was approached by the medical registrar one day, who asked me if I was interested in doing a locum on the cardiology ward. Which is how I met one of the giants of Brighton health care, Dr Douglas Chamberlain, consultant cardiologist, honoured by the Queen, and now Emeritus Professor.

I have never warmed to cardiology, and I never ever really understood the ECG machine or those bits of paper which it spews out. So, for some unknown reason, but probably my quaint sense of humour, on the very first ward round with Dr Chamberlain, at the first patient's bedside I decided to deliberately hand this famous cardiologist the ECG printout upside-down.

He took it, upside-down, read it in an instant, then turned to me straight-faced, and said,

"Although it is no problem for me to interpret an ECG upside-down, I do prefer them the right way up!"

That is how I became close friends with a very wonderful and humorous man. Every time I am back in Sussex I always go and see him and drop him and Jenny a bottle of the finest extra-virgen from my local olive-oil mill at Pinos de Valle. Then we go and have a meal at his local Italian restaurant in Hove. He is knocking on now and is becoming progressively more bionic in his joints, and is fed up with decrepitude, but his mind is still razor-sharp.

We both remember his striding up the stairs of the Tower Block to the ITU in the County every day, followed by his cohort of would-be cardiologists. Never the lift. Douglas would say, quite seriously. "If they can't keep up with me, they won't get the job! In all my life at the County only one registrar beat me to the 8th floor – and he didn't get the job either!" Another roar of laughter.

When, after an enjoyable and educational month on the cardiology wards I left Hove, Douglas said to me, "Stick to general surgery: I think you'll do better there!" and laughed his head off again. He knew my heart was not in cardiology.

I spent the last of my six-month rotations with Nigel Porter, a very good general surgeon who specialised in breast and endocrine surgery, including thyroid, pancreatic and adrenal surgery, which is a very fine art indeed.

Nigel was a very correct surgeon, and a gentleman whom I had great respect for, so when my time came to leave, and he said to me, "I don't think you will ever be a consultant general surgeon in England, because your attitude is not right", I was not unduly surprised, once I had thought about his words.

I know absolutely that I was born to be a surgeon, but of a different ilk. More revolutionary, and far less conservative. Always a voyager. Taking unreasonable risks, quitting the hierarchical ladder to the top and loads of private surgery and much dosh, preferring the life of a vagabond surgeon in Africa.

Uncle Nigel understood this unorthodox desire of mine but still saw me as a decent technical and humane surgeon. That was all the accolade I ever wanted from this very fine general surgeon, and we parted in June 1978 on very good terms. I admired this man who had the courage to just tell me the truth. Strangely, I have found this is quite rare within the profession.

The windsurfer which he gave me as a present is still sailing on the lake at Deanlands Farm where I grew up, and has now entertained three generations of my family. Sadly, Rick told me that Uncle Nigel died last year, so I salute another great general surgeon and teacher.

My two years at Brighton were drawing to a close and with my FRCS degree I would normally have started applying for a senior registrar job, but instead, I had decided to quit the NHS in favour of Africa. I had just obtained a three-year contract with the Danish International Development Agency (DANIDA) as provincial surgeon for Northern Frontier District, Kenya, and I had decided to drive there from Brighton, rather than fly.

It was a momentous decision as it would effectively rule me out from ever getting a consultancy with the NHS, but I had remembered Nigel Porter's words, and Africa is where I wanted to be. It was a place where I could fulfil my destiny as a bush surgeon and once again enjoy the delights and dangers of the Dark Continent.

I bade farewell to my many friends and colleagues, some of whom I am still in close touch with. It had been a great two years by the seaside, and I had achieved a great deal which has always stood me in good stead.

On June 27th 1978, I left the County hospital in Dennis, my long-wheel base Land Rover, and headed south to the ferry at Newhaven and three months on the open road, heading for Mombasa.

13. THE ROAD TO MOMBASA

I spent much of my free time in 1978 re-building and restoring a Series 3 long wheel-base Land Rover which I had bought cheaply at a car auction in Southampton, in preparation for a three-month road trip to Mombasa. I soon found out why Dennis came to me so cheaply, for this was a vehicle which had already crossed the Sahara once, at least.

It was the small sand dune behind the dashboard which gave the game away. That, and the fact that everything from the swivel-joints to the back axle was completely worn out. It took three solid months to do the necessary repairs. During this time, I also joined the fraternity of Land Rover owners, and a jolly bunch they were. There was no corner of the world they had not driven their robust wagons, and they were full of tips and valuable advice.

I also did a 5-day course at the British Leyland Special Services Division in Coventry on Land Rover Maintenance. We were nine on the course, of whom three were females. Each one of us was going somewhere exciting, and I found we were kindred spirits in spite of our disparate origins, all of us intent on becoming competent Land Rover mechanics. Our teacher was called Dennis, and such a good tutor was he that I christened my own Land Rover Dennis.

Two years later, on the banks of Lake Victoria, by pure chance I met Tanya, one of the three girls on the course. She was driving a short-wheel base Mark 2, and when she told me she had christened her wagon Dennis I split my sides laughing.

From off-road racing to Land Rover Surgery

I had already spent much of my life with a spanner in my hand, since the age of 14 when I got my first motorbike – a Mark 1 LE Velocette 125cc, one of which is presently residing in the Science Museum, next to an Ariel Square 4.

During my years at Lewes Grammar school, I also used to race Austin 7s with my two friends, John and Victor. This involved all sorts of advanced mechanics – such as fitting twin SU carburettors and a straight-through exhaust. The car then metamorphosed into a very scary machine as we drove flat out over the fields of East Sussex, particularly because the brakes on these off-road racers were still rod and hinge on these specimens of 1937 British engineering.

Dennis, our lecturer, was a teacher with a dry sense of humour, mostly relating to the catastrophes which Land Rover owners had suffered over the years. Some were hilarious, but a few of his stories had us thinking seriously about what we were about to drive into, for when you are out in the Greater Bhundu by yourself and catastrophe strikes, there is no AA or RAC to phone up.

After five days we had all stripped an engine, repaired a swivel- joint, changed a half-shaft and a host of other essential pieces. Dennis also gave each of us a copy of the Series 3 workshop manual, which was an indispensable aid during my three years with Dennis the Land Rover. I had several major breakdowns in Dennis during the next three years, but every time, with this manual and a lot of luck I was able to retrieve the situation. Dennis was a hardy machine and went everywhere without groaning too much, but regular daily checks and maintenance were essential. Our tutor Dennis had taught us that.

On the Road to Africa

I was sorry to leave Brighton and the County boys and girls, for I had enjoyed an excellent two years there. But once again, Africa was calling me, and so I bade farewell to all my friends. The Evening Argus came and took a photo of me leaning out of a heavily loaded Dennis at the main entrance to the hospital, another treasured moment. Then we were off, south to Newhaven and the ferry to Dieppe, and the first step of another long voyage.

I had rigged the back of Dennis to accommodate a comfortable bed, with some jazzy curtains for the windows. That night I had *moules mariniére* and *frites* at ´Entre Deux Mers´, my favourite restaurant in Dieppe, much visited by me and the kids over the years, and still going strong. After a carafe of decent vin rouge, I wasn´t going anywhere far, so I retired to Dennis, parked cosily in the shadow of the ancient church of St Jacques which guards the main square.

I was awoken around 0530hrs by the Saturday street market setting up. It was great to see all the farmers coming in with their waggons loaded with fruits and vegetables, the ducks, chickens, geese and the wonderful arrays of cheeses and other goodies whilst I had an early morning café crème and croissant. The French take their food and drink very seriously, which is why I have always been in love with France and the French, and my voyage through France and Switzerland was a gastronomic delight.

Basle. First breakdown.

My good training in Land Rover maintenance came into its own in Basle, barely two days into my voyage. I had been staying with Peter, an old friend from Kenya days in 1975, who had first come to me in Voi as a young medical student and was now training as a paediatric surgeon.

When I did my morning checks under Dennis´s bonnet, I was surprised to see the cylinder block covered with a fine, silver powder, which seemed to be coming from the distributor. One of Dennis the tutor's axioms had been, "If you find a problem – Sort It ! – DON'T leave it for tomorrow!"

So, I disconnected the five high tension leads and removed the distributor. When I took off the plastic cap, I was surprised to find the inside of the aluminium base covered in aluminium dust. I then completely stripped the points out and removed the plate they were on to find one of the two counter-balance springs below had broken, and the small weight had eaten a hole in the aluminium base of the distributor. Along with many other spares I had a brand-new Lucas distributor which I installed with no problem, and soon was heading east again, giving thanks for Dennis's good advice.

From Switzerland I travelled to Luxembourg. I wanted to visit this tiny country, partly for the ancient memories I had of listening to Radio Luxembourg on my first home-made crystal radio. I also wanted to see the place where so many millionaires kept so much money. The whole place stank of richness.

I was very amused the following morning to climb out of Dennis and step onto an army of snails covering the pavement, all heading for the banks in the centre of town.

I continued east to Vienna where I had another fun night with two nurses I had met in Brighton, Denise and Charlotte. They proudly showed me the handsome marijuana plant growing on their kitchen windowsill and surprised me by saying that this was a common practice in Vienna.

HipHip! thought I, who had previously regarded the Austrians as rather dour, bourgeois mid-Europeans. But the food I ate in Austria was some of the richest and the best I ever had on the trip. Viennese coffee, which is blended with dried, crushed figs was another delicious discovery.

There is no doubt that travel broadens the mind. I had only been on the road a week or so, but I had already seen and learned a great deal.

I had also learned just after crossing the frontier into Hungary that even a heavily loaded Land Rover can get a speeding ticket. Within a kilometre I found myself in a small queue of foreign-registered vehicles, and from each one the Hungarian police were extracting $20 in foreign exchange for an unintelligible speeding ticket.

Hungarian has to be one of the most difficult languages in the world, whose roots are all shrouded in mystery. So, there was no chance of having a polite discussion about possible discounts with this gang of heavily armed, mean-looking police.

I realised that there was simply no option but to pay up. It was the only speeding ticket that Dennis ever earned, and is another valued memento of this voyage.

As I headed east towards Budapest, I was thinking how enterprising these Hungarians were, being so strapped for foreign currency in those days of East European Communism.

This sort of blackmail I found more than once on my voyage. Travelling in a strange country in a vehicle always excites interest, especially at frontiers. Drugs and other contraband were often carried across borders in vehicles, and I soon got used to the long waits at frontiers, which became wilder the more I headed east.

That night I went to sleep with a belly full of excellent *gulyás*, looking at the shining lights of Budapest from my perch inside Dennis. We had come to rest on Margaret Island in the middle of the Danube, and it was the gentle sound of flowing water which sent me to my dreams.

Looking for Dracula in Transylvania

Then it was onwards and eastwards to Romania and Transylvania. The further east I drove, the poorer everything became and the more obviously communist. I spent one night in the mountains by a huge, hidden castle straight out of Dracula, the same one where Prince

Charles now has a roost. The building was also garnished generously with tall spires which rose out of the green forest like red rockets. All in all, it was a very grand edifice which spoke of a previous era of great wealth.

Bucharest was ugly and bleak. Ceausescu´s palace was a huge, completely square concrete eye-sore, as was much of the city. So, I kept driving, and the following day came upon the astonishing mediaeval churches and their frescos in Suceava.

These paintings were over 500 years old and covered the outer walls of these old buildings. Remarkably, the colours were still well-preserved. The one which stays in my mind is that depicting Jacob´s ladder. From the ground to the eaves of the church the whole ladder was rising heaven-wards, complete with devils and angels and archangels. These forgotten jewels were rarely visited in those days when I passed through, and I was often alone at the seven churches I visited.

The rain never stopped, though the tarmac often did, and twice I had to use the winch to pull me out of a mud-hole.

Many of the roads in Romania were in a poor state

I awoke one morning after a night of torrential rain, to find my box of 10 audio cassettes completely water-logged, and then spent the next two hours drying them all out whilst I listened to the drumming of yet more rain falling onto Dennis´s roof. Not only did the cassettes survive their soaking, but I am still playing them today, some 40 years later.

One significant expense in Dennis´s rehab was a top-range Pioneer audio cassette player, and I had also put 4 x 40 watt Sony speakers inside. Music was always a necessary adjunct to driving, whether listening to Bob Marley in a wilderness or to Bob Dylan as I mounted the long slow road to Mount Ararat, watching out for brigands.

Romania was becoming more depressing for the weather and the general air of fatigue in this poverty-struck communist country. The towns often had just one single shop, which sold everything from wellington boots to ersatz coffee, so disgusting it made me retch. Yet there was also much that was beautiful. Great carts pulled by two big shire horses were a common hazard on the poorly maintained roads, many of which were just dirt tracks. I also saw oxen pulling harrows and ploughs whilst women, all with brightly coloured headscarves were planting potatoes in the furrows.

Shingles. Not the viral sort, but the hand-sawn wooden tiles which covered the roofs of the churches and also many houses all over rural Romania. They were cut with a variety of primitive tools, including ancient saws. The Romanian craftsmen rendered the church roofs very beautiful, and the porticos were also often cut in wooden friezes with great skill and much fine decoration.

Then further east to Bulgaria, a very strange country with another difficult language and a Slavic population which again was mostly involved in agriculture. It was only when I reached the shores of the Black Sea at Constantin that I found any signs of tourism, and they were bleak. All the hotels were concrete and square and full of well-padded Russians. The one shop I went into was full of large jars of marinaded gherkins – and nothing else.

Another Near-Death Experience

It was on the way south from Constantin to Turkey that I had another close encounter with death. Crossing a narrow humpback bridge in the dark of night I was suddenly confronted by a massive combine harvester. In fact, there were five. Fortunately, I was not going fast but there was nowhere to go except the ditch, and that's where Dennis and I ended up – wheels in the mud, but upright, even if I was sweating and swearing.

That frightening moment taught me another lesson. I never again drove at night unless there was a serious reason. I always stopped and made camp as the sun started to fade and did my cooking as dusk fell. Then I went to sleep, awaking with the dawn and setting off as the sun rose, after making my essential thermos of tea. It was a great way to travel, and as I continued east the summer temperatures were rising noticeably, so the early morning hours were a refreshing prelude to a broiling day. I had usually done 100 kms before I made my first stop around 0800hrs.

From Europe to Asia Minor

I love Istanbul and have visited that fair city three times. I lingered there for two days, getting a flavour of the east before heading to Ankara and the central Turkish plateau. I was now in Asia Minor, and everything was very different.

In my sights was Cappadocia, a region of Anatolia south of Ankara, with most unusual geography and geology. Its history was also long, from its early inhabitants, the Hittites in the 6th century BC to the Persians who were then defeated in 323 BC by Alexandra the Great, and it later became the largest province of the Roman empire. In 1399 the Sultan Beyazit added Cappadocia to the Ottoman empire. From this era there are many fine examples of Byzantine art and culture still existing, in particular, several well-preserved Orthodox churches and monasteries.

Through Cappadocia runs the Silk Road, uniting the occident with the orient as it has done since mediaeval times when the Seljuk empire stretched from Anatolia to the Hindu Kush. The Seljuks developed the area considerably during mediaeval times, and built a long series of hans, or caravanserai every 20 kilometres along the way, this being considered a reasonable day´s travel in those days. The caravanserai were hostels for travellers, lodging them and their animals for free for three days and nights. Many of them were constructed by philanthropic local sheiks and were on a grand scale, with a large square behind devoted to the pack animals and their loads.

In this area, erosion over many centuries had created towers of stone, so eroded that each tower was shaped exactly like a penis. Within many of these towers troglodyte dwellings had been established and over centuries a system of underground tunnels and even small towns had been created, of which Kayseri is one of the best known. The architecture was some of the most unusual I had ever seen, with whole townships carved into the caves and monoliths which dominated the landscape, united by the tunnels, the longest of which was over a kilometre in length.

I camped out in this fertile region for two days while exploring the area. The food was excellent with lots of vegetables, such as aubergines, okra and courgettes to make a delicious form of *ratatoullie*, and lamb was the meat of choice. I drank fresh lime juice, which I loved, and gallons of mint tea to combat the fierce heat. Surprisingly I saw very few tourists at the time I was in Cappadocia, which added to my pleasures in this weird corner of the world. The further east I now travelled, the fewer tourists there were, and soon there were none.

Since then, Goreme, Kayseri and the other small villages dotting the Cappadocian plain have become the centre of a vast tourist industry. Today, honeymooners now float above those rocky penises in hot air balloons, no doubt having a good laugh as they look down on their cave-riddled shafts.

Once I had left Goreme, I never saw another tourist until I hit Mombasa six weeks later. Instead, there were increasing numbers of Army roadblocks as I approached the border with Iran, and this is where my voyage very nearly ended prematurely.

On the Dangers of Trafficking Drugs

As a concession to tourism at that time, BP garages across Turkey often had an adjacent ´campsite´. These were usually just a space off the road, but with no facilities. It was at one of these that I made my next night stop, four hours east of Cappadocia, on the way to Erzerum, the last large town in Turkey before the Iranian border.

Imagine my joy when I found a good part of the camping space taken over by a plantation of mature marijuana plants. Ever since I discovered the joys of maryjane in The Congo in 1974 I have been a devotee of this medicinal plant, and to find this treasure, all going for free was too much a temptation. So, without considering the possible consequences, the following morning I took two of the ripest plants with the biggest buds and stuffed them under the front bench seat of Dennis to dry out. The herbal stink as I drove along merrily was an added delight. Until I came to the inevitable army roadblock. Panic!

Very fortunately, I found myself at the end of a queue of traffic, and thus had ample opportunity to get rid of the plants surreptitiously. The control passed with no problems after a cursory glance into Dennis, and then it was just 50 kilometres more to Dogubayazet and the Iranian border.

This was a real frontier outpost, where the Iranian authorities held public executions every week for the drug smugglers coming from Turkey, where every sort of drug was obtainable for trade. When I rode up in Dennis there was a lot of activity, but I got through the Turkish side without any problem. I also got through all the immigration, currency and passport business on the Iranian side, and even got my immigration stamp. There was just the final barrier, a red and white-striped post across the exit road. By it was lounging an innocuous looking fellow in a suit, who approached Dennis.

"Open the window!", he ordered. I slid my driver's side window back, whereupon he stuck his nose in and breathed once, very deeply. At that moment he reminded me of a bloodhound I once knew.

"Out, out!", he cried excitedly. Then I stood and watched in horror as he ransacked Dennis. He was worse than a bloodhound. He was more like a pack of African wild dogs, and I was terrified. All the stories told to me in Istanbul by veteran travellers were true, and suddenly I was in deep shit.

My problem, as usual, was a total lack of insight and awareness. This time, of the consequences of being caught with weed in Turkey, or Iran. I had at least got rid of the weed from Dennis, but he still stank like a herbarium inside, something I had been enjoying until this bad moment.

Hercule, for that is what I had now christened this human ferret, was stripping everything out of the two cupboards I had built into the rear ceiling. Then he went to the front of the waggon and began rooting once again through everything, including the three front seats, under which I had stashed the grass.

Then he turned to me, looking me straight in the eyes and said,

"I know that you have got something in your car. Show me, and we will go lightly with you. Perhaps you will not join our shooting party this week, just do 20 years in our local jail. They are not so pleasant for foreigners like you!"

There is a lot of my father in me, and he was a bomber pilot. I also knew that I did not have any drugs on board, even if Dennis still stank of weed. So, I turned on the attack.

"You have been searching my car for two hours and have found nothing. The reason is because there is nothing to find!" And in a moment of pure inspiration, I followed with,

"What I think you are smelling is my patchouli oil, which has leaked from the bottle".

Like all hippies, I was never without candles, joss-sticks, flower-power clothing – and patchouli oil. It was my Liverpool girlfriend, Mo, who first introduced me to this great oil way back in `69, and along with tea tree and Olbas oil, I am never without it. I have always found the aroma of marijuana to be quite similar and harmonious with that of patchouli.

I got my wash bag and stuck it under his enquiring nose. Indeed, it was saturated with the stink of patchouli, and eventually after a further scrutiny of me and my machine, he let me go.

It was during my BSc Hons. classes in Psychology in 1965, under the tutelage of Dr Mancini, our lecturer, that I learned how to lie fluently. It was all to do with the eyes and the face, and the posture and movements of the body. Today, it is commonly known as 'body language´, and it is extremely important.

So, I gave Hercule the eye, every second I was speaking to him. What I do is to visualise looking through the person's eyes, and into the very brain itself. And that was the look I was giving Hercule, whilst praying mightily.

I am sure it was that straight, honest look which finally convinced him to let me go, but once again, I had learned a life-long lesson. Never under-estimate the opposition, and never, never ever think of taking drugs across frontiers.

I was so trembling and incoherent after this traumatic experience that I could drive no further. For the first and only time in three months on the road, I paid $20 for a night under clean sheets in a road-house just out of Tabriz, where I feasted on slow-roasted lamb on a bed of Basmati rice with broad beans – *Khoresh Torsh*. When I say slow-roasted, I am talking about five hours or more over hot coals. But I did have a lot to celebrate, that first night in Iran.

Iran, Khomeini and the Revolution

Iran was in turmoil in the summer of 1978, for the exiled Ayatollah Khomeini was on his way back to Iran from France, and the Shah was on his way out. There were roadblocks all along the road from Tabriz to Teheran. When I entered the outskirts of Teheran, I suddenly found myself in an anarchic mess of traffic, coming from all directions, never observing the traffic lights and all out to kill me, it seemed.

One reason for my long voyage to Africa overland was so that I could visit my sister Lizzie, and her husband Shahrokh in Teheran. I had first met this Persian prince in 1975 when I was doing general surgery at Frimley Park hospital. I went up to Putney where they lived, and Shah cooked a delicious meal of lamb with aubergines. I said to Lizzie, "if that guy can cook so well, he can´t be bad".

And so it was. They got married and moved to Teheran. Lizzie became a Moslem and learned fluent Farsi – which is no easy language to learn. She became totally integrated into Iranian culture and life which, for a blonde-haired woman in that radical city, was no mean feat. She always wore the chador when she went out, and I was walking with her along Pahvlavi Street one day when she was spat on by two young Persian men. I was shocked, but to Lizzie with her long blond hair, this was part and parcel of being seen as an infidel in such a religiously ordained country, now in a state of civil war, as the Revolutionary Guard tried to unseat the Shah of Iran.

On the Effects of Opium

Back at Shahrokh´s house, I was given a rapturous welcome by his family. His uncle was in the kitchen, heating an ornate porcelain pipe with a long wooden stem over the cooker flame. Then he turned and offered it to me.

"Shah, what am I about to smoke", I asked.

"Opium", he replied, as I took the first long drag. I had never tried opium before, nor ever did again. After the third long toke I began to feel woozy, and the last thing I saw as I collapsed into coma onto the futon was Lizzie`s terrified face, which I did not see again for 12 hours.

Once I realised what had occurred, it was an easy decision to never go near the poisonous stuff again. Since then, as a doctor I have injected many doses of refined opium into sick patients, but then it is called Morphine.

I spent a week in Teheran with Shahrokh´s family and had a whale of a time, eating some the best food I had so far tasted on the trip. Iran was a fascinating blend of Arabia, Asia and the Orient. The main souk was a spectacular emporium of oriental delights, including gallons of bottled lime juice, which became my favourite travel drink – until I arrived in Kenya, and drank Tusker beer again.

This was my first break from driving since leaving England a month before. With Shahrokh and Lizzie as my guides I was introduced not just to Shahrokh' s extensive family, but also to Persia's magnificent history. There were very few foreigners on the streets of Teheran during the summer of `78, and I was very glad to be in Shahrokh's company as we passed bands of students shouting for Khomeini and the revolution.

The Grand Bazaar was not quite as big as Istanbul's, but was stuffed with all manner of beautiful objects, and was a delight to meander in. Shahrokh took me to his uncle's carpet shop where I lounged on exquisite carpets worth thousands of pounds, whilst pulling on a hookah and drinking mint tea, brought on a copper tray by a little boy.

We also visited the Shah´s summer palace in the northern suburbs of Teheran. It contained all manner of treasures, including a huge Persian carpet on the ground floor – at just under 250 sq.m, the biggest ever created in Persia. There were also two great malachite orbs guarding the entrance to the stairs, two metres tall and exquisitely carved, the luminous green of the stone polished to brilliance. I wonder if they are still there after the revolution, when so much to do with Reza Shah was destroyed.

I often visited Shahrokh´s parents, who lived in a modest house nearby with a grapevine which sheltered half the garden. There we drank home-made grape juice whilst enjoying the antics of Mama´s two white ducks in their pond. It was warming to see the way in which this Persian family had taken my sister Lizzie into their lives. They were the kindest, most hospitable people you could ever wish to meet, and I was sorry when my time came to leave.

The temperature in Teheran was in the `40s as I headed out of the rather ugly city through the mad and terrifying traffic. I was already feeling paranoid, for in Iran if one was involved in a car accident you were thrown into jail immediately, whether guilty or innocent, and I had many miles to go.

It was while I was in Teheran that I fitted Dennis with the extra radiator cooling fan I had brought with me. I was about to go south from Teheran into the Zagreb mountains, hitting the coast at Bandar Abbas and following the Persian Gulf to Khorramshah. Then via Kuwait to Saudi Arabia and across the Arabian desert to Jeddah. These are some of the hottest and most inhospitable terrains in the world, and I intended to be prepared.

South to Shiraz and Isfahan

My adventure had really started in earnest now, and as I headed south towards Qom, a major religious centre of Shiite Islam, I could see that I had left Europe far behind.

Donkeys became increasingly visible, carrying everything from humans to massive piles of vegetation, and even household furniture. The countryside was arid, and the traffic was as anarchic as it had been in Teheran, which kept me on the *qui-vive* every metre of the road. Overtaking vehicles were a constant threat, especially on-coming vehicles, whose drivers seemed to have no sense of perspective nor relative speed. I had already seen several crashes before I came to Qom, barely 100 kms from Teheran.

The town of Qom was where Khomeini had his base whilst he prepared the revolution which would terminate the Shah's reign, and that of his rich, royal family. A harsh Shiite theocracy followed, as well as the return to Sharia law. A violent youth movement, the Revolutionary Guard, murdered many hundreds of innocent Iranians. Tragically, this included Shahrokh´s young nephew, Shahria, who died in Evin jail, still in his teens.

The further south I headed, the drier and hotter it became. The ambient was never less than 40 C, and by the time I reached Isfahan I was ready for a break from the road.

Isfahan was a city with an ancient history, and some of the most magnificent architecture I had ever seen. Even Ely cathedral could not compare with the Shah Mosque, built in the 14th century AD, totally covered inside and out with exquisite turquoise tiles. The main cupola dwarfed the whole town. Hundreds of devotees were passing in and out, but I was an infidel, and contented myself outside with taking some good photos of this wonderful building.

There were many other architectural wonders in Isfahan, all constructed during the reign of Shah Abbas, who came to power in 1585. He was determined to make Isfahan the most beautiful city in the world, from whence comes the saying that all Iranians know, "*Esfahan nesf- e- jehan*" – Isfahan is half the world!

The food was always good wherever I went in Iran. It was easily available and cheap. The delicious aroma of roasting lamb was everywhere, as the Persians barbecued their *kofti* and *shwarma* kebabs, and I noticed that chickpeas were now more and more common in their dishes. The more I travelled, the more I could see that this was a country with a huge history and culture. I already knew much about Iran from the time I had spent with Lizzie and Shahrokh in Teheran, and I was eager to learn more.

After two stimulating days in Isfahan, I hit the road again, continuing south towards Shiraz. The route I was driving had been suggested by Sharokh, in order to take in some places of special interest, of which Isfahan had been one.

Shiraz was another Iranian jewel, with a history going back to mediaeval Islam. During the Zand dynasty from 1753 – 1794 the city briefly became the capital of Persia and many of its beautiful buildings were constructed during this period. It became an important centre of learning, hence its ancient crown as *"Dar-ol-Elm"* – the seat of learning.

Famous poets such as Sa´di (1206 – 1290) and Hafez (1320 – 1390) lived in Shiraz, and both have elaborate tombs in the city. Omar Khayyam is said to have his written Rubaiyat here, but in Iran he is best known as a Master of mathematics and astronomy. The medical school is still one of the most famous in all Iran, as is the university. Even though the West knows little of Persian history, the practice of medicine and health care was advanced in Persia, even before the Middle Ages, when Europe was only just awakening.

I wanted to spend more time in Shiraz, but the second day I was there an armed conflict began. Army helicopters appeared amongst the spires and minarets, and things started looking dangerous, so I made tracks.

The Magnificence of Persepolis - and another breakdown

That night found me about 50 miles south, in the ruins of Persepolis, where I was replacing Dennis´s burnt-out starter motor. How I cursed Dennis, this dying donkey.

There was even a starting handle to turn the heavy 2-litre Rover engine over, but in the terrible heat of southern Iran in August, it became a nightmare. Once again I was forced into my old man´s ex-RAF overalls, and slid underneath Dennis with my spanners. It was a horrendous experience. Sweat poured from me and got in my eyes and made them sting. I also bashed my knuckles heavily, causing me to use bad language.

All Dennis´s electrical parts including the starter motor were made by Lucas, GB. I already had my doubts about this British manufacturer, ever since the distributor had melted in Basle. How grateful I was for the advice of both Dennis my lecturer and my closest Land Rover aficionado, Gordon. Neither trusted Lucas components very much, so I had got a spare for every electrical part of Dennis, and was mighty glad, for there was small chance of the Royal Automobile Club rocking up to Persepolis, Southwest Persia in mid-August.

My reward after two hours of awful, sweaty labour, was to sit in the 5-star Persepolis Palace hotel, which appeared completely free of any tourists, and drink my way through two large gin and tonics. Six months later this would have been impossible, for by then Ayatollah Khomeini held the reins of Iran, and the Shiites just hated alcohol.

Going to sleep slightly drunk, amongst the ruins of Persepolis under a star-lit sky of indigo has to be another crystal moment of my voyage. When I awoke the following morning, savouring a rare hang-over, I was awed by the grandeur of the buildings around me. These were constructed by Darius I around 500 BC. and were once encircled by a massive wall, nearly 20 metres high. Most were in ruins, for this wonderful city had been razed in 323 BC by Alexandra the Great in one of his lesser moments. But there was still much to admire.

The Grand Staircase was lined with a stone frieze of Assyrian warriors, all mounted on horseback – brilliantly carved in black stone. There were massive porticos and columns which must have been at least 10 metres tall – similar in size to the temples of Karnak, on the banks of the Nile in Egypt which I last saw in 1975.

I spent the best part of a day within the ruins of Persepolis. The single guard/guide, Mohamed, was a great chap and very keen to practice his English with me. He told me I was the first genuine tourist he had seen in a month, the revolution having scared everyone away from Iran. Mohamed was only 22 but had been a guardian here for two years, and he knew a lot about the history of Persepolis, which he was happy to share with me.

We shared a lunch of kebab and excellent bread with olives and a very fine red wine from his father´s farm nearby, under the shadow of the Apadana, the meeting hall of the kings. This is a massive auditorium, which was originally supported by 36 stone columns, more than 20 metres high, of which only 14 were still standing.

I am a great one for ruins, and places like Memphis, Palmyra, Karnak, Petra, Persepolis and Machu Picho need to be visited and seen by the public, just to appreciate that there was greatness, and there were real empires millennia ago.

The recent destruction of Palmyra by Islamic extremists was an historic outrage, but even if they destroyed the beauty of the construction, the building blocks will still be lying on the ground as evidence in a thousand years' time, so massive was its construction. Palmyra existed in its magnificence because it had become an important town on the Silk Road, that magical, meandering path of merchants for centuries between the Occident and the Orient. Now it is no more.

The subterranean water systems and cisterns which the Persians developed millennia ago in this most arid of lands, are marvels of hydrology, and are what allowed these ancient cities to thrive and grow. In Jordan, the palace of Petra and its town of 40,000 inhabitants were supplied with precious water during the same era via an eight- kilometre *acequia*, and it is still in operation today.

Water was also now becoming a major issue for me, and for Dennis. The temperature was over 45 C when I hit the Persian Gulf at

Bushehr, and the temperature gauge on the dashboard never went out of the red. Thank God I had thought to install the extra fan in front of Dennis´s radiator.

I had started for Bushehr at daybreak, after a second night amongst the ruins of Persepolis. Now I was heading down through the Zagros mountains towards the Persian Gulf. This mountain range covers some of the most arid country in the south-west of Iran, and soon there was nothing to see but the occasional malnourished goat and some stunted bushes.

The road was a real nightmare, as many mountain passes can be. On one side there would be a cliff, and on the other a precipitous drop into a ravine far below. These valleys were littered with the crushed corpses of vehicles which had run off this road, and were a constant reminder of the danger, as were the small shrines which appeared by every serpentine bend.

Why the British so loved the Shah

Once I hit the torrid coast, I was in Oil country, the heartland of Iran´s wealth today. The British and the Americans had always been interested in Persia for political reasons, and when oil was discovered in the early 1900's they made heavy investments in developing this wealth, as well as becoming firm friends of the Shah.

At the end of the Second World War, the Teheran Conference marked a most significant alliance between the British, the Americans and the Russians. All three had huge interests in Arabia – because of its oil reserves, and also because of the strategic access to the Gulf which Russia had always eyed enviously.

Today, all there was to see were massive chimneys spouting flames a hundred metres high and all the ungainly elements of the petroleum refining and storage industry. All in all it was an ugly scene, and a big contrast to the beauty of Isfahan and Shiraz. So, I kept driving, north along the Gulf towards the road which crossed the northern Gulf.

This was by far the worst part of the voyage so far. This road is 95 miles long, completely flat, and completely straight. It passes over enormous salt pans where there was no visible life. What there was in abundance was heat, a heat so harsh that I could feel it with every red-hot breath I took. My own thermometer read 50 C. I was terrified of breaking down, for I would very likely have died of heat-stroke.

I was taking a swig of water after every 5 breaths, so dehydrated was I. One of the best bits of all my travelling gear was the 2-litre leather *bota* I was never without those days, and I had now slung it around my neck, so the spout was in my mouth as I drove.

It was a fearsome journey, and when I arrived at Khorramshah that evening I was flaked out. What is more, the whole place was in uproar, police and emergency vehicles with sirens going were racing around, for reasons I did not know until the following day, after a night in the Seaman's hostel. The genial manager, Farokh, told me there had been a huge fire last night at a cinema in Khorramshah, and there were rumours that over 400 people had been burnt to death. It appeared to be related to the ongoing revolution, which was becoming increasingly violent.

It was Farokh, whose help eventually got me onto a dhow going to Kuwait City, after three days of anxious waiting and bargaining. The problem was that there was nowhere else to go now, and the only way to Kuwait was across the head of the Gulf, past the Shat- al- Arab to Kuwait City by boat.

I had planned to get to Basra in Iraq, and I had the necessary visa, but the Iran-Iraq war was in the making, and that border was now closed.

Across the Persian Gulf by Dhow

The dhow-owners were a tough lot to deal with – apart from my lack of Farsi. They all knew that I was at their mercy and adjusted their prices accordingly. But once again Lady Luck came my way.

I came across Ishmael at the moment when I was about to give up. He was the Head of Customs for the port. Not only was he a very nice chap, but he was a fervent Anglophile, surprised to find an English doctor on his doorstep. I spent that night with him and his family, ate like royalty, and the next day by midday I had a done a deal, through the great assistance of Ishmael, who knew every dhow owner in Khorramshah, with an Arab pirate to take me across the Gulf to Kuwait.

When Ishmael took me down to the dock where we were to embark with Dennis, I was shocked. Amongst a row of decrepit– looking dhows was the one I had paid for. It was not very big, being about eight metres long and three metres wide, and getting Dennis on board was going to be challenging. In order to arrive at the dhow, it was necessary to negotiate a very narrow pier about 100 metres long, composed of two - metre planks on top of 40- gallon oil drums. It was worse than precarious, but I had to do it.

Steeling myself and focusing every nerve, I took Dennis at 3 mph along this deadly track, rocking and rolling from side to side as the drums swung to the tide. The last three metres were the scariest, as I had to take a well-judged run at the dhow, lying athwart to me, and jump Dennis off the planks and across the thwarts of the dhow – without over-cooking it and ending up in the Shat al Arab.

When I reviewed this dangerous moment, I was amazed and horrified at what I had achieved, which was to land smartly on top of some huge sacks of millet which Ahab and his pirate gang were shipping to Kuwait. Both front and rear bumpers stuck over the thwarts of this small dhow. The only way Dennis was ever going to leave this quaint ferry was with the help of a crane. Which is what happened when we arrived in Kuwait City two days later, after a stimulating trip across the Gulf.

In spite of hardly a single word of common language, Ahab and his gang of four did me proud. They were the kindest of people, sharing their lentil soup and flat breads with me. I cracked a couple of cans of baked beans the second day out at sea, and introduced this happy crew to something British, which had them all smacking their lips. Mohammed was about 12 years old and was the cook. Each morning he was crouched over the small brazier, roasting fish they had caught overnight.

The toilet facility was unusual in its construction and design, being just a tiny wooden cage suspended over the stern. The first time I was forced to use it was enough to render my anal sphincter into spasm as I watched the limpid waters below my naked bum, in which no doubt swam hungry sharks. This was no Hilton Hotel. Ahab and his gang were all politely amused as I clambered on board again, shaking slightly.

From Kuwait to Saudi Arabia

I was sorry to leave this jolly gang of pirates when we docked in Kuwait City. A giant crane came by and rudely hooked Dennis off the sacks and onto the quayside. Then came the Customs inspector, very neat and well-rounded in his impressive uniform.

"Six books", he barked out. "Have six books?", he asked me.

"I´ve got about 20", I replied, at which he got really excited and started jumping around. I opened up my travelling library and showed him my fine collection of literature.

"Six!", he shouted at me, now looking stressed. God Almighty, what was going on.

Only when this obese guardian of the port showed me a porn

magazine he had with him did I realise there had been a communication problem. After giving Dennis further scrutiny, he let me go to Immigration, and an hour later I was about to jump into Dennis when I noticed a ship off-loading several enormous, vase-like stainless steel containers. Later, when I was staying in Jeddah with my knowledgeable friend Eric, he told me that these containers were full of whisky and other spirits for the Islamic Arabs of Kuwait, where alcohol was so strictly prohibited.

Then it was through the port control and cruising through Kuwait City, which all looked modern and ugly to me. The only noteworthy things I saw as I headed south and out of town were the Kuwait Towers. These are three tall concrete towers bearing great globes, one of which was a water storage cistern and another a restaurant and viewing platform. And that was all I remember of interest in Kuwait. Except the heat.

Fortunately, it was a dry heat, but even so, everything was an effort. It was well over 40 C during the day, and not much less at night. I was going to have to get used to it, for I was about to cross 600 miles of Arabian Desert. As I drove Dennis from Kuwait City, 200 kilometres south to Dammam and the Saudi Arabian border I was already preparing myself for a challenging trip.

Ever since I had passed Bandar Abas on the Persian side of the Gulf, the unpleasant smell of oil had been everywhere. The whole area around Ahvaz and Khorramshah at the head of the gulf was blighted, as was the Arabian coast from Kuwait to Damman. You could easily see the huge investment in petroleum production and the power of Aramco, the multi-national company which had benefited enormously from this black gold, as had the Saudis.

The Aramco City at Dammam was a little piece of America, hidden behind steel fences with armed guards at the gates. It was the only place in this Arab kingdom where women could legally drive. And although alcohol was forbidden throughout Saudi Arabia, it was easily available within this fortified island.

The heat had been oppressive since I left Kuwait, and I was ripe for some cool luxury. Another strain had been the continuous need to be on high alert ever since leaving Europe and crossing into Turkey. So, imagine my joy, after facing up to the guards with their Armalite rifles at the entrance to Aramco City, to find myself in an air-conditioned hall where about 100 youngish Americans were line-dancing, something I had seen before in Houston in 1974, but not warmed to.

I got chatting to a young American teacher called Julia, and she invited me to spend the night at her air-conditioned house on the campus, which made a very pleasant change. Julia proved the point. There are good people wherever one goes. She was well educated, and liberal in all things, and a very refreshing change from my conceived notion of Americans. I was sorry to leave her air-conditioned house, but Riyadh beckoned, and I had 600 miles of dangerous desert to drive.

Riyadh was like Kuwait City to me, a mass of ugly concrete and endless highways with unintelligible Arabic wording on every direction sign. Driving down the main street of Riyadh at 2300hrs after seven hours crossing the desert from Damman, I was shocked to see a MacDonalds sign appear. Good God!

And that was how I found Saudi Arabia, an empty nothingness, full of dust and sand and Arabs who, a generation ago had been the pearl-fishers of the Gulf, thin people, until the riches of oil were discovered in the 1920´s. Today I was struck by the obesity they exhibited as they strolled through the gold-filled bazaars and souks in Riyadh.

It was a family friend who got me into the King Faisal hospital, then on the outskirts of Riyadh. I had previously read about this unique hospital, which only treated millionaire princes of the realm. Henry was a British refrigeration engineer and oversaw all the air-conditioning for this refuge of Arab princes. He was therefore a most important person, and an excellent guide.

I was struck by the fortifications which surrounded this millionaire's hospital in the desert. The fence was electrified, the guards were all armed with automatic repeater rifles, and we had to have our photo taken before being allowed inside. During our guided tour, Henry led us into a corridor with doors leading off, whose walls and floors were lined with fleecy white carpet. "What the hell goes on in this high-spec ward", I asked Henry.

"This is where we dry them out", he replied, giving me a very old-fashioned look.

That is the problem with any religion. It forces us feeble humans into hypocrisy. Inside the 20 fleece-lined private rooms there were Arab princes, drying out from their alcoholic excesses.

The expats in Saudi also had access to booze, and many even manufactured it in their garages, but for them the penalties were severe. I later met one expat who had been caught making and selling booze, and he told me he had spent hours in a Jeddah jail standing on a huge block of ice, under a sun which heated the ambient to just under 50 C., as part of his punishment. He was luckier than some other criminals, for in Saudi Arabia Sharia law prevailed. Eric had told me that thieves and other criminals were still having hands axed off during the Friday punishment sessions of the feared religious police.

After my enlightening hospital visit, I drove on south and spent the night in a transport park 100 kms south of Riyadh. During the night, under enormous white tents, transport trucks of all descriptions were being repaired. All this industry in the middle of the dusty Arabian desert, in a temperature of 45 C + left me feeling weak. It was an inferno, with welders sending out fountains of sparks, and a bellows-operated forge glowing like a volcano as well as the sound of hammers bashing metal. It was not my most restful night stop, but I felt safer in company at night in Arabia.

The following day I steeled myself and drove the rest of the 600 miles to Jeddah. The only problem was, approaching the Red Sea coast in the dead of night, I took the turning to Medina by mistake, and ended up in front of two armed soldiers, at the gates of Mecca. They were as surprised as I was, but accepted my explanation of the transgression with good grace. Having scrutinised my various documents, they pointed me towards Jeddah and the house of my old friend Eric.

Eric and I had been in the choir together at St Marys, Warbleton back in the `50s, and he was now the representative of Eagle Star Insurance, doing re-insurance on the huge oil-drilling platforms in the Gulf. To have an old friend in this outpost was indeed a great thing. Not only had Eric been in Saudi for three years, but he knew Jeddah well, and during my enforced two - week wait for my Greek cargo boat to Mombasa, he showed me a lot of this ancient port.

Jeddah was fast becoming modernised. When I saw the destruction of the beautiful old buildings in the old part of Jeddah, to make room for more neo-Arab architecture, it was sad to see. Most were constructed of wood and were several stories high, with exquisite wood carvings and dated back centuries. The many new buildings included a very fancy shopping arcade, air-conditioned and full of jewellery shops stuffed with gold objects, tax-free cameras and other baubles. That was all that many Saudis seemed capable of – getting rich by doing nothing, then spending their lives getting fat and spending all that oil wealth on trinkets.

The Saudis knew who the bosses were, because any blonde like me was a *feringee*, and by definition second class. More than once I was in a shop being served when an Arab came in, and the merchant just dismissed me and went to his Arab client. After my frugal desert days in Arabia, this explosion of vulgar consumerism was a shock, but that was how Arabia was developing, under the rich umbrella of petroleum.

One day Eric took me into town to see his office. Inside a big room there must have been 20 secretaries and administrators working. But there was not one woman in sight. All of Eric's business work was done by men, mostly from India or Pakistan. All the masses of construction work going on in Jeddah was done by cheap, imported labour, mostly from Asia, and the dreadful conditions under which they worked and lived smelt of slavery. It was clear that the Gulf Arabs had become so rich that they no longer needed to work, only invent new, and more outrageous ways of flaunting their unearned wealth.

After a recuperative week with Eric, I started to get twitchy. I had seen all of Jeddah that I wanted to, and there was still the area south to explore, including the Asir mountain region, said to be very beautiful, cool in the summer with peaks over 2,000 metres. I had a visa for Yemen, but whilst we were in Saudi Arabia another war had started between north and south Yemen, and what with the Iraq – Iran conflict and the Iranian revolution, I had experienced enough of armed conflict. I decided to explore more of Saudi Arabia.

Once more I did the checks on Dennis, then pointed his bonnet due south. Taif was the first town or any significance. It was one of the summer residences of the Saudi royal family, being high in the hills and relatively cool after the stifling heat of Jeddah. The further south I went, the higher and craggier the mountains of the Asir range became. It was wild and barren country, although there were forested areas, and it was on the outskirts of one just north of Abhar that I felt the call of nature.

The sun was setting in glorious colours over the mountains, and the Red Sea was just visible to the west. It was a magnificent vantage point, just perfect for my needs. Certainly, a great advance on my fear-struck evacuations on board the Persian dhow. With my pants round my ankles, I was considerably shocked to see a white apparition advancing on me from the gloom. It looked like a dancing Dervish as it approached. Suddenly I was in a tricky position.

It was another anal spasm moment for me. Expecting the worst, I jumped up, grabbing my pants, heading for Dennis. When this apparition spoke to me Arabic, he did not sound threatening, so I paused in flight and listened. By his indications, he gave me to understand that he was inviting me to his home, and so, instead of having my throat cut by mountain bandits, I spent a memorable night with Mohamed, my new friend, his wife Fatima and their three children.

Mohammed and his family. Abhar. Saudi Arabia

It turned out that he was a Berber, and a farmer in the small wadi where I found myself next morning. It was a magical small valley, made fertile by the run-off from the peaks of the Asir range, and Mohamed was the owner. In this small hidden oasis, all manner of sub-tropical plants such as citrus, grapes, millet, maize grew, along with many other foods. His wife tended the herb garden, and every day she baked *khobs,* the bread I found all over Arabia.

It was the only time in Arabia that I ate a meal with the women and children, as well as the males. In every other place there was a strict separation between the men and women, who always ate after the men had been served, and then apart, in the kitchen, with their children. But this Berber farmer had a very liberal attitude to life, and he was only a loose follower of Islam. He even made a delicious, sweet dessert wine from his grapes, as well as wonderfully juicy sultanas which Fatima put into the lamb tagine she cooked over the coals that first night.

I collapsed into Dennis after a monstrous meal, fit-to-bust, and slept like a log, waking to the sounds of the children leading the goats out to pasture. Not much Primary Schooling around these parts of Arabia. The three kids were hilarious. They had never seen a *feringee* before, and they delighted in all the toys and tools I had inside Dennis, including my Pakistani fighting kite, which worked very well in these high altitudes. I also had the crazy mask Peter gave me in Basle after the Carnival, which everyone wanted to try on, even Abdullah the grandfather.

We spent two glorious days together, and this short respite completely changed my attitude towards Saudi Arabia. There was another country, which did not run on oil wealth, and I had been most fortunate to find it, together with Mohamed and Fatima and the children. I was sad to leave this warm family, hiding out in their wondrous hidden wadi, so green and full of goodness after the lifeless, arid desert I had been driving through. I knew I would never see them again, but when I look at the photos I took during my stay with them, they confirm this magic place I came upon by pure chance, within the dry and dusty deserts of Arabia.

The return to Jeddah was an anti-climax, but Eric had a last moment to share with me. This was a trip to the Corniche, a concrete esplanade over-looking the Red Sea, where at sundown every day the great cannon was fired, to signal the end of fasting, for we were still enjoying the sparse joys of Ramadan.

What Eric particularly wanted me to see were the queues of air-conditioned Rolls-Royces, most of them with a tv on the bonnet and a hungry Arab family within, enjoying TV Riyadh. At the first echo of the gun, I was impressed to see them all reaching for the big hampers they had on the back seat, and begin stuffing themselves with luxuries, freshly arrived from Europe, as they watched the latest news on TV. So much for the good life of the rich Gulf Arabs, but it was not anything I wanted any part of.

I was happy to get a call from Giorgio, the captain of the good ship ´Athaena´, five days later. I said fond farewells to Eric and Saidi, his fuzzy-haired young house-boy, who was gay – a very rare and dangerous state to be in Saudi Arabia in 1978. Eric himself was not gay, but he cared a lot for Saidi, and protected him as best he could from the Saudi authorities.

Steaming to Mombasa

Then to the port of Jeddah, and the hassle of getting Dennis winched on board the ancient Greek tramp steamer.

It took two weeks to get to Mombasa, and during that time I must have eaten kilos of Kalamata black olives, moussaka, stifado and kleftiko – all cooked by Georgio's magnificent wife, Analiki. She never stopped cooking during the time I was on board, and my belt was tight when we docked in Mombasa.

I was the only passenger on this cargo-passenger vessel, and spent amusing hours with Giorgio at his captain´s table as he steered us south down the Arabian Sea. We stopped for a day in Djibouti to pick up some cargo, and there I once again saw the French kepis, smelt Gauloise and garlic and ate a whole, freshly made baguette stuffed with tuna and salad.

Djibouti was a tiny French colonial outpost with the usual pretty fort, and guns all pointing seaward, for the Straits of Hormuz controlled every vessel passing up and down the Gulf. It was a very strategic area of the world – and as hot as hell.

The good ship 'Athaena' arrived in Mombasa on September 7th, shortly after President Jomo Kenyatta had died. Daniel Arap Moi, from the minority Kalenjin tribe had already taken over the reins of power in Kenya.

Giorgio rolled his eyes. He had his own Greek opinion about Africa and the Africans. He still found it hard to believe that I actually wanted to spend three years in the *bhundu* treating Africans. Analiki gave me kilos of Kalamata olives, and a great chunk of their aged goats cheese from Kefalonia as well as a big hug. She and Giorgio had been the perfect hosts.

In Jeddah I had changed the cross-ply tyres with which Dennis began his voyage, for the Michelin radials which Gordon had kindly sold me very cheaply after the Land Rover course I had attended. Not only were they a vastly superior tyre, but they greatly improved the handling of Dennis, and were much better for the dirt roads of Kenya I was about to enjoy.

Once again, I had arrived in Africa, and I would not return to England for seven years. After my recent adventures in Dennis, over 5000 kilometres across unknown territories, it was hard to imagine experiencing any more stimulating voyage. But my trip to Garissa to start my new job as provincial surgeon was to prove every bit as stimulating and demanding.

14.   GENERAL SURGERY IN EAST AFRICA   1978 – 81

September 1978. Mombasa. Kenya.

Kenyatta was dead and Daniel Arap Moi was the new president of Kenya when I set foot on the quayside at Mombasa harbour. A dockside crane lifted Dennis, my trusty Land Rover out of the hold and bounced him onto the quay. I was on the final stretch of my three-month journey. Europe, Arabia and Persia traversed, and now Africa to enjoy once more.

I was glad to be back inside Dennis and on the road again, after two weeks on board ´The Athaena´. I thought that Dennis felt the same as we headed north out of Mombasa, parallel to the coast, past the long lines of Africans offering us mangoes and coconuts along the highway out of town. The outer suburbs of Mombasa were always depressing, like the slums of Kinshasa which I had explored with Pastor David, head of the Presbyterian Mission in the Congo, 1974. At that time those city slums were the largest in all Africa, but today Kibera in Nairobi is vying for that position.

I was just 32 years old, and ripe for another adventure. I now had seven years of post-graduate general surgery in various parts of the world under my belt, my newly won Fellowship in General Surgery, and also a three-year contract with the Danish government (DANIDA) as Provincial Surgeon for Northern Frontier District, Kenya, based at Garissa.

After my four months with the Flying Doctors in 1975 I had decided that I would only take two or three-year contracts in future. Only then would I have time to properly understand and appreciate the language and the culture of the people I served.

The Dangerous Road to Garissa

Garissa was to be my provincial headquarters. It was a desert outpost on the banks of the Tana River which flowed east from Mount Kenya to the East African coast just north of Malindi. It had been my base for three months in 1975 when I was a general surgeon with the Flying Doctor Service, so I knew what to expect. Dust, torrid heat, a variety of wild animals, venomous snakes, and nomadic patients. Just my cup of tea.

I have always been drawn to the deserts and the tribes that inhabit them. They are amongst the hardiest humans I have ever come across in my travels. Living as they do on the outer borders of humanity, with their goats and camels and donkeys and their religion, and not much else. They were also a joy to operate on because obesity was unknown, except in the richest Somalis. All these nomadic people, Boran, Omras and Somalis were fit and resilient, and were also proud of their harsh life.

Garissa was a government outpost that existed only to protect north-eastern Kenya from Somali bandits, and incursions from Ethiopia. One of my regular twice-monthly surgical safaris was to the confluence of these borders at Mandera, possibly the most volatile and dangerous corner of Africa at that time. Twenty years later, the 1999 edition of The Rough Guide to Kenya begins the section on Garissa thus,

"Do not attempt to travel east of Garissa by road. Armed robberies and murders have become weekly, if not daily events, and are now hardly worth a mention in the national press." This was the same road I was now travelling, as I went north towards Kilifi Creek and Watamu Bay, one of my favourite haunts on the coast, where I spent a real African night on the roof of Dennis, looking up at the stars glistening over the crashing surf of the Indian Ocean.

Malindi was my next stop. It was always a haven for the expats, and was a delightful seaside town, typically Swahili, shaded by palm trees and coco palms and banks of brilliant bougainvillea. I sat in the shade of a seaside bar, admiring the brilliant orange/vermillion flowers of the Casuarina tree over my head as I enjoyed a pint of Tusker. Africa is so full of vivid colours.

Then I turned inland along the southern bank of the Tana River, following the B8 to Bura, passing the small village of Hola on the way. It was certainly a B road, being mostly mud after the recent rains. The potholes were enormous, and very risky to get stuck in, as traffic was always very sparse along this dangerous track. Large and aggressive wild animals were prevalent, wandering bandits were always around, and there was no sign of any AA or RAC support in this forgotten part of the planet.

The heavy winch I had bought from AutoSpares, London Road, Brighton at some considerable cost, was once again proving itself after my recent Romanian adventures in the mud. I used a metre long shaft of steel driven deep into the mud to peg the end of the rope, and then started the electric winch motor. It was always a minor thrill to watch Dennis winch his way out of a muddy pit in first gear, low ratio. The Michelin radials also came into their own and provided far better grip than the cross-plies I had used on the tarmac roads from Brighton to Jeddah.

The tarmac roads had not really tested Dennis, but now his sturdy engineering became evident. I had never used low ratio gear in anger until I hit this road, but now I was using it every hour. The strain on the half-shafts was tremendous, and progress was very slow. Strengthened half-shafts were a particular feature of the Series 3 Land Rover, and I never had one go on me, even when ascending much of Mount Kenya.

It took two days to reach the junction with the A3 from Nairobi, during which time I saw barely 20 people, but a wide variety of wild animals. I was back in safari country, and it was all magnificent. The birds were astounding in their colours, from egrets to Marabou storks, raptors of all sorts and many others. I also saw elephants, giraffes, zebra and even the occasional long-necked gerenuk. It was like a free holiday, and apart from the need to keep a constant watch out for bandits, the journey went well.

Doing Dennis' daily checks with my assistant

Thwarted at Garissa – and back to Nairobi

It was only when I arrived at the hospital in Garissa, that the Provincial Medical Officer told me that my contract had been voided and I was to return to Nairobi. Just like that. But that was independent Kenya in 1978.

Apparently, the Kenyan government badly needed a surgeon at Voi, a town on one of the most dangerous highways in Africa in terms of deaths per kilometre from traffic accidents.

I had no choice but to head back to Nairobi, where Karin, my contact at DANIDA HQ gave me my new marching orders.

I then had three glorious days in Nairobi with all my friends from the Flying Doctors, including Hugh, my pilot from my previous Garissa days. We used to meet at the Flying Club at Wilson Airport, and always had a serious Full English breakfast there, before reviewing the planes.

Hugh took me round to the Flying Doctors hangar so I could renew my acquaintance with Harold, the chief engineer. He was checking the new Cessna 402 which had just arrived. It was a beautiful twin-engine monoplane, the same model Hugh and I were flying when we were attacked at Mandera, and nearly died.

Once again, I stayed with Hugh and Annie in their old *cortijo* in Karen, a beautiful and tranquil suburb of Nairobi then, nestling in the foothills of the Ngong mountains. After a round of visits to various Ministry of Health officials, my papers were stamped, my FRCS certificate was examined and then it was south to Voi and three years in the East African savannah.

To Voi and Much Major Trauma

After my previous adventures at Garissa, Voi was almost a paradise. The climate was far better, being hot but dry, and I now found myself living in the middle of the largest game park in Africa.

Voi was a smallish town which had importance as the junction for the main Nairobi-Mombasa railway, where it divided and sent a spur westwards 100 kilometres to Taveta on the Tanzanian border, a place I was to get to know well. Apart from tourism, much of the local economy was based on the production of sisal, a plant similar to agave, which provided the strong fibres used to fabricate ropes and the hessian sacking used all over East Africa. The economy was mainly subsistence farming. Most people drove through Voi without stopping, and in 1978 there was not even a hotel in the town.

Vinu Shah was an enterprising Indian who ran much of the local commerce, having a large emporium full of sacks of posho, maize meal, chickpeas and lentils and a thousand other useful things. He and his wife became good friends of mine, and taught me a lot about Asian cuisine.

There had been no surgeon at the hospital for some time, in spite of Voi being a busy route centre. All the locally qualified doctors wanted to be in the city centres, so the districts were often short of any specialists, and I was soon to find out why the Kenyan Medical Service wanted an experienced general surgeon in Voi.

Voi District General Hospital,

I now had a total of 15 years medical and surgical education behind me. Also, considerable experience of working single- handed in remote situations. Now I was in my element, responsible for the surgical care of over a million people, deep in the heart of Africa.

From the daily journal I always kept, I have tried to create an image of the following three magic years as a bush surgeon in Africa.

The hospital at Voi was a very typical government establishment, built by the British after the second world war, and had a capacity for about 100 patients. Most of the staff were of the Taita tribe who inhabited this area, but there were also staff from other tribes, including the Kikuyu, Kamba and Luo. Everyone seemed to get on together, which was just as well, because the influx of patients never ceased, and being a government institution, logistics was a constant problem, as was staffing.

This was the major difference between the public government hospitals and the private mission hospitals wherever I went in Africa. The missions usually had far better access to resources than the government hospitals. After my early experiences with the missions in Cameroun and Congo, I now felt the need to practice in a more authentic Africa, within the government service, even though it would likely be much more demanding.

The first thing I always did at a new hospital was a major ward round, not just to survey the human pathology, but to assess the nursing care, cleanliness and organisation of the wards.

It was always a stimulating experience, as I never had any idea of what I was going to find. As things turned out, I did not actually complete that first ward round, because the second male patient I saw, who had been admitted two days before with an obstructed inguinal hernia was looking decidedly peaky, with a tachycardia of 120 bpm, and temperature hovering around 40 C. He was toxic with peritonitis, so we just took him straight to the operating theatre and within half an hour I was doing my first small bowel resection at Voi.

At Voi, as in every other bush hospital I had ever worked in, the process of referring a patient to a higher centre was virtually impossible. There were simply not the funds for an airlift out. So, I became used to dealing with all sorts of serious injury and other major surgery, in the knowledge that if I did not do something, that patient would probably die. It was a great way of learning, but nerve-wracking at times.

When I did finally conclude the ward round of 93 beds in all, I could have written a book on the pathology I had seen. About 10% of the patients had some sort of wound – an animal wounding, burns or osteomyelitis draining pus from a bone. TB was also common. It is such a ubiquitous and variable disease, appearing anywhere and everywhere, and often presenting in strange ways, such as a renal mass or deep bone infections. There were 15 cots and beds in the children´s ward, but 22 patients, with everything from bronchiolitis to broken bones, and a primigravida in obstructed labour on the labour ward. All in all, it was a fairly typical array of the patients to be found in any district hospital in East Africa.

I then inspected the laboratory and Xray departments, both of which were simple but adequate. Outpatients was a frightening mass of humanity, of whom most were mothers with crying children. Fortunately, much of the routine work was performed by well-trained clinical officers, who referred only the more tricky cases to me. Communications were relatively good and there were many outlying villages, so we often saw more than 200 outpatients a day, and as the word went out that there was now *a mzungu* surgeon at the hospital, the number of patients increased considerably.

Finally, I inspected the operating 'suite', which was a misnomer, as the facilities were as basic as could be. The operating table was adequate, but the autoclave belonged in a museum, being just a tin drum with a lid, heated below by two paraffin-fuelled Bunsen burners. There was a prototype Boyle's anaesthetic machine which would also have looked good in the Royal College's museum. Lighting was once again by light bulb, just as in Garissa. This was always a major problem in these peripheral hospitals and was why I was never without my battery-powered headlight.

The first 'relocation of resources' which I ever carried out in Kenya was to find a lonely mobile operating light in the Kenyatta hospital in Nairobi a week later, and carry it back to Voi, where it impressed my staff and revolutionised my surgery.

My operating theatre for the next three years was enhanced by the view through the windows. Just outside I could see the wooden rafters which supported the extended roof, hanging comfortably from which was a large family of pipistrelle bats. These became my constant companions, and often joined us inside the theatre when the windows were open.

Living in the Wild

One of the big benefits of being the District Surgeon at Voi was my comfortable old colonial house with its wide terrace and wilderness garden, which was also part of Tsavo East and West Game Reserve. My house was in the middle of these two big reserves, and as a result I soon became immersed in every aspect of African wildlife, from the highly amusing antics of the dung-beetles to larger and more dangerous animals.

All kinds of wild animals used my garden as their preserve. In the tall euphorbia tree by the kitchen lived a black mamba, the most poisonous snake in Africa. The snakes are silver, and the black bit is actually found in the mouth, but I would strongly advise against anyone attempting to check this fact. We lived together in perfect harmony for three years, and the only time there was a slight friction was when one of these long, silver snakes came into the kitchen one evening, slid into the living room and then exited onto the terrace.

Another ugly and more ungainly of the animals was the monitor lizard. They were also vicious, with a poisonous bite, and they were for ever trundling over my vegetable garden and dope plantation. I did not usually take umbrage, until the night one invited himself into my house.

I was entertaining myself shooting flies and mosquitoes with the fly gun I had been given as a birthday present, whilst listening to Nairobi FM on the radio. There were no luxuries like television then, nor did I need them. The African nights were full enough of noise and life.

The monitor lizard appeared through the kitchen door and headed for the couch where I had left the remains of my evening feast – the bones of a roasted impala shoulder.

I sat perfectly still as this metre- long reptile demolished every remaining morsel, gave me a brief nod, and then exited the living room door on to the terrace.

I was beginning to learn that if I did not react instinctively to these animals, they often disregarded me, and then I saw some astonishing natural behaviour from time to time.

After this particular intrusion I placed a wire mesh barricade across the bottom of the doorways. I always used to leave the doors open in the evenings, to invite the cooler breezes of night after the desiccating days, but it was also an open invitation to all the wildlife I shared my small estate with at Voi.

Once a month a lorry arrived outside my house from the nearby Manyani jail with two prisoners and a mass of hard wood for firing my Tanzanian tank. This was a 40-gallon drum mounted above a fire pit, into which I threw the occasional acacia trunk. The tank provided my hot water supply. It was primitive, but it worked like a dream. Much of the survival technology was of this ilk in Kenya in those days.

On Call from the Swimming Pool

Voi was the only town of any size between Mombasa and Nairobi, and was also home to Voi Safari Lodge, an upmarket tourist lodge a kilometre out of town. By virtue of my position, I was allowed free access to this lodge on the borders of Tsavo East and West game parks, which were full of wild animals and birds of every genus.

The elevated swimming pool at the lodge had been especially constructed to give a spectacular view overlooking a waterhole, from where one day I filmed over 300 ochre-coated elephants coming to drink as the sun went down.

On a bad day I would see the immaculate white jacket of Kibaki, the senior pool waiter approaching with a kilo of Bakelite telephone on a tray. He would then plug the brass jack on the end of the phone cable into the conveniently situated socket within arm's reach of me, and hand me the earpiece. It was usually either a Caesarian section which needed doing, or else another road traffic accident which dragged me off my pristine perch at Voi Safari lodge. I didn´t mind too much, as the privilege of being on call from such a great vantage point was a big bonus in my busy job.

Taveta – an Introduction to Bubonic Plague

Every month I used to drive Dennis west to Taveta, which lay on the Kenya-Tanzania border. Taveta was the most dangerous of my two peripheral hospitals, for bubonic plague was endemic in the surrounding area, and had occasionally burst into an epidemic form, killing hundreds as the disease evolved into the pneumonic form.

I will explain.

Yersinia pestis is the causative organism, the same which caused The Black Death over 600 years ago. The animal vectors were rat fleas, and nowhere was free of rats, especially Taveta.

More commonly, this bacterium infected humans causing inflammation within the lymphatic system, and hence the development of ´buboes´ - abscesses of the lymphatic glands. These often presented as perineal abscesses and much of my surgical work at Taveta was the incising and draining of these abscesses, as well as giving antibiotic treatment.

All microrganisms have the power to evolve into something even more toxic, and this was the case with Yersinia.

Pneumonic plague was a terrifying evolution of bubonic plague, which rapidly caused a wide-spread pneumonia with a near 100% fatality rate, and once a month I found myself in the centre of this potential nightmare.

There was a small brick shed by the hospital with a United Nations – World Health Organisation notice on the door. This was the emergency store in case there was another pneumonic outbreak. Inside was everything required to treat 100 severely ill patients. From plastic sheets to boxes of Erythromycin and Tetracycline to iv lines and litres of Dextrose and Saline. I was impressed that at this remote outpost there was such a UN-WHO emergency facility. It showed forward thinking as well as a certain commitment – which was not so common in these parts.

My prayers were answered, for not once during my three years did I need to broach the contents of this hidden shed. As it was, I was always slightly scared of getting infected by bubonic plague from the patients I was routinely operating on every month. As a doctor, that was the risk I had to accept, as did all my other nurses and health workers.

On the Last Steam Train to Taveta

One Sunday afternoon I was called to the hospital where I found a young local couple with their three-month old baby who had an incarcerated right inguinal hernia and signs of intestinal obstruction. I called my main man, Justin and an hour later the child was on the operating table.

All went well and we discharged the baby the next day, and that was how I came to meet Bombo, and travel on the last ever steam train from Voi to Taveta. The year was 1980.

Bombo was just 25 years old and was the father of the baby. He was also a train driver and drove steam trains all over Kenya, including to Taveta. With this common interest we became instant friends. He said he would call me the next time I was going to do my clinic at Taveta, and that I could travel in the cab of the engine.

It was like a dream come true, for I have always been in love with engines, especially steam engines, ever since I took off for Ely at the age of 8 from Newquay station. All the years at Lewes Grammar we travelled on the Cuckoo Line from Horam to Polegate in a steam engine, but sadly they were gradually replaced by ugly diesel engines.

There was something romantic and even scary about this steaming great mass of steel on wheels sparking red-hot coals and shooting out clouds of poisonous smoke and soot, which diesel locomotives never achieved.

Sure enough, one early morning during the small hours Bombo called me, and an hour later I was in the cab of the old steam locomotive with Bombo and his fireman, Wilson, who was just setting the teapot over the entrance to the glowing furnace which powered the loco.

The locomotive was a Garrett-Beyer, of which there were dozens spread across East Africa. First conceived by Herbert Garrett in 1907, they were unusual in that the power train was in three parts, the boiler, cab and fire-box being the main unit, attached flexibly to two water tanks, in front and behind. This gave them the advantage of being able to run on winding rails.

This engine not only had an enormous headlight but an armoured cowcatcher sweeping the rails in front. Wild animals were a big problem, and in fact it was more an elephant-catcher than cow-catcher, because these big animals were our greatest threat. At night they became almost invisible and were a constant menace.

The savannah plains were full of game and the rail track was not fenced off, so many animals were coming and going as we headed west, jumping so daintily across the rails like the impala and the Thomson's gazelles as we looked on, drinking our morning chai. We had to stop at Bura to take on water and more passengers, which allowed me the chance to have a look around this remote village which only existed because there was water to re-fill the steam engine´s boiler.

On the platform of this tiny station, I was amused to see not just one, but two toilets. One for First Class and the other for the *watu* – the proles. It took a good half hour to fill the trains' boiler and squeeze all the passengers inside – along with a large amount of livestock, for the Taveta market was on the border with Tanzania and was an important centre of commerce.

Three hours later we arrived at Taveta after a terrific trip across the African veldt, which even a millionaire's safari could not beat. At one point a big troop of baboons crossed the line, forcing us to stop.

"These *wananchi* are not coming on board", shouted Bombo to me, "for they have not paid the ticket!". He was a really entertaining companion and became my good friend till I left Voi, introducing me to all kinds of interesting things, for example, how to roast a goat at speed.

I shot off to the hospital leaving Bombo and Wilson to do their thing while I attended to another list of bubonic patients, performed one Ventouse vacuum extraction for an obstructed labour, operated on two inguinal hernias and circumcised five Masai children under local anaesthetic.

Every time I looked up from the patient I was operating on I could see the massif of Mount Kilimanjaro through the window of the OT, and I thought, " one does not see this sort of view from the heady heights of Guys Hospital, London!", and I rejoiced to be where I presently was, operating in the wilds of Africa, in spite of the constant risk of being infected by the plague.

By 1700 hrs I was through, and left the hospital in the care of Dr Kanjeni, the local District Medical Officer. By then I had also done a two-hour outpatient clinic, during which I saw 32 patients, from paediatric problems to pelvic tumours and more. Two patients who needed major operations were coming back on the train, but otherwise I was now free until the train left, so I went to explore the market which was still in full swing.

I love all African markets. They were the real base of African society wherever I went. From Agadez to Zanzibar they were a vivid living image of life. They were places where everyone met to socialise, sell stuff, buy stuff and generally have a good time, and Taveta was no exception.

On Roasting Goat at Speed

I caught Bombo negotiating with a Masai for the price of a goat, which was immediately dispatched, eviscerated and handed to Wilson who carried this fresh corpse back to the train which was being readied for its return trip to Voi.

I thought Bombo was just going to take it back to Voi for his family, but no.

"By the time we get to Bura we shall be eating roast goat", he shouted as he climbed up onto the boiler of the engine and placed the corpse over the copper whistle just in front of the cab.

Meanwhile Wilson had been banking up steam, and inside the cab was like the entrance to Hades, with the red-hot glow from the furnace into which Wilson was shovelling big lumps of coal, and hot steam coming from every direction.

Then Bombo gave a shout from above, Wilson let me pull the whistle cord and enjoy the magnificent sight of the goat wrapped around the whistle, being gently steamed up. I had never in all my years seen such antics on British Rail.

Sure enough, by the time the big water tube at Bura was once again filling *Mzee*, (old man), as Bombo had christened this ageing locomotive, we three were tucking in to delicious fresh-roasted goat. It was past midnight, but who cared? I was having the time of my life – all in the cause of saving lives, and I was feeling fine. That was until

our headlight went out.

On Locomotive Engineering - in the dark

The huge headlight on the train was American, being manufactured by General Electric. It was powered by a clever hydraulic motor driven by the engine and normally gave a brilliant glow to the track ahead which also acted as a warning to the wild animals.

The elephants moved slowly and were like rabbits in the light, becoming paralysed as the light approached. "We don't want Mzee to have an argument with a jumbo", said Bombo, and I could not disagree.

So it was that we spent the best part of two hours in the dead of night in the Taita plains while Bombo got his soldering kit out and did the repair. The steel tube carrying the pressurised oil had fractured. The hydraulic fluid had all escaped from the fracture and we were not going anywhere until this was fixed.

I held the two ends of the tube together while Bombo ignited his primitive paraffin-powered fire-torch and melted the solder. He slowly welded the two ends, both dosed heavily in flux. It really was a work of art when finished, and I gave Bombo a big hug. He was a champion, and soon we were off again at a steady 30 mph, the headlight illuminating 100 metres ahead of us once again.

During all my time in East Africa I continued to be amazed at the resourcefulness and skills of the indigenous people. Somehow, they always managed to keep stuff moving. From a wrecked *matatu* to this old locomotive, the Kenyans were masters in the resuscitation of dead motors, and Bombo was no exception.

We got back to Voi just in time for me to start the morning ward round, and I was bleary-eyed, for I had now been awake for 48 hours. But I did not actually feel too tired, for my recent train ride had been a super-stimulating African moment.

It really was the last steam train to Taveta, because in 1980 all of the Garrett-Baley engines were retired and replaced by diesel locomotives, which were never so beautiful.

Human Resources at Voi

Between the regular number of road accidents and wild animal woundings, there was every other aspect of general surgery to be dealt with. My catchment population was over a million and the nearest other surgeon was Mohammed, 100 miles south in Mombasa, so there was masses of work to be done, and not so many material resources.

My human resources were mostly excellent. I always treated every ward round and clinic as an opportunity to teach the nursing staff clinical methods and new skills, such as sterile dressing techniques for burns. My clinical teaching always paid off and relieved me of a great deal of work in the end, for everyone was keen to learn more.

Six months after I started at Voi, a young female doctor arrived, looking for work. Thus, it was that Martha joined my team, and a year later we got married.

In the OT I taught much minor surgery to Justin, who was my main man in the operating theatre, and was also well used to dealing with the antique autoclave. He always got rid of the bats which occasionally flew into the room while I was operating. He was a State Enrolled nurse, with two years of formal training, but was now very experienced. He was an excellent surgical assistant, a first-class nurse both in and out of the theatre and was a very fine person in every way.

Jocelyn was his right-hand man and took care of the cleaning and sterilising, and then came Rosalind, a very young nursing assistant who was quite inexperienced, but she was with us in the OT for two years and became a valued member of our small team. With her natural intelligence and her great enthusiasm, she turned into one of the best young nurses I ever did know. But she still always ran screaming out of the OT when the bats flew in. I hope that now, some 40 years later, she is the matron of some bat-free District hospital in the Greater Bhundu of East Africa.

Dafton Mwaita was my clinical officer anaesthetist. He was already a qualified nurse, and had done another year learning anaesthetic techniques, and was now also very experienced. Together over the three years, he and I must have done hundreds of operations, with never any disaster. He was quiet and very competent, and made do with a very ancient Boyle's machine, ether and Trilene being the anaesthetic gases of choice for us. Only in Nairobi or in some mission hospitals was it possible to find halothane or fluothane, which were the modern, risk-free anaesthetics in routine use in England then.

I remember how impressed my old friend Ian was when he visited, seeing Dafton's expertise with Trilene, so old-fashioned a drug that Ian knew little of it, except that it was also explosive.

Ketamine was an injectable anaesthetic drug that we used often. I could use it myself when necessary and I never travelled without a bottle in my kit. It was particularly good in children, and could be used intramuscularly or intravenously. It produced general anaesthesia without paralysing the vocal cords and was therefore relatively safe to use without intubating the trachea, which was a big advantage. We also did many operations using spinal anaesthetic, and a lot more using local anaesthetic, such as countless circumcisions on local boys, for which the government paid 10 Kenya shillings per foreskin excised.

To me these minor operations were socially necessary as these boys were all Moslems, but they were inconvenient, and Justin did them just as well as me. So, we came to a comfortable arrangement. He did them all, 10 every Wednesday morning when I had a surgical outpatients' clinic, and he kept the 100 shillings, which he certainly needed, as all Kenyan nurses were poorly paid.

Voi being around 1000 metres altitude and having a dry climate, many of the common tropical diseases such as malaria were less prevalent, except in the rainy season. I also noticed that wounds healed a lot quicker in Voi than in the humid jungles of Cameroun and Congo. To make up for this there were a frightening number of road traffic accidents, many involving fractures and other severe injuries.

Burns were also typically common wherever I went in Africa. The ubiquitous use of *jikos,* the charcoal-fired cooking stoves, inside a crowded hut was always an invitation to disaster. The high prevalence of people with epilepsy, usually as a result of obstructed labour leading to a hypoxic infant, often resulted sooner or later in an epileptic collapse over an open fire.

The pathological results which I had to then face were highly demanding, and invariably involved months of skin grafts, daily dressings and often, infection. Even on a dedicated plastic surgery ward, infection is a dreaded complication, and at Voi I also had my fair share. Infected grafts were not uncommon, however hard we tried to maintain sterility, and they were always difficult and time-consuming to treat, even with the few antibiotics we had.

On the Healing Powers of Plants

Then I came across an article describing the use of papaya as a wound dressing and disinfectant. The papaya fruit grew everywhere around us at Voi. It cost nothing, and with pineapple and a banana it regularly made me a very fine and nutritious breakfast.

I started my own experiment on the female ward where we had three burns patients. First, I scraped out the soft papaya fruit and then compressed it within a gauze dressing which I placed over the wound. The ward sister was at my side as I explained this unorthodox treatment. She changed the dressing every day, and after three days the wounds were clean and free from apparent infection. We were both impressed, and then began a trial involving all our burns patients, the results of which we recorded in detail every day.

The results were spectacular. All the infected wounds benefited, and they all healed well after further grafting. Then I started using a papaya dressing prophylactically, as soon as I had laid the skin graft onto a burn wound in the operating theatre. This also reduced the rate of post-operative infections in my grafts, and quite soon all presenting wounds received a dose of mashed papaya. I also found that the papaya skin is equally effective in cleaning infected wounds. There was no waste, and a papaya sold for 5 cents.

My later research explained this magic antiseptic property of papaya. The fruit contains proteolytic enzymes, one of which is papain, which is the same as the powder commonly sold as 'meat tenderiser'. It hydrolyses proteins into smaller components, and I found it was a very effective de-slougher of infected tissues.

It has recently been discovered that papaya also contains an enzyme called carapaine, which is an effective compound against intestinal parasites and amoebae.

Pineapple is another tropical fruit which contains a different proteolytic enzyme, bromelein, which I learnt is also an effective disinfectant and de-sloughing agent of wounds.

This was the beginning of my extensive research into natural plant alternatives in medicine, which continues today.

On Road Traffic Accidents (RTAs)

It turned out that shortly before I was posted to Voi, a local MP had been killed on the outskirts in a road traffic accident on the main Mombasa road. He had run into an elephant at high speed, the elephant being almost invisible in the dead of night on the tarmac. There was no surgeon at the hospital at that time, and an outcry was raised. That was exactly why my contract at Garissa had been cancelled, and I ended up at Voi.

I have previously referred to the dangers of driving in Kenya, and now I was in the thick of it. I was now a full-time orthopaedic surgeon, even though I had no formal training other than my work in A+E departments. Fortunately, I did have some experience of orthopaedics, and knew the basic principles. I also had one very good book on general orthopaedics which became my bible.

The vast number of road traffic accident victims who arrived with clockwork regularity at Voi District hospital, and the variety and complexity of their injuries was staggering and continuously taxed me. A whole team of orthopaedic surgeons would have been kept busy with the multitudes of splintered bones which arrived almost daily on the surgical wards. Yet, facilities such as X-ray and laboratory were very limited. Also, the technical instruments necessary for treating limb fractures were never available. Fractured lower limbs were a common occurrence, so I determined to sort something out, having at one point no less than five patients in traction for lower limb fractures.

On Fractured Femurs and the Kuntschner Nail

Even the traction weights I had to invent. A litre of water weighs a kilo, so a bucket on the end of a traction rope became a common sight on the wards. I simply could not afford the bed space for all these fractures, so after a rapid visit to the Flying Doctors, I came back from Nairobi armed with a bunch of stainless-steel rods, known as Kuntschner nails.

This was another great operation which my old friend Don Gilchrist had taught me. You make a lateral incision in the fractured thigh, insert the Kuntschner nail into the proximal end of the fractured femur, then push it proximally until it cracks through the top of the femur and becomes subcutaneous. Then, incise the skin over it, push the nail through the skin until it is flush with the fractured end of the proximal femur. Then align both fractured ends, and then give the nail a bash from above, which forces the nail into the distal medullary canal, and binds the fractured bone ends together.

If all went well, these patients went out walking after three days of post-op physio. We made terrific crutches out of acacia wood – the sort of thing Long John Silver would have been proud of, and then I saw the patient a month later in outpatients, by which time they were fully mobile and also had good flexion and extension of the knee.

The traditional, conservative treatment using traction meant three months of recuperation, and bed-occupancy, which I could not afford as I had road traffic injuries coming in almost every day. The only serious complication from this otherwise excellent invasive implant operation was infection. Therefore, absolute cleanliness and sterility were essential.

The Crash of February 1981 - managing 93 injured alone

The Nairobi – Mombasa highway is one of the 10 most dangerous in the world, in terms of deaths per mile, according to the annual Christmas edition of 'Time' magazine. A combination of ineptitude, drunkenness and the miserable state of this road led to countless deaths and injuries. The most terrible and memorable accident occurred in February 1981, just one month after Martha gave birth to our first child in Mombasa hospital.

Vinu Shah called me at 0200hrs one Sunday. There had been a bad pile-up between a bus and a lorry. Bad pile-up was an understatement, for that night we admitted 93 wounded and 11 dead. There was little chance of performing any useful triage with my miserable resources, but I did what I could, and amazingly, not one of the wounded died. But I spent three days in the operating theatre, sleeping on the examination couch, with no other surgeon to help me.

It reminded me of my time in Biafra in 1968.

The inmates at Manyani prison were magnificent, queueing up to give blood. My companion surgeon in Mombasa, Mohammed

Siddique, did send some help eventually. But on the fourth day we were out of every single useful dressing, bandage, splint and blood. I really could do no more, and I was utterly exhausted. I told Fernandez, the Provincial Medical Officer who arrived from Mombasa, that I was feeling tired, and would he like to carry on. Then I went to my bed, and did not care if the world fell in.

Shortly afterwards, after yet one more call for another RTA I was surprised to find Adelia, the matron of Mombasa Hospital lying on a bed in the Female ward, obviously in a lot of pain. I knew her quite well after frequent trips to Mombasa. She was a great, old- style Irish nurse who had spent years in Kenya, so she knew the score. I had only just finished dealing with another major pile-up. Justin had told me we were out of plaster and bandages – once again, and now this. Adelia had a compound fracture of her left femur, so using the last of my sterile battle packs I bound the wound and splinted the two legs together with a board. "Adelia", I said, "We are out of everything except morphine", of which we always had buckets for some reason.

"Give me 60!", were her immortal words.

"Grams or grains?", I replied, laughing, then shot her up and saw her relax into the arms of Morpheus. There was no more I could do except get our ambulance to ferry her back to Mombasa with a nurse escort. Two months later I met her in Mombasa, on crutches still, but smiling.

On the Causes of Infection

In between the trauma cases I was performing a wide variety of other operations, including many inguinal hernia repairs, and I was suddenly concerned after one ward round to find that three of my recent post-op patients had wound infections. In a clean, elective procedure this was most unusual.

Justin and I went over everything – and eventually found that the rubber seal on our antique autoclave had perished, and it was barely making one atmosphere of pressure. This was a serious problem for me, the district surgeon.

I left the hospital in the hands of Dr Kotek, the District Medical Officer and rushed to Nairobi to find Don. He was still flying all over Kenya with the Flying Doctors, and maybe knew of a spare autoclave, because it was extremely unlikely that the Ministry of Health were going to be of much help.

Don took me up to the Nazareth hospital just north of Nairobi in Kikuyu country, to the home of Jomo Kenyatta, where a gang of jolly Italian and Irish nuns ran this small but impeccable hospital. Sure enough, they did have a spare autoclave – and it was electric – a vast improvement. I also got a spare rubber seal, then set off back to Voi.

I have always been a hunter-gatherer and forager, but one must also have luck. I have always been lucky, and this time was no exception, for Justin nearly burst into tears when he saw my trophy from the nuns. From then on, we never had a problem with sterilisation or infections.

Interestingly, some while later a young man presented with an infected Kuntschner nail in his left femur – inserted one year before at another hospital. This steel foreign body had caused a serious problem, as there was infection, and also non-union of the bone at the fracture site. In the end I had to open his leg again, get rid of the Kuntschner nail and do a radical clearance of all infected bone and tissue, and then leave the wound to drain before I filled the cavity with tetracycline powder and closed the wound. He was two months in traction and then spent a further three months on crutches.

I learned that the morbidity from infected implants was considerable, and in the end, this knowledge tended me towards conservative, rather than operative solutions to simple fractures of long bones.

On Mind over Matter

One of great joys of being a bush doctor was the extraordinary variety of problems which I was faced with which I had never encountered before, which meant that life was always stimulating. From routine fractures to tricky obstetric problems, to some patients whose diagnosis was a complete mystery.

Of all the patients in the hospital, Mwasi had the strangest story. Two years before he had fallen off a lorry whilst loading sisal. He had presented at the hospital, paralysed from the neck down. He had to be fed by the nurses as he laid flaccid in his bed – but he had never developed any form of bed-sore, which I found amazing. My initial examination had confirmed a flaccid paraplegia.

One of the greatest fears of nursing staff anywhere was the development of bed sores in any paralysed patient. A combination of lack of movement plus inadequate nutrition of the skin made them almost inevitable in most cases, and once developed, they are the devil to treat adequately.

In any patient with a spinal cord injury, which is what I assumed Mwasi was suffering from, the chances of avoiding these decubitus ulcers, or pressure sores was miniscule. I simply could not understand how Mwasi had managed to avoid them for two years. It was only when I talked to Justin about this exceptional patient that he mentioned money.

It transpired that Mwasi had started a claim for damages because of this accident, and was still awaiting the outcome of his case. Justin said, "Daktari, we shall see how his health goes when his case is resolved".

Justin was a wise man, and sure enough, within two days of the award being made, Mwasi walked out of Voi District hospital, apologising for his illness, saying he was now better.

How a person can feign paralysis for two years is a miracle to me. But no bed-sores? I knew that something was fishy, but it took an African to explain the nub of this clinical problem.

Ward Rounds with my Mother-in-Law

In the spring of 1979 my prospective mother-in-law, Jadwiga, came out to stay for a month with Boris, her Polish ex-submarine commander husband. Viga, as we called her, was fascinated by the hospital at Voi and our very basic clinical setup. She was a senior consultant in obstetrics and gynaecology from a London teaching hospital but was unfamiliar with my own novel approach to obstetrics and gynaecology.

One week, I took Viga with me to my other local hospital at Wundanyi, an hour's drive away in the Taita Hills, in order to further educate her in matters of bush surgery. This hospital was situated on the top of a minor mountain full of luxurious vegetation, something which was lacking in the arid area around Voi. I always enjoyed my two-weekly visits there for the radical change in scenery, as well as the company of Robin.

Dr Robin Mogere was the local medical officer. He and I were the surgical/medical/gynae team at Wundanyi District hospital, and we were starting to perform some major surgery in this small hospital. Before every visit Robin would prepare a list of cases for me to review, which would include pelvic tumours and other gynaecological problems, including on one very rare occasion, a patient with a *lithopaedion* presenting as a pelvic tumour.

Bear in mind that we had no X-ray facility at Wundanyi, and the laboratory was very limited in scope, so most of our diagnoses relied on a good history and clinical examination.

"Why don't you send them for X-ray, just in case", asked Viga sagely on her first ward round with me in the heady heights of Wundanyi.

"There is none", I replied. "Up here we do it all on the touch of a finger – it's cheaper as well", which left her rolling her eyes. She was rapidly learning that this was no London teaching hospital. However, she warmed considerably to Robin.

Robin had arrived on my doorstep one day in 1979, having just completed his houseman year in Mombasa. Now he was to be the Medical Officer at Wundanyi for two years. He was very unusual in every way. For a start he was a Kisii, but spoke the Queen´s English as well as I did, much better than any African I ever met, and better than a lot of the British expats in Kenya.

He was also of a very cheery countenance and was rarely put out by anything – a useful attribute in these sparse outposts of humanity. He had just qualified from Makerere Medical School in Uganda – at that time one of the best in all Africa. He was determined to become a consultant obstetrician – until I disabused him of that most stressful discipline, in favour of general surgery.

As I said to Robin, "Look at me. I am terrified by obstetrics, yet I am doing at least one Caesarian section a week, forceps and vacuum extractions, and all the gynae in between, as well as orthopaedics, paediatric surgery, emergency abdominal surgery and everything else. If you do obstetrics, you will just spend your life in the female pelvis."

So, Robin started coming to Voi once a week for a taste of general surgery. He was a clever and able student, and soon became proficient in a variety of procedures, as well as an increasingly trusted friend. His wife Grace was a physiotherapist, and always prepared a great lunch whenever I was up in Wundanyi.

Today Robin is a consultant urologist in Nairobi, and their first-born child is named Viga, after Jadwiga, my mother-in-law. She was instrumental in getting Robin to London in order to prepare him for his own London Fellowship in General Surgery. For her great generosity and kindness, I can never thank her enough. I was there with her to join in the celebrations when Robin succeeded and became like me, FRCS. It was a triumph for this young African, who is still my dearest friend from Kenya days.

A Dose of British Corporal – Flogging the Prisoners

One other major responsibility I had at Voi was as Medical Officer and surgeon to the 700 prisoners in Manyani jail, 20 kms up the Nairobi road.

The table I am writing on today was made in the carpentry workshop at this prison in 1979, and I have been writing on it and eating off it for over 40 years. It is dark, solid, African mahogany, and takes two strong men to lift it. The prison workshops at Manyani were a legacy of the British colonialists, as were the bi-monthly floggings I had to attend there.

Every two weeks a crucifix was erected in the prison yard, and I then endured the spectacle of 20 or so unfortunates being flogged on their buttocks with a bamboo cane.

My role was mainly to give each prisoner a brief check-over to make sure he was fit for a dose of ´British Corporal´, as it was called. Only once in three years did I manage to exclude a prisoner from this primitive form of Behavioural Therapy. He had an abscess on one buttock, into which I stuck a scalpel later that day, and for which he was eternally grateful to me.

This prisoner was called Jakob, and had been arrested for sheep and goat rustling, a common enough pastime amongst the rural Taita tribesmen. Jakob took a shine to me, and when he was let out of jail he later became my gardening assistant. It was he who later brought me 10 fine seeds of marijuana, which I planted amongst my tomato plants.

On Snakes, Snake Bites and Snake Jokes

I had a fright one day when I lifted the corrugated iron sheet which covered my firewood behind the kitchen, to find a happy family of 12 tiny mamba babies. I never killed snakes, in spite of having that natural human fear of them. Alastair, my Australian dentist friend from Mombasa once said to me, "Kill one, and there are 100 more within reach", and he was probably right.

This reminds me of another amusing interlude during my days at Voi. Dave and Heather were both medics from County days in Brighton during the long hot summer of '76, and in 1979 they came out to spend a couple of weeks at Voi.

It was easy to have a good time at Voi, in between the daily chores of work, and we had just returned to the hospital after another game safari in Tsavo park. Dave and Heather wanted to have a stroll around the hospital, so I drove Dennis back to the house to prepare the evening barbecue.

On safari in Tsavo game park with Dennis and friends

Then I saw a big snake lying across the dirt track. It was a black mamba which had been run over by someone and was patently dead. I stopped and grabbed the snake and drove with it to my house – for I am a collector of *objets trouvés*. Then I decided to play a joke on Dave and Heather.

I opened the back door and placed the snake half in and half out of the kitchen. I then retired to my terrace with a bottle of Tusker to await Dave and Heather, directing them to the kitchen when they arrived.

"There´s a bloody great snake!", came the expected cry from Dave. Excellent!

I got out of my comfortable chaise longue on the veranda and turned the corner to see the tail of a long, grey snake emerging from the kitchen door.

"Don´t touch it! It´s a mamba", I shouted, but Dave and Heather did not look at all interested in mixing it with this venomous reptile. I stepped forward, grabbed the tail of the serpent and swung the snake around my head before smashing its head on the terrace floor, twice, just for effect.

I could see that Dave was impressed. "Hey, man!", he said, looking astonished, "I would not have done that".

"It´s ok when you know how", I replied nonchalantly as I hung the twice dead snake from the clothesline.

The strange thing is that whilst I meant to explain my prank to Dave and Heather before they left, for some reason I forgot. Over a decade later we were together again in Brighton at a big County boys and girls social do when Dave started describing the mamba moment at Voi. "Dave", I confessed, "that mamba was already well dead. Do you really think I am such a suicidal idiot!",

Dave gave me such a venomous look. "You big bastard" was his response. "Of course you´re stupid enough!".

A Diabolical Dilemma

It was another venomous snake, but this time a viper, which caused my single greatest surgical crisis during three years at Voi.

A 15- year-old boy was admitted, having been bitten on the right hand by a snake the day before. When I examined him on my 0800h ward round I could see that his hand and wrist were already swollen and the child was mildly toxic. This looked like a viper bite, but we had no anti-venom. I was worried because the haemolysis caused by viper venom can cause so much swelling that the main blood supply to the limb can become strangulated. The limb then becomes gangrenous, and the patient inevitably dies from septicaemia – without some form of radical surgical intervention.

When I went back to review the boy at midday, the swelling had now reached the elbow and I could no longer feel the radial pulse. His right hand was cold as well. The only way to stop this arm from becoming gangrenous was some urgent surgery to open up all the tissues and relieve the pressure on the radial artery.

The problem was that this child had come in alone, he was under 16 and there was no relative to give consent. That was the Kenyan law I had to abide by under normal conditions – which this was not.

I went to Kotak, the district medical officer and explained the situation. My only hope was the MDU – the Medical Defence Union to whom I had been paying my 25 pounds a year for professional indemnity insurance for years. I knew they had an office in Nairobi and asked Kotek to urgently call them whilst I was opening up the child´s arm, for every minute counted now.

Dafton anaesthetised the child, and I began to open up the arm from wrist to elbow – and was horrified. Every tissue plane was solid with extravasated blood, and the radial artery felt thrombosed. I could not save this arm. To save this child's life I would have to do an above-elbow amputation, urgently. Justin took the pre-operative photo of the right arm, for I was already thinking of the law, and evidence just in case. If I did not sort this problem correctly, I would surely have to face a government enquiry, and who knows what may happen then in independent Kenya.

By the grace of God, Kotek had found and spoken to the MDU lawyer, who would call me within the hour – which he did, and gave me the go-ahead, understanding that this was a life-or-death situation.

Two hours later the child was back in bed, minus much of his right arm, but already less toxic. I had very mixed feelings, for although his life had been saved, I just hated doing amputations, for the life of penury which they inevitably led to. A week later the boy's father arrived to take him home. Justin explained to him what had been necessary, and I could see that the father accepted the sad truth. He well knew the implications but was grateful his eldest son was still alive. I had mixed feelings. I was glad that I had saved this child's life, but mortified to know that in the process, I had turned him into a cripple.

On Wounds and Woundings

There are surgical wounds and there are animal woundings, and they are very different, particularly since animals do not much mind where they make their wounds, or how. So, I was not too surprised to be called by Justin one peaceful Sunday afternoon to find two young shepherd boys in various stages of disrepair. Being the boys they were, when they came across a pair of rutting warthogs fighting, they intervened with their catapults, at which point the warthogs disengaged and headed for the boys.

One of them was limping from a tusk wound which had opened up his left leg from hip to knee, and the other had something sticking out just below his left eye, which turned out to be a broken tusk, which had deeply penetrated the maxillary antrum, just two millimetres below the eye and was now tickling the base of the brain. Amazingly his eyesight was unimpaired, and he was fully conscious.

At Alder Hey children's hospital they would have called the whole neurosurgery team out for this, but I had just Justin and Jocelyn with me, and all three of us were perplexed at what to do. Then I remembered the boy with the dart in his head at Alder Hey. The surgical team had pulled that out with no problems, so I seized the bull by the horns, in a manner of speaking.

I grabbed a large forceps and told Justin to get some one-inch ribbon gauze in acriflavine ready. Jocelyn held the boys head, I prayed and yanked, and out came copious blood plus three inches of filthy warthog tusk, a trophy which I still possess. I rapidly packed the maxillary cavity with the acriflavine ribbon gauze, then checked all eye movements before sending the boy to the paediatric ward.

It took us another two hours to put his friend's leg back together, and I laughed to hear Justin admonishing these two boys the next day on the post-op ward round, warning them of the dangers of rutting warthogs.

Another type of wound is caused by weapons, from cutlasses to cannon and I have seen many of these. One particular patient at Voi comes to mind. He was a Masai cattle herder who had been shot in the chest by rustlers two days before and had walked all the way to hospital with a collapsed right lung. Fortunately, the bullet had passed clean through the chest wall and exited posteriorly. For a change, our Xray machine was in full working order, and I have photos of three good films, one taken on the day of admission, the second at one month and the third taken three months later. I treasure them because they clearly show how the body can heal itself, given half a chance.

I had quickly put a chest drain into his right chest and drained a litre of blood, which re-expanded the lung. A week later I discharged him, with good air entry on both sides of his chest and no signs of infection, and when he arrived for his one-month follow-up the Xray only showed a small opaque area. At his return visit two months later the Xray looked normal, and the patient was in good health.

I had done little more than put in a chest drain and given a course of antibiotics, and this herder´s body had done the rest. But these were fit and resilient people I was working with, and obesity and diabetes were rare in those parts.

The Natural Wonders of Kenya

Within my busy schedule I still found time to explore the magnificent country around me and it´s fauna. The dusty plains which surrounded Voi were loaded with all kinds of wild animals, from the classic ´Big Five´, to the voles and bush babies and civet cats which used to appear at night.

The birds were also magnificent in their variety and colours, from the Superb starling to the lilac-breasted rollers, the raptors and vultures and the Marabou storks, the ugliest bird in the world, which constantly circled overhead, looking for carrion.

Using a 20cc syringe and some tubing I had made a fountain within a hollowed-out tree trunk in my front garden, with a small pond below which also attracted a lot of birds.

The Marabou storks are the only birds I have never had any affection for. Not only are they physically repulsive, but their behaviour is equally. To see them fighting over the rotting corpse of a water buffalo is not so picturesque, nor was the sight of these ugly birds digging up my latest offerings from the OT.

Managing Lions on the Wards.

The surgeon's house at Voi was a half kilometre stroll through dense bush from the main hospital, and there were never any fences, so this stroll was always slightly tempered by the possibility of some big, wild animal jumping out of the bush.

One day, during a severe, seven-month drought, I arrived at the hospital to do my usual 0800h ward round and was surprised to see the TB ward terrace completely devoid of patients. Maybe the Rifampicin we had just started using had effected a miraculous, overnight cure. But my optimistic wish was not the reason for this sudden glut of empty beds on the Male ward.

It transpired that one of the TB patients had awoken in the middle of the night to find a male lion staring at him. I imagine that he gave some form of warning to his fellow patients, and then jumped over the open terrace and went for bush, closely followed by the rest of the patients.

Must get a few more lions around here, I thought to myself as I started a somewhat depleted ward round. That afternoon Kioku, the Taita District Commissioner came by. He and I drank Tusker together and occasionally played draughts on his scratched old board.

"Daktari," he said, "we are having a problem with lions". "Anything I can help with?", I said jokingly.

"You must take care coming to the hospital. The lions have come to town because of the drought. One herdsman was taken last night". He laughed when I told him about my vacant TB ward, but his warning was serious. From then on, I always took my ebony killer-stick which I got during my Congo days. I reckoned that a clout from that would make a lion think twice, but mostly I just prayed as I walked.

Continuing Medical Education in the bush

It is hard for me to imagine how life is for the district surgeon at Voi these days, with the advent of the internet. Keeping in touch was a constant problem during all my years in Africa. A bush surgeon was, by definition, isolated. Resources, from libraries to my professional colleagues were far away – which was the loss I felt most.

However, there was in Kenya at that time a really great bunch of fellows, known as the East African Society of Surgeons, of which I am still a proud member. We even had our own tie – crossed scalpels over a zebra. Every one of us was a general surgeon, from as far north as Makerere in Uganda to Dar-es-Salaam in Tanzania and south to Harare. Many were teachers at Makerere or Nairobi medical schools, but there were many others who, like me, worked out in the sticks. We had three meetings every year, which I found vital for my professional sanity, as well as introducing me to other surgeons.

Gerald Neville, Mike Wood, Imre Loeffler, Don Gilchrist and many others were the most excellent people you could ever want to meet, each one a master of the scalpel and the most willing of teachers. I remain indebted to them all.

We also had the journal, 'Tropical Doctor' published four times a year, and edited by my friend, Hugh de Glanville of the Flying Doctors in Nairobi. We all contributed to it over the years, and it did help to stop me from vegetating out in the *bhundu*, teaching me some useful tropical medicine as well as some exotic pathology.

From Death by Coconut ....

For example, it was in this worthy mag that I learned of the dangers of sleeping on East African beaches. A regular, annual paper from Tanzania described the major causes of head injury around Dar-es-Salaam, in the top three of which was always 'Death by Coconut'. I was nearly killed by a falling coconut in Mexico, at Palenque in 1974. Thirteen deaths were recorded in 1980 along the pristine Tanzanian beaches. It was not the sort of thing I had been used to seeing on Brighton promenade.

Head injuries were a constant and stressful problem. In those days no one in Kenya knew what a car safety belt was, and with the high rate of road accidents, I soon got used to using the Kenyan equivalent of the Glasgow Coma Score once again. The problem was not just the need for skilled nursing staff, but the occasional accident victim with an acute subdural haematoma.

Like obstetrics, neurosurgery used to terrify me, and the thought of it still does. Cracking a skull in the dark hours under local anaesthetic and praying I had hit the right spot was always nerve-wracking.

One of the vital surgical tools I had brought with me from England was a stainless - steel box containing a hand trephine set. I knew how to use it and did probably save a few of the many head injuries I had to cope with, but it was a part of general surgery which I preferred to avoid. Give me an ´acute abdomen´ any day.

……To Obstetrics, and Teaching a Life-Saving Skill

Obstetrics was another of my major surgical fears in Africa, for the need was never-ending. Kenya' s birth rate was high in spite of the International Planned Parenthood Federation' s best efforts. Ante-natal care was always sparse, so there were often complications during the delivery process. Furthermore, I had never had any formal training in obstetrics and gynaecology. It was small wonder that Jadwiga, my mother-in-law, had been in a near-constant state of shock as she observed my sparse obstetric skills. I had learned all my obstetrics on the run, so it was also often stressful. I relate just one example.

It was yet another Caesarian section, and we had just lifted the newborn baby from the mother´s open uterus. I had the Duval' s forceps on the lateral edges of the uterus when the attending paediatric nurse said, "this baby will not breathe", always a bad moment for me.

I told Justin to lean on the bleeding hysterotomy incision, grabbed my precious neo-natal endotracheal tube and laryngoscope and in a few seconds had intubated the infant, sucked out the larynx and slammed the Ambu bag onto the tube for the nurse to squeeze. Then back to close up the wound after an alcohol wash of my gloves, breathing rather heavily. This is what bush surgery is all about. Another close shave.

Justin closed up the skin while I wrote up the operation notes, and then I had a moment of inspiration. We were still losing some new-borns as a result of respiratory insufficiency at birth, but I was the only one who knew how to intubate a neonate apart from Dafton, and we were often tied up in the OT.

I had learned this life-saving skill at Alder Hey in 1974 when I was doing Paediatric surgery, and it is a very handy skill. The neonatal anatomy is very different from the adult, and the establishment of an adequate airway is absolutely critical within seconds of the child being born. The whole of the child's future life depends on these precious few seconds, and sticking a suction tube into the mouth was simply not adequate in some cases. The trachea had to be directly visualised, sucked out and intubated – a very delicate procedure in a new-born.

I had learned to intubate patients in Cameroun when I worked with Jack and had used it to good effect later in The Congo, but those patients had been adults. Neonates were very different. I decided to teach every obstetric and paediatric nurse this skill, starting with the nursing sisters, who were all very well-trained in those days, and were willing students. Then, I taught the sisters how to train the other nurses. We had so many deliveries every day it did not take long to train all the nurses how to directly visualise the vocal cords and insert the special neonatal ET tube.

In this manner we reduced the neonatal deaths to almost zero, and the nurses were all pleased to have learned this vital skill.

Voi was also where I learned to use a vacuum extractor. This is a very good instrument for delivering a babe who is a bit stuck - (one of my personal obstetric terms). Place suction cap on presenting scalp (hopefully ´tis not a leg), get the pump going, and pull – very gently, with the contractions.

Usually – Bazooka! One more live child, squawking loudly, if things went well. If things didn´t work out, then there was always a rapid Caesarian section, 25 minutes from skin incision to skin closure on a good day.

A Visitor from Liverpool Days

Shortly after I started work at Voi my friend Ian from the garrett at Percy Street days came out to stay for a month, bringing with him an electric ice-cream maker as a gift. It fast became a treasured kitchen item, and the luxury of home-made mango and pistaccio ice-cream became a regular treat.

I am still not quite sure what Ian thought about my rustic African surgical setup, for he was now a senior registrar in anaesthetics at a major London teaching hospital. Our antiquated equipment and limited resources must have been a revelation to him, but he was not fazed.

For me it was great to have my old friend and colleague at my side again. We had hardly seen each other since we got Fellowship three years before. It was also the first time I had had the privilege of a second opinion for two years and it made me realise how isolated I was, so I was sad to see him go.

Even though we had been blood brothers since those days in the freezing garret at No 9 Percy Street, it was astonishing how widely separated had become our medical trajectories. Ian was now single-minded on becoming a consultant neuroanaesthetist – a career for only the bravest hearts, whilst I continued to enjoy the life of a bush surgeon in wild Africa. But that is the joy of medicine. It provides an infinite number of possibilities for a fulfilled life in health care.

The Birth of RHeMU

One big problem wherever I worked as a surgeon in Africa was the maintenance and repair of equipment. From a broken sphygmomanometer to the anaesthetic machine, to the hospital generator and transport, there was a total absence of this essential maintenance and repair facility in every government hospital I visited. The religious missions usually had an engineer on site, and as a result, the whole hospital functioned a lot better, but the Kenyan government health care system had nothing budgeted for maintenance and repair.

So, I went to Karin, always my most valuable asset at the Danish Embassy in Nairobi. I put a proposal to her which she passed on to Hans, the main money man. I called my project RHeMU – Rural Health Maintenance Unit. It says much for the Danes that within six months the old hospital mortuary had been converted into a garage and engineering workshop, and a most able young Danish volunteer, Kjeld had arrived, with his wife Hanna.

Kjeld was one of the most industrious people I ever met, never happy unless he was buried in a mass of broken metal. I donated him our old mortuary to use as his workshop. Hanna was a nurse, and she became an extra asset in the Mother and Child Health department. The first thing Kjeld did was to start digging a car examination pit in the centre of the mortuary floor. The fact that 1000 dead bodies had been dissected in this space did not bother him. Then he concreted everything. The final result was highly impressive.

Then I gave Kjeld his first serious hospital project. It would affect every ward and outpatient nurse, every day, and to me was extremely important. It was the maintenance and repair of every sphygmomanometer in the hospital – as well as the checking of their accuracy. By the time my "extraordinary request" for Danish funds for 10 decent quality new stethoscopes had been attended to by Karin, my gang of nurses were smiling fit to bust, and after that we never had a problem measuring basic clinical parameters which, in our poorly equipped hospital were so vital for so many acutely injured patients from the road traffic accidents.

Kjeld even made a reading frame for Mwasi, my 'paralysed' patient so he could read the 'Daily Nation' every day.

By the time Karen and the Danish Ambassador arrived at Voi some three months later to review the project, Kjeld and I had a pristine government district general hospital to show them, which included a fully equipped and functioning workshop, with the first local apprentice already in training. We even had two infant incubators – 'relocated' from the main Nairobi hospital and repaired in Kjeld's Aladdin's cave in the old mortuary, which now also had a metal-working lathe and a small blacksmiths forge.

The Ambassador spent half a day with us, and was clearly impressed with our maintenance project, to such an extent that he committed DANIDA funds to develop more RHeMUs in other provinces of Kenya. Kjeld was soon promoted to become the manager of these satellite projects.

If you want to plant a seed, fertilise the ground first. Karen was the planter of my seed with the Danes, and she was a brilliant administrator. After two years in Kenya, she not only spoke Swahili like a native, but was living with a 2-metre tall Masai warrior half her age. She had become immersed in my various revolutionary activities, and by now was a good friend, so RHeMU was no big surprise to her, and it was not our last successful co-operative project.

An Introduction to Thoracic Surgery

Just after Christmas 1980 Justin came to me and told me that Dafton was unwell. Apparently, he had been having difficulty swallowing for some time, and it was getting worse. Dafton had always been tall and thin, and I had not noticed any obvious weight-loss in him. But when I went to speak to him, I saw that he was indeed thinner.

From his history it seemed there was some obstruction around his oesophagus or stomach – a place I had rarely visited, except with an endoscope.

Suddenly I was in a fix. Not only was Dafton my trusted anaesthetist, but over our years together he had become a very good friend. Yet here he was with the possibility of a cancerous tumour in a very inaccessible place. All I could think of was Dafton's need for an urgent operation if I was to have any chance of saving his life. I was even prepared to take him to the Kenyatta Hospital in Nairobi myself, but we both knew that was not a good option. I had never excised an oesophageal cancer by myself, and I was in no way a competent thoracic surgeon.

So, Dafton and I drove down to Mombasa to see Mohammed, the consultant surgeon, and he organised the barium swallow which confirmed my clinical diagnosis of a low oesophageal tumour. But Mohammed was working alone at that time, snowed under with work, and sadly told us he had no chance of operating on Dafton. Reluctantly we drove back to Voi, where Dafton had expressed his wish to die.

It was a terrible drive, as both of us now knew the diagnosis, and were fearing the worst. Then I had another of my inspirations.

"Dafton", I said, "if you don't mind risking it, I'll have a go". He knew as well as me my limited thoracic experience, but surprised me by replying, "Of course, daktari. Who will be my anaesthetist?" Oh God! Suddenly I was full of fear as the reality of my offer sank in. But by the time we reached Voi, I had a solution, and called a friend.

Gerald Neville was a very experienced general surgeon and had become a mentor to me. I rang him at home in Nairobi and explained my problem, and within two days he was at my side in the OT at Voi, with his own experienced anaesthetist from the private Nairobi Hospital. And Dafton was unconscious on the table.

First, I performed a laparotomy through a midline incision and palpated the gastro-oesophageal junction, but felt nothing inside the stomach. However, there was something bouncing off my right index finger, which was extended into the lower oesophagus.

"Gerald, I think the tumour is in the distal oesophagus", I said, and handed over to him. After a detailed examination inside the abdomen, Gerald nodded his head in agreement. So, it was to be a thoracic approach to remove this tumour, and suddenly I was very glad indeed that Gerald was here to perform it, for I had no experience in this very specialised field of surgery. I closed the laparotomy incision, then we re-positioned Dafton on his right side and re-placed the sterile towels. All was now ready.

"What are you waiting for?", asked Gerald.

"You, of course", I answered, handing him the scalpel.

"Indeed not" replied Gerald, refusing it. "Dafton is your patient. I am just the assistant today".

I briefly looked outside the OT window, praying for guidance, but all I saw were our family of bats hanging upside down in the rafters.

It was a magic moment. I was about to perform some major thoracic surgery on my own friend and anaesthetic colleague. Thank God for Gerald! Under his skilful and confident guidance I did complete the operation, something I doubt I could have achieved alone. Almost miraculously, the tumour turned out not to be malignant, but a rare, benign gastric leiomyoma – a non-malignant tumour of smooth muscle fibres.

One of the last procedures I performed at Voi was to remove the nasogastric tube from Dafton, two weeks post-operatively. It was a wonderful moment for us all, and we did celebrate. Dafton, with a small bowl of soup, but the rest of our jolly team with Tusker.

If my praise of great teachers occasionally sounds repetitive, then please forgive me. I was in the shadow of great teachers, from Socrates to Gerald Neville, and I have always done my best to emulate their efforts. However, after three hard years at Voi, being constantly on-call, even though I was becoming a master of bush surgery in all its forms, I had had enough of non-stop surgery. I needed a rest.

I completed my three-year contract with DANIDA in March 1981. Our son was nearly three months old. After some joyous departure celebrations with the hospital staff, and promises to re-visit friends, we retired to a 22,000-acre ranch just 30 miles south of Nairobi, where Joni, an artist friend of mine had a house. She was off to Japan for a year to study their traditional art.

It was there in the Athi plains, that my Danish friends came to find me two months later. They had a project I might be interested in. It concerned building a hospital in a place called Lesotho, and then running it for three years. "Carsten", I said, " you know that I am just a simple surgeon. What the hell do I know about hospital construction and administration, and where on earth is Lesotho?"

15. TO LESOTHO AND THE MAGIC MOUNTAINS 1981 – 84

Life on Athi Ranch

It was March 1981. I had just celebrated my 35th birthday on the ranch at Athi, having finally finished my work at Voi after three hard but enjoyable years. It was wonderful not to be on call, and there was the added delight of a new baby. Wojtek was now three months old and starting to behave more like a human, and Joni´s house was a great place for us to be.

1981. Phidelia and Wojtek at Athi Ranch

Joni was an American artist who had been years in Kenya, living in this most extraordinary edifice which she had constructed. She was leaving on a year´s sabbatical to Japan, and we were welcome house-sitters.

It was hard to call it a house because Joni had designed and built it without a single right-angle. It looked more like an abandoned ruin than any normal dwelling. Even the windows were shards of broken glass. The shape was in no way geometric, but was most poetic. The walls were of solid rock and the roof was made of reeds and palms supported on wildly crooked acacia beams. I had also created a hammock for Wojtek, hanging from the huge beams above, in which he spent happy hours swinging.

The facilities were basic, but the house was comfortable, and the outdoor composting toilet faced a panoramic vista which was pure Africa. We were surrounded by 20,000 acres of Kenyan savannah and the lights of Nairobi were a distant 30 miles away. We would sit on the terrace in the evening watching the sun fall out of the sky, drinking gin and tonics. Sometimes Don came out to see us, but otherwise we were very isolated, which was exactly how I wanted things after my three turbulent years at Voi.

We had also inherited a menagerie, and I do not use this word loosely. Dune was the name of our camel, and he was the guardian of a flock of 14 ostriches. There were also three horses, four dogs and a flock of chickens. A pair of prize mynah birds serenaded us with a host of vulgar Swahili idioms, until for some strange sad reason they both fell off their perches within a few days of each other, and swore no more.

There was also an extensive herb garden which Joni cherished, of which a quarter consisted of her marijuana plantation. Outside the confines of this crazy house was Africa, with every wild animal imaginable, including a herd of 17 giraffe and one zebra called Spot, who all ran together with us when we were out on horseback. Even the cheetah cub Simba we helped look after shared the dogs' food from time to time.

One day I persuaded a big male giraffe to eat one of Joni's dope plants, which it did with gusto, only spitting out the root. I could not follow the full evolution of this original experiment as we were already into our second G+T, but the last I saw was the herd disappearing minus the bull, who was leaning against an acacia tree looking rather apathetic.

We used to go out most mornings at daybreak on the horses, leaving Wojtek swinging in his hammock under the watchful eye of Phidelia, our constant house companion, who had come up from Voi with us. To ride across the sun-kissed plains, wild and free with only the wild animals to contend with was a daily pleasure. The early morning dew made glistening patterns on the cobwebs hanging off the plants and there was a freshness in the air which would disappear within an hour as the sun rose.

There was one great danger apart from large carnivores that we occasionally encountered. Honey badger, or ant-bear holes. The tunnel entrances were sculpted by these ferocious mammals, and if a horse put a foot into one of these holes, a fractured leg was the least to expect.

Wherever we rode there were antelopes of every species. Impala and Thompsons gazelles abounded, and there were herds of zebra and hartebeest as well as the occasional gerenuk. This antelope's neck was an elongated marvel of design, enabling it to feed off the upper branches of the fever trees and other savannah shrubs and trees, which Thomson's gazelles and impalas could not reach.

Of all the wild animals which surrounded us at Athi, the bees were the most numerous and dangerous. Joni had omitted to tell me that her house was infested with honeybees. Wherever we moved there were bees, and I was concerned for Wojtek and all of us as the risks of getting stung were considerable.

It took a while to find their nest, and when I did, I was amazed. It occupied the whole of the hull of Joni's 20 ft sailing boat, which was quietly desiccating outside under the tropical sun. When I opened the hatch, all I could see inside was a mass of bees climbing over mountainous stacks of honeycomb, and there was a powerful and ominous hum all around. It was not a place to linger.

I did not want to kill these bees, and I also fancied some of their honey, so I worked out a cunning plan. I would anaesthetise them using the exhaust from Fifi, my trusty Renault 6. Connecting a tube to the exhaust, I led it into the hull via the hatch, then started up Fifi and stood back. There was little effect, in fact the bees seemed to get more lively. So, I waited until midnight when things had cooled down and the bees were quiescent, and gently opened the hatch again.

I had a panga with me and quickly cut a big slab of honeycomb and then withdrew. But I still had to get rid of the bees and in the end, I did have to poison them, which saddened me as I do so love their honey. Nevertheless, it did improve life inside our dwelling.

A visit from the Vikings

When the short rains came, the whole plain turned into a muddy quagmire, known as 'black cotton mud', and became almost impassable. So, I was surprised one damp and dismal day to see a Land Rover approaching. Inside were Karin, my main contact at the Danish Embassy and two senior diplomats whom I did not know. Once inside and out of the teeming rain I asked them how I could help.

"We are wondering if you would be interested in another project?", said Carsten, the senior.

"To be honest, I've had enough of surgery for a while", I said. "Oh, this is not so much surgery", he replied.

"Exactly what, then?", I asked.

"It's to start a new hospital and then run it in", said Jacob, and I imagined myself moving from our comfortable hide-out at Athi to some frenetic Kikuyu town. No way, thought I.

"Whereabouts is this place?", I asked.

"Lesotho" replied Carsten, leaving me wondering, for I had never heard of that country. "It is in southern Africa". I had not yet travelled south of the equator to work, and when offered a map I was interested to see that it was a tiny land-locked blob in the middle of apartheid South Africa.

"What qualifications do I have to build and run a hospital?", I enquired, beginning to feel out of my depth, for I still considered myself a bush surgeon and nothing else.

"We have a Danish architect and engineer who will be responsible for the construction", he replied. "We would like you to be responsible for the clinical and administrative side of things, and it would be a three-year contract".

My immediate response was negative. I was enjoying my freedom on the ranch and the joys of fatherhood and had no intentions of changing things.

I apologised, explaining my reasons. "Well, just have a look through these", said Carsten as Karin handed me a thick sheet of papers. "Maybe you will change your mind". Then they left, skidding sideways down the track of black mud.

I went to Nairobi to seek advice from some friends. I talked to Mike and Don at the Flying Doctors and also to another surgeon friend, Gerald Neville He was the surgeon who had come to help me with Dafton´s thoracic surgery during my last days at Voi. Their vote was unanimous. I should not change track, but continue my work as a surgeon.

In spite of this advice, I was still interested in the possibilities this proposed project offered. I had absolutely nothing in mind as far as work was concerned. The sterile corridors of the teaching hospitals seemed a million miles away and my NHS career was already blown, so I was effectively a free agent without an agenda and still had enough money to survive on the ranch for a few months. I could not travel halfway down Africa to some completely unknown place to work for three years without knowing what was expected of me, so I began to read the papers Karin had given me and became more and more interested.

Lesotho – the Mountain Kingdom

Originally called Basutoland, Lesotho was an independent country, and was a genuine African kingdom with a live king, Moshoeshoe. Previously it had been a British protectorate. It was also the only country in Africa united by one tribe and one language – Sesotho, which already made it interesting. It was one of the highest countries in the world, as nowhere was it less than 1000 metres above sea-level, and it was full of mountains. It was also poverty-struck and landlocked, surrounded on all sides by apartheid South Africa and its *bantustans*.

The project was to build, develop and run a 100-bed hospital at a place called Qacha´s Nek on the southern border of Lesotho with the Transkei, one of the bantustans which the government of South Africa had created. The job involved taking responsibility for all the clinical needs of a widely dispersed population of 100,000 mountain dwellers, amongst the very poorest people in the world.

The job title was, "Medical Superintendent and District Medical Officer, Qacha´s Nek District, Lesotho". Surgery was certainly not top of the list of my responsibilities according to this document, and that did pose a real problem for me.

I had done nothing but surgery for the last 10 years, even though much of it was not on the London RCS curriculum. I had already spent years studying surgery, and a lot more hours performing it under every imaginable condition, and I still wanted more. On the bright side I already knew that within the population of some 100,000 Basutos there would always be some requiring surgery.

In the meantime, David, the young white Kenyan owner of Athi ranch and a good friend of mine, was devising a new plan which he wanted to share with me. He was a most enterprising person, totally in love with Kenya where he had been born, and he was about to launch into a revolutionary type of business. Selling game meat.

It was a brilliant idea, and I was immediately interested. The end result is now called ´The Carnivore´, one of the most visited restaurants in Nairobi, and now world renowned. Vegans and vegetarians are never seen there, but what you can always see is a mass of roasting game meat, spitted over an open fire of glowing acacia wood coals.

In April 1981 I was out with David in the back of a short-wheel base Land Rover, he with his Mannlicher ,375 and me with my camera as he laid into a herd of impala. He needed an extra pair of hands, and I was happy to oblige, as long as it did not involve me killing the animals.

We made sausages with the first meat he shot, and then he started selling cuts, made by a butcher friend of his in Nairobi. That is how ´The Carnivore´ evolved, and I was happy to be a part of its evolution, because I was never without fresh game meat as a result.

The Return of the Vikings

I was still tempted by the possibility of a radical career change when once again I heard the sound of a Land Rover ascending our now non-existent track, after a month of heavy rain.

"GudTag!", said Karin, giving me a peck. "Dr Jensen has come from Copenhagen to talk with you". He turned out to be the director of DANIDA, the Danish International Development Agency, and he would not easily take no for an answer.

"If you have come to Athi all the way from Copenhagen, then I assume you are serious", I said. "So am I. I shall not move anywhere unless I have the opportunity to see this place and make an informed judgement before I commit myself. It is not a surgical post, and I am a surgeon".

They agreed, and gave me a six -week consultancy, all expenses paid. And that is how I arrived in Lesotho, in June 1981.

From Savannah to the Snow

As soon as I stepped out of the Twin Otter which had brought me from Johannesburg, and onto the tarmac of Maseru airport, I knew I was now in another orbit altogether. The air was crisp and dry and cold, yet the sun shone down brilliantly, lighting up the snow-covered Maluti Mountains in the distance. After the tropical heat of Kenya, this was a revelation. Sitting on the 45th parallel south, Lesotho's winter begins in June, and today there was snow everywhere. I could have been in an Alpine ski resort. Was I really still in Africa?

Kristin and Kjeld from the Danish Embassy were there to greet me and take me off for some refreshment at their modest office, whilst they filled me in on the local situation. I had a stiff itinerary to follow for the next three days, meeting various government officials including the Minister of Health, 'Me Moshoeshoe, a relative of the Queen.

(Note : In the Southo language, *'Me* translates as 'mother', and is the polite way of addressing a woman. *Ntate* translates as 'father' and is used in the same manner to address a man.)

I was to stay in the Maseru Hilton Hotel, which sounded rather upmarket for my taste, and so it turned out. There was a lot of American influence in South Africa, and their hotel chains was just one. There was even a small casino within the Hilton hotel, and in this poor city of just 100,000 inhabitants, a brand-new Casino had just been opened. I had never come across this anywhere else in Africa and was perplexed, but the reason soon became apparent.

I have written earlier about the conflict of religion and human nature, and the genesis of hypocrisy. Here in Lesotho I suddenly found myself in the middle of a very strange paradox.

The South African Boers originated in the Calvinistic atmosphere of 17th century Holland, and had remained fervently low church ever since, with outwardly strict moral scruples. But human lust being what it is, a way was found to export it just outside South Africa´s own borders – into the surrounding bantustans, and the three independent countries of Botswana, Lesotho and Swaziland, whilst maintaining the high moral standards demanded by the Dutch Reform church within South Africa.

Every weekend, crowds of white South Africans out for a good time would cross the borders for some immoral fun and games. Hence the many prostitutes I saw in Maseru, and the shining new Casino which, at the moment I arrived, had become the centre of a national scandal. This was related to the opening of this casino one week before, when, to entice the punters, the owners had offered the chance of a $16,000 bonanza, for a stake of just one maluti – equivalent to one South African rand. It would be a huge prize for any Basuto.

One day later a Basuto man from the hills dismounted from his pony outside the casino, entered and placed his one maluti bet – and won the prize, which was the front-page news in the Maseru Times that week. Mostly because the casino had refused to pay up. Everyone was outraged. Even the president became involved, and eventually the prize was paid out, but I was left shocked at the whole story. This was a side of apartheid which I had never imagined, and it left me wondering even more about men and their morality.

The next morning, I was surprised to find a tailored chauffeur waiting for me outside the hotel by his shining Mercedes. I thought it was over the top, but I allowed myself to be driven to various ministries during the morning and had some productive meetings with health officials. Lunch was at the Danish embassy, where I told Kristen that

I was uncomfortable in the Hilton, which to me was like a slice of America. She fixed me up at the Victoria Hotel where all the government officials stayed, and that suited me much better.

That evening I went for a stroll round Maseru in order to learn more about this mountain kingdom. It was not a pretty city and did not extend very far. It had evolved from being a small police post in 1869 when Basutoland became the British protectorate of Lesotho, and was now the capital, with a population of around 100,000. As I walked down Kingsway, the main street, I came across the Tourist Centre, which was the only beautiful building I saw. Its shape was based on the traditional Basutho hat, being tall and conical with a roof composed of long grass reeds on top of a round stone wall, and it stood out from every other building in town.

The influence of South Africa was plain to see wherever I walked. From the new casino and the Hilton Hotel, to the many small stores, all of whose products were manufactured in South Africa, from food and drink to machines and a lot more. There were numerous white South Africans around. I later discovered that they controlled every border crossing in and out of Lesotho.

By the time I returned to the Victoria hotel I had seen and learned a lot. It was clear that Lesotho was dependant on South Africa in every way, and in that sense was little different from a bantustan, being land-locked, even though it was proud to be known as an independent nation.

The next morning, I rid myself of the chauffeur-driven Mercedes. I told Kristen it was just not my style. Did they not have some wheels they could lend me? And that was how I came to spend the rest of my six weeks in Lesotho aboard a 500cc Honda trail bike, which I christened Eric the Viking.

Lesotho on Two Wheels

Although the motorbike was dangerous on the icy roads, which were pock-marked with potholes, it was a great way of getting around, and for a biker like me it was a perfect means of transport.

It was during my explorations of Maseru that I came across Billy Gibson. He was a young white man, born and bred in Maseru, where his father ran a hardware store. Billy was a hippy like me, but his hair was down to his shoulders, and so was his beard. He taught me a lot about Lesotho in the few days I was in Maseru, and he later became a close friend with whom I later shared a few memorable adventures.

I also took the opportunity to explore more of Lesotho on Eric the Viking, and sometimes I went out with Kristen and Kjeld in a project vehicle. They were a fine young couple, and we became very good friends. They knew a lot about Lesotho and its people and shared it all with me, so by the time I arrived in Qacha´s Nek one week later, I was well-informed about the general situation.

Dick Zaal was the Dutch doctor caring for Qacha´s Nek when I arrived, after a perilous flight across the mountains in a single-engined Cessna. He met me at the airport – a fenced off area on top of a mountain, where the control tower was a corrugated shed. The views were unlike anything I had seen in Africa before. We were on a plateau ringed by snow-covered mountains, of which Thaba Souru was the highest at 2,830 metres above sea-level.

I had often seen the snow-covered peak of Kilimanjaro when I did my monthly visits from Voi to Taveta, and I had climbed Mt Kenya in 1975, but they were rare and isolated snowy outposts in the African veldt. Here, all I could see were snow-covered mountains and it was very hard to believe I was still in Africa.

Qacha´s Nek – and my first emergency laparotomy

As we drove from the airport to Dick´s house, we passed the beginnings of the new hospital. The foundations were being dug and some buildings were already erected. The whole area looked just like a building site, and it was hard to imagine a 100-bed hospital there.

Dick and his wife Marie and four lively kids lived in a stone house in the old hospital compound which had been built by the British in 1925. The hospital was a collection of sandstone-walled blocks, all with tin roofs, and all with a coil of smoke rising into the freezing air.

Those plumes of smoke came from imported South African coal. This was the root of the reason I was here in Qacha´s Nek. Whilst Lesotho may have been a politically independent nation, being land-locked, it was dependent on apartheid South Africa for everything from maize meal and beer to coal and petrol, and even the oxygen bottles for the anaesthetic machine.

The Danes were working quietly to combat apartheid, and the new hospital was a part of their plan, for it was to have solar-powered heating and thus avoid the dirt and cost of imported coal. Until the new hospital was ready, I would continue using the resources of the old hospital – which were very limited. In addition to the hospital, I was to be responsible for eight outlying mountain clinics, as well as the inevitable TB ward.

The doctor´s house was typically colonial, with walls of sandstone and a wide terrace under a corrugated iron roof. It had recently been renovated and now contained a fine coal-fired cooking stove in the kitchen, where ´Me Emily was in charge. She was a diminutive Zulu grandmother who cared for Dick and his family, and later became a precious member of my own family, as well as Wojtek´s greatest friend.

After a rich meal of Dutch pea soup, Dick took me down to the old hospital for a ward round. I always enjoyed the first ward round in a new hospital, because you just never knew what to expect, and this time was certainly no different.

As we entered the male ward, which had both medical and surgical patients, Dick asked if I would look at a sick boy who had come in three days before with abdominal pain. The boy, called Mhotse, was 15 years old and looked ill. Even from the end of the bed I could see he was toxic. He was sweating and barely conscious and his pulse was racing. Strangely, he was hardly breathing, but when I lifted the bedclothes, I knew immediately why.

His abdomen was tense and bloated and had a sheen to it. It was tympanic to the touch, and when I gently percussed his abdomen there was a lack of liver dullness, indicating the presence of free gas inside the abdomen. Clinically he had peritonitis, from a perforation somewhere in the gut. In my mind there was no doubt, unusual though it was in a 15 - year- old, but there was always appendicitis to think of. Always expect the unexpected, I was taught early in my career.

"Dick", I said, "this boy needs a laparotomy – now! Is that possible?"

All thoughts of my Danida contract disappeared. This was a genuine surgical emergency. Both Dick and I could see that this kid was dying in front of us, but Dick was not a surgeon, good doctor though he was. Outside, there was a snowstorm and a freezing, howling wind. No planes were going to fly today, and there was no chance of any referral.

"I'll see if I can find Ntate Mpoe", said Dick and disappeared. Dick had already got an intravenous line in, which I switched full on. This child was very dehydrated and needed some rapid resuscitation before his operation. I put another iv line in his other arm and ran in a litre of 5% glucose. I also gave him a gram of ampicillin iv, and 80mgm of gentamycin. Then went to find the operating theatre.

Great Scott! It was Listerian in its starkness. Dusty ancient glass bottles sat on shelves, and the anaesthetic machine also looked Victorian. A lonely 100- watt bulb hung from the ceiling and the rudimentary table was bricked up at one corner as one wheel was missing.

Suddenly the lightbulb flickered into life, and I mean flickered. As the hospital generator cranked into life, but not for long, the alternating current frequency could almost be counted as the bulb filament waxed and waned.

Within the hour I was scrubbed up, facing Dick across the table. I had done a spinal on the child, which had been particularly difficult as he was rigid with peritonitis. I held a Swan and Morton 23 blade in my right hand, and thought,

"I have no professional insurance. I do not have any remit from the Danes, nor from the Lesotho government and no consent from his father, who is presently mining for the Boers outside Jo´burg. Lady Luck be with me". Then I incised the abdomen from xiphisternum to the umbilicus. Choosing the correct incision is a mixture of skill and luck. The upper midline is the one most favoured by the general surgeon as it could always be lengthened if necessary.

As soon as I opened the peritoneum a foul stink erupted, and I knew I was on the right course. The sucker was full on, but rancid bowel contents were still pouring over the table and onto the floor. "Where the hell was this bowel perforation?" In the middle of all this carnage and fluid it was impossible to see.

The years of training then kicked in. I must do a logical search. I started from the diaphragm to the greater curvature of the stomach, and then the lesser curvature, inch by inch. At the pylorus, where the stomach joined the duodenum, I found the hole.

It was at this point that the lights went off and the generator died.

It turned out that Ntate Mpoe had not checked the oil. There was none and the engine, a big old three-cylinder Lister had seized up. The anaesthetic nurse had a torch, and someone lit an oil lamp. I had learned never to travel without my headlight, which was retrieved from my bag, and this was how I completed my first operation at Qacha´s Nek.

Having liberally washed out the abdomen with several litres of normal saline, the last thing I did before I closed the peritoneum, was to spread a gram of tetracycline powder over the inflamed intestines. We sometimes also used sulfadiazine in Kenya, more in hope than anything else, but it did seem to make a difference in cases of severe peritonitis, even if there was no scientific evidence that I knew of.

When I left Qacha´s Nek three days later Mhotse was still alive and taking oral fluids. Two weeks later Dick sent me a telegram at Danida HQ in Maseru, to tell me he had been discharged,

It was probably this first clinical case which persuaded me to come back to Lesotho for what turned out to be three of the best, and most stimulating years of my life. I could still be some sort of surgeon, but the challenge of starting a hospital in these inhospitable surroundings I also found rather exciting.

During my stay in Qacha´s Nek I had found the Basotho people I got to know to be full of good spirit and humour, in spite of their straightened circumstances. ´Me Malisema was the hospital Matron, and a proper mother of all her flock, which was soon to include me. The nurses I met were all very well trained, and I could see that morale was high.

Arthur was in charge of the laboratory, and was one of the finest colleagues I worked with at Qacha's Nek. A kind and educated man, he also had a beautiful baritone voice and ran the hospital choir, which started every day with hymns and prayers on the wards. Even in the mission hospitals I had not come across this, but I found it a great way to begin a new day in the hospital, even though I was in no way religious.

Stig and Søren were the Danish architect and engineer, and we bonded quickly. They spent two days showing me the plans and the details of the new hospital, including its 120 square metres of solar panels and the computer-controlled central heating system. Out in this back of beyond it was extraordinary to find such high-class technology, and the skills to make it happen. I was beginning to have a lot of respect for the Danes.

It was not just the old hospital that was in a state of disrepair, so was the town. There was not one metre of tarmac and only one general store along the rocky high street. Everyone was either walking or on horseback, wrapped up to the hilt in woollen Basuto blankets of rich colours. We were in the middle of winter, and both rain and snow were falling copiously. It was freezing. Everywhere coal fires were burning, but the Sesotho also used dried manure from their cattle and donkeys as fuel, so the night air was richly perfumed.

The female ward was grim. In the middle of the dark room was a coal-burning stove, or what remained of it after half a century of use. The lower half of the stove was absent, and all I saw was a pile of red-hot embers falling from it onto a sheet of metal on the floor. Surrounding the stove, on the floor were the blanketed bodies of more female patients, the 12 beds already being more than fully occupied. Coal dust coated the entire ward, which was impossible to keep clean under these primitive conditions.

A part of the problem was related to the extreme geography and isolation of this corner of Africa. In winter, many of the tracks became impassable, and villages and clinics were cut off for weeks at a time. Pregnant women then made their way to the hospital as best they could, in order to have their 'lying in' safely. As a result, there were always a dozen or more women needing shelter and food as well as ante-natal care, in addition to the regular influx of female patients.

The male ward was similar in its Dante-esque appearance, with another corroded stove dropping red-hot coals onto a steel sheet. The walls and windows were also covered in coal dust, as were the patients. I began to see why a new hospital might be a good idea.

The final nail in my coffin as a full-time bush surgeon came in the form of a Basuto pony which Colonel Chaka lent me for half a day. Colonel Chaka was the senior officer in the Lesotho Mounted Police, who did his work on the back of a Basuto pony, and he became one of my greatest friends. It was he who later chose the big white stallion, Phakiso, which I rode on for three wonderful years. Its name translated meant 'like the wind', and he did ride like the wind.

I have ridden all sorts of things from scooters and motorbikes to camels and donkeys, but the hours I spent getting saddle-sore that day convinced me that I must come back. I had never been in such wild, untamed country, with its snowy peaks and running rivers of freezing spring water. Everywhere I looked was a delight to the eyes.

Lesotho was a true wonderland

Even when I had been riding across the Kenyan Athi plains on horseback, I did not have the spectacular backdrop which Qacha's Nek offered, and the thought of working in such an environment became increasingly attractive.

The villages were also very pretty. The houses, called *rondavels,* were round and the walls were of stone blocks, with straw and reed-covered roofs. Many of them were painted in bright colours.

The people were also great. They were very humorous, full of music and dance, and spoke English with the sweetest accent I had not heard before in Africa. They were of the southern Southu tribe, neighbours of the Zulu, the Xhosa and the ancient San peoples, whose languages were interspersed with a variety of clicks, which I never really mastered.

I was sorry to leave Qacha's Nek after one month, but I had much to organise in Maseru. ´Me Malisema came to see me off and told me she expected me back quite soon. She was a great lady, very perceptive and a good hospital matron as I was to find out.

From general surgery to public health and primary health care

Back in Maseru I de-briefed with Kirsten and Jens, the Danish head of mission. It seemed to me that whilst a new hospital was badly needed, the peripheral clinics also needed to be improved and better supported. Each clinic was run by a nursing sister qualified in midwifery, but there was no electricity in these remote clinics and deliveries at night were done using candles and oil lamps.

If I was to be the District Medical Officer, I wanted the clinics developed as well as the hospital, and the Danes agreed. The 40,000 extra dollars they provided was enough to supply every clinic with solar panels and lights as well as power for a single side band radio.

I was well received by ´Me Moshoeshoe at the Ministry of Health when I reported my findings. At that moment I held all the cards, and I was determined to squeeze one major concession out of the government. I wanted to make sure, if it was possible, that I would be followed at the new hospital by a local Basutho doctor. There were very few in this thinly populated country, and many of them quit Lesotho as soon as they were qualified in order to work in better paid jobs in South Africa, so it would not be an easy ask. ´Me Moshoeshoe assured me that she had every intention of placing a local doctor when I left.

It was the best I could hope for, and I did trust her. She had been very helpful during my visit, and I knew that relations with the government health officials were going to be critical if the hospital project was to be a success. I was feeling optimistic as I boarded the plane back to Johannesburg after a busy and interesting six weeks in Lesotho, and I was fairly certain I would be back. Kirsten and Kjeld came to see me off and did not seem to doubt this.

I had a great deal to think about on the way back to Nairobi, even though I was fairly sure I would take the contract. Once again, I held the aces. It was clear to me by now that the Danes were committed to a very complex project, which would require not just an experienced doctor with multiple skills, but one who could also administrate the project´s development. And there were not so many qualified candidates around.

How much could I negotiate with the Danes to improve the terms of my contract? I knew I would be employed as a specialist consultant, so my pay would be fine, but I also wanted an expatriate contract for Martha, who would be looking after Mother and Child Health. In Kenya she only had a local contract, which was poorly paid. If I was to administer a whole health district, I must have another capable doctor at my side, and they would merit being well paid.

I was also determined to get a decent project vehicle for my use. The government vehicles were mostly either dead or dying. There was a creaky old Nissan ambulance at Qacha´s Nek, but that was it, more or less. I had in mind a 4,7 litre, turbo-charged Toyota Land Cruiser, the very acme of off-road travel. I had driven one in Kenya once and they far surpassed a Land Rover´s performance.

I would also insist on a two-week language course in Sesotho for us before I started. The Danes had been kind enough to pay for one in

Swahili when I started at Voi in Kenya, and it had made a huge difference to my work and social life. The missionaries always learned the local language and I saw how important it was. I had also loved languages ever since I had learned Latin at the Kings School, Ely.

Back at the ranch I discussed my recent visit with Martha. She was up for it, and Wojtek also appeared to be in favour of this radical move I was planning as he lay swinging in his hammock, sucking his thumb.

A few days later I went up to Nairobi and paid the Danes a visit. After some extensive negotiations, I left with a contract for three years in Lesotho as District Medical Officer and Medical Superintendent of the Qacha's Nek Hospital Project, to be funded to the tune of $ 250,000 by DANIDA. My other requests were also agreed.

Thus, it was that I changed track. After 10 years of full-time work as a surgeon, I was about to enter the realms of hospital management and public health, and begin a life-long interest in all aspects of social medicine and healthcare which still continues.

Back to Qacha's Nek : Living under Apartheid

Within two months I was back in Qacha's Nek, driving a five-ton Mercedes truck full of building materials down a muddy track. It was to be the first of many adventures in Lesotho. The asphalt road had run out 20 kilometres outside Maseru. The rain was sheeting down, and large chunks of the main road to Qacha's Nek were dissolving in front of me. I have driven in all sorts of conditions over the years, but never quite as ferocious as this dark night. I was actually thinking of stopping and sleeping the night in the lorry cab when I saw a light in the distance. As I approached, I saw it came from an isolated rondavel, so I stopped, jumped out of the cab, and knocked on the door. As the door opened, a cloud of sweet marijuana smoke preceded the face of a young man with a big smile on his face.

That is how I came to meet Sankomota, one of the only rock bands in Lesotho. Moruti was the bass player, and it was he who greeted me and invited me in. The lead guitarist, Banjo, was stirring a pot of stew on top of an old coal-fired Victoria stove, whilst 'Stix', the drummer was flaked out on a mattress. I was well-received by these strangers, especially when I retrieved my own guitar from inside the Mercedes' cab, along with my stash of food.

We spent the night playing music and getting to know each other, and by the time I hit the road again the following day, I had gained four excellent friends. It was Sankomota who came and played at the 'Music in the Mountains' festival which I organised to celebrate the opening of Machabeng Hospital. Three years later they were invited to play in England, and spent several days with me in Brighton whilst playing sessions in local clubs.

Dick Zaal was staying on for a month to settle me in before he left for Zimbabwe, where he was going to study surgery. Although I still had medical responsibilities, I could really begin to focus on the development of a plan for the establishment of the new hospital.

It was a daunting task and one I had never faced before. However, my years in Africa since 1964 had taught me a great deal, and I did know a lot about how these remote hospitals functioned and what their needs were. But in Lesotho at that time there was an extra major problem to contend with.

In 1981 South Africa could reasonably be described as a fascist dictatorship, apartheid being just one facet. The Boers saw anyone not of the extreme Right to be suspect, including Leabua Jonathan, the Prime Minister of Lesotho. The Lesotho Liberation Army (LLA) was the Boers proxy army to menace and destabilise Lesotho. As Qacha's Nek was on the border between independent Lesotho and the bantustan Transkei, there was quite a lot of military action, often directed against the local civilians.

A favourite trick of the LLA was to throw a grenade in through the door of a rondavel. The resulting carnage took me days to sort out, and I was always on my own, because referring a patient was almost impossible. Even though it was a wrench to know I could no longer honestly call myself a full-time surgeon, the on-going guerrilla war with South Africa supplied a regular list of surgical patients.

To Denmark : an introduction to GammelDansk

18 months later the structure of the new hospital was almost complete. I then went to Denmark with a long list of every item required to run a 100-bed hospital. I now needed to organise the supplies and equipment. It was a huge task and took me some time, during which I learnt more about the Danes, whom I respected more and more.

Whilst the Danes were happy for me to spend my budget on Danish products, they were liberal in their general approach to foreign aid and did not object to me buying from other countries. This was not the case with British-funded development projects.

Outside Copenhagen near Helsinger was a surgical instrument factory where high quality instruments were manufactured, some of which I intended to purchase for my surgical needs. It was at this factory that I was introduced to Gammeldansk one chilly winter's morning. The directors and I were sitting around a large antique mahogany table with a small cup of coffee in front of us, about to start the wheeling and dealing, when a strange dark bottle appeared. It was passed reverently around the table, each person pouring a shot into a small glass, and I did the same. Then came a loud 'Skol!', and down went the black liquid, at which point I became breathless, tears rose in my eyes and I could not speak, only choke, for this was rocket fuel and I was on fire.

The others all thought this a huge joke, and once recovered we began this important meeting in good humour, but I never drank Gammeldansk again. Like the tequila in Alabama, I could not face it, such a shock it was to my well-tuned system. Just as Kenya runs on Tusker beer, so Denmark runs on Gammeldansk, and in that frozen country I could see why, but it was not for me.

Back in Lesotho I started making trips to Durban to buy more equipment and check the arrival of goods from Denmark. It was there that I realised the true position of the Asian businessmen I was dealing with. In Kenya and other places where the Indians ran commerce it was always possible to ´do a deal´, i.e. obtain some discount. But never in South Africa. Every aspect of commerce was ultimately controlled by the white South Africans, and I never met an Asian who really was the master of his business. It was another example of the reach of apartheid, even if the whites did not regard the olive-skinned Asians as lowly as the black Africans.

Just at the moment that tons of hospital equipment started arriving at Qacha´s Nek, like a miracle arrived Shari, a young American from California on a year´s sabbatical from UCLA. It was she who did most of the checking and cataloguing of the piles of materials I had ordered. Between her and Malisema, we equipped the new hospital with everything from beds to an Xray unit, and a lot more besides. I was now working hand-in-glove with Malisema, and she proved to be my greatest help in organising the equipping of the hospital.

A New Voyage : around southern Africa by road

Finally, I was satisfied, but by now I needed a break as I had been full-on for nearly two years without a holiday. And then, as has happened so often, an omen arrived in the form of a letter from Cape Town, South Africa.

The letter was from an academic medical friend of mine, inviting me to an anthropology conference in Cape Town. It was too good an opportunity to miss, and I was already using this chance to hatch a plan. I went up to Maseru and spoke with Tom ´Motsi´ Thabane, the new Minister of Health. He and I had always seen eye-to-eye throughout the hospital project, and I knew he was pleased with how things had evolved. He had already told me that Queen Moshoeshoe was coming to open the new hospital in six months' time.

He agreed to let me have a month off, and that I could use Hercules, the project vehicle to drive to Cape Town for the conference. That was a big concession. My plan was another safari across Africa, but this time to explore more of southern Africa. Tom also promised to send Dr Mosotho down to cover my absence. He was the young Basuto doctor who was to become my replacement when I finally left, so this would be a fine opportunity for him to familiarise himself with Qacha´s Nek and the new hospital.

I was also in the middle of converting the old hospital into a rural Community Nurse Training Centre. From the first day I had considered what to do with the old hospital, which even though rundown, was well-constructed and deserved to continue functioning in some manner. I hit upon the idea of a rural-based nurses training school as a means of providing a steady flow of nurses for my district, and also because most training centres were based in the cities and big towns. The Ministry of Health thought it a great idea, and the Danes agreed to fund the necessary changes.

I left Stig and Søren in charge of this conversion while I started to prepare Hercules for a long overland voyage. Within two weeks I had said goodbye to Martha, ´Me Emily and Wojtek, and was on the road south, heading for Durban, for I had planned a very round-about route to Cape Town, via Zululand, Swaziland, Mozambique, Zimbabwe, Namibia and Botswana. My planned route covered almost 5000 kilometres, compared to the direct route to CapeTown which would have been less than 2000 kilometres.

Zululand : Rorke´s Drift and King Shaka of the Zulus

I spent the first night on the beach just north of Durban, alone under the stars. It felt really good to be on the road again and after a steak grilled over my small barbecue, washed down with a decent bottle of wine from Meerlust, a vineyard in South Africa I intended to visit, I easily fell into a deep, refreshing sleep.

I was on my way through the Zulu kingdom to salute the memorial of King Shaka of the Zulus at Shakaskraal. He was king of the Zulus in the early 1800´s and was the one who created the feared Zulu army of impis with their stabbing assegais and battle formations which decimated the opposition, including the British Army.

From this iconic memorial I drove to Isandlhwana the site of a great British defeat by the Zulu army in 1879. Then I carried on to Rorke´s Drift where the British fought another famous battle with the Zulus.

It was easy to see that KwaZulu was a rich and prosperous country. The land was rich and well-farmed and there was light industry in the towns I passed, but the influence of the white South Africans was everywhere, in a manner which I had not yet seen in Africa. From the pristine roads to the giant grain silos and electricity pylons marching across the veldt there was an air of activity and development. The only problem was apartheid and the inherent racism of the whites.

Then I drove further north and into Swaziland, another independent country within South Africa, like Lesotho, but visibly richer in agriculture. I wanted to get to the capital, Mbabane and the king´s thermal baths, which an old African had told me about.

I eventually found them after some difficulty, and late one night I found myself in the shadow of the palace walls, completely alone, luxuriating in these hidden and private royal thermal springs under a brilliant silver moon. I did not stay there long as I did not want to be arrested for trespass, but I slept nearby in Hercules, just outside the royal compound.

The following day I made a brief excursion into Mozambique, just to say I had been there. Even there the influence of South Africa was evident, for it was the major trading and commerce country throughout the whole of southern Africa. After my brief visit to Mozambique I continued north to the Kruger National Park, one of South Africa's main tourist attractions.

It was the lodges which fascinated me for they were all managed by whites and were exemplary African versions of a Holiday Inn. Everything was correct, clean and well-ordered, too much so for my liking. Even the barbecue area was pristine. I was beginning to see exactly how the whites wanted their adopted country to be, but it was certainly not any part of the Africa I had been used to.

Across the Limpopo and into Zimbabwe

I continued north and entered Zimbabwe, crossing the Limpopo River at Beitbridge. As children we all learnt from the Just So Stories of Rudyard Kipling about the Kolokolo bird who spoke of 'the great grey-green greasy Limpopo', so I had high expectations. Sadly, these were rudely dashed, for whilst the Limpopo was indeed grey-green and greasy, great it was not. A prolonged drought had reduced it to a small and turgid stream easily passable on foot.

Zimbabwe was enjoying its first years as an independent African country under the leadership of President Mugabe. It was full of life and industry and a very well-educated population. There was a well-developed mining industry, but it was the agriculture which really impressed. Huge ranches grew everything from maize to high grade beef, most of them still being owned and run by white settlers, born and bred in what had been Southern Rhodesia.

Whilst I was enjoying my traverse of this rich and pleasant country, there were two places I particularly wanted to visit. The Matopos Hills just south of Bulawayo and, of course, the Victoria Falls.

The Matopos Hills, now known as The Matoba, cover a large area of the southern province of Matabeleland and are composed of the most remarkable granite rock formations as a result of erosion, many of them being round in shape, balanced precariously one on top of the other. This area was first inhabited 40,000 years ago by the San, who were the original bushmen. 20,000 years ago they started their unique rock paintings, using only plants and natural dyes, which can still be seen today all over southern Africa.

High on these weird round rocks, looking over the vastness of the southern African veldt is the grave of Cecil John Rhodes, the founder of Rhodesia. It was he who colonised both Zambia and Zimbabwe for the British Empire of the 19th century, and so became a British hero at that time. During colonial times they were known as Northern and Southern Rhodesia in his honour. He also had the vision of a Cape to Cairo highway and was responsible for the construction of the railway and the bridge which still crosses the Zambezi River at Livingstone. Today people think very differently about this early colonial adventurer, many now regarding him simply as an imperialist. However, like many other Europeans at that time, he did much to open up and develop the riches of Africa.

From the Matoba hills I continued east from Bulawayo on a good tarmac road, 450 kilometres until I reached the Victoria Falls, where, on the border with Zambia the Zambezi River forms a mile-wide torrent which cascades 100 metres into the gorge below.

Mosi-oa-tuniya - the Smoke that Thunders

This is the description which the local Kololo tribe use to describe the Victoria Falls. The same Kololo who described the Limpopo River.

The words that Dr David Livingstone wrote in 1855 best describe the falls ………..

"It has never been seen before by European eyes, but scenes so wonderful must have been gazed upon by angels in their flight."

It was he who named them the Victoria Falls in honour of his monarch.

The sound of the crashing water was deafening. The multiple rainbows dancing brilliantly in the sun were like an illusion. The sheer volume of water flowing over the edge of the cliffs, which spread for more than a kilometre, was more than I had ever seen.

For the fact finders, the falls are 1,700 metres wide, falling 100 metres over nine enormous ramparts into the gorge. On a good day more than six million cubic metres of water falls – every minute. No wonder the Victoria Falls are amongst the greatest wonders of the natural world.

The Zambesi rain forest which borders the gorge is also unique. It is the only place on earth where a rain falls continuously, seven days a week and 52 weeks a year, being mostly composed of spray from the falls.

Then there was the Victoria Falls Hotel, 5-stars and reeking of opulence and antiquity. In all my African travels I had never seen the like. Since the days of ´The African Queen´ a multitude of famous people had come to stay, and for good reason. A room there cost well over 200 dollars a night and was out of my price range. Instead, I settled for a char-grilled kudu steak and the trimmings, sitting out on the verdant terrace while I listened to the sounds of the Victoria Falls Band as they played their drums and *marimbas* outside on the hotel terrace, the roar of the falls a continuing and rhythmic background.

I still have the vinyl record I bought of their music, and from time to time I put it on my turntable at 33 rpm, just to remind me of a great two days under the never-ending spray from those magnificent falls, and being lulled to sleep on the roof of Hercules by their incessant roar.

To Botswana, the Chobe desert – and a serious breakdown

I then headed east to Kasana, and from there to the Ngoma bridge where I briefly crossed into Zambia. But did not linger there for long, for I still had many miles to go.

I crossed into Botswana and entered the Chobe desert at a remote village called Kachekabwe, and that is where my luck ran out.

The Chobe desert covers a large part of northern Botswana and melds in the south to become the Kalahari Desert. In between these two great deserts lies another marvel of the natural world, the Okavanga Delta and Swamp, and this is where I was aiming.

Even in the deserts it rains from time to time. Exceptional seasonal rains had just hit Botswana, and the Chobe desert was now flooded. The last sign of humanity I saw for over 24 hours was a forlorn signpost outside Kachekabwe. Thereafter all I saw was flooded desert, and patches of sand forming islands in huge lakes of floodwater of unknown depth.

For the first time I felt alone in the wilderness. But I kept heading Hercules south and west towards Maun, the main town serving the Okavanga Delta and its evolving tourist market. The going was exceptionally slow due to the clinging mud and sand, and the many lakes I had to negotiate. Many of them contained the submerged carcasses of acacia trees which made the drive even more perilous, and it was one of these that I hit around midday.

The water in this particular lake was already up to the doors in Hercules. I was in low ratio and going very slowly when there was a loud explosion, and we came to a sudden halt. Oh God! I thought. What now? Looking out for snakes, I stepped out of Hercules. The water came up to my groin and was black as ink. I could not even see the wheels, which were submerged, but at the front end I found the problem. A branch of dead acacia had driven itself into the offside front tyre and was now completely wedged between tyre and wheel rim.

The bottom of this fetid lake was composed of rotting vegetation and provided no firm base, which was another big problem, as I was certainly going to have to jack up Hercules and change the wheel. Thank goodness for the Hi-Lift Jack. It was one of the tools which I removed from Dennis before I sold him. It was another important part of my emergency equipment, and had cost me over £100, but that day it more than paid for itself.

The jack is composed of two 2-metre bars of steel with cogs which can be slowly hoisted, lifting up to two tons, and had sat padlocked onto the back of Dennis when I left England, never used in anger until today. I threw another spare wheel into the morass to use as a base for the jack, and then started pumping. The first time I tried, the whole arrangement collapsed in the mud, which only made me angrier and more determined. It took another two hours to remove the punctured wheel and replace it, by which time I was not looking or feeling my best. I was also covered in flies, attracted by my shawl of rotting vegetation – and I had little water to spare for washing.

After this episode I was even more anxious about the remaining 200 kilometres to Maun, and I was also exhausted, mentally and physically. I had learned never to drive if I felt tired, especially in strange environments, so I stopped at the next group of trees which gave shelter and made camp. Dusk fell as I lit the stove, and the desert was silent apart from the cicadas above me in the trees. For the first time in my life, I had not seen a single human being since early morning when I left Kachekabwe. It was an interesting thought I took to bed with me, lying on the roof of Hercules under a canopy of stars.

When I awoke in the morning, I had no clear idea of where I was, for the best map I had was inadequate. There was not even a constant, clear road, only a sandy track, interrupted with dark and dangerous lakes. I estimated that I still had another 200 kilometres to go before

I arrived at Maun, but with no road signs and only my compass to guide me, it was an anxious journey as I now had only one useable spare tyre left.

Sleeping Sickness – the curse of the Tsetse fly

The first sign that I was approaching Maun was the cloud of aggressive tsetse flies which started entering Hercules and attacking me. Then, an extraordinary steel fence appeared out of nowhere, stretching mile upon mile beside the track I was driving along. I even had to pass through a long shed on the outskirts of Maun where Hercules was sprayed with anti-parasite chemicals before I could enter the town, such was the fear of sleeping sickness, not just in the humans, but in their domestic cattle.

I found out later that day in Maun that the flies and the fence were connected.

I have written previously of ´dudus´ in East Africa. The tsetse fly is not just a big ´dudu´, but is also very dangerous, as it is the vector for sleeping sickness, or trypanosomiasis. This is a serious and often incurable infection caused by the flagellate plasmodium, Trypanosomiasis Brucei. The tsetse fly is the intermediate host in the life cycle of this parasite, whose adult forms can infect the blood of a wide range of vertebrates, including birds, fish, cattle – and humans. The disease causes wasting, lymphadenopathy, weakness, coma and eventually death in thousands of animals and sub-Saharan Africans, and inevitably has a significant effect on many economies.

The South Africans were clever people. They had millions of acres on which to produce food, including beef. But the global sanctions against their apartheid regime had reduced much of their export potential, including meat. So, they now grew their beef within sanctioned South Africa, then walked it into neighbouring Botswana, which had tariff-free access to Europe and the world, and sold it from there. This explained the great number of abattoirs I saw in Botswana. But the tsetse fly was endemic in Botswana, and any meat contaminated by trypanosomiasis was rejected for export. This explained the long fence I had encountered, which separated the domestic animals from the feral vertebrates, which were always the prime host for the tsetse fly.

Maun : gateway to the Okavanga Delta

I liked Maun. It was like a cowboy town, whose main street was a dusty track, enhanced by two bars and the Maun Hotel, run by Mike, the uncle of my flying friend Hugh. That is where I spent two restful days recovering from my adventures in the Chobe desert, in the most pleasant surroundings. Mike´s son Ralph was another bush pilot and close friend of Hugh, and it was he who flew me to a lodge in the centre of the Okavango Delta where Mike had arranged for me to spend, for free, a further two days fishing in the crocodile-infested rivers and exploring some of this huge inland delta from a fragile pirogue. They were two magic days.

Botswana was already captivating me. It was a big country which had many attributes as well as the beautiful Okavanga, the delta in the middle of a desert. Regretfully, I said my farewells to Mike and Ralph and headed south past Francistown, the capital and on to another historic ruin, right on the border with South Africa.

The siege of Mafeking took place during the Boer War, and started in October 1899, lasting seven months. When I arrived at the site of the siege, I was disappointed to find only a line of stones marking the boundaries of ruined buildings. Nevertheless, it was a pretty place to make camp, whilst I meditated on what might have been going on here 82 years before.

I was now on the last stretch of my journey to CapeTown and the anthropology conference, which was the justification for my long, meandering *safari* in Hercules.

To Cape Town and the Cape of Good Hope

As I entered Cape Province everything became more developed and alien to me. The capital, Cape Town was dominated by Table Mountain. The city was pretty in its floral avenues where the wealthy whites lived, but driving thorough the suburban townships where the black Africans survived, I could see that things were very different.

Although the Portuguese were the first Europeans to set foot on the Cape, around 1485, it was the Dutch who established the Dutch East India Company there in 1652. They became the first colonisers and remained so until 1806 when the British began to take an interest in this rich domain.

My voyage had been well worth it, as I found the day-long conference fascinating. My friend Jonathan was a lecturer in anthropology at Cape Town university, and he gave the introductory address. It covered the whole history of the San people, the forerunners of the Bushmen, who spread themselves over the inhospitable deserts of southern Africa some 40,000 years ago and later left their exquisite rock paintings for the world to wonder at.

Over the years the Boers had hunted them down relentlessly, deeming them sub-human, and forced them from their deserts. Only in the 1950´s did Laurens van der Post bring them to the public´s eye through his exceptional book, "The Lost World of the Kalahari", published in 1958. But by then any pure-bred San were virtually extinct.

Jonathan took me out for a short tour of the city that evening, and I could see that the whites lived very well in their fortified villas, although he told me there was now an increasing amount of violent crime. We had an excellent fish meal in a plush downtown restaurant, where the only diners were white. This was my first personal experience of the daily, social aspects of apartheid, and it left me feeling uncomfortable, yet again.

I left Jonathan and Cape Town the following day, still heading south, as I intended to stand on Cape Point, the rocky cliff which separates the Atlantic and Indian oceans. At this point I would be over 7000 kilometres from Cairo.

(A note : it was a Captain Kelsey who first attempted to drive from the Cape to Cairo in a motor-powered vehicle, in 1913. On July 19th 1913, the Marconi Transatlantic Wireless Telegraph signalled from London to the New York Times that Kelsey and five companions were about to set off on their great adventure. They estimated it would take one year. Sadly, Captain Kelsey did not manage to complete this voyage, as he was killed and eaten by a leopard in Rhodesia.)

As I stood on the high cliff looking down onto the angry sea more than 100 metres below, I reflected deeply. It had taken me over 10 years to travel from Cairo to the Cape, by very wayward means, but at least I had not fallen prey to a leopard. Now, here I was on the southern tip of Africa, the seabirds appearing like floating feathers, so far below me were they. The coastline was dark and rugged, contrasting strongly with the rounded summit of Table Mountain. An endless chain of restless waves was crashing onto the shore, spraying a cloud of spume. It was a far cry from the Chobe desert, and it was a far cry from Cairo.

The memento I took back with me from this unusual place was a photo I took of the lonely bench I sat on, overlooking this merging of two great oceans. It had a large sign on the front saying, "Whites Only" in English and Afrikaans.

North to Meerlust and the ´dorp´.

I now had to head back to Lesotho, for I had a bare week left to travel. I turned north into the wine country, aiming for the famous vineyard of ´Meerlust´, which had provided my first bottle of red wine outside

Durban at the beginning of this trip. Apart from its renowned wines, this vineyard was remarkable for the big wooden dovecot at the entrance, built in the late 1600's by the first Dutch settlers. It was in perfect order, still home to dozens of white birds.

The vineyard itself was a revelation. I could have been in France for the vegetation which surrounded me. The estate contained a small forest of deciduous trees which bordered the precious vines as well as avenues of flowering shrubs. Johannes was the young white manager I met, a person sympathetic to the cause of the black Africans, and it was he who explained to me about the 'dorp'.

Dorp, translated from Afrikaans, signifies town or settlement, but in the South African vineyards it also represented the manner of paying the workers – which was in wine. It was small wonder that many of the local African workers were alcoholics, living in misery and great poverty. The vineyards of the Western Cape such as Stellenbosch and Meerlust were now major tourist attractions, in spite of the apartheid sanctions, but I doubt that many of the visitors knew anything of the lives that the workers lived.

Johannes kindly allowed me to camp in the vineyard that night and bought me a very fine bottle of red wine which we shared as I cooked my evening meal, as he educated me further into the workings of the South African wine industry.

I left the next day, still wondering about the bizarre workings of apartheid. Whilst it was comforting to know that there were some whites who felt differently towards the black Africans, the 'dorp' was just one more ramification of an evil national policy. Wherever I went in South Africa I saw the evidence of apartheid, and it always disturbed me.

Crossing the Great Karoo

I had one more desert to cross before I saw Lesotho again. The Great

Karoo. It was a great desert, composed of little but sand and rocks, which went on for many dry kilometres until I spotted a town on the horizon, and the desert started evolving into arable land. Approaching the town, I passed a field in which were two oxen pulling an ancient plough, which seemed strange in a country where every farm had a tractor. The primitive wooden plough was guided by a strangely clothed person, whose clothing was reminiscent of the images of the Puritans I had seen in books. And this turned out to be the near truth.

Just as the Amish had done in the USA, a group of the original Dutch settlers had broken away in order to live a life unchanged from the 17th century. This explained the oxen ploughing and the lack of any modern machines.

I stopped in the town, needing to make some purchases, and was astonished when the woman in the general store refused to serve me. Not only that, but she refused to speak English. She also wore the strangest clothes, as did all the other people in this strange town, which must have been all the rage in the 17th century. These people did not even speak Afrikaans, but an archaic mixture of Dutch and Hugenot which was unintelligible to most South Africans.

I was glad to escape this creepy place and continued driving east and south towards Port Elizabeth. All along the way I kept meeting big flocks of ostriches, which surprised me. I later learned that this is the main area where ostriches are farmed, in earlier days to supply the fashion market with their feathers, but today for their meat, which though dense and tough, has a fine flavour and also makes good quality biltong.

By now I had seen all I wanted to of South Africa. From Port Elizabeth I drove east along the coast to East London, and then 450 kilometres non-stop until I hit Matatiele on the Transkei border, just 30 kilometres south of Qacha´s Nek.

I was struck in apartheid South Africa by the quality of the roads, which were generally excellent, as they were in Botswana and Zimbabwe. It was all to do with trade and commerce. In South Africa I had driven on good tarmac almost all the way, which was never the case in any other African country I had visited.

Back to Qacha´s Nek

As soon as I crossed the border at Matatiele, I was no longer in South Africa, but in the bantustan of the Transkei, where the roads were very different. The 30-kilometre dirt track which led to Qacha´s Nek was always dangerous and was never maintained. During the winter rains great parts of it often just disappeared down a ravine, and the remainder was often covered in sheets of ice and snow. And there were also the terrorists of the Lesotho Liberation Army to contend with.

It took me an hour and a half to arrive at Qacha´s Nek, where I was joyfully received by ´Me Emily, Martha and Wojtek. After a voyage of 5000 kilometres and so many vivid experiences, I was ready for a short rest in order to digest the events I had just enjoyed during a month on the roads of southern Africa. But first I needed to review the state of the project and the hospital.

I found Dr Mosotho and ´Me Malisema, who took me on a tour of the old and new hospitals. Everything was in order and there had been no crises during my absence, for which I was relieved. The conversion of the old hospital was also going well. The chief nursing officer had been to make an assessment, and had already appointed a senior nurse to be the director of the new training school.

All in all, things were looking good, and soon we would be ready to receive Queen Moshoeshoe for the formal opening of the new Machabeng Hospital. I had insisted that the new hospital had a proper name, and it was at another *pitso* of all the senior district officials that the decision was made to name it ´Machabeng´. In

Sesotho this translates as ´ for the people´ and was a name which everybody found most appropriate.

Satisfied after my extensive review of the hospitals, I went back to my house and poured a beer. Then I sat down on the terrace, gazing at the peak of Thaba Souru in the far distance, and started re-tracing my steps of the last month.

16.   FROM LESOTHO TO LONDON AND TRAGEDY   1984

After one year in Qacha's Nek I was beginning to know the lie of the land. The new hospital was slowly rising from the ground, whilst I looked after the clinical work in the old hospital with Martha. At the same time, I was concerned with the planning and logistics for the operating of the new hospital including staffing. I was determined to make the most of my position to improve as much of Qacha's Nek District health as I could, so I was still making regular visits to Maseru.

Skiing in Africa

These visits allowed me to renew my friendship with Billy, who happened to be a keen skier. When he suggested a weekend of skiing, I was most interested, as the idea of skiing in Africa appealed greatly to me. Even though Kilimanjaro and Mt Kenya are amongst the highest of the African mountains, there are no facilities there for skiing.

We took off towards Buthe-Buthe on the Saturday morning, heading for the Maluti mountains and what has now in more recent years become known as the 'Afriski Ski Resort'. Hercules, my Toyota Land Cruiser was loaded with suitable provisions for a few cold days. Every weekend during the winter months, a group of South Africans would cross the border and come skiing. They had formed a club named The Maluti Ski Club, which at that time consisted of a winch with a 500-metre cable and some ancient skis and boots.

Billy and I spent hours being towed up the mountain one at a time, on the end of the steel cable. We were dwarfed by the huge peaks around us, most of which were 3000 metres or more. As a rare African diversion, it was unbeatable, and remains one of my more unusual African adventures.

By New Year 1984 the new hospital was complete and ready for occupation. It had been an immense job but one which had been thoroughly enjoyable, apart from the continuous fight with the white South Africans and BOSS, their secret police.

Fighting against Apartheid – and the consequences

The main source of income for Lesotho came from the men who worked in the South African mines, where working conditions were not good. They lived in big dormitories with poor sanitation and hygiene, surrounded by destitute women prostitutes. They were often robbed of their precious earnings when they arrived back in Lesotho in December every year, so their existence and that of their families was always precarious.

The economic plight of the Basuto also led to the horrific practice of infanticide – a mother killing her baby. In all my life I had never imagined this, but in 1981 in Lesotho it was common. The women spent 11 months without their men, and during this lonely time the inevitable often happened. As their husbands began returning from the South African mines in December, pregnancies were terminated in back streets and infants, newly born, were disposed of. When I became aware of this, I determined to try and mitigate this horrendous social problem, as best I could.

A major part of my routine work was vetting a group of up to 50 Basutho men every morning before my ward rounds for any significant medical condition which could prejudice their mining work in South Africa, before they were flown out to the mines. Once I realised the dreadful social situations they were reduced to, I started using this time to also educate them in certain matters of public and personal health. Strangely, the Boers considered this 'subversive' and placed me on their list of undesirables.

Shortly after I started this educational programme, I jumped off my motorbike, back at my house after a midnight Caesarian section, to be greeted by a camouflaged soldier with a machine gun.

It gave me a big fright, even though I was well-used to weaponry, having been in the middle of a civil war for two years already. It turned out that Colonel Chaka had ordered a 24-hour guard on our house because he had intelligence that the Boers were going to try and kidnap Wojtek in order to silence me.

Things soon got even worse. Christopher, a young Canadian medical student had found his way to me from Vancouver and was spending some educational weeks with me in Qacha's Nek. He was with me the day I did the monthly trip in Hercules to collect new oxygen bottles from Matatiele, on the Transkei-South African border. Until that day I never had any problem, and I used to use the chance to phone England as the telephone lines usually worked in South Africa.

I was in the local garage using the payphone when I suddenly felt hard steel against my right temple. I looked round to see a heavily built Boer in plain clothes ramming a Colt .45 into my head and I knew immediately that he must be an agent of BOSS, the dreaded South African secret police.

Chris the Canadian suddenly went pale. My own knees were shaking as well. The bull-necked primate ripped the phone from me, stuck the muzzle of his shooter into the nape of my neck and marched me out to Hercules.

"Yew com bak´ere agin and we kill you!" was his parting shot as I headed for the Transkei border, wondering why I had decided to leave the relative safety of Kenya.

Poor Chris was shell-shocked by this new entry in his c.v. and left for more peaceful pastures shortly afterwards. I was more concerned about how we would now get our vital oxygen for the anaesthetic machine, as there was no chance of any plane from Maseru flying to Qacha's Nek with cylinders full of oxygen. In the end I negotiated with the hospital at Matatiele, and they arranged to send the oxygen up on one of the trucks which carried supplies to Qacha's Nek.

A visit from old friends

During our three years at Qacha's Nek we had very few visitors due to our isolation, but one of my friends from Brighton in the summer of '76 did come out to see us. Nick was an embryo eye-surgeon who had just taken his family to Vanuatu for two years of Pacific Island medicine and had arranged to visit us on the way back to England.

He arrived with Caroline his wife and three young children, whom we accommodated in our adjacent guest house. The next day I took Nick and Caroline on a tour of my two hospitals, and they were impressed by the development of the new one. The 120 square metre solar collector was almost completed as were all the ward blocks, and it was beginning to look like a regular new hospital.

The following day Nick and I took off on the horses to explore Qacha's Nek and the surrounding mountains. I had been longing to share this excursion with Nick as he was also an intrepid adventurer, and the sights were magnificent on this crystal-clear day. There was still a lot of snow about as we left the plain and headed up the flank of Thaba-Souru. Many of the narrow tracks we rode were icy and very dangerous, but our Basuto ponies, Phakiso and Phela, were extraordinary animals. They had been born and bred in these mountains for centuries, and nothing was more sure-footed than these ponies.

After a couple of hours at altitude skidding in the snow, we descended to 'Me Phakosi's house on the outskirts of town. She was a brewer of beer and when she had a brew on the go, she always hoisted a yellow plastic bag on a pole above her house. This time it was maize beer we sat and drank under a cloudless sky whilst being entertained by the village children. Many of them knew me by now since I had started teaching HealthCare at their primary school once a week. Like all African children I met, there was nothing they loved better than singing and dancing, and in us they had a willing audience.

When we finally got home after several hours in the saddle, I could tell Nick´s gluteal muscles were aching by the way he walked, and we laughed. He recognised the fact that I was now a 'hard-arse' after the hours I now spent in the saddle, and I could tell he was warming to the eccentric life I was leading in the mountains of Lesotho. That was until later the same evening.

As a grand finale to our day´s outing, I took Nick on a ward round by horseback, something I did every Sunday morning with Wojtek sitting in front of me on Phakiso.

My greatest human resources at Machabeng Hospital, 'Me Mohlome, 'Me Malisema and 'Me Old, and another snowball fight

Getting ready for the Sunday ward round with Wojtek

We slowly patrolled the grounds outside the wards as the sister-in-charge gave me an update on each patient. Even at the age of three Wojtek loved horse-riding, and all the Basutos loved to see him in the saddle. Nick was duly impressed by my novel take on ward rounds.

An explosive dinner

Once we were back home, we un-saddled and fed the ponies. Then it was time for a gin and tonic on the terrace before we retired inside as night fell. We all enjoyed a serious catch up whilst the lamb stew cooked on the stove, as we downed glasses of South African *tinto* in front of the open fire. I particularly remember our tapas that night because it was the first tasting of my home-made biltong, with local bread and Spanish olives – a rare and precious commodity in those parts.

The butcher in Matatiele had taught me the fine skill of marinading and conserving beef, or any game meat for that matter, and turning it into biltong. The crisp, dry mountain air of Qacha´s Nek was ideal for curing meat. It is still my favourite food for travelling, being high energy and very durable, and this evening it went down with no complaints.

The aromatic stew was on the table, and we each had a glass of tinto in hand to toast our friendship when the machine gun opened up.

"Oh, sod it!", was my first thought. "I hope there is no midnight Caesarian section tonight".

The problem was that my surgeon´s residence was not only a dangerous kilometre from the new hospital, but was also facing the Lesotho Mounted Police HQ, directly below a 100-metre bluff above our house. It was from there that the Lesotho Liberation Army had decided to attack that night. Soon the front garden began to look like a firework display, but this firefight was more intense and deadly, with flares and grenades going off and the staccato rattle of machine guns.

"What about my children?", enquired Caroline, looking stressed. It was a killer moment. I had to do something about the children next door in the guest house. We had to get them back with us at least, and there seemed no option but to go and get them.

"Don´t worry Nick", I said, "I´ll tell them to stop while we get the kids out". My words are included in that well-worn tome, "Famous Last Words". When I opened the front door, all I saw were the yellow-red spouts of flame from guns as everyone opened up.

Suddenly things were serious. I was back inside within five milliseconds, with a pulsating tachycardia and mildly dyspnoeic after this shock. We had a council of war and decided to simply rush out to the guest house, grab the kids and rush back. And that is what we did. We did not get shot, but I have rarely been more terrified.

Nick and Caroline left on the next plane out, and I could understand why, but I still had months to enjoy in Qacha´s Nek.

It was only because of the resourcefulness and resilience of the Basutos that Machabeng Hospital was successfully completed. To live under the yoke of apartheid was bad enough. But the violence and warring of the LLA was an added problem which I was inevitably involved in, both as a trauma surgeon and medical administrator. Apart from the trauma I had to manage, from horse-riding accidents to war injuries, I was also responsible for performing post-mortems, sometimes in the most unusual surroundings. One of my most taxing cases had involved a day-long trip on horse-back into a remote corner of the Maluti Mountains. This dangerous horse-back journey made such an impression on me that I shall describe it here, as I wrote it up in my daily journal in April 1983.

In Praise of the Basuto Pony.

It gets cold up in the mountains of Lesotho in winter and yesterday was no exception, even though spring was in the air. The early morning sun was shining but it was still bitterly cold outside. Today it did not seem to bother me for I was about to embark on an authentic African adventure. I was full of anticipation and a certain degree of excitement.

I was going to a village so remote and so small that I could barely find it on the large-scale map of the district. All I knew was that getting there and back involved a day's journey on horseback over some difficult mountain terrain.

As district medical officer I had been asked to accompany a patrol of the local police to a village called Qabané, across the Orange River, several hours ride north of Sekakes where one of my peripheral rural clinics was located. I had been asked to perform an exhumation and post-mortem on a member of the chief's family who had died earlier in March and was now known to have been murdered.

At this time I was extremely busy as we were finalising the arrangements for the transfer of patients from the old hospital to the new Machabeng hospital, now ready for occupation. So it was with mixed feelings that I received the request from Lt. Colonel Chaka of the Lesotho Mounted Police.

Thus it was I found myself at 0630 hrs filling two saddlebags with a varied assortment of articles, from my mortuary dissection kit to a tin of beans and a bag of biltong plus my thermos flask, always an essential part of my travelling kit in these frigid mountains.

Just after 0700hrs I am on my way to Sekakes, the village where I shall leave my Toyota Land Cruiser and take to horseback. The early morning sun is magnificent and the peach blossom is ubiquitous – pink islands on the barren rocks of the mountains competing with the mimosa for a share of the bright colour on the otherwise barren hillsides.

Smoke is curling in the early morning light from the roofs of many of the village huts that I pass. Trees are very scarce in Lesotho, so the primary source of fuel for cooking and heating is compressed cow or goat dung which is found lying on the walls of the compounds to dry. It is like peat in quality and burns slowly if well prepared, and the smoke emitted has a pleasant smell.

There is little traffic on these twisted mountain roads at the best of times, and I do not meet a single vehicle on my way to Sekakes, a drive of over 90 minutes.

By 0900hrs I am mounted on a fine, black horse supplied by the police, sitting on the saddle I use on Phakiso. I sling my saddle bags over the pommel and then we are off. My escort consists of a sergeant from the Criminal Investigation Department and a detective trooper, both heavily armed with pistols and submachine guns. They tell me that things can get ´awkward´ in the mountains, which is why they always carry arms on these trips. Furthermore, most of the time they go ´footing it´ since it appears that the mountain people can recognise a police horse from afar and can then take early evasive action if required.

It takes over an hour to make the long descent to the point where we shall cross the Orange River, and passing down the narrow bridle path we start to meet a few people. There are small groups of men on horseback, women carrying all manner of goods on their heads, from their own shoes as they cross the river to such interesting items as two chickens, a six-pack of beer, and also a door complete in its frame. Then comes a line of mules slowly winding up the tortuous track, carrying great sacks of maize and barrels of *joala,* the locally produced beer.

I have travelled to work in Africa by a variety of means – canoes in Cameroun, aeroplanes in Zaire, and on the footplate of a steam train in Kenya, but the mode of transport I was forced to adopt today is possibly the most pleasant of all. I had never spent more than three hours on horseback continuously before, but this morning I spent four hours riding to the village of Qabané where the exhumation was to take place. I found that there was ample time on horseback at a steady walk to take a good interest in the wide variety of things new to me on this trip.

The sergeant and the trooper were fine company and told me many things of interest as we passed along the way. At every bend in the winding track there was something new to see and reflect on. I remember catching sight of a strange bird that closely resembled an ibis, having a long, curved beak. It was a dull grey-brown colour, but it was the brilliant purple irridescent sheen over its brown wings which caught my eye. I had not seen this variety of ibis in other parts of Africa. I later discovered from my books at Qacha's Nek that this was probably the onomatopoetic named Hadadah ibis (*Bostrychia hadedash*), so-called because of its loud cry, " Ha Da Dah ", and is common all over sub-Saharan Africa. It is rare that we travel here without seeing something of interest.

The Pitso (meeting) at Qabané

When we finally arrived at Qabané just after 1300h it was obvious that something special was going on, for I could see over 200 Basuto men plus their horses gathered in the centre of the village. Each man was covered in a large, brightly-coloured blanket – the traditional garb of the Basuto people. The sight made a marvellous spectacle against the gaunt backdrop of Mt Qabané (2,500 m) which is where we were soon heading.

The chief was telling the amassed people what was about to happen, speaking in Sesotho. It is a hard language to grasp well, derived as it is from the Bushmen dialects of the desert wastes of southern Africa, full of clicks and grunts. In spite of the two-week course I had done when I arrived at Maseru and speaking it daily, I was still not fluent, so much of this talk passed me by, but I got the drift. I was just glad to sit on the ground and rest my aching muscles after the ride.

I was disconcerted to learn from the sergeant that as soon as the pitso had been terminated we were all to walk to the top of the mountain, whose peak I could see only dimly in the distance. Just below it was a cave from which flowed a small stream, and it was here that the victim was buried. It looked miles away, and I could hardly bear the thought of a further hour's exercise, being suffused with sartorial and gluteal aches and pains after my ride to the village.

The pitso soon terminated and I was invited to re-mount as the hordes of Basuto men emerged from the meeting. Together we began to ascend the mountain in a truly biblical kaleidoscope of colour and shouts. About halfway up the terrain became increasingly steep and soon to my dismay everyone began to dismount and walk towards the site of the grave. At this stage in the saga the only thought that kept me going was that unless the reluctant grave diggers were incredibly lucky, they were unlikely to recover the body in less than 15 minutes, and to my relief I was proved correct.

The corpse discovered – but where were the missing bits?

In less than half an hour I was standing at the grave site – a small cave crudely blocked off with large boulders, through which issued a trickle of water. Under the instructions of the police, one of the accused began digging, heaving mud and rocks about as he searched for traces of the body. I sat on a large stone in the sun drinking coffee from my thermos and giving thanks for the rest.

Suddenly I heard an audible sigh coming from the mountainside, and on turning was amazed to see the whole side of the mountain covered by the Basuto villagers, their blankets hard against their faces as they tried to keep out the cold wind which had sprung up. There were countless scores of them, all silently waiting for news of the body – the brother of their chief who was now thought to have been murdered by revengeful villagers for his part in the murder of his brother's daughter.

The sigh was in response to the sight of a partially bleached skull being raised aloft by the grave digger. This was where I was supposed to make my entrée, and I suddenly realised that I was in a unique position. Being privy to this remarkable spectacle was a rare privilege. Here I was, sitting on the side of a mountain thousands of miles away from the tiled Victorian mortuary behind the Liverpool Royal Infirmary where I had first been introduced to the art of post-mortem examinations. I was about to embark on my first high-altitude post-mortem in Africa.

The skull was intact and showed no sign of external violence. It was shortly followed by the appearance of the mandible, and then both lower legs and half of one foot. What had emerged so far was badly decomposed but was clearly human – but where was the rest of the body? The whole of the thorax was missing as well as both arms and the pelvis. Despite further excavation no more bones were found. I explained to the CID sergeant about the missing body parts, and he retired with the main suspect for some further interrogation, without any positive result.

We assembled all the bones, and I made a comprehensive list, cataloguing them all. Even though all the flesh had rotted away some of the bones were still connected by ligaments and fibrous tissue which, as I explained to the sergeant, indicated to me that this corpse was months old rather than years. But as I stressed to him, I was no expert in pathology. Further analysis would take place back in Maseru at the Queen Elizabeth II hospital where there was a qualified pathologist.

We were now faced with the problem of transporting all the bones back to Qacha's Nek, there being no sack available in which to carry them. With true inspiration the sergeant solved this in a trice by inviting the detective trooper to remove his overalls and then knotting both legs and filling his home-made sack with the rattling mass of bones.

I never ceased to wonder at the ingenuity of the people I was working with – though no doubt the trooper was thinking other thoughts.

Before the remains were placed in the sack, the chief rose and addressed his people, who were sitting on the mountainside, wrapped tightly in their blankets. He was inviting them to come and view the remains of their clansman. So it was that more than 200 curious men came to gaze in wonder at the pile of bones, exclaiming loudly when they saw the skull, for they could not believe how it could be so large. The sergeant told me that none of them had seen a bare skull before – which on reflection is not so unusual.

Afterwards, in a picturesque convoy we all moved slowly down the mountain to the village where after another short discourse with the chief the pitso broke up, everyone dispersing in a cloud of dust and flying hooves. By now it was after 1600 hrs, but I was still optimistic that we could reach Sekakes by 2100 hrs, and I could then be back in Qacha's Nek in time to start work the next day. I was to return with the trooper while the sergeant made his own way back with the prisoner and the sack of bones.

I bid a friendly farewell to the chief and his family, who had fed me well and were fine and courteous people. He invited me to come back again and visit them, saying I would always be welcome. Even though I never did, I still remember Qabané as a beautiful village, hidden amongst the folds of the Maluti mountains.

We had not travelled more than a few kilometres before the sky began to darken and I noticed a big double rainbow in the eastern sky. Following us was an even larger cloud of rain. Suddenly I was concerned, for torrential downpours were common in the mountains. Flashfloods caused deaths every year, and we still had the Orange River to cross.

As dusk fell the rain started, slowly at first and then a steady downpour. By 1730 hrs we were alone in the darkening mountains with only the hissing rain and the clip-clop of the horses' hooves for company. At this point the trooper left me, saying he had to go by a village to collect a blanket he had left there, but I was not to worry as he would soon re-join me on the bridle path. To this day I have never set eyes on him again.

Now I really was alone. Night was falling, and the rain was sheeting down onto an invisible track which I had never travelled before. I had only my faith in my big, black horse to comfort me, and I was full of fearful anticipation.

With no other options open, I carried on along the twisting track. To my left was a precipitous drop of over 50 metres down the gorge of the Orange River, and to my right was a barren cliff face. The time passed, pleasantly at first in spite of the rain, and there were still the occasional shadowy outlines of villages and the smell of burning dung from the cooking fires of the houses I passed. Just before the light failed completely, I spied a lone figure on horseback in the distance, and I hurried to catch up with him.

He was an old man, heavily cloaked against the rain, and he told me he was also on his way to Sekakes. My spirits lifted immediately, for I had been feeling very isolated and the darkness was only broken by frequent bursts of dazzling lightning. Neither did I have any clear idea as to where I was heading, but I knew that we had at least another two hours of riding before we arrived at Sekakes. By now I was beginning to appreciate fully the daily hardships of these mountain people as I sat on my good horse, seeing nothing and only trusting blindly that the horse knew the way better than I did.

By 1830 hrs we were in the centre of a violent storm, with flashes of lightning and deafening bursts of thunder. The bridle path had not been so easy to ride during the daylight hours. In the darkness it became something of a nightmare as both horses occasionally slipped on the greasy track. I felt helpless as I had no way of guiding the horse, but the horse knew better as he followed my companion unerringly. From time to time he drew ahead on his horse, and in the total darkness he became invisible. Then I would shout out loudly, frightened that he would just disappear for good, but each time he would slow down so I could catch him up.

The rain fell continuously, and I was soon starting to feel cold in spite of my two jerseys and the thick, handwoven woollen poncho over my shoulders. I could not remember a time when I had been so scared for so long, but there seemed little else to do other than stay on my horse´s back at all costs and not to dwell too much on what would happen if we did slip over the edge of the gorge.

Slowly we began the descent of the gorge to the banks of the Orange River, and after many a slip and a stumble on the stony track I heard the sound of rushing water. It was frightening in its intensity, and I could tell that the level of the river had risen dramatically. I could not believe that I had to traverse this raging torrent on horseback, but that is what we did, my silent companion leading the way.

As we began the crossing, I could feel the water flowing over my boots and then up to my thighs. It was a fearful moment. Every year in Lesotho many people and animals drown in the flash floods which occur with the rainstorms, and we were in the middle of one, with the water still rising as we approached the middle of the swollen river. I could not even see the far bank and had no way of knowing what lay ahead, but my brave horse was nose-to-tail with my companion, going strongly. I sat tight and tried to think of sunny days and blue skies, whilst making promises I hoped I would never have to keep.

When we finally hit the southern bank I was exhilarated, knowing that the worst of the journey was now over and Sekakes was just over an hour away. But I felt drained and exhausted after my heroic ride. By now I was wet through, cold and tired, and only the reassuring presence of my companion kept me going the last few kilometres. Who was he, I wondered, and where was he coming from? Was it just chance that we met, or was it something else? I shall never know, for he left me at the door of the police station at Sekakes and gently faded into the night. I like to think he was St Christopher's African brother.

I entered the police station and sat down gratefully beside the glowing coal stove. I could hardly believe my good fortune in having arrived safely after such a dangerous trip and such an extraordinary day. My jeans were soaked but surprisingly my poncho, although also very wet, had kept my upper body dry. The police brought me a cup of chai which was well received as I rested my aching body. It took half an hour to recover from the ride, before I felt capable of driving back to Qacha's Nek. My legs still felt distinctly wobbly and both arms and wrists ached – probably from the force of fear with which I had been gripping the reins.

I was asked to give a lift to a trooper returning to Qacha's Nek. As I prepared for the return journey I told him about the hard day I had just experienced. But he did not sound impressed. He told me that the Basuto ponies were bred to cope with extreme conditions and gave me to understand that I should have expected nothing less than a safe return, but I was not so convinced.

Before we set off, I went to the stables and gave my unnamed horse a loving embrace, which seemed to surprise him. I bless and thank the big, black horse on whose back I had spent nine hours this day. He never tried to cheat or frighten me, a stranger and relative novice.

Whilst I was often startled by the flashes of lightening and the thunder, he remained calm and knowing, and passed some of his confidence onto me. I suppose he does this work quite often and is therefore familiar with the whims of the elements in these mountainous parts of Lesotho. He was as sure-footed as a goat and as strong as an ox, but more intelligent than both.

And what of the hardy mountain people who experience these things every day of their lives? I can only say that this trip has given me a deep and lasting respect for them and their way of life. Patients often arrive at the hospital on horseback. There are no ambulances to help them on their way, so their lives depend utterly on their horses, just as mine did this day.

I arrived back in Qacha's Nek after 2200 hrs, too tired to relate my adventures to Martha, and collapsed into bed. My head was filled with many vivid images, still fresh in my mind, of a beautiful black horse bearing me up the jagged mountains of the kingdom in the sky.

I suppose one could say it was just another day's work, but here in Lesotho every day was an adventure in one way or another, and the life we led was as vivid as a rainbow in the sky. I was not in a rush to change this mode of life, for I appreciated living a little closer to the earth than I ever did before.

In February 1984 our daughter Anna Palesa was born, shortly before my contract was due to end. It was like a very special gift to reward all our labours. She was the second of my children to be born in Africa, something which I was proud of. Martha had gone to the mission hospital at Morija, near Maseru, to deliver Anna Palesa. I was not too concerned as I knew she would be in capable hands there, and indeed it appeared that all had gone well and that both she and the babe were fine.

When I drove Hercules into the mission compound at Morija on February 14th, Valentine's Day, the sun was shining, the sky was a brilliant blue above and birds were singing in the pine trees which shaded the hospital. Also, for some extraordinary reason, from the loudspeakers hidden within the trees which usually gave out Jesus messages to the Basuto patients, I could clearly hear Marvin Gaye singing 'Sexual Healing'. It was quite astonishing in this Catholic mission hospital to be listening to such an excellent song, one which was a favourite of mine, and not a religious hymn, and I took it as a good omen. After all, I was about to set eyes on my new-born second child.

Mother and child were both sitting pretty in the bed when I arrived. It was truly a joyous sight and lifted my heart after all the hard graft I had been doing in Qacha's Nek. The following day we were off back there, arriving just before dark. We had a great time introducing Anna Palesa to 'Me Emily and Wojtek, who appeared much moved by the arrival of his little sister.

'Me Moshoeshoe had kept her promise to me, and Dr Mosotho had recently arrived to take over the reins. We had planned a one-month handover, and he had already taken over most of the daily hospital routine, leaving me to cope with the outstanding 13 ritual murder cases.

On Ritual Murder

At this time Lesotho itself was under investigation by the United Nations as a result of the prevalence of the weird and evil practice of ritual murder. Only the most gruesome horror stories come near to describing it, but during three years in Qacha's Nek I had seen more than enough to last a lifetime, and at this moment, one month before I was due to leave there were over 10 outstanding murder cases still to be dealt with, which included doing all the post-mortems.

The object of ritual murder appeared to be to obtain the magic power contained within certain human organs including the heart, and one horrific time, a full-term foetus. These organs were often excised from a living person in order to gain more magic power, which made the whole business more shocking in its cruelty. This was yet one more responsibility of the District Medical Officer at Qacha´s Nek, and I had done dozens of post-mortems on these unfortunate people by the time I left.

Within a few weeks Martha was going back to England with two children more than she started out with six years before. I was staying a further two weeks in Lesotho to complete the handover and also make a final tour of my District – this time on my big 420cc Suzuki trail bike Sayonara, with my friends, Hugh and Joyce, in their Land Rover. I had been asked by Save the Children Fund to do a follow-up on the Extended Programme for Immunisation (EPI) and had decided to combine it with a final tour around Lesotho on motorbike.

Before then we had our going away party at the hospital. Queen ´Mamohatha had only just left after a wonderful opening ceremony, one of my memories of which was urinating together with Motsi Thabane, the Minister of Health, onto the back wheel of the regal Land Rover. It had been a fantastic night of celebration and goodwill amongst the Basutos with us, one I shall not forget in a hurry.

My other outstanding memory of that celebration was of Queen ´Mamohatha squatting on her knees with the kitchen staff performing the *mojiba*, a unique and rhythmic Basutho dance to the accompaniment of the hospital choir in full voice. Hard as I tried, I could not imagine the Queen of England doing the same. This celebration was followed by a three-day concert by Sankomota, playing southern Southo rock and roll outside the new hospital, surrounded by a ring of mountains. It was such a celebration that I have never forgotten it. After three years of very hard work, it was a very fitting end to a successful project.

The last thing which I did at the hospital before I left for England was to plant 36 floribunda bushes, which were to be our present to this wonderful African mountain community where we had spent the last three happy years. The rose bushes varied from peach to red and they lined the entrance to the hospital as though it were a garden centre, surrounding the hospital garden which I had started two years before. Every woman who entered our Mother and Child Clinic did her turn in this fruitful vegetable garden.

The day I finally left, at least one floribunda bush could be seen from every ward against the backdrop of Thaba Sourou, the big black mountain which had been watching over us every day for three glorious years. Machabeng Hospital, the Hospital of The People was not only functioning well, it was beautiful. To me, that was the greatest accolade I could receive.

Interestingly, I heard some time later from DANIDA that the Machabeng Hospital project had won some international recognition.

Two days later the twin-engined Fokker came cruising in for a perfect landing on the tiny strip, lost and encircled by the vast Maluti mountains, which was the last sight Wojtek ever had of Qacha's Nek.

I waved my small family off with 'Me Emily, and as I watched the plane wheel against the sun and start heading north for Maseru I experienced a tangible feeling of loss and change which was hard to explain. It was a very strange feeling to be without my mate of the last seven African years of adventures, and now also my two kids, the youngest of whom I hardly knew.

The following day Hugh and Joyce appeared, and we spent the evening packing and preparing for a wild trip across the mountains of Lesotho, me on Sayonara, and Hugh and Joyce carrying all the gear in their short-wheel-based Land Rover.

Round Lesotho by bike

The first night we spent at the clinic at Sethlebathebe, the wildest corner of my domain, with Puleng, one of our most experienced sister/midwives. She was practically in love with me since Brad, the electronics engineer and I had fixed the solar power system and given her not just a working radio, but a good light 24 hours a day for her deliveries which came at all hours in this isolated clinic. It was the one really good thing that I did for the eight rural clinics we served. God bless DANIDA for giving me the extra 40,000 dollars to develop solar systems in every clinic for light and radio. With the help of Brad, who was the most gifted of the many American engineers I ever met, we completed all the clinics before I left.

Sethlebathebe clinic also had a solar oven made out of a Huntley and Palmer biscuit tin which we were experimenting with. There was also a solar-powered vaccine refrigerator for the Extended Programme on Immunisation (EPI) programme which I had been evaluating for Save the Children. After we had all enjoyed a rich lamb stew, Puleng then presented a great cake which she had made in the solar oven. She really rated the oven, even though it could only be used in the heat of the day when the ambient temperature was over 30 centigrade. It was yet one more innovative item in this fuel-poor country, which seemed to work and cost no money.

We left the next morning at first light as Puleng´s first patients were arriving on horse-back. We were heading for Mokhotlong which was the next town where we had two Dutch friends who were running the small hospital there. But before then we were off into the park at Sethlebathebe to do a spot of trout fishing.

I had been serving this clinic outpost for three years and enjoyed nothing better than to pass a couple of days in this wild domain bordering on South Africa where the rare black wildebeest grazed and brown trout were just waiting to be caught in the bubbling waters which ran through the park. Wojtek caught his first trout there at the age of three, and I still remember his smiling face at the moment he lifted this shining fish out of the water on his small rod. We also did well that morning, catching four. Then we hit the rough road away from the border and north towards Mokhotlong.

The road was empty of traffic but full of rocks and potholes and was hard going on the bike, but there was a great sense of freedom and space as we wended our way slowly north. Darkness fell on us before we reached Mokhotlong, so we just set up camp and while Joyce heated up the rest of the lamb stew which Puleng had given us, I stretched out in my Blacks Icelandic sleeping bag under a canvas of twinkling stars and gave thanks to Allah for another good day.

A strange thing occurred at dawn, when we all awoke to the sound of galloping hooves. By the time we had opened our eyes we were surrounded by about 20 rough looking Basuto horsemen, wrapped in their colourful blankets and all armed to the teeth. I was interested more than afraid, for there were very few white people in these wild southern parts of Lesotho, and most of the locals knew of us expatriate doctors. In spite of the on-going civil war and all the problems of apartheid I had never received anything but kindness from these people.

So it was in this case. Hugh and Joyce spoke far better Sesotho than me, but I was able to get the drift. They were a local partisan patrol out looking for a South African guerrilla force which had crossed the border the day before. Shouting greetings, they all bid us a good journey before they wheeled their ponies and galloped off across the barren plateau towards the Orange River. It was an interesting start to a new day. While we brewed up some chai in the freezing cold, we discussed our plans for the day.

I would start first and we would all meet up at the hospital later that day and spend the night with Hank and Lidie, the two young Dutch volunteer doctors. There were only eight hospitals in the whole country so we doctors who ran the districts were all in touch, and we used each other´s houses freely when we were travelling, for there were no hostels or hotels in most of our impoverished towns.

Around 11 o'clock I stopped by a small stream flanked by aspen and birch. Just to see any trees in Lesotho was rare, but this spot was exceptional because the trees were full of weaver bird nests and the bright yellow male birds were getting busy setting up homes for their prospective brides.

There are quite a few different species of weaver birds, and the males all build different types of nests. Some have just a small entrance hole, but others like these in Lesotho had a long, curved entrance hall hanging from the nest. It was so beautifully woven that it was hard to believe that an armless bird could achieve such a marvel. The amazing thing about these birds is that if the female arrives and doesn't like the nest, the poor male has to get busy yet again and build another. And often yet another, until the female is satisfied and then becomes his bride.

I was sorry to leave this perfect spot. It was so rare in Lesotho to be adjacent to both water and trees that it even made me think of the greenness of England for a brief moment, where I was soon bound. Over the centuries the whole of this rocky land had been continuously denuded of trees, leading to ever greater soil erosion until large areas of the country were simply bare rock, incapable of sustaining life. So this was a very precious place.

The only form of agriculture in these barren wastes was pastoral. Dotting the mountain slopes were the shepherds, often just young boys dressed in rags and their flocks of sheep from which came the famous, hard-wearing wool, but there was little for them to graze on as I looked around me. Only the Orange River gave life to this eroded land.

The twittering of the weaver birds was still ringing in my ears as I kicked Sayonara into life and continued across the barren plain which led to Mokhotlong. Two hours later I cruised into the hospital compound and parked up. I was looking forward to a good session with Hank and Lidie as well as doing a ward round with them, just for fun, but when I saw the look on Hank's face as he approached me, I became concerned that not all was well.

Disaster strikes

"Thank goodness you are here", exclaimed Hank, "we've been trying to find you since yesterday. You have to get back urgently to Maseru because the Danish embassy called to say your new baby is very ill." At that moment I felt my comfortable world changing. A black cloud of fear fell on me and was still cloaking me two days later when Martha met me at Heathrow. Looking back, I now know that was the moment that my life changed for ever.

The Danes had been magnificent as always and had done everything to get me back fast, including persuading the Boers not to arrest me in Johannesburg as I passed through. They were still hunting me as a terrorist and agitator and I was still banned from South Africa, with a price on my head. I had to spend two hours in the cell which they called the Transit lounge, which was where all troublesome passengers were incarcerated until their flight to freedom left. I was surprised and amused to find Motsi Thabane, the Lesotho Minister of Health was also one of my fellow prisoners in this minimalist space between freedom and the torture chambers of BOSS, the dreaded secret police.

"Xhotso! Ntate", I cried out, "Greetings! Father, how good to see you in this fine hotel". It was indeed good to find someone I knew at this dark moment. He had helped me enormously during the three years of developing the new Machabeng hospital at Qacha's Nek and had become a good friend. Motsi was the last Basutho I was to see for a long time.

Martha was distraught when we met at Heathrow. It was bad enough to be back in UK, but to arrive under these circumstances was terrible. Anna Palesa had been off her evening feed two nights before and the following morning had started fitting. Now she was in the throes of a full-blown, virulent pneumoccocal meningitis, and we both knew what that meant. When I looked over the cot at her tiny body in the paediatric intensive care unit at Lewisham General, I just felt empty inside. She had been anaesthetized to prevent further fitting, but I could see her brain waves on the EEG machine, and they were hypsarrhythmic, being wildly out of control and looking like an electric storm on the coil of paper as it slowly unfolded. I knew then it was a disaster for us both.

Boris and Viga, my Polish in-laws could not have been kinder or more welcoming, and their big comfortable house in Greenwich was always a haven for our family. But we were all paralysed at the thought of Anna's suffering and the likely bad outcome. The doctors did their best to reassure us, but I had seen too much neonatal meningitis during my paediatric training at Alder Hey and then seven continuous years in Africa not to realize that Anna Palesa's case was extremely serious and could be fatal.

Even if she did survive, she was almost certain to suffer some degree of disability, from deafness and blindness to total mental incapacity. Anna's grandmother, Viga, had been a consultant obstetrician all her life at Lewisham, and she also knew exactly how very serious this illness was. So, there was an air of gloom and fear around, which was impossible to dispel and affected us all to a varying degree. Boris, my father-in-law, the old Polish submarine captain sat in his chair and said little, but he too was suffering. Likewise, my own family down on the farm in Sussex. Fortunately, they had seen Wojtek and Anna Palesa just a few days before she fell ill.

When we saw the series of brain scans some weeks later, we could easily see large lacunae, great big holes where there should have been brain. It was a terrible thing for us to see, but it was no more than I had already dreaded. Then Anna developed hydrocephalus.

If there ever was a worst nightmare for anyone, then this was it for me. Hydrocephalus causes the forehead to become swollen and embossed over the eyes, which become shrunken as the whole skull expands. For any parent it is heart breaking, and for me it was even worse because I knew exactly what was going on and what the likely outcome would be, and so did Martha.

It was exactly 10 years before that I had performed my first ventricular shunt on a hydrocephalic infant at Alder Hey under the tutelage of Professor Peter Paul Rickham. The actual operation was not so difficult. It consisted of implanting a small tube from the lateral ventricle of the brain into either the carotid vein or into the abdomen, in order to drain the excessive spinal fluid, and thus reduce the swelling of the skull.

The great problem was the blocking of these tubes and the subsequent need for further revisions in most of such cases, and so it was with our daughter. The pain of watching her come out of the operating theatre, her head swathed in bandages and her eyes staring out of her swollen and deformed skull was almost too much to bear. I now knew that we would be caring for a severely disabled child for the rest of our lives, and that was a very grim thought.

We tried to find solace in ourselves, but it was hopeless, for Martha´s heart was broken. She knew just as well as me what the likely outcome was going to be. She became cold and shut herself off from me, which increased my own sense of fear and foreboding.

Then came the day when Anna Palesa was discharged from hospital. Looking back on that dreadful day, I still find difficult. I shall never know if it was a secret, unspoken choice we were being offered, but at that time Anna was even incapable of swallowing any nourishment. And she had been discharged without any intra-gastric feeding tube in place.

Viga the grandmother, Martha the mother, and I, stood together looking at our terribly damaged child. Without any sustenance she would die within a few days. It was a killer moment which I can never forget. Then Viga said in her strong Polish accent, "Ve must put a tube down!" But neither she nor Martha were able to, for the sheer emotion of the moment. It was I who slid the nasogastric tube through Anna's nose and into her stomach.

Now, we really were committed to caring for a severely brain-damaged child, and that was a heart-breaking thought for all three of us doctors.

Whilst in Lesotho Martha had managed to get herself an attachment to a GP in Brighton so she could start her general practitioner training, and in late 1984 we moved down to the house at 15, Arundel Street with the two children. For months I had not even thought about work. I had left Lesotho without any plan for my future. In my heart I was still in Africa, but I was now so reduced by present circumstances that my normal boundless confidence had been shattered. Fortunately, we were not short of money, but I had to find some work.

Back to Academia – at the London School of Tropical Medicine and Hygiene

Just when all the chips were down, along came Dr Murray Baker. We had met years ago in Lokkichoggio on the Sudan-Kenya border during yet one more border war, whilst I was up in Turkana country. He had spent his life in the colonies providing health care to the locals. Now he was the senior medical advisor to the Overseas Development Agency. It was through his kind help that my life took a right turn, as far from clinical surgery as one could ever get in health care.

"I'll see what I can do for you", he said after our chance meeting at the Royal College of Surgeons in Lincolns Inn Field. "You need a rest from surgery after the last seven years. You've done a lot, you know". As he said it, I realized that I had indeed been busy 24 hours a day for the past seven years, often alone and exposed, and I cried when I thought of the beauty of Lesotho, its wildness and its people who lived their lives on horseback in a land that was mostly mountain rock.

Three days later I received a letter stating that I had been awarded one of two annual Medical Research Council scholarships. This would support me at the London School of Hygiene and Tropical Medicine for one year in order to study for a Master's degree in Community Health in Developing Countries. God Bless Murray, as he was known to all of us bush doctors. Once again, the old boy network had been in action, saving my bacon and allowing me back into academia once more, a place that I did occasionally enjoy.

The one thing that kept me going during this bleak time was the London School of Hygiene and Tropical Medicine, where I could bury myself in books and briefly forget the catastrophe which enveloped me. There was also the sanctuary of my small flatlet in the house of my oldest mate from Liverpool, Ian, in Clapham. This comfortable refuge became my base for several months, and Ian was always my supportive friend. He was now a senior neuro-anaesthetist at the Hospital for Nervous Diseases in Queen Square. Our warm companionship during these bleak times was one thing that helped to keep me on the straight and narrow, in spite of feeling so isolated and alone, and unloved by my partner.

The School of Hygiene was in Malet Street, just off Goodge Street and it was there that I re-entered the world of books and study. It was quite something just to be doing a 9-5 day with no on-call commitments, and to be free in the evenings to do my own thing. Sitting and being lectured to on such erudite subjects as biostatistics and epidemiology was gripping stuff, and with the other half of the course being pure tropical medicine, I was in my element.

My student companions were also excellent company, being 32 from over 20 different countries around the world, from Mexico to Kashmir and beyond. Over the course of the year we all became good friends, and I learned a lot from them. Our teachers at the School were of the highest quality and delighted in teaching us. I began to realise the great mountain of knowledge and experience in all aspects of tropical health care which was contained within the School of Hygiene. It really was a world centre worth its salt, and I felt privileged to be a part of its alumni.

It was Arturo, a young, recently qualified doctor from Mexico who taught me an invaluable lesson concerning the expectations of patients. After he qualified, he was posted to a small town in the wilderness of Guadalajara, where some rural doctors had already been murdered over the years by certain dissatisfied patients. Within days of his arrival, he had been called to see the chief of a neighbouring village, who was suffering upper respiratory symptoms. Arturo's diagnosis had been a simple infection but, knowing how the land lay, he threw up his arms, declaring to the chief's family and entourage, "There is nothing I can do. This patient will surely die unless a miracle occurs. I have only one medicament which may help", proceeding to give the old man an aspirin.

He was not so surprised, two days later when he re-visited the chief, to find him sitting comfortably outside his residence with his wives. "Thank you for saving my life", said the old man, and Arturo left the village, not only alive and well, but with a fine fat chicken under his arm.

I later improved on Arturo's excellent approach during my years as a GP in Hailsham. I began to greet each decomposing patient as they entered my consulting room with the uplifting words, "My goodness, Mr/Mrs Go-Lightly, how very well you are looking today".

I liked to believe that these words alone may have reduced the patient's burden of pathology. Possibly wishful thinking, but I could see Arturo's point. Patients' prognoses should always be guarded.

The Wellcome Tropical Institute

Shortly after getting my Master's in Community Health in Developing Countries (CHDC) in 1985, I obtained a very good job for one year as Assistant to the Director of the Wellcome Tropical Institute at Euston. This was a new institute, funded by the Wellcome Trust, whose main aim was the production of educational materials for healthcare workers in developing countries. My main responsibility was producing distance learning teaching aids for doctors working in remote situations. But I also had other interesting responsibilities, one of which was teaching battle surgery to the SAS.

I was sitting in my extensive office one morning when in walked Prof Parry, closely followed by a colonel from the SAS. "The colonel was wondering if you could teach some of his friends from Hereford a thing or two about battle surgery", Prof addressed me. "I'm sure I could", I replied, somewhat surprised at this unusual request.

So it was that one week later I was sitting in the lecture room inside the Museum of Medical Science on the south side of Euston Road in front of 22 very fit young men, all with very close haircuts. I honestly had no clear idea where to begin, so I handed each soldier a blank piece of A4 paper. "Write down the one thing you would like to talk to me about", I said, and was considerably surprised to receive 11 requests to discuss domestic problems concerning their own children's health.

So, I did oblige these young fathers, believing that this would earn me their confidence. I held a one-hour GP surgery, with them all firing questions at me from skin rashes to circumcision and a lot more. It touched me that these battle-hardened soldiers put the care of their children first, even though they were normally off shooting brigands and terrorists during working hours.

My novel consultation paid off, and during the weeks that followed I established a great *camaradie* with these young warriors. I imparted some necessary medical and surgical information, whilst sharing some of the SAS´s secrets which are not in the public domain.

Another special moment was the arrival of the Chief Nursing Officer of China, with whom I spent a memorable day. She was a sprightly 82 years old, petite and full of fun. She told me that when her delegation arrived at Heathrow, she was surprised to be offered a wheelchair at the foot of the aeroplane's stairway.

"But I do not need that thing", she said definitively to the British Council representative who had come to meet her, and we laughed at the thought. She spoke very good English and was interested in everything the Wellcome Museum had on show. She invited me to come and visit her in China, and I regret that I never did. But I still have the postcard of the terracotta warriors which she later sent me.

At this point I moved from Ian's flat, and for six months I lived on board 'Baroque', the Bristol Channel pilot cutter I had bought a half-share in some years before with my friend James. She was now berthed in St Catherine's dock in the shadow of the Tower of London. This reduced my daily commute to Euston to just 20 minutes on the Tube, which was almost bearable, and 'Baroque' was a most comfortable residence, deep in the heart of London.

The winter of 1986 was freezing, and I spent it ice-bound in St Catherine's dock on board 'Baroque'. Carrying sacks of coal down the ice-clad ladder of the dock to the icy deck of 'Baroque' was always dangerous but had to be done. The small cast-iron stove in the galley not only cooked my food but kept me warm and comfortable below decks. I even 're-located' a large blue Wilton carpet from a skip, which helped to insulate me from the freezing dock water.

In this manner I managed to pass one year in London, even though my heart was not in this city. The continuing domestic catastrophe with Anna Palesa never went away. It was with me every day I was in London, and whenever I went back down to Brighton. There was no way we could ever regard our new daughter as a normal child after all her suffering. All her development goals were wildly off track, and she was so unresponsive that we also feared that she may be blind. There was no minute of the day when I did not feel fear and sadness.

In spite of all the many problems, clinical and other which I had surmounted in Africa, there was nothing within my power I could do to assuage this nightmare which had suddenly enfolded me and rendered me so unhappy and insecure.

Fortunately, there was still 'Baroque' to escape on, and when Spring arrived, James and I often sailed across the Channel to Fécamp and

Honfleur along the French coast. Only on the deck of 'Baroque' with the sails filled by the wind and the decks heaving in the swell, surrounded by the sea, did I manage to forget the turmoil in my life for a while.

'Baroque'

She became a refuge for me during my bleak years

Then, shortly after the birth of our third child Sarah, Martha divorced me. There was no absolute reason, but the tragedy of Anna Palesa had forced us apart rather than together.

I was left alone inside the echoing walls of No 15 Arundel Street. It was a dreadful moment, and it was only the great kindness and understanding of my good friends which enabled me to survive the subsequent dismal years.

17. FROM TRIBULATION TO TRIUMPH 1986 – 2000

Even though I was now drifting like a rudderless ship, I had already made some decisions about my new existence. I knew I would never go back to London to work. I was also determined to continue to take an active part in my children´s lives, even though Martha was now living a mile away with the children in Queen´s Park.

´Baroque´ - and Mike the Navigator

I needed to find some employment locally which would allow me to live in my house in Arundel Street, which had always been a comfortable refuge for me. Brighton Marina was just 100 metres south of Arundel Street. During the summer of 1986 James, my partner in ´Baroque´, and I, sailed her down the Thames from St. Catherine´s dock to the marina, which became her base. I now had a second comfortable refuge within easy reach, and I subsequently spent a lot of time on ´Baroque´ dreaming of empty seas and skies, and freedom from my woes.

James and I had an extensive nautical library on board, and by now I knew a lot about Bristol Channel Pilot cutters like ´Baroque´. Most were built around the turn of the last century and were specifically designed to sail into the Western approaches of the Atlantic in all weathers and guide the huge passenger steamers from America safely into port. They were built very strongly and were crewed by just the captain and a boy. The pilot occupied most of the comfortable space below decks, which is where I had made my home.

'Baroque' was one of the most famous of these beautiful boats, for the voyages she made with Major Harry Tilman into the northern Arctic wastes during the post-war years. I was sitting on the deck one day, enjoying the anaemic autumn sun, when an elderly, but very upright old man approached me and asked if he could come on board with his little dog. And that was how I met another of the Giants of Men.

Mike Richey had just retired as the Director of the Royal School of Navigation at Greenwich and was already a famous person within the ocean sailing fraternity. He was also a contemporary of Major Harry Tilman, 'Baroque's previous owner. He told me that after some disagreement many years before, Harry Tilman had refused to let Mike set foot on 'Baroque'. So, this was a very special moment for Mike, whom I was already warming to.

I led Mike down into the living quarters, which he had never seen, where we split a bottle of Burgundy whilst I listened, enraptured by his sailing adventures. Now I had a new friend, and one of the highest calibre. Even though there were 30 years separating us, we became close friends and used to meet every week on Thursday evenings at 'The Rock' in Kemptown where we drank Harvey's Best and related adventure stories in the Snug, which always had a glowing fire on the go during the winter months.

Mike was 70 years old when I first met him, but he stood over six feet tall, with a ramrod back and a crushing handshake. He was an ascetic, a practising Catholic, and one of the most modest men I ever met.

Born in 1917, Mike's life was one of pure adventure and exploration on the high seas. During the Second World War, his expertise in navigation was recognised by the Royal Navy, and during that war he also developed his skills in astro-navigation, which is what he became most well-known for. His erudite papers on all aspects of navigation were published in the most respected journals. After the war, for over 30 years he was the Director of the Royal School of Navigation at Greenwich, for which he was honoured with an MBE.

He owned two sailing boats. 'Jester', a 25 ft Nordic *folkboat* in which he made his famous Atlantic crossings, and 'Ballerina', a 12-foot, clinker-built sailing dinghy, which he gave to me on his 90th birthday, saying he was getting a bit too old for small boat sailing. But it was Mike who taught me to sail that beautiful dinghy.

On my 50th birthday in 1996 Mike presented me with a rolled-up scroll of paper. It was a copy of the certificate from the Guinness Book of Records confirming Mike as the oldest person to have sailed across the Atlantic, single-handed. He did it in 'Jester', and was then 80 years old, but he made little of this stupendous achievement.

It was this friendship, and others, which enabled me to begin to enjoy my life in Brighton during these dark times, in spite of being physically separated from my children, following our divorce in 1987.

In spite of doing some crazy and dangerous things during my life, I had never been suddenly brought up short by any disaster – until now. But my abrupt return from Africa after seven idyllic years, to face the grave illness of Anna Palesa and then the separation of my family, had totally deflated my ego, and with it my drive and confidence had left me. The one thing I felt I had been born to do, surgery, was something I could no longer face, and that was a very frightening thought. I still had to earn a living as a doctor but had no idea where or how I was going to begin my new career.

On Learning to cope with Bereavement

Living with this uncertainty was a killer, and I entered a long period of depression, which pills did not help. I was suffering all the signs and symptoms of bereavement, though I did not realise it at that time.

Every loss is a bereavement, whether it is a child's toy, or one's own health. The loss of a family member is one of the greatest bereavements, and I had just lost several. It was Rick, my old friend from County days, who had now become my GP, who introduced me to Jackie, one year after my family had broken up. She was a counsellor, an experienced Gestalt psychotherapist. It was she who over 10 years helped me to pass through the inevitable five stages of bereavement, and finally to acceptance and peace of mind. She and her husband Keith became life-long friends and their comfortable terraced house in Newhaven was always a refuge for me. She died at the ripe old age of 84, and I came over from Spain to attend her funeral, which was not a sad affair. It was a happy meeting on a sunny day, of many old friends celebrating a life well lived. In her earlier life Jackie had been a ballerina, and to her, life was a dance, and we were all the dancers. Her photo is beside me as I write.

50 years ago, after six years of medical study I had never heard the word bereavement mentioned. Yet every one of our patients is bereaved in some manner. Today the value of psychotherapy is well-recognised, PTSD is now in common parlance, and there is also now a large cadre of trained counsellors who provide ´talking therapies´. After my own experiences I can see their great value.

Another thing that helped to keep me sane were my regular weekends with the children. Wojtek was now six years old and studying at St John´s primary school in Kemptown, and Sarah was soon to follow him. Anna Palesa was in a residential care home in Portslade, which made visiting easy, and I used to go every week, often with Wojtek and Sarah in tow.

The family farm was another great refuge. My parents had just retired and moved to a flat in Eastbourne and my brother Mark had taken the farm over with his wife, Suzie. Most weekends we would meet up there with our children. My sister Lizzie and Shahrokh would also come over with their two boys, Ali and Adam. There were always a couple of old cars on the farm, bought cheaply from Heathfield market, and the 5-acre field is where the children learned to drive, before they had reached their teens.

Re-kindling my Pyromania

The farm was still a place where I could create explosions without the anti-terrorist police interfering, and so I started a series of voyages across the channel on the Newhaven-Dieppe ferry with the boys, in order to purchase large quantities of fireworks which we christened Chinese High Explosive, unavailable in England at that time. These were a variety of explosive devices of varying potency – from the relatively benign Bisons to the terrifying Tiger 3´s, which looked and sounded exactly like a stick of dynamite going off. Even the Catherine wheels were like revolving rockets.

Adam and Wojtek were willing aides, and whilst I bought the dynamite, it was they who humped the haversack, full of explosives, back to Newhaven. I shudder when I think of what our penance would be today if arrested. But in the mid-1980´s Customs seemed less excited about the importation of Chinese explosives by school children.

Whilst their childhoods passed into the teenage years, I was happy to be reliving my pyrotechnic past in the company of such admirable young people. In the summer months I used to take the boys for a weekend´s biking in Normandy, which we all enjoyed. Wild camping in a field, consuming charred meat and sleeping under the stars, what could be better. I also took up mountain biking with Rick, and we travelled the South Downs from north to south and east to west over the years. Biking, blading, badminton and ´Baroque´ became my releases during these difficult and uncertain years, as well as keeping me fit and sane.

Biking Brighton sea front with Wojtek and Sarah

Blading Brighton sea front with Irene

The seafront from the marina to Shoreham power station became another playground for me and the children. Carrots Café in the shadow of the power station is where we used to have Sunday breakfast together. Wojtek had just fallen in love with skate-boarding and Sarah had her pink bicycle, and with me on my rollerblades we used to spend hours traversing the sea-front from end to end.

Brighton is a seaside town which is full of interesting diversions, from Volks electric railway, built in the 19th century, but still ferrying tourists between the marina and the Palace Pier every day, to the museums and theatres and clubs. On the lower Marine Parade there was a rich mixture of shops, bars and cafes, gypsy fortune-tellers and tiny, old-fashioned stalls, including the Penny Slot Machines, into which my children poured hundreds of pounds worth of my pennies during their formative years.

On the road to General Practice

In order to earn some money, as well as regain my confidence, I soon started doing a series of six-month rotations as a Senior House Officer in and around Brighton in disciplines from A+E to Geriatrics, with the aim of becoming a general practitioner. A career as a GP in England seemed to be a reasonable alternative to surgery, which I knew I could not go back to at that time.

I started back again as an SHO in Accident + Emergency medicine, a discipline I had first encountered 15 years before at Broadgreen hospital in Liverpool. It was there in 1971, after just one week as a doctor, that through ignorance and inexperience I nearly killed my first patient. But by now, I had a wealth of clinical experience behind me.

Once again, I became a junior doctor, amongst seven others. All of us working under the watchful eyes of Kevin Baker, the senior registrar in A+E, who was a fellow motor biker like me. He was the friend who introduced me to Buddhism, a path which I have subsequently always tried to follow. Carlos Pereira was our consultant. He had just been honoured by the Queen for his work in the A+E department after the IRA bomb went off in the Grand Hotel, Brighton in 1985, and was a good boss to work for.

I noted the lack of experience of my fellow SHO´s, who were fresh out of their first houseman year, and had never been exposed to A+E medicine except as a student. I was often asked by one of them to help with a patient, and sometimes mistakes were made through ignorance and inexperience, just as had befallen me, and many other young doctors in training.

The Genesis of COITIS – and the Gunderson Prize

My year at the Wellcome Tropical Institute had taught me a great deal about all aspects of pedagogy, and I put this to good use. I constructed a special training course for my fellow SHO colleagues. Then I went to Kevin in order to discuss my plan, which I called "Casualty Officers Integrated Training : In Service", or COITIS for short. The acronym had a nice ring to it, I thought.

The plan involved using the SHO´s who had just completed their six months in A+E to mentor and teach the new, incoming SHO´s for a period of one week. There would be two hours of formal teaching in class each morning, then the new SHO´s would go on to their normal clinical duties, with we more senior doctors acting as mentors.

Kevin and I developed a series of specific goals which had to be achieved within the week, such as suturing a wound, managing a heart attack, correct referral procedures and many more. Then we went to Carlos, who was all for the plan. He was the person who persuaded the Health Authority to devote the funds to enable my plan to flourish.

That was when I met Dr Jenny Bennett, the Director of Public Health for East Sussex.

"You cannot possibly call this project COITIS!", she said definitively, giving me a wry look. She was not a woman to argue with, and so my project became COIST, "Casualty Officers In-Service Training", which never had the same ring. Nevertheless, it was a great success, and the course continued to be run every six months. It also netted me the Gunderson Memorial prize, worth £400, for innovation in medical education. More importantly, this successful experiment showed me that I could still make an effective contribution to medicine beyond surgery.

Promotion to Director of Hamster Therapy

I then became SHO in Geriatrics at Southlands hospital, Shoreham, where I learned a lot about the care of the elderly. Even as I did my nightly ward rounds with the geriatric patients I was constantly yearning for the wild hills of Africa, still so deeply meshed into my soul. Yet amidst all the gloom there were the occasional humorous episodes.

Just before Sarah's fifth birthday I asked her what she would like as a present. "I want something soft and furry", she said definitively, which is how I came to be the part-time owner of Sammy the Hammy.

My original three-pound investment eventually cost me a lot more, as the first thing this rodent did was chew through the cables of my central heating system. Then there was the purchase of a cage and toys and plastic tunnels, bedding material and food. With the help of Chris, my guitar-playing friend, we even made a truck for Sammy, and I guess the photo I have of Sammy smiling in the driver's cab makes up for a lot of the damage and grief he caused me.

During my alternate weekends on-call at Southlands hospital where I was doing Geriatrics, I used to have to look after this creature in my on-call room. One night just before I set off for my night-round I stuffed Sammy into the white coat pocket which held my Littman´s stethoscope. He loved sleeping in pockets of every description.

Sister Bernadette was taking me round when we came to a very ancient patient, and I was astonished to see a small furry thing jump out of my pocket and onto the patient as I got my stethoscope out. Sammy made a beeline for the sheets as Sister Bennett' s eyes bounced in and out. Oh God! I thought. More trouble.

Then a smile appeared on the face of the old lady, and she produced Sammy from below the sheets, clasping him in her hands. I quickly grabbed him and stuffed him back in my pocket, apologising to sister for this professional lapse, but she was also smiling.

The following morning at the nurses´ handover Sister Shirley gave me a piece of paper. "You´d better have this", she said. There, on this crumpled piece of paper was a shaky but recognisable image of a hamster. "She used to be an art teacher", said Shirley. And that is how I began a new career as honorary Director of Hamster Therapy at Southlands hospital.

Every night I used to take Sammy with me on my ward rounds, put him on a bed and let the old ladies play with him. They really loved it and Sammy seemed to enjoy his ward rounds as well. The Night Sisters could see the difference that this small animal made, even though they all knew, like me, that this was not orthodox practice. Twenty years later, my old mum was at Berry Pomeroy old people´s home behind the Grand Hotel in Eastbourne. Every Wednesday she would come alive in joyful expectation of the arrival of Rusty, a genial golden Labrador who was a regular visitor to old people all over Eastbourne, along with a tribe of other animals.

We all need someone to love, and the age of someone makes no difference. From Sarah at five years to my mum at 93, we all need someone to cuddle now and then, even a dodgy hamster.

An Unorthodox Approach to General Practice

In 1988 I obtained my Vocational Training Certificate in General Practice and that summer I began a new career as a general practitioner in Hailsham, 10 miles north of Eastbourne in my home county of East Sussex. The surgery was only a 30-minute drive from Arundel Street, so my regular outings with the children could continue as before, and that suited me well.

Being a GP in rural Sussex was a far cry from the bloody operating theatres of Africa I had been used to for so long. But it did stimulate my developing interest in social medicine and community care, and the great differences between preventive and curative healthcare. In general practice I found the perfect match of academic and clinical medical practice.

Hailsham had originally been a small but thriving Sussex market town. My father bought his first calves there in 1957 at the Wednesday morning market, which was then the hub of a thriving farming community. But during the early 1980's, large housing estates had been created around Hailsham in order to re-house hundreds of people from south London. It had become a town with many of the social and health problems associated with poverty and unemployment, and I could see I was going to have my work cut out.

After my years in Africa working with a population of mainly fit, thin Africans, I was shocked to see the levels of obesity in the population of Hailsham and their sub-optimal lifestyles. Well over 30% of my patients were obese. Half my patients with diabetes were obese and also smoked, and very few did much to maintain their own health. I was rapidly becoming aware that much of a GP's work revolves around some of the life choices that people make, and then dealing with the consequences.

Within my small surgery I had two staff to assist me. Jenny was 18 years old, the youngest daughter of Barry, my old friend from Lewes Grammar days. She had recently achieved maximum grades in her administration and secretarial exams but was finding it impossible to find work. She became my PA and fixer, and there never was a finer one.

Rita, "Tweetie" to us all, was my Practice Nurse. She was a vivacious nurse from the Seychelles and was also a qualified swimming coach. She was also a very caring nurse whom all the patients admired and could never say no to.

The evolution of the HALO Project

We were a good team and had some memorable adventures together during our three years at Hailsham, of which the greatest was the HALO project, which began to take shape one night over the bar of my local, ´The Merry Harriers´ in Cowbeech.

As I downed a pint of Harvey´s Best, I was thinking about my new responsibilities as a general practitioner. Whilst the routine minor problems were manageable as well as the more challenging urgent cases, the never-ending queue of patients with chronic disease who faced me every day was depressing. I was convinced that much of the chronic disease I was looking after, from obesity to shortness of breath and insomnia to depression, was a result of unhealthy living. I also believed that diet and exercise were the bedrock of any formula for improving the health of my patients. Pills were not the best answer.

In a moment of inspiration, I realised that facing my surgery was the answer. The Oasis Leisure Centre, owned and operated by the local Wealden Council, with its swimming pool, squash courts and exercise gymnasium, café and bar, all managed by my friend Mike. He was a fellow guitar player, of Caribbean origin, and we had started playing rhythm and blues together at the leisure centre bar every Thursday night.

I left the surgery and walked over to the Oasis to expound my idea to Mike. He willingly agreed to offer my patients subsidised exercise sessions for £1 each. Few of my patients could afford the standard rate of £3, but as part of their commitment to the project I wanted them to pay something. In the end it proved to be a perfect deal. Mike got a lot more clients for the leisure centre, and later on their children also came. My patients got a cheap aerobic workout three times a week, as well as the chance to form new social groups in a healthy environment.

The following Monday, having briefed Jenny and Rita, I began to prepare a small scientific study to determine the effects of regular aerobic exercise on certain chronic diseases. My year at the London School of Hygiene had not been wasted. I now knew how to design and run a trial. For one week I asked every patient which form of exercise they preferred, if any, and was surprised to find that 80% of the women and 50% of the men enjoyed swimming.

My first trial patient was Gay, a middle-aged lady I really liked because she was normally a healthy jogger. Today, six weeks after having a hysterectomy, she was not looking her best. "I hit John yesterday", she said, and burst into tears. John was her husband of 25 years and I had always seen them as a happy couple, so what was going on?

After taking a full history my diagnosis was post-hysterectomy depression, a not uncommon sequel after removal of the uterus. "Right Gay", I said, "I think I have the cure for you, and it is not a pill! It is a free session at the Oasis Lagoon".

Half an hour later Gay was doing lengths in the pool with Rita. And that was just the beginning. Within two weeks I had signed up 15 patients to a contract. They would go to the Lagoon three times a week for swimming with Rita, at the subsidised price of a pound a session. We did experience problems at the start. Fear was often a major factor. For example, some of my 15 trial patients had a strong fear of exposing their bodies to the public.

Rita told me one day that a female patient had arrived to start her three weekly swimming sessions, saying, "So sorry, but I have forgotten my costume." Her ruse to avoid the coming challenge was foiled at the moment Rita opened a locker door to expose a multitude of costumes of every size. "Just have a root around", she said, "I´m sure you will find one your size". And we both laughed our heads off when she recounted this tale.

Nobody escaped Tweetie. She was a demon motivator, and the patients all loved her, so what could they do but follow. Because of her aptitudes I knew that she was critical to the success of this project, and it could not have succeeded without her.

Rita and I recorded various significant parameters such as weight and blood pressure at every patient´s visit, and we used a linear analogue score to assess their mental state, from depression to elation. I spent hours at night recording and collating all the data, and I still possess those records. After one month Rita and I had a meeting with all 15 trial patients in the Oasis. Mike provided tea and biscuits.

The results were striking. Thanks to Rita, the compliance of my 15 trial patients during the month was 100%, and every patient had benefited from the exercise prescription. Not only had every patient lost some weight, but their mood and sense of self-worth were much improved. Blood pressures were also significantly reduced in the at-risk patients. Gay had even started running again. But the most unexpected finding was that out of seven smokers, four had stopped voluntarily. I had specifically said to Tweetie that we would never mention smoking in this small experiment, so I was gratified to find this unexpected result. All 15 patients became friends, and quite a few later chose to exercise together. This was the genesis of my later development of 'Pathology Gangs´.

I went to Mike and told him of these most interesting results, and he saw their worth. I wanted to extend the scope of the exercise programme because many of the men preferred to work out in the gym, so Mike introduced me to Jim MacLaughlin. He was a super-fit Canadian who was the first graduate of the American College of Sports Science I had ever met. He ran the Oasis gym, and it was he who introduced me to Sports Science, from the science of aerobics to the psychology of endorphins. He was a great teacher and motivator and soon became an integral part of my team.

With Rita, the three of us devised the Health and Leisure Organisation, which soon became HALO. Its main aim was the safe medical referral of patients to a programme of physical exercise. At this stage everything was informal and involved only my own practice. Then Dave Hanratty, another Hailsham GP, joined HALO and started referring his patients for exercise. This increased the number of my subjects, as well as helping to convince me of the validity of what was then a revolutionary idea.

Rita, Jenny and I spent hours recording the results for every signed-up patient, and when I had collated the data from the first 50 patients, I presented my findings to the Eastbourne GP association. This resulted in the interest of the East Sussex Health Authority, and £5000 of vital seed money from Dr Jenny Bennet, the Director of Public Health, who, having scoured my data confirmed the validity of my idea.

She became a mentor and the central figure of this evolving project, and with her long experience in public health she provided invaluable advice and support.

I must also give due thanks to Dave Robertson who was the senior administrator from the Health Authority who did so much with Jenny Bennet to organise my project and integrate it into the health care system. He was the person who spent painstaking hours with me, as we composed the vital protocols for the safe referral of patients to exercise. This standard set of guidelines is what allowed the HALO project to spread nationally.

Reference : *HALO. Exercise on Prescription: a Protocol for Collaboration. Dr S.Ramsay Smith and David Robertson*

ISBN : 1 899064 00 1 (© *East Sussex Health Authority*)

January 1994 Version 3.1 DR

Nothing is ever new

My friend Alex, from Anatomy days at Liverpool in 1966, was now Senior Lecturer in Public Health for Merseyside. He invited me to Liverpool to spread my idea to the local Merseyside GPs. He also introduced me to 'The Peckham Project'.

This revolutionary project was started just after the Second World War by two enterprising GPs in south London, who created a unique community surgery. Apart from the consulting rooms, there was also a garden, a swimming pool and areas to relax for the post-war, poverty-struck people, as well as many other social benefits. My HALO project was just a later version, but the ethos was the same.

In 1989, one year after I had started HALO I made another revolutionary move. With Mike's blessing and also that of the East Sussex Health Authority, I shifted my GP surgery into his leisure centre, and thus became the only GP in Britain with his surgery inside a leisure centre. The evolution of this novel form of health care, and the results, were once again significant.

My consulting room was in the basement of the leisure centre. The waiting room was the café-bar, where all patients were offered a free cup of tea or coffee while they were waiting to be seen. They were also offered a free hour of exercise at the time of their choice. Soon we all began to see the great benefits of this approach to community health care. Some patients even turned up to the Thursday evening music nights where Mike and I jammed, and joined in. I have always believed that music is therapeutic, but when it is performed in an arena where one can just go for a swim between verses, it is incomparable.

Today there are some supermarkets which have a GP surgery inside them. They are even found in some railway stations, but they are all privately run for profit. If I were King of Britain, I would have an NHS doctor's surgery inside every leisure centre.

I also started a series of support groups amongst my patients, which we called 'gangs', in order to make them less formal and medicalised. The first was the post-natal gang, (the PNG) where all post-natal mothers met once a week at the Lagoon, most importantly, along with their partners. Post-natal depression was a relatively unrecognised problem at that time, but throughout Britain many new mothers suffered, and some even tragically committed suicide as a result. Soon, the combination of a neutral environment, music and exercise exerted their effect, and post-natal depression in mothers declined significantly.

Later we started cardiac gangs and obesity gangs, with weekly meetings in the Oasis. Their togetherness worked magic in motivating changes in lifestyle. Some of them even had T-shirts made proclaiming their membership of these informal health clubs. The heart of all this social change was the leisure centre, and Mike .... and our music. The rest of what happened had its own energy and flowed on its own. Over 30 years later, the process I started in Hailsham continues to be budgeted for as part of the national health policy.

It was Dr Jenny Bennett, who later became my boss for one year, who told me a profound truth concerning health care. Until the moment that a government provides budgets for a health and social development project, it is not 'real'. HALO was just such an example. In 1990 for the very first time, East Sussex Health Authority included 'GP Referral to Physical Exercise ' in its annual health budget. Both Jenny and I considered that a triumph.

Two years ago, 20 years after HALO started in Hailsham, I was gratified to find in Lewes Leisure Centre that they are now offering patients with dementia free access three times a week. Referral to exercise is now an integral part of every healthcare budget, and I am proud that I had a part in the genesis of that. One of the proudest moments of my medical career came in 1992. I was standing in the group of graduate students from Sussex University, at the Chelsea College of Physical Education in Eastbourne with Rita, Jim and Dave

Robertson. After severe scrutiny by the Higher Education authorities, my HALO training course, was about to become a legal, integrated module within the BSc (Hons) in Exercise Science course. I then handed the reins of HALO over to Dr Nick Webborn who was a specialist in sports medicine.

In the end I found that general practice was not the career for me. It was not in my blood, and the thought of another 15 years as a GP did not appeal to me in spite of the success of the HALO project.

Whilst I enjoyed every aspect of medicine, one in particular had always appealed to me more than others. Surgery had always been my natural bent, and the discipline I felt most comfortable with. It mattered less where I performed my surgery, whether it was excising a wart in the Minor Surgery unit at Brighton or performing an emergency Caesarian section in a bush hospital during a dark African night, I was happiest when I was holding a scalpel in my hand.

Once again, at another moment of indecision the gods smiled on me. Jenny Bennett offered me a post in the Public Health department as Health of the Nation Coordinator for East Sussex. I was to be based in Brighton, where I spent an interesting year attending to local public health problems, from drug and alcohol dependency to the teenage pregnancy rate. Jenny had even developed an alcohol-free pub, but it soon died a natural death. After my two years in clinical community medicine, I had now become a public health administrator.

My most memorable moment came at the end of the year when I presented the year's results in my annual report. When I presented the graph of the incidence rate of teenage pregnancies, Jenny was visibly impressed at the ascending red line.

"Do you realise that you are responsible for that!", she said, indicating a doubling of incidence during my years tenure.

"Jenny", I replied, somewhat hurt, "if I fornicated day and night, I could not achieve those heights!"

Jenny had a way of giving me 'wry looks' when I erred from the straight and narrow, which always reduced me. But that day there was also a twinkle in her eye. She remains the person who did most to encourage and guide my work in public health, and is still a good friend.

My career had now covered the whole spectrum of healthcare, from acute emergency surgery in war zones to tropical medicine, general practice and finally public health. My recent years in Brighton had been a fascinating educational voyage, but I had still not found myself where I wanted to be.

Returning to my Roots ; the Victoria Hospital, Lewes

It was Rick, my friend from my County days in Brighton in 1976 who told me that there was a post available for a surgeon at the Victoria hospital in Lewes, where he was now a GP/anaesthetist. So it was that I re-ignited my career in general surgery, becoming the resident surgeon at the Victoria Hospital, Lewes. It was the same town where I had done my secondary schooling 25 years earlier. At last, I was once again in a place where I felt I belonged.

The Vic, as it was called by everyone, was a small community hospital, built during the 1920`s, next door to the granite walls of HMP Lewes. It was a satellite of the County hospital in Brighton, eight miles away, where we performed elective surgery of all sorts, from general surgery to gynaecology and urology. There were just 50 beds on three wards.

Rick took me round the wards on my first day, to introduce me. On entering Poile ward, which housed the female medical patients, I was astonished to find a bottle of claret on every bedside table. In all my years of hospital medicine I had never seen the like of this before. Turning to Sister Winstanley, I asked, "Does all this wine come on an NHS prescription?"

"Sadly not", she replied, "but they do like a glass with their evening meal".

"But what about the male patients?", I asked.

"Oh", said Sister Winstanley, "they prefer a tot of whiskey".

Good grief! This was not the NHS I had known before. I knew I was going to enjoy working in such a civilised hospital, and so it turned out. Rick then introduced me to Peter the Porter.

Peter was possibly the most important person in the hospital, and certainly one of the most modest. Born and bred in Grimsby, he had started out on the fishing boats aged 13, before later moving to Sussex. He was a very clever and educated person and had trained to become one of the very first para-medics – obtaining the highest possible marks in the stiff exams: more than every doctor.

He was part of the very structure of the hospital and was respected and loved by us all. With the help of two young assistants, he did more than anyone to keep this unusual health facility functioning on a daily basis.

The porters' lair, where I often used to spend some pleasant hours, was up in the attic of this Edwardian edifice. Under the wooden beams Peter had arranged the most comfortable of abodes. It was reminiscent of a cross between a Turkish caravanserai and an exotic night club, with a TV and a coffee percolator, and a chaise longue in which to lounge. It was Peter's own private domain, and only certain people were ever invited, but Peter and I were kindred spirits, and I was always made welcome.

Staff turnover was almost unheard of at the Vic, and everyone was a friend. As the resident surgeon, I was always looked after extremely well. I even had my own doctor's mess, minus the bar but with a garden outside and a dovecote with 12 white doves to entertain me. There were no night emergency admissions, which allowed me a full night's sleep – almost unheard of in my previous life as a surgeon, and in the summer, we had barbecues on the lawn – just as we did in the summer of '76 at the County in Brighton.

In the mid-90's the Minor Injuries Unit was established at the Vic. It was run by experienced nurse practitioners and local GPs and took a great load off the A+E department at Brighton. I also did minor emergency surgery there for patients referred by their GPs. I had no waiting list, and so they usually got sorted out on the same day, which would not have been the case in Brighton. Thus, the hospital helped to maintain very good relationships with all the local GPs.

The theatre team was led by Sister Ruth Kennedy, a young Irish nurse with a wicked sense of humour, who very sadly died of bone cancer just before I left for Spain. Ruth was like a mother to us all and brooked no nonsense. Discipline was always correct, and morale was high, but she was always up for a joke.

Another tense staff meeting at the Victoria Hospital, Lewes

We always had the best quality coffee, made in a cafetière. None of the usual brown dust which the NHS normally offers its staff.

Caroline, a consultant anaesthetist, always brought a home-made cake when she did a list, improving our morale even more. Rick was often our anaesthetist for the general surgery lists which Bob Gumpert and I did every week. We three were the same team which had been operating together in Brighton during the long hot summer of '76, and even though we are now far apart, we remain the best of friends.

The Victoria hospital was not just a great place to work, but it was very efficient. The local community have always been very active in supporting its work, and still are. Rick is now the chairman of the Friends of the Victoria Hospital, helping to raise necessary funds and actively supporting its work. Long may this jewel of the NHS continue its valuable work, in spite of the onslaught of so many recent budget cuts to the NHS.

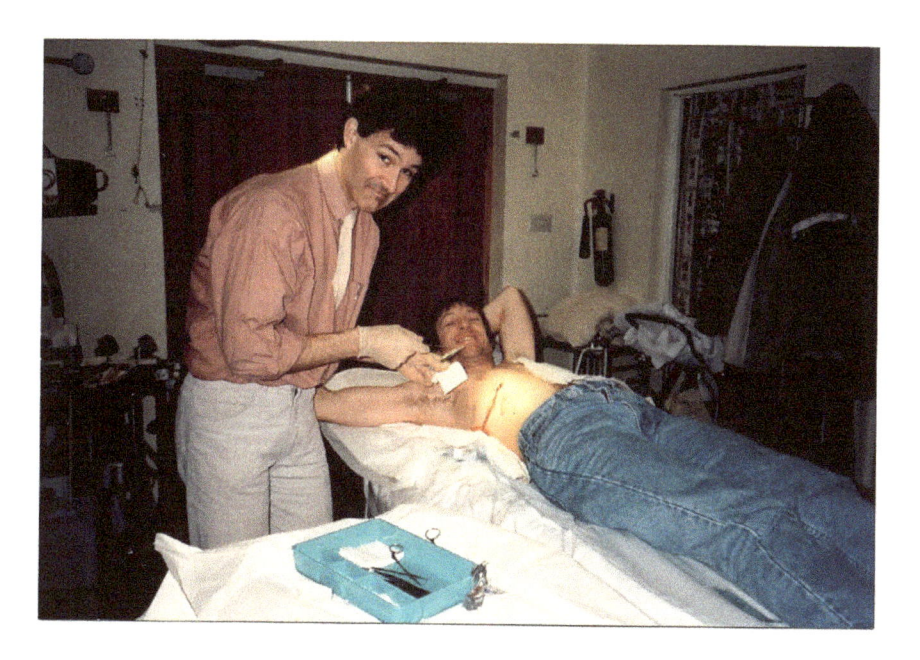

I even let Rick operate on me once. How could I have been so dumb?

It was a great privilege to spend 10 years working with such a dedicated team, whilst my three children grew up in Brighton. The photograph of my nursing team from the John C Robinson (JCR) surgical ward, is by my side as I write, John C Robinson having been a local philanthrope who personally funded the construction of this ward.

By now Wojtek was 12 years old and at secondary school in Brighton. He was still addicted to skate-boarding, but every Sunday morning he and I played badminton together at the sports centre in Wilson Avenue. Sarah had developed an interest in horses and went riding at Rottingdean every weekend. Anna Palesa was happy in her residential care home where she was very well cared for.

Anna was now 13 and had been diagnosed as severely autistic, which was no big surprise after her sufferings. Even though she could not speak, she had been taught Makaton, the signing language, and in that manner she could communicate in some fashion. She also recognised her family and friends and had a generally good humour. Physically she was very able and did enjoy her walks on the sea front, especially if we were heading for Carrot´s Café, where she could easily demolish a full English breakfast. But she would always need 24-hour care.

RollerDoc – on the Thrills and Spills of Rollerblading

It was during my years as the resident surgeon that I earned my nickname, RollerDoc. Janice, my girlfriend at the time, got me into rollerblading, a brand-new advance on roller-skating. The rollerblades were much faster, having four in-line wheels with well-engineered bearings on each blade. But with the speed came danger.

I fell and fractured my right forearm on only my second blading sortie with Janice. It wasn´t just the acute pain of the fracture which shocked me. It was the fact that I could no longer operate, nor even drive my car safely. I even tried to convince myself it was just bruising, but on my next operating list Rick, who was the anaesthetist, put me right immediately and sent me off for an Xray, which confirmed a distal fracture of the right radius.

I was signed off for at least six weeks. There was the inevitable Hospital Enquiry, and I was accused of irresponsible behaviour. I did mention the recent absence of one surgeon, wearing a full-length cast on his left leg after a recent skiing holiday, but apparently that was different.

Dave was the Senior Plaster Technician at the County hospital in Brighton. He had been one of our crazy gang back in ´76, and was delighted to see me, even fractured, after a gap of several years. He laughed when I told him about the origins of my fore-arm fracture, and then I told him of my problem. I was off work for six weeks at least and needed to be mobile and able to both rollerblade and drive a car. A plaster cast would not allow that.

"No worry", he said, "I'll give you a resin cast".

Thank God the advances in Medicine continue at every level. The heavy kaolin plasters of old were being replaced by lighter materials, including this remarkable resin sheet which Dave began to warm up using a hairdryer. The resin soon became malleable, and Dave formed a tube of it around my fractured arm, pressing it gently into every part. Then he bisected the tube along its length and attached Velcro tapes. Within 30 minutes I had the most amazing cast, which weighed nothing but allowed full movement of thumb and fingers yet held the fracture completely immobile when in place.

The first thing I did was go down to the Hove seafront and pay Blade Marc 25 pounds for five blading lessons. Then I drove to Lewes, picked up Janice and had another mad evening in the back streets of Lewes before collapsing at her house in Lansdowne Place.

I now had six weeks in which to perfect my blading technique. I have always loved wheels of any sort, except my old man´s wheelbarrow on the farm, always so full of manure. But rollerblades had eight in-line wheels, and they were practically friction-free. We are now talking of the thrills of speed, balletic grace and the dangers of wheels.

I still give daily thanks to Fred and Wilma Flintstone for all they did to invent and promote The Wheel.

Blading from Arundel Street to Hove Lagoon, or even Shoreham Power Station when we felt strong enough, became a habit which Janice and I indulged during this enforced period off-duty from the Victoria Hospital in Lewes, and which I continued until I left Brighton in 2000. The Brighton and Hove seafront deserves to be famous, all eight miles of it, and blading was certainly a brilliant new way of keeping fit, even if risky.

A Timely Diagnosis

Janice had a mother who was a dragon, and I was mildly surprised to be called at my house in Arundel Street one day by Sister Paula from the Vic whilst I was enjoying an afternoon off, saying there was a sick patient in Acute Admissions asking for me.

It turned out that Janice's mother had had 'a turn' whilst out shopping and was now crippled with chest pain. She had just arrived at the Victoria Hospital. Paula had called the Cardiac ambulance, which had just deposited her in A+E at the County Hospital in Brighton.

Then Janice rang me asking for help, and suddenly I was in a moral dilemma. Her mother trusted me for some opaque reason and insisted on having my opinion. But in the County hospital I no longer had any responsibility, even though I still had friends working there.

"I'll go up to A+E and have a look at her", I said to Janice, "but I promise nothing". I got into my car and headed for the County, dumping my car in the ambulance and medical parking before opening the doors to A+E.

The first thing I did was look at the Incoming Patients board, to find Janice's mother sixth on the list waiting to be seen by the

Medical/Cardiac houseman. I knew that it represented a wait of at least an hour or two before being seen by a doctor, so I introduced myself to Helen, the sister-in-charge and asked a favour.

"OK", she said, "but five minutes only!", and so it was that I faced a much-reduced old woman in Cubicle 6, in such pain that she could not breathe properly, nor could she speak.

I could see immediately that she was ill, even though her face lit up when she saw me enter. I tried to forget that this decaying dragon could one day become my mother-in-law and focused on the problem in hand.

The main problem was that I could not get a history out of her because she could not speak for pain.

I have talked about pain previously. There are all sorts, from a trivial ache to chronic debilitating pain, to death-inducing pain, and this is what I saw in front of me. Faced with such a situation, orthodox medicine then had only opioid analgesics to offer – which render any patient incoherent, if not unconscious. However, since being introduced to the path of Buddhism some years before, I had learnt about Breathing and breathing techniques. Breathing is fundamental to our being, so fundamental that even extreme pain can be controlled by correct breathing techniques.

For five minutes I coached Janice's mother in this little-known technique, until the time when she could speak again and thus recount her history.

She had been putting her shopping in the car three hours before when she experienced a sudden pain right in the middle of her abdomen, around the xiphisternum. The pain had just got worse and worse till she could barely breathe, and now the pain was everywhere, including her back.

It did not sound like a typical heart attack to me, but I was no cardiologist. Then I told her I was going to examine her. She had a raging tachycardia, but her heart sounds were normal and regular. As soon as I laid a hand on her abdomen, I knew the diagnosis. One just does after many years of clinical examinations.

She had generalised peritonitis, not a heart attack. Yet she had been admitted under the physicians, not the surgeons, and I had no authority.

I went to sister Helen and explained my findings. I had to speak to the Medical SHO urgently, and she understood the urgency. Janice´s mother was well over 60 years old, and for every hour´s delay in this sort of emergency, the mortality rate in the elderly doubles. If my diagnosis was correct, all speed was essential if this dragon´s life was to be saved. By then it was 1800 hrs.

Within a few minutes a young medical SHO appeared and listened to my story. All of this was on trust, but she was good enough to call the Surgical SHO, a fine young doctor who did a quick examination, then said he would call the Registrar at once. Paul Farrands, whom I knew well, was the consultant general surgeon on call. He would call me later.

With that I went to thank Sister Helen for her great help and then retired to Arundel Street to call Janice. Blimey! I was in some shock after this extra-curricular adventure, and I still did not have my diagnosis confirmed.

Paul called at midnight. "We´ve just closed the perforation", he said. "Good diagnosis, Goodnight and sweet dreams". It was over 12 years since I had saved the life of Mohtse, the 15-year-old boy I operated on at Qacha's Nek hospital for the same diagnosis, a perforated ulcer.

I went to bed, dreaming of dragons.

Some 25 years later I met my old blading partner Janice at a party in Lewes. She told me that her dragon mother was still alive, now aged 93. We had a hilarious reunion, mostly concerning rollerblading. It took me right back to the Victoria Hospital, Lewes and the 10 happy years I spent at this unique community hospital where everybody knew everybody, and everyone got looked after. It was life on a small scale, but the *camaraderie* and professionalism made my life a joy, in spite of the occasional frustrations, and this is how I ended my medical career in the NHS.

To a Roost in Andalucia

Ever since I had arrived back in England in 1984 and seen the social changes occurring under Margaret Thatcher's regime, I had felt more and more that I did not like what was going on in Britain. The creed of this millionaire's wife seemed to be, "Get off your butts and work. Everybody can get rich!"

But all I could see was the poor getting poorer, whilst even more millionaires appeared on the rich list every year. I did not like Britain's class system, nor the inherited privilege of the rich landowners, nor its sense of national nostalgia. I also detested the deeply ingrained racism which had been a part of Britain's culture since the days of slavery. Even my own parents were guilty of that. I could also see that social equality and justice in Britain had waned after the Second World War, and today things have only got worse in that regard.

So, I decided to retire to another country, one where there was less racism and more social justice and equity, and in 1988 I started exploring Hispania, starting with the Canary Islands.

I had enjoyed the parts of Hispania I had already seen, from Mexico to the Spanish mainland. I liked the people and their culture. In Spain there was no class system and far more social equity, and very little racism as far as I could see. Spain was also firmly within the European Community, which Britain no longer is. The British still regarded the withered remains of their empire with a mixture of pride and nostalgia, something which never appealed to me. I have always believed in a united Europe

In the end I could not settle in the tourist-infested Canary Islands, and I turned my eyes towards the Mediterranean coast of Spain. Between the Sierra Nevada and the Costa Tropical is where you will now find me, basking on Mediterranean shores, two hours' drive from the ski slopes of Pradollano.

In 2000 at the age of 55 I was offered the chance of early retirement from the NHS and took it like a shot. The children already knew that the day Wojtek started at Bristol university, I would feel free to leave Britain and head for Andalucia. And that is what happened.

That is where I found the ruined stable which I spent two years rebuilding, and where I have now lived for 22 years. It is a wild place. The folds of the Sierra de la Contraviesa lie above me, enveloping rocky ravines where wild boar and *cabra montesa* roam. The hills which surround me are dotted with carob and almond trees, and in December the first white almond flowers burst out. By the end of January these hills form a green carpet, punctuated by thousands of flowering trees, brilliant white under the sun. Sometimes buzzards and vultures fly overhead, and in the summer the rambla is full of hoopoes, bee-eaters and swallows returning to their old nests.

Yet, just five kilometres south of the stable lies the Mediterranean, blue and inviting. And Africa is just a four-hour voyage on the ferry from Motril to Melilla.

Two years later I sold my house in Brighton, knowing I would never come back to live in Britain. My children and friends come out to see me now and then, and I make the occasional foray back to England, but I know I shall die in Spain, *mañana*, as we like to say.

Three years after I had completed the restoration of the stable, I knew that I now had a secure base, in a place where I felt comfortable, and in 2004 I began to look around for some other stimulating adventure.

Back to war with Medecins Sans Frontières

I suppose I could have done anything, but somewhere within me the love of surgery still lurked. I was fit enough, and still had my wits about me, so I started making enquiries. The first thing I did was attend a week-long course in Geneva on War Surgery, run by the International Committee of the Red Cross, (ICRC), following which I was accepted by them as a war surgeon. But the ICRC had few functioning hospitals in war zones, and after six months I was still waiting for a posting. So, I applied to Médecins Sans Frontières (MSF), which is how in 2005 I once again found myself in the jungles of West Africa.

At the age of 60, when most chaps are dreaming of warm slippers by the fireside and a good book, I found myself in the company of Los Medicos, dodging bullets and mosquitoes, and had some of the most exciting and demanding adventures of my whole life during the next three years, from the Ivory Coast to Sri Lanka.

It seems that I really was born to be a surgeon, but one of an unusual breed.

18.   MAKING IT WITH LOS MEDICOS (1)

Médecins Sans Frontières. Ivory Coast, West Africa 2005

After five tranquil years in Andalucia, I began to feel the need for another challenging project. I may have retired from the NHS, but I had not yet retired from life, and I was still young and fit enough to enjoy a change of career.

So, I left my donkey Matilde and the nine goats, and the almond-studded hills of Andalucia, and found myself treading the gold-lined streets of Hatton Garden one cold January day in 2005, searching for the London office of Médecins Sans Frontières.

I still wanted to do something useful with my life. I also wanted to travel, and in Médecins Sans Frontières I found the perfect solution. It was as independent of politics and religion as a humanitarian non-government organisation could be, which was important to me. I had always followed MSF since its inception after the Biafran war in 1968, and I admired the work they did in some of the most dangerous corners of the world.

From London to Amsterdam

After a demanding hour with Marleen, the Dutch head of MSF Human Resources in London, and a very thorough perusal of nine pages of curriculum vitae representing 35 years of medical experience, I was pleased to be welcomed into that band of valiant brothers and sisters a few days later as a war surgeon and trainer for MSF.

Thus began a stimulating series of tropical adventures, starting in Africa and ending in Asia, taking me back to West Africa where I had performed my first hernia operation in 1965, aged 19.

Under normal circumstances no MSF volunteer would go on any mission until they had passed the 10-day Preparation Primary Departure course, the PPD.

PPD is only three letters of the alphabet, but the Preparation Primary Departure course was an obligatory and demanding regimen lasting 10 days, to prepare MSF health workers for the many challenges of a war-torn country. Everyone had to do it, including 24 hours out in the wilds practicing survival skills.

In view of my previous lengthy experience in the tropics, and because of the urgent need, I was sent to West Africa almost immediately and without my PPD certificate.

My contract was for two missions of six weeks duration each, with a six month separation between them. My first mission would be to assess all the medical and surgical resources of the district of Danané, in the Ivory Coast of West Africa, and to make recommendations to MSF-Holland. I would also be responsible for the clinical surgical care of the district. During the following six months MSF would be responsible for ordering and delivering the material resources I had identified. Then I would go back to Danané for another six weeks to manage the allocation of the new resources provided by MSF, whilst continuing my clinical and teaching duties.

My voyage back to Africa began in Amsterdam, my favourite city, which was the headquarters of the MSF-Holland surgical team I was to work with. There were two days of briefings and procuring visas, whilst I was lodging in the comfortable 3-star Hotel Arena, before I set off in the company of two young Dutch nurses, Janine and Andrea, who were to work with me at Danané.

From Amsterdam we flew to Paris where we picked up the Air France airliner to Abidjan, the capital of Ivory Coast. It was a good policy of

MSF to always try to send volunteers out to mission in the company of others. My two companions were both first timers and had never been out of Europe, whereas I had my previous years of experience to share with them during the voyage. They were excellent company, and we were already a jolly team as we entered the body of the huge airliner to be greeted by absolute bedlam.

It was as though we were already back in Africa! 90% of the passengers were Africans going home, dressed in all manner of rich and beautiful robes. Many of these passengers were children, careering around the aisles between the legs of the prim but slightly flustered Air France flight attendants. It was just like an African market, with all the colour and the babble and the children running everywhere.

By the time we arrived over the Ivory Coast many hours later, I was eager for a decent meal and a bed. As I waited in the torrid humidity and heat of the Customs hall with Janine and Andrea, I could see a small group with MSF sweat-shirts waving wildly in greeting.

I was impressed by the eagerness with which I was welcomed by Lauren, the Australian nurse, forever afterwards known by me as the Bird from Bondi Beach. She was the Medical Coordinator (MedCo) in Ivory Coast for Médecins Sans Frontières, and there was a particular reason for her pleasure in seeing me.

First Acute Abdomen – a rare diagnosis

There was an acute and serious problem for which Lauren needed my advice. The Logistics coordinator (LogCo) from Danané, an Italian called Dario had suddenly been laid low two days before with acute abdominal pain. It was so bad that he had been crash-evacuated the 750 kilometres back to Abidjan for a qualified surgical opinion. This had resulted in him being imminently prepared for abdominal surgery by a local surgeon.

After my previous experiences in Africa, it was no great surprise for me to be dragged off by Lauren to a private clinic in the centre of Abidjan whilst Andrea and Janine went back to the Residence to eat a bowl of pasta and go to bed. It was after midnight and all three of us had now been awake for almost 24 hours.

Passing through the entrance to this private clinic Lauren and I eventually found ourselves inside Dario's private room, where I found a sickly looking 35-year-old Italian lying prostrate in the bed.

It appeared that the local surgeon was keen to operate on Dario immediately, but Lauren was worried about the possible consequences, and whether or not this was the most appropriate course of action. Although she was a very experienced nurse, this problem was out of her natural orbit, which explained her joy at seeing me coming through Immigration at the airport.

The Problem with Private Practice

I have always been suspicious of private medicine in all its forms, and despite many opportunities, have never ever practiced privately. It often led to compromises in care, and above all I remain a socialist at heart, and simply do not believe in the unequal sharing of such vital resources as education and health within any social system.

I had my own minor problem to contend with at this moment. For the previous five years I had been hiding out up the Rambla of Rubite in southern Andalucia, and had never performed any surgery, apart from three memorably dangerous veterinary interventions on Matilde the donkey with Paco as a very unqualified first assistant.

During the previous 10 years at the Victoria hospital in Lewes, although I had been a full-time surgeon my work was only elective, non-urgent cases, and I was currently out of practice in the emergency department. So, it was back to basics. As Jack had said to me all those years ago in the primaeval rainforest of south Cameroun, when I first ever faced a patient across the operating table,

"First make the patient comfortable, then yourself!" An early lesson in healthcare, whose value I have never forgotten.

"Dario, *buon giorno*", I said, introducing myself to my new patient with a shake of the hand, which is how I always greeted a patient. With a finger on his right radial pulse, I knew at once that he had a tachycardia.

The first question was critical in these undiagnosed acute cases, in order to elucidate an accurate history of the problem.

"Tell me", I asked, "when did you last feel perfectly well?" This is always the first and most important question I ask in any encounter with a new patient.

Slowly and carefully I elicited a history going back several weeks of primarily left-sided abdominal pain and bowel dysfunction, culminating in this recent episode of increasingly severe pain and vomiting which led Dario to this private clinic. There was no significant family history of similar disease, and he was otherwise healthy apart from a diet of Sportsman cigarettes and alcohol. Then I began my examination.

There was no doubt that Dario was ill. He was toxic with a mild temperature and tachycardia and had signs of local peritonitis over his left lower abdomen.

"Did the doctor stick his finger up your bum?", I asked Dario.

"No way!", said Dario, as the colour drained from his face in horror at the thought.

"Well, turn onto your left side and take a deep breath", I said, "for I am going to do just that!" With Lauren looking on I put on a rubber glove and proceeded to examine carefully the rectum and pelvic area of the groaning Italian. As I had thought, there was a tender swelling deep in the left pelvis, palpating which caused Dario to jump about the bed and speak some particular words in Italian.

I was satisfied that I had a diagnosis, even though it was a most unlikely one, and had confirmed it by the rectal examination – an important part of this particular diagnostic problem, which the private surgeon had failed to perform.

I had always been taught in my student days at Liverpool that if you did not put your finger in it, you put your foot in it – speaking of the need to perform a rectal examination in every patient with an acute abdomen. The fact that this surgeon had not done such an exam made me suspicious, and the fact that we were in a private clinic immediately made money an issue. Any operation was going to net the surgeon a tidy sum, and in Abidjan during these days of civil war, money was hard to come by, so the temptation to perform an operation was there. I thought that we could at least wait the night out to see how things evolved over the next eight hours.

"Dario", I said, "I think you've got an inflammation of the large bowel, possibly what we call diverticulitis. I think you will live till morning without needing an operation, and then we'll see how things are tomorrow".

"I'd better have a word with the surgeon", I said, turning to Lauren, who was looking less stressed after my opinion on Dario. "Fine", she replied, "I'll go and find him", and disappeared.

So it was that I got to know Dario and also the lie of the land at Danané, where I was soon bound. After an awkward conversation with a disappointed African surgeon, Lauren and I went off to the MSF residence, driving through the city of Abidjan in the middle of the night, still full of traffic and enormous piles of stinking garbage along every road.

It was a familiar return to the Africa I had known so well. The terrible smell which we experienced on our journey that night turned out to be not just the ubiquitous garbage on the streets, but a ship full of toxic chemical waste from Holland which had recently been discharged at Abidjan.

As a direct result of this toxic waste dumped in the Ivory Coast from Europe, during the weeks of my first mission at Danané several dozens of citizens died and many more were terribly injured. There was always an economic agenda in the dealings between the western global capitalists and the third world, which included the trade in rubbish and waste from these rich countries. I found out later that this Ivorian tragedy was only surpassed by the similar one at Bhopal years before.

The torrid heat and humidity of Abidjan hit me like a wall. When we finally reached the MSF residence I was also greeted by a sweet and sickly smell as I exited the MSF pick-up. It was quite awful and pervaded every corner.

"What on earth is that horrible stink?", I asked Lauren who was busy investigating a half-empty pot of cold pasta.

"It's the Nestlé chocolate factory", replied Lauren, "remember that when you eat your next Mars bar!"

At three o'clock in the morning I finally fell onto my bed, sweating in the 95% humidity and starving hungry – for I simply could not face the unappetizing pot of congealed spaghetti and the smell of melted cocoa beans in my nostrils. This is how it was with MSF.

Four hours later an anxious Lauren woke me with a life-saving cup of tea. "Giddup yer pommie bastard!" was her congenial greeting. Andrea and Janine were still fast asleep after their long day, but at least, I thought ruefully, they had something solid inside their stomachs whilst I was already feeling serious pangs of hunger.

"Is there a banana in this joint?", I asked Lauren, who directed me to the kitchen where I found a huge bowl of fruits.

I knew from all my previous experience that one could travel four or five hours on one banana. It truly is a miracle food. A banana contains not just sugars for fast energy, but also oils for more sustained energy, and in addition the banana is completely protected from outside infestation by its easily removable skin and can also be eaten without the use of any tool.

With one banana inside my stomach, Lauren and I were soon standing once more by Dario´s bedside. I looked at the floor, which was now covered in a thick carpet of what had recently been Dario´s body hair. It looked as though we had arrived in the nick of time. At that moment a nurse appeared with a fresh razor and was about to render Dario even more naked when I intervened,

"Arretez, s'il vous plait", I ordered the nurse, and invited her out of the room. I then turned to Dario and studied his face and comportment briefly, but intently. He did not appear to be any worse, and on checking his chart I saw that his vital signs were stable.

"Buon giorno, hombre", I greeted Dario in my personal version of Esperanto. "How are you feeling this morning?" Dario flapped his hands, *"Comme ci, comme ça"*, he replied.

I briefly examined Dario' s abdomen, which, though still tender showed no signs of spreading peritonitis. It would be a fine decision, but I reckoned Dario was fit enough to be flown back to Europe for his further care. I wrote out a prescription for a course of broad-spectrum antibiotics, then I beckoned Lauren outside, and said,

"I think we can get him back in one piece, but we need to make sure he can be admitted somewhere in Paris, rather than go all the way home to Milan, and for sure he's going to need an escort – but not me!", I said, suddenly realizing that it was a possibility. But my good karma continued, and it was Andrea who found herself on her way back to Paris later that day, having not even been long enough in the Ivory Coast to unpack her bags. She carried with her a letter from me to the admitting physician in Paris, committing me to a diagnosis of diverticular abcess with local peritonitis.

In a 35-year-old it was a rare and unusual diagnosis to make. I had never been faced with such a case before during my 30 years of surgery, for diverticular disease of the colon is a usually a disease of later age. Nevertheless, the clinical signs and symptoms all pointed to this diagnosis.

The only other likely possibility, and a very common one in all the countries in which Medecins Sans Frontières operated was an amoebic abscess. Pathological amoebae lurked in every source of contaminated water, which was often all there was to drink in these impoverished parts of the world. On occasions, instead of the more usual acute presentation with abdominal pain and diarrhoea, the amoebae can become encysted and cause granulomatous disease and abscesses in unusual places, from the brain to bone and the bum.

That night Pierre, the Head of Mission in Abidjan invited us out to a Lebanese restaurant not far from the residence, where I ate an excellent meal of tagine and kebabs and drank mint tea. It did not sound as though there was much in the way of *haute cuisine* in Danané, so I made the most of this Middle Eastern feast.

The Road to Danané

The following day a white Toyota pickup left the MSF residence in Abidjan with Janine and me on board. We were heading north and west along 750 kilometres of good tarmac road through the teeming suburbs of this West African city and into the evergreen forests and plantations. Andrea was to join us on her return from Paris.

It was over 20 years since I had last worked in Africa and as we travelled past the villages which lined the road, the smell of charcoal cooking fires and the sights of rural Africa on the move brought back many memories dating back to 1964 when, at the age of 18 I had first set foot in Africa.

I noted many changes. The most striking was the decimation of the rain forest, and the huge lumber lorries which passed us carrying enormous trunks of hardwood trees bore witness to the continuing plunder of these ancient hardwood jungles, most of which no longer existed.

The other remarkable sight was the forest of satellite television antennae which sprung from almost every mud hut along the way. The French colonialists had done much to develop an infrastructure in Ivory Coast during their tenure. Apart from laying a tarmac road from the capital, which now ran to the western border with Liberia where I was now heading, they had also harnessed large amounts of electricity using hydroelectric power from dams around the enormous Lac de Koussou north of Yamoussoukra. This now provided light and power for all the villages strung along the road.

There were many roadblocks along the way, most of them just huge tree trunks placed strategically across the road, manned by armed soldiers. Fortunately, the MSF logo was well known along this road and we had no problems, but they were a constant reminder of where we were heading.

We arrived at Danané in the late afternoon, 10 hours after leaving Abidjan, and were relieved to find a hot meal waiting for us at the MSF residence.

Danané - Surrounded by Four Armies

Danané lies in the extreme west of the Ivory Coast, just 40 kms. from the border with Liberia. At that time was in a state of latent war, surrounded by not just one, but four armies.

First was the Ivorean national army, which faced a rebel army made up of tribesmen from neighbouring countries such as Burkino Fasso and Mali, who had come to Ivory Coast years before as economic migrants. These two warring factions were held apart by 1,500 French legionnaires and a UN contingent of Bangladeshi ´Blue Helmets´. The morning commuter traffic along the kilometer of road from the MSF residence to the hospital was therefore interesting, and not what I was used to in the Rambla de Rubite, Andalucia.

The Africans drove anything they could get their hands on, from clapped out buses to camouflaged Land Rovers, whilst the UN went around in white Scout armoured cars. But the prize-winners were the French legionnaires, who paraded the town in massive, armoured personnel carriers. Each one carried a gun which looked big enough to demolish the whole hospital with one round.

The French legionnaires all looked as though they would quite enjoy cutting someone's throat, while the Bangladeshi soldiers were quite approachable and behaved very well as a rule. The African warriors in their ragtag uniforms were quite another matter. Manageable when sober, but dangerous and unpredictable when drunk – which they often were. The numerous roadblocks which they manned were always a testing time for the MSF team, particularly because the only bribe that MSF ever offered these soldiers were condoms, of which MSF had a huge stock. What the Africans ever did with the hundreds of condoms we handed out over the weeks and months I shall never know, but it certainly was not for their original purpose.

I was now a surgeon working in a country where the prevalence of AIDS was 15% and condom usage was minimal, in a population where sexual activity was high. To make matters worse, the quality of the MSF surgical rubber gloves I was soon to use every day was poor. During all my time with MSF it was not the fear of being killed in the war that concerned me as much as the fear of contracting AIDS from one of my patients. All of us surgeons had that threat to face every day.

On arrival at the MSF residence, we had been greeted by Steve, the project manager. He was a young Canadian, already experienced in humanitarian work, and he turned out to be a good team leader with a dry sense of humour. Life in Danané was generally good for us in spite of the war, and we were well cared for in the residence. The most important thing was the high morale, friendship and trust among the MSF team, and also between MSF, the local militias and the local staff and townspeople.

The town itself was forlorn, in an African sort of way, being mostly a collection of mud-walled huts with rusty corrugated iron roofs, every one of which sported a television aerial. There was a lot of visible war damage wherever I went. There were some well-built villas from the colonial era, but these had fallen on hard times and were also in a state of slow decay, quite a few being decorated with pock-marked walls from shells and bullets.

There was rubbish everywhere, but today it was almost all plastic, from the inevitable carrier bags to water bottles and even babies' dummies. The open drains and ditches were also full of ordure. Stagnant patches of water from the rains were all over the place, each one a breeding ground for mosquitoes. (The prevalence of malaria among under-5's in the peripheral clinics which MSF ran was consistently over 90%.) There had been an outbreak of cholera only a month before, and the generally poor state of the town made me think there would be many other infectious diseases to cope with in these war-torn parts.

I do not know whether it was just the after-effects of civil war or whether it was just Africa, but in one of the richest countries in Africa – self-sufficient in petroleum, as well as the world's greatest exporter of cocoa and a major supplier of hardwoods and coffee, I wondered why things generally appeared so shabby and uncared for.

The Hospital

The hospital was in a similar state. The whole place needed a coat of paint, and in spite of the tropical rainfall there was no running water in the hospital, which I found most surprising, and unnecessary. Nor was there any working X-ray machine.

Danane. Surgical facilities were primitive

There was a brand new Xray machine, which had arrived weeks before, but it was still inside the wooden crate it had arrived in. Why had it not been put into use? Every air-conditioner had been ripped out of the walls by the retreating rebel troops months before, leaving gaping holes and bare cables poking out. The wards themselves were clean and in reasonable order despite the usual overcrowding.

My first impression was of a typical government district general hospital, built by the French during their colonial rule, and there was a familiar aura about the place. At this point I had no knowledge of the resources I would have available, so it was with eager anticipation that I entered the male surgical ward with Janine, ready to meet the staff, do my first ward-round and generally size up the situation.

On the male surgical ward, we met the bespectacled Coubaley, the only nurse in the hospital with any formal surgical training. He was a good nurse and became my staunch ally during my time at Danané. There were also two young Ivorian surgeons working with me. Alex, who had trained in the Ukraine, and Edgart who had studied in Abidjan. Though relatively inexperienced, they were both good doctors and they seemed to run a fairly tight ship, in spite of many problems. We also became firm friends and learned a lot from each other.

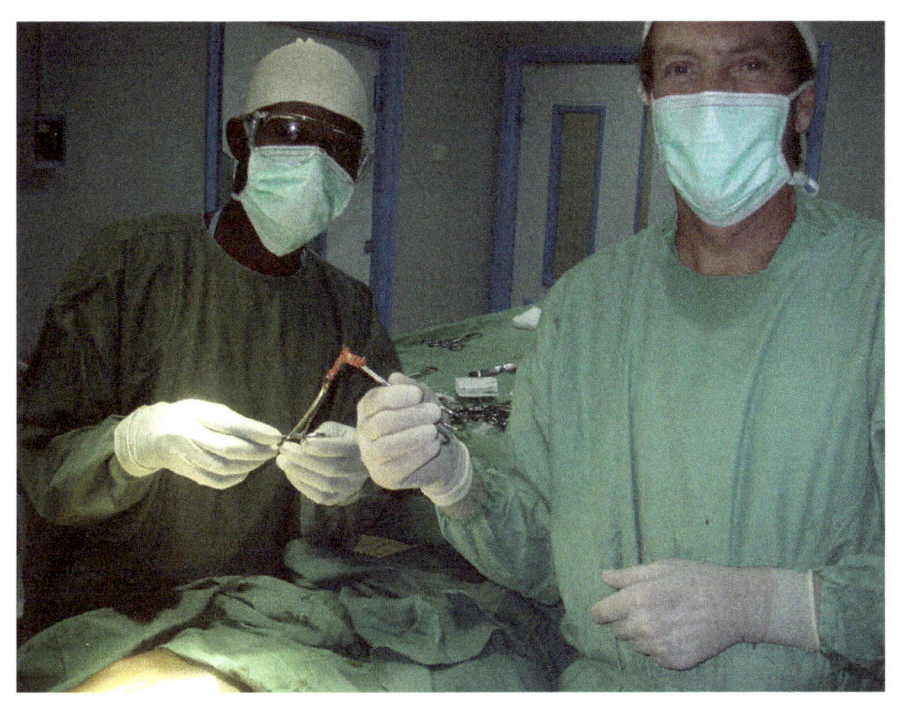

Another appendicectomy with Edgart

On Alternative Orthopaedics

Even before we started the ward round, I saw a young man sitting by the nurses' station with an obviously fractured forearm, not even in a sling. I was even more surprised to learn that he had been admitted the day before following a traffic accident.

"Is there a reason why he has no sling to elevate the arm?", I asked, "and is there an X-ray?", which is when I learned that the nearest functioning X-ray facility was at the MSF-Belgium hospital at Man, 50 kilometres away.

"He is not having treatment here", said Coubaley, "he is going back to his village".

"Why?", I asked, somewhat non-plussed.

"These people do not like the treatment here, they are going back to the village healer for fractures", he replied, which is how I came to terms with yet one more cultural idiosyncrasy.

It may also have had something to do with the fact that neither Edgart or Alex had any training in orthopaedics. During my time with them I did all I could to share my knowledge of this essential surgical speciality, as well as other surgical skills which they had yet to learn. Never in my life before as a tropical surgeon had a patient with a fracture refused treatment for this reason, and I was already interested to know what the results of this rustic approach to trauma therapy were.

Alex and Edgart then told me about Tomas. He was one of our theatre assistants and had fractured his left tibia last year playing football. In spite of working in the hospital, he still insisted on going back to his village for treatment and when we later met him, he obviously still had a significant limp and deformity of his lower leg, but he seemed quite content.

Janine and I were both surprised at this revelation, but as I had said to her before the round, "We really have no idea what we are about to see, so let's just try and be observers". As the round progressed, I could see Janine's eyes growing rounder and rounder as the extreme pathology in every bed revealed itself. She had never worked outside Holland, so Africa was something very different indeed.

To my eyes, all was more or less as I had expected. Some good people trying their best under very difficult circumstances, with an overwhelming demand on their very limited resources.

From Obstetrics to Burns

As we progressed it became apparent that obstetrics was a major part of the surgical workload, averaging about one Caesarian section every day or two. There was only one operating theatre, so before any operation we did it was always vital to check with Maternity that there was no woman in danger of going into obstructed labour.

There was virtually no ante-natal care available to any female who lived outside Danané town, so we were often presented with cases *in extremis*. These included patients in obstructed labour, where both the mother and child were in imminent risk of death. In many cases the child was already dead, and the mother moribund. It was a desperate situation, never seen in the West, and often the only option was a lifesaving, emergency hysterectomy, as the uterus was so often ruptured by the time the poor patient arrived at the hospital.

Another big load on the surgical side were burns. Wherever I have been in the world there have been burns. My very first post-registration job was on the Burns Unit at Alder Hey Childrens Hospital, which at that time was the largest Paediatric hospital in England. It was there that I first saw the terrible effects of burns as I began my studies in Plastic and Reconstructive surgery. Most of those burns were related to domestic accidents and house fires.

In the developing countries one of the main causes of burns is related to epilepsy, a common and mostly untreated condition in Africa.

Epilepsy is commonly associated with hypoxic damage to a baby during birth, especially where there are any delivery complications. Therefore, the standard of maternity care, both ante-natal and during labour is extremely important. It requires a high degree of skill as well as an adequate peripheral community health service. In Africa this was practically non-existent, and as a result I was used to seeing the most terrible burns in these epileptic patients, who often fell unconscious sometimes onto an open fire inside a hut.

Danané was no exception. There were six patients with burns which needed skin grafting when I arrived, but neither Alex nor Edgart had any training in plastic surgery. Nor at that time was there any skin grafting knife. So these patients had just been left, having dressings done on their mostly infected wounds. There were also quite a few cases of major infected wounds and tropical ulcers, always common in these humid latitudes. By the time Janine and I left the surgical wards we both knew that there was an awful lot of clinical work to be done.

Knowing what I might expect I had packed my father's old bread knife. It was made in Sheffield by George Butler & Co around 1895 and was made of high- quality carbon steel which took a good edge, and still cuts my bread today. But in April 2006 I was using it to cut skin grafts deep in the West African jungle. The fine steel blade was not perfect, but I was able to cut thick, full-thickness grafts with it – and there was nothing else any better to use at Danané at that time.

We went all round the hospital, noting the lack of any running water in all wards and the operating theatre, which was a serious problem. The sterilizing facilities were the most primitive I had seen for years, being simply three pressure cookers on top of a gas fire. I was surprised, considering that MSF had had a presence at Danané for two years. But the circumstances of civil war changed all the normal rules. Nevertheless, these logistic limitations were going to affect the surgery I was expected to perform.

After our grand tour of the hospital, we went back to the residence, walking the kilometre through the busy market street full of traders.

Both women and men were selling all manner of food, clothes and plastic utensils opposite the ominous-looking UN headquarters where the white Scout armoured cars were parked up, ready to go. This busy street was flooded by the pervasive smell of groundnuts cooking, for peanut soup was a staple of the diet in these parts. Then up the hill past the Gospel Hall, a poor wooden shack in which every day a large group gathered to sing loudly and enthusiastically, swaying and jogging to the rhythm as we passed by.

On 100% Nut Allergy - in a Land of Peanuts

Along the way the children came up to laugh and joke with us. They were so happy and so free and full of good energy it delighted us all and it became a welcome part of our daily commute by foot to and from the hospital. But Steve, our Project Coordinator never made that walk with us. He suffered from total nut allergy, and one breath of peanut stew could have killed him, so he always drove to the hospital and back. He was the first person I ever met who lived with an Epi-Pen strapped to his body. What courage it must have taken to know that every second there was the risk of anaphylactic shock and possible death in this country where peanuts formed a major part of the peoples´ diet.

Back at the residence the big steel gates were opened by Jacob, one of our guards who let us in, welcoming us with his huge grin.

"Bienvenue a tous!", he cried, pointing us towards the tall gas fridge full of morale-boosting bottles of beer – plus Fanta for the more sober members of the team.

We were nine in all, led by Steve. He was a good administrator and became a good friend. He still is and has been out to stay with me in Spain. Amongst other attributes he was a great one-liner, and I always have remembered his first words to me, after the stimulating ward round with Janine, which I repeat,

The Certainty of Uncertainty

"Just remember", Steve said, "that with MSF only one thing is certain – and that is uncertainty!" He was certainly right, but for me that was precisely part of the fun. You never did quite know what was going to happen.

Two days after I arrived, a Sunday afternoon when all should have been tranquil, just the creaking of the swinging hammock and the clucking of our chickens disturbing the tropical afternoon, the emergency phone went off. An hour later we were sorting out the results of a local church roof collapsing onto the congregation. Some 35 people were injured, three died and suddenly every bed in the hospital was full.

It took Alex, Edgart and I more than four hours to do all the first aid necessary, with the good help of Andrea and Coubaley and a few other nurses. We managed, but it was exhausting, and left Koulo, who was our main man in theatre with two days-worth of soiled linen to clean. The next Caesarian section was performed that night using the same soiled linen. It was an unthinkable thing, in English terms, but here on the war front we were just doing the best we could with what we had to hand, and it was not very much.

I really had my work cut out, not just because I was out of practice, but because I had several responsibilities, the most important of which was to make an assessment of all human and material resources relevant to the surgical unit in order to upgrade and prepare the hospital for a possible new outbreak of war, which was rumoured. I was also contracted to train staff, both medical and nursing, to develop a triage system in case of mass attack, as well as perform necessary operations, so there was not much free time during the day. It was certainly a big change from my hedonistic existence in Spain.

Malaria was endemic everywhere within the Equatorial belt. After my previous experiences in Cameroun with malaria, in spite of taking prophylactic anti-malarials, I had decided to do without them in Danané and rely on citronella oil and covering up, which had previously served me well. Lauren reluctantly agreed, but I still had my mefloquine (Lariam) tablets with me. Because of the very high incidence of malaria at Danané I did start taking mefloquine for my second mission, but it led to disaster, as we shall soon see.

My First Caesarian Section - after 23 years

It was quite a shock for me the first time my emergency phone rang at four in the morning, calling me to Maternity where there was a case of obstructed labour. I had not been on emergency call for over 10 years, so just the nocturnal disturbance was a shock, and what followed was even more of a shock to my system.

This was to be the first time I had to perform a Caesarian section for 23 years, since I had left Lesotho in 1984. I well remember beginning the horizontal incision, with Edgart, one of my two young Ivorian colleagues looking on as first assistant, but also sizing me up.

I prayed a quick prayer to God that all would go well, and so it did. When I had put the last skin suture in after 24 minutes of operating and then heard Edgart say *"Pas mal, mon chef!"*, an immense wave of relief passed through me.

All those Caesarians I performed during 10 years in Africa had not been forgotten, even after 23 years. I was so emotional that I had no idea even of the sex of the infant we had delivered. But it was a fine boy who lay on the resuscitation mat crying lustily as I left the operating theatre to write up the operation notes.

I was also relieved when a few days later in Danané I received an email from MSF confirming my diagnosis of Dario following an abdominal scan, saying that Dario was improving on a regime of conservative therapy.

On Tropical Ulcers

Apart from all the burns cases I also had a large collection of tropical ulcers to manage, with not many resources. Wherever I had worked within the hot and humid Equatorial belt, there were tropical ulcers, usually affecting the limbs. Sometimes they evolved from a minute insect bite, or a minor abrasion, but they were extremely difficult to cure, and often spread in spite of all I could do. Quite a few were very extensive, and sometimes involved the whole limb. As a result, I spent hours debriding infected wounds in every part of the body. Even if I did manage to clean the wound and ready it for skin grafting, the grafts often became infected, no matter how careful I was. It was very time-consuming and frustrating surgery.

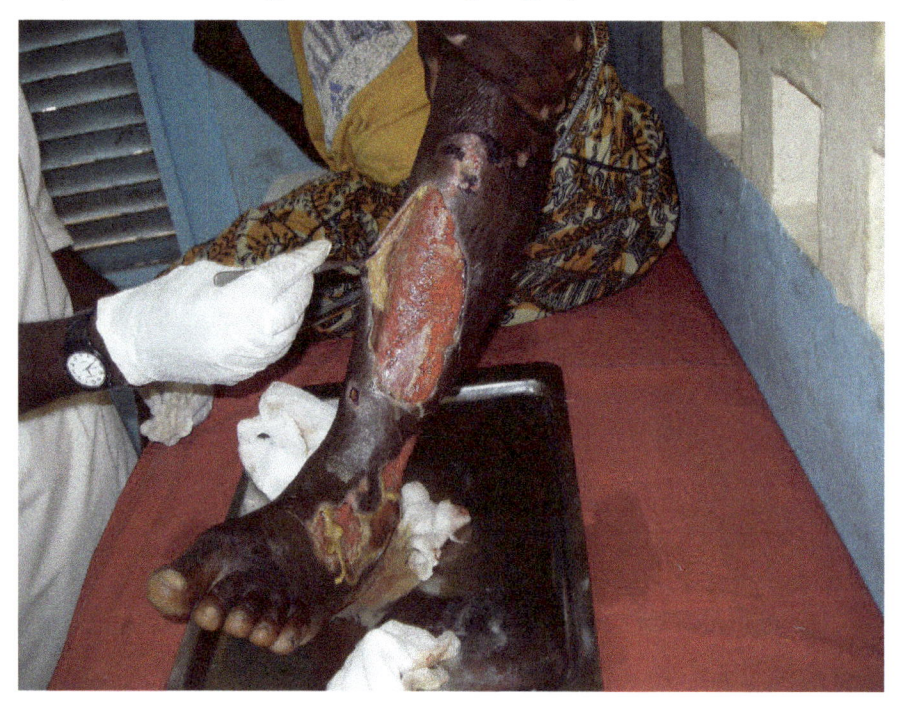

A typical tropical ulcer

One of the most insidious and persistent of these tropical ulcers was Buruli ulcer, caused by a Mycobacterium, the same genus which causes tuberculosis. I saw several cases in Danané in patients also suffering from AIDS. These ulcers never healed, the patients became increasingly wasted and just faded away. There was nothing we could do, as there was no available treatment for AIDS at that time in Danané.

Another common problem was elephantiasis. This disease mainly affected the lower body and was caused by blockage of the lymphatic system by micro-filarial worms. This led to swelling of the genital organs and the legs, which often became so swollen the patients could no longer walk. To complicate matters further, the skin and subcutaneous tissues often decomposed, forming deep ulcers which even involved the long bones. It was not uncommon to find the base of these ulcers crawling with maggots.

These unfortunate patients invariably presented with open wounds, for in the villages there were no dressings available, and the flies had been busy laying their eggs. In fact, maggots in an infected wound perform a useful job in consuming the infected tissues, but the sight always used to make me silently retch. Alex and Edgart were always amused by my obvious discomfort.

In order to improve the cleansing of these wounds I started using a super-saturated salt solution. A kilo of salt mixed into a bucket of warm water, into which the patient placed the affected limb for an hour was a simple but effective treatment – until the hospital kitchen ran out of salt. By the time I completed my first mission at Danané we were using over 10 kilos of salt a week, and Sam's Super-Saturated Salt Solution had become a standard treatment, known by all as the 5-S regime.

The Paediatric Ward. Teaching Thoracostomy and Drainage

Every morning after my surgical ward rounds, I did a round on the Paediatric ward. There was always work to do there, from burns and fractures to the ravages of tuberculosis and many other problems, some of which were complex and took me into unknown territory.

Ngwama was a 14-year-old boy who had been admitted by the physicians with severe breathlessness. After two weeks of antibiotic therapy, he was no better, and I was asked to review him. As usual in these parts the history was vague. Ngwama had become increasingly listless and breathless over a period of weeks, and I could see that the child before me was now in extremis. I did a thorough examination and found that the left side of his chest was completely dull to percussion. This could be either a solid tumour or fluid, but sadly our new Xray machine was still pristine in its box, and it was a 50 km drive to Man to the nearest functioning Xray machine. So, I decided to make a clinical diagnosis.

I took a 20cc syringe and a long spinal needle and inserted it into the 7th intercostal space and sucked. I was rewarded by the sight of yellow pus. There may also be a tumour, but I now knew for sure that there was pus within the chest cavity.

Neither Alex nor Edgart had any experience in chest surgery, so I decided to use this opportunity to teach them a valuable procedure – thoracostomy, opening a conduit into the pleural cavity, and the insertion of a chest-tube. So much of my work involved teaching new skills, and every ward round and every operating session was a teaching opportunity for the doctors and nurses.

It took half a morning to collect the equipment I would need, including a sterile chest tube drain mounted on a 40 cm steel shaft with a sharp, pointed end. This was the end I was going to penetrate the chest wall with, hopefully missing the heart. I was in no way an expert in thoracic surgery, but I had put a few chest drains in over the years, and this was a case which urgently required one inserting.

I had an audience of four doctors, including Alex and Edgart when I began. Coubaley was also there to learn, for he was a very competent nurse, who also did minor surgery. He held and comforted Ngwama, who was now sitting upright on the edge of the bed, very breathless indeed.

I filled a 20cc syringe with local anaesthetic and plunged it deeply into the pleural cavity. Then I slowly withdrew it, injecting anaesthetic as I went, until I reached the skin, which I thoroughly infiltrated. With a No 22 Swan and Morton scalpel blade I then incised a cross in the skin, to ease the insertion of the steel tube and drain. Saying a silent prayer, I firmly grasped the tube and steel shaft and forced it through the wound and into the pleural cavity. Then came the magic moment when I withdrew the steel shaft from inside the drain, which was followed by a stream of stinking yellow pus. I immediately clamped the chest tube, to stop any air entering the chest cavity, and connected the tube to an underwater seal in a two-litre glass bottle. A round of applause greeted me at this point, and I took a bow as my audience clapped their hands, for I was not so used to this appreciation of my art.

As the pus flowed out, I explained to the staff how to manage the underwater seal, and how to check it was working correctly. Over two days, 1,5 litres of pus drained from Ngwama´s chest, and by day 3 he was visibly better and breathing more normally. We decided that the most likely diagnosis was pulmonary tuberculosis, and he was started on TB therapy.

In these extreme working situations, my teaching mantra was always, 'See one, Do one, Teach one'. One week later it was Edgart who inserted the chest tube into a soldier who had been shot in the chest, with me looking on. But this time it was blood he drained.

Performing one operation may save one life, but teaching that same procedure will save many more. I know that both Alex and Edgart were grateful to me for what I taught them over the few months I was with them, but I had also learned a great deal from them. Such is the power of teaching.

Every afternoon I held a short, formal teaching session. I also spent some time developing PowerPoint teaching programmes for the surgical staff, using images of the patients we were caring for at that time. Alex and Edgart were keen students, and later some of the surgical nurses also joined our teaching sessions. I felt it was the best thing I could do for these good people in the short time I had with them. I knew a lot about working alone, and I felt for my isolated colleagues. Access to information and education was a lifeline for them in these remote places.

Every Sunday if things were quiet, the MSF team would take a walk around the town, where we were always well-received, especially by the children. They all loved posing for photos as well as dancing and doing tricks for us. In this dilapidated, war-torn town, the children always appeared happy and full of fun, and delighted in entertaining us.

Exploring Danane town

Back to Amsterdam and the PPD Course

After six weeks of intense work at Danané I went back to Amsterdam to make my report to MSF. My recommendations were agreed and accepted, and the ordering process began. I then went up to Bakkum in northern Holland in April 2006 where, after 10 tough days I attained my PPD certificate. This is where I met Fons, who was a finance officer based at MSF-HQ in Amsterdam. We soon became good friends, and still are, united by a love of rock and roll.

During the PPD course I also met Lidie, who became another special friend. She was a nurse and had previously been in the national Dutch volleyball team. She was one of the fittest women I ever met, but when we met at Bakkum she had just been evacuated from Sudan having narrowly avoided being raped by a soldier. Wherever we went with MSF there was danger, and much of the PPD course was to help protect ourselves from everything from malaria to murder.

Andalucia again, then back to Danané

I then flew back to Spain, knowing that in six months´ time I would be heading back to Danané once again.

I always remember opening the heavy old stable door when I arrived home. I stood in the doorway, listening to the silence which surrounded me, broken only by the whistling of the bee-eaters, and I just drank it in. After the previous three months with MSF the contrast was profound, and I felt very relieved to return to my tranquil Spanish existence.

Back in Amsterdam six months later, Fons and I had a couple of stimulating days together exploring the many delights of Amsterdam before I grabbed my bag and headed for Schipol airport on December 3rd for my second mission to Danané. There, I was delighted to find a rejuvenated Dario, now fully recovered from his recent illness. As a tribute to me, so he said, the new Xray machine was now in working order, and there was also running water in the operating theatre. Things were looking up.

Steve had moved on to another project, so it was Asha, a young American who was now our Project Manager. She was also an excellent administrator and a source of ribald humour when we went out on our rare forays at night to La Temple de la Joie, one of the few night-club/bars which was still functioning.

As well as the constant demands on me from surgical patients, I now became involved in cataloguing and distributing the mass of equipment which had arrived at the hospital.

Imagine my joy when I found the wooden box containing a brandnew skin grafting knife – and one single-use grafting blade within. Imagine my frustration and anger on discovering that the 100 extra blades I had ordered were absent, and never did arrive.

With the one single-use blade that I did have, I did 12 skin grafting procedures on different patients, until the thin blade became totally unusable. I then reverted to my father's Victorian breadknife once again. Such were the joys and tribulations of working with MSF.

Poisoned by Mefloquin

Because of my own fears of getting malaria, and the policy of MSF, I had reluctantly started a course of mefloquin (Lariam) during my last week in Spain. Less than one week after arriving back at Danané, and two weeks after I had started taking Lariam, I began to suffer insomnia. I have never suffered from insomnia, so this was a new and disturbing problem. Then my hands started shaking, to the extent I could not hold a scalpel properly. I was suddenly very frightened, and went to see Asha, who called Lauren in Abidjan. Lauren drove up the next day – all 750 kilometres, and I recounted my story to her. By now I could not even think coherently, and she immediately put a stop to me operating, and I stopped taking Lariam.

It was a bad situation to find myself in. Alex and Edgart already worked like Trojans, and they needed my help, but I was so reduced that for some days I could do nothing. After a week I decided to start work again, even though I still felt shaky and still had insomnia, but I was never in the same groove as before. I had lost my edge.

When I returned to Spain I researched Lariam, and was horrified to find out what a very poisonous drug it was, and how many people had been profoundly affected psychologically by its side-effects, some even committing suicide as a result of taking it. I suffered these side-effects for years, including depression and palpitations of the heart, and it is only in the last two years that the symptoms have declined. It was a heavy price to pay for the joys of working with MSF, and a rude awakening to the power and dishonesty of some drug companies.

´Beat-Boxing´ with Damolo

The very last operation I performed at Danané was on a 12-year old epileptic boy who had fallen into a fire, severely burning both feet. Damolo had been on the ward for six weeks already whilst we prepared his burns for grafting, and he had turned out to be a star. He had a strange gift which amused every one of us. Using just his hands, feet and mouth he could create the most incredible music, a mixture of sounds and rhythms which was pure Africa, and which today is popular world-wide, now known as ´Beat-Box´. It was a most unusual talent, and Damolo loved performing for us, so on my last ward round I invited him to give us a short concert, which I filmed. Both his feet were now bandaged after the skin grafts, so the music he produced was slightly compromised, but the huge smile on his face as he entertained us was a gift for us all.

During my time in Danané I had taught both Alex and Edgart the art of taking skin grafts, and it was they who actually performed this operation, one of them doing each foot as I looked on. I was proud to see their work, and so were they. When I was back in Spain I received an email from Edgart saying that Damolo had walked out of hospital a month later, still playing his one-man band.

On Roasting Pigs. Party Time at Danané.

Soon after I arrived back in Danané, Dario threw a big party to celebrate his return to health. One thing that every MSF Logistics Coordinator knew how to do was to organize a barbecue, and Dario was no exception.

From somewhere within the ravaged town, he found a pig, then slaughtered and gutted it. He then crucified it on a steel frame and slowly roasted the spread corpse during two days over a hardwood charcoal fire. The feast that followed was well remembered by the 20 odd MSF warriors who arrrived from various corners of the Ivory Coast to enjoy this event.

It was always a total mystery to me how booze and edible delicacies would appear out of the blue at these rare MSF get-togethers, whether in the darkest jungle of the Congo or the empty deserts of Sudan and Somalia, these resourceful MSF warriors would drag a bottle of gin out of their backpack or a pack of Struppen Waffles without which the Dutch members could not function. The party went on for hours, and all the while the sporadic shelling and machine gun fire continued in the humid African night, melding with the sounds of a million cicadas.

Then came the moment that Dario proposed a toast to the English surgeon who had saved him from the jaws of death in Abidjan six months before. I was already feeling comfortably mellow after my generous plateful of roast pig and several glasses of good Chianti, my present from Dario.

"But, you pommie surgeon", continued Dario in his thick Milanese accent, "you ever sticka your finger uppa my bum again, I phukin keel you!", at which point people started falling off their chairs, and I retired to my bed, praying I would not get called for a Caesarian section. I fell into a deep and therapeutic coma to the sound of the cicadas, thinking how great it was to be back in the jungle with my brothers and sisters of Los Medicos.

My life continued to be both a challenge as well as an opportunity to do what I had been destined to do many years before. And with that thought I fell asleep.

19. MAKING IT WITH LOS MEDICOS – (ii) 2007

Mannar Island, Sri Lanka

I had enjoyed my two missions in West Africa with MSF Holland despite being severely poisoned by the venomous anti-malarial drug Lariam, and I was keen to go on another MSF mission. Since I was officially resident in Spain I decided to sign up with MSF-Barcelona, on the understanding that this time my mission would not be in Africa. By now, much as I loved Africa after 10 years travelling and working in that vast continent, I wanted to see more of the world.

Thus, I found myself standing in the muggy tropical heat of Colombo airport with Ana, another first-time volunteer. She was a Spanish ITU nurse from Madrid and had never been outside Spain. Ana was to become my surgical companion during six months at Mannar Island in the north-west of Sri Lanka, where civil war had been raging for several years.

There had been problems between the Singhalese, who represented 80% of the population, and the Tamils, ever since Sri Lanka gained independence from the British in 1948. Since the 1970s the Tamils had been increasingly disenfranchised by the politically powerful Singhalese. This had led to increasing demands by the Tamils for their own state in the north of the country, which they called Tamil Eelam (Precious Land).

It was a young Tamil activist, Velupillai Prabhakaran, who created the Liberation Tigers of Tamil Eelam (LTTE) during the mid-1970s, more commonly known as the Tamil Tigers, and it was he who led the fight against Tamil repression. The sporadic violence between the Singhalese and the Tamils increased until in 1983 open civil war broke out. The tragic war which followed turned this fertile and prosperous island, previously favoured by so many tourists, into an arena of violence and destruction.

Mannar

At the time of our arrival the Tamils were in retreat. They had been forced by the government Singhalese army northwards into the Jaffna peninsula in the east and Mannar in the west.

Mannar was a small island with a population of 35,000, most of whom were Tamils. It was connected to the mainland of Sri Lanka by a three-kilometre causeway which was often under attack. As a result, the surrounding area of Vavuniya was rapidly filling with internally displaced people (IDP) from the south who had lost everything.

Mannar Island was also an important base for the nautical branch of the Tamil Tigers, and periodically they would attack government military installations in boats loaded with dynamite. There were also frequent terrorist attacks throughout the island at that time, so there was a lot of miitary action, and I could see that I would be busy.

The journey in the MSF Toyota Hi-Lux from Colombo to Mannar was continuously interrupted by roadblocks. Armed soldiers were everywhere, and we saw a lot of military hardware. The Singhalese army appeared to be well-disciplined, and I did not see any drunken behaviour as had been the case so often at Danané in the Ivory Coast.

I had never visited any part of Asia before and found the journey most interesting. Sri Lanka was clearly a fertile country and there was a lot of small industry going on in the towns we passed, though it became progressively poorer as we headed north into Tamil country. We arrived safely at Mannar just as the sun was setting, casting a sheet of luminous orange over the waters of the Bay of Bengal, on which were bobbing a small fleet of traditional fishing boats. As we crossed the narrow causeway and onto the island, we began to see extensive fortifications, a reminder of what was awaiting us.

The MSF Residence - an Explosive Arrival

Our residence was about a kilometre from the hospital and was a modest but comfortable building. After meeting Giovanni, our Italian Project Coordinator and being briefed on the current local situation, we decided to start work proper the following morning, and meanwhile arranged ourselves within the residence.

That was when I had my first surprise. I went into the bathroom to relieve myself and found a pretty green frog perched on the china bowl, not shy at all. When I went to the sink to wash my hands, I found another frog sitting on the soap. There were also two in the shower. In fact, there was a small frog family occupying the room, whom we christened 'The Froglets'. They did not appear to be venomous, and rather brightened up the room I thought. They did have the strange habit of hiding under the china rim of the toilet, and periodically hopping out, causing occasional screams from the bathroom.

On our first night at the MSF residence there were six of us gathered around the table. Giovanni, our project manager, Othman from Columbia, who was our WatSan (Water and Sanitation) specialist, with whom I played many games of chess over the six months. He was also a big expert at the barbeque, and we all enjoyed kilos of local fish grilled over the red-hot coals of Othman's barbie.

The other members of our gallant band were my nurse, Ana from Spain, Carolina, my anaesthetist from Santiago, Chile, and Marty from Dominica who was coming to take over from Carolina.

Mannar. With Ana and Carolina – my surgical team

We were all enjoying a fine meal when there was a mighty explosion, such that the whole house shook, and windows rattled. The three women sitting opposite me hit the floor in terror, and I was not too surprised, for that was how it was to be in Mannar, June 2007.

Exploding mortars became a common part of our day. Although we soon got used to the sound of exploding munitions, we were nervous when the Tamil Tigers started launching attacks close to our residence. In case of desperate emergency, we had a form of bunker into which we periodically retired while the battle raged outside.

Following our first explosive dinner together, we were all asleep when the emergency alarm went off just after midnight.

First Emergency - a Catastrophe

Ana, Carolina and I rushed off to the hospital, which I had yet to visit, and into the operating theatre suite where I found three badly injured government soldiers including a senior officer.

Even as I was doing a rapid triage, the first soldier exsanguinated and died. Of the other two soldiers the major was the most severely injured, with two bullet entry wounds right over the xiphisternum, no visible exit wounds and an unrecordable blood pressure.

That was the moment when I met Sister Shwarma. She was the theatre superintendant, and it was she who rapidly prepared the OT for some major surgery. In these totally new surroundings and under these desperate conditions, I was praying that all would go well, for there was not a second to lose. During my six electric months at Mannar, it was Sister Shwarma who was always at my side, along with Ana. Tonight was just the beginning of a long and most wonderful professional relationship.

The acute problem I had at this dramatic moment was whether to perform a thoracotomy or a laparotomy. Even as Carolina and I were stuffing large-bore infusion cannulae into this severely injured soldier, I was worrying about where to make the incision. In the end decided to open the abdomen, whereupon a gush of bright red blood shot everywhere, completely obscuring my vision.

Even with the sucker going full on it was impossible to find the source of the heavy bleeding at first. Then I found three holes in the stomach, the left kidney was completely pulverised, and there was still more blood welling up from the retro-peritoneal area.

Carolina used up every pint of O +ve blood in the hospital but it still was not enough. In spite of all we did, the blood pressure kept falling and falling and suddenly the scary straight line of asystole appeared on the monitor screen.

I was the person who had to make the decision to stop resuscitation. It was one of the most difficult decisions I have ever had to make. The nurses were crying, Shwarma was looking stressed, Ana was rather shell-shocked, and I was feeling bad as well. Dr Pryah, my first assistant did not say much. But he was a Tamil, and he knew as well as I did, that this dead patient was a senior Singalese army officer.

It was hard to stomach – my very first case at Mannar and my first ever death on table, and a senior goverment soldier at that. There was no doubt at all, I was back where I belonged with Los Medicos, but for me it was a very painful entrée into a world of war and death on this tropic isle.

After this catastrophe I still had to operate on the other soldier, who had been shot through the left shoulder. It was 0400h by the time we had sorted him out, and by then I was physically and mentally exhausted.

Death On Table

Sometimes a simple acronym can signify a whole life, and such is D.O.T.

Death on Table is the most feared complication that a surgeon has to face. Yet, in over 30 years of surgery all over the world, I had been most fortunate never to have experienced this heart-crushing moment, until now.

That first night in Mannar, I had watched a major in the Singalese army die in front of my eyes on the operating table. It was a terrible moment for me – quite apart from the political consequences. A formal enquiry was held later by the government, and I had to attend some interesting meetings with powerful people. In the end, probably for want of any other surgeon, I was allowed to continue my work at Mannar District hospital. But I will never forget that night.

The Hospital - First Ward Round

By 0830h I was back on the male surgery ward to start my first ward round, having hardly had time to collect myself after the dreadful night I had just experienced. I did it in the company of the four young Tamil doctors who managed the surgical patients with me. They were a good team, well-trained and a pleasure to work with. During six hard months we never had any serious problem or falling out. Ansela was the only female doctor, a most genial lady, who had in tow with her a young 4th year medical student, Rosalind, who was on attachment from the medical school at Colombo. We always did the morning rounds together, and also the busy outpatients, so there was a constant teaching process going on as well as all the clinical work, of which there was loads.

The 35 patients on the male ward represented practically the whole field of surgery. There were five orthopaedic cases, three burns to be grafted, two head injuries – one very serious, whose conscious level was diminishing by the hour, an elderly man with urinary retention who probably needed a prostatectomy, and a young man with an incarcerated inguinal hernia whom we put first on the operating list as he was clinically obstructed. There was a miscellaneous collection of other patients, including a palm-tree tapper who had fallen some 10 metres from a tree whilst harvesting arak, the toxic booze which too many of the Tamils got drunk on. And we had not even got to the female and paediatric wards.

It took three hours to complete the ward round, by which time I had a good idea of how things were in the Surgery department, and they were generally good – certainly a lot better than at Danané. There were no chickens on the wards, as had been the case sometimes in Africa, but there were sparrows nesting in cardboard nesting boxes in the eaves, and the hospital cat, called Shiva who slept all day in the female ward wheel-chair. Outside the wards were donkeys grazing amongst the debris, as well as a vocal collection of yellow-beaked mynah birds.

I was always impressed by the way in which the Sri Lankans approached education at every level. From the training of the four young doctors I was now working with, to the crocodiles of small children with their white blouses, blue trousers and skirts, everyone proudly carrying their satchel to school, the Asians were streets ahead of the Africans. It showed wherever I went in the hospital, which even had a small, 2-bed intensive therapy unit, something I had never seen in the African bush.

The equipment I was now working with was also vastly superior to what there had been in Africa. The maintenance and repairs were of a very high standard, and were all managed by the Sri Lankans. The state of public health was also far better, in spite of the raging war.

I was also charged with the Obstetric department. This was always a high-stress area for me, as I was only usually called for some surgical intervention for obstructed labour, such as a vacuum extraction or Caesarian section.

After two missions at Danané I was becoming fluent once again at performing Caesarian sections and hysterectomies, tubal ligations and other gynaecological surgery. At least I never saw a ruptured uterus in Sri Lanka, so horribly common in Africa where the peripheral ante-natal care was non-existent.

At Mannar all the obstetric staff under the frightening Matron, Sister Paulina, were very well trained, which helped enormously with this tricky area of my surgical responsibilities. It was a big relief to me when a qualified MSF obstetrician, Costa the Greek arrived, halfway into my mission. He was a great addition to our multinational team, with a very Greek sense of humour, and he always had a smile on his face. He was also a master of the barbecue.

Our MSF team had very good social relations with all the hospital staff. We used to have regular volleyball games in the garden behind the hospital where everybody joined in, and barbecues and dancing at the weekends when work allowed. Morale was very good, in spite of the ongoing war outside.

We did have a lot of laughs as well when circumstances allowed, but all the important stuff got done correctly, and that was very important to me, as the surgeon in charge, for it was indeed a heavy responsibility to bear under these circumstances. Particularly when the nearest help was in Colombo, hundreds of kilometres to the south.

Ana was magnificent, and soon started teaching nursing classes on a daily basis, which were much appreciated by all the nursing staff. She was an excellent nurse in all ways and worked harder than anyone, whether on the wards or in the operating theatre, where she proved to be a very able assistant.

I always operated with one of the young doctors at my side in order to teach as much as I could of all aspects of surgery. In the end we MSF doctors are just passing through, and the best legacy we can leave in such a short space of time is to freely share our acquired knowledge and skills.

The experience of a general surgeon is so valuable in these war-torn zones where the only certainty is that the next patient will have a completely different problem, calling on a whole new area of skill and knowledge. I do not think I would enjoy the life of a specialist surgeon. The variety and cut and thrust of general surgery has always been stimulating and challenging to me, and it is where I have always been most comfortable.

On Geographical Pathology

I have talked before of geographical pathology – one of my favourite disciplines in the whole of medicine and health care, which has been my life now for over 50 years. The study of global patterns of disease has always fascinated me. Just passing from Africa to Asia with MSF had provided me with a pile of new clinical problems which I had not seen in Africa, as well as the ubiquitous diseases of the tropics such as malaria, dengue fever and tropical ulcers. In Mannar, as in Africa, the population was generally fit, and very few were obese, but I found that diabetes was much more common than it had been in Africa.

The most demanding and horrific problem which I found uniquely in Mannar was self-immolation. I never once saw this in Africa, but amongst the Tamil women it was fairly common, and a terrifying thing to behold.

Self-immolation was mostly associated with various forms of abuse committed by the men, commonly associated with drunkenness, which was surprisingly common amongst this deeply religious community.

The poor abused wife would go out and buy five litres of paraffin or petrol, invert the can over her head, and apply a match. The resulting burns were amongst the worst I had ever seen, and I have seen many.

This self-immolation usually rendered the whole upper torso a mass of infected scar tissue. In some cases it contracted the neck tissues so severely that the chin came to lie on the anterior chest wall, fixed there by dense scar tissue. As a result, several patients died of starvation because they could no longer open their mouths, as they were cemented shut by a dense mass of scar tissue. I had never seen the like before. But on the female ward there were three female patients awaiting me, all with similar, dreadful burns.

The reconstructive surgery I had to perform subsequently was extremely difficult, and often required up to five or even 10 separate operations over a two or three month period. This effectively blocked a valuable bed for weeks and months.

At the same time there was a steady stream of injured civilians being admitted, including many children with terrible wounds from bullets or shrapnel. There was hardly a free moment, what with the heavy clinical load, the teaching of medical and nursing staff. I also had direct responsibility for developing an effective triage system for the whole hospital, as I had done in Danané, in case of a mass attack leaving many dead and wounded patients.

On MSF and Advocacy

One other important responsibility I had as a senior surgeon with MSF was advocacy. In short, speaking up for the disadvantaged and disenfranchised. This had always been one of the founding principles of MSF since it was formed in 1971, following the experiences of two young French doctors during the Biafran war in 1968. One of them, Bernard Kouchner, later went on to become the French Minister of Health.

The exact reason why MSF was created is interesting. Kouchner and others became concerned at what they saw as complicity by the ICRC and the Nigerian government in the neglect of the Biafran population during the war, even when the Nigerian army was deliberately attacking Biafran hospitals where they were working.

The 13 founding doctors of MSF swore allegiance to a code which ignored any political or religious boundaries, hence their name, 'Doctors without Borders'. Their aim was to provide humanitarian aid in all forms, to the civilian populations affected by war or natural disasters, and that resonated with me.

Advocacy became an important part of their work, as MSF was often the only independent channel to publicise the truth of what was actually occurring. This was the case in Mannar, where atrocities by both sides were very common.

Some mornings we even had to go out in the Hi-Lux pickup and collect bodies and body parts before I started the morning ward rounds. Therefore, my accurate personal records of surgical procedures and post-mortem findings for victims of war were of great importance. These data were collated every week by both the hospital authorities and MSF and were sent to MSF headquarters, where they were later used to inform the general public.

Since 1968, when I went out to Nigeria and Biafra during that civil war as a medical student, and to other countries in later years as a war surgeon, I have always experienced what the Americans like to call ´collateral damage´. More clearly put, this is the physical and mental trauma inflicted on the innocent civilian population. Food famine and malnutrition were also an inevitable cost of war. Most victims were women and children. It is quite inhuman what men will do in fighting their cause.

Mannar was no different. There is something very ugly and horrifying about a civil war, where no quarter is given. It becomes tribe against tribe, and none of the civilian population are immune from the dreadful effects of this violence, especially the children. Some of my own most traumatic moments in general surgery have been in the care of innocent wounded children and all the sequelae.

Children - The Innocent Victims of War

It was a relatively quiet Sunday noon when they brought in the body of a 10-year-old boy, named Thomas. He had been shot three hours earlier with a Kalashnikov, the bullet passing clean through his anterior right chest wall and exiting posteriorly.

He was literally at death's door when I first saw him in the operating theatre. Marty and Ana put in iv infusion lines while I scrubbed up. I was slightly concerned that I was about to re-enter the field of thoracic surgery, another area where I had little previous experience, and no formal training.

I asked Shwarma to lay out both the laparotomy set, and also the Caesarian instruments. I had no idea what I was going to find, but I knew I was going to be working down a deep, dark hole, full of damaged lung and blood. After my terrible experiences of the first night in Mannar, I was already fearful, but there was no time to fret, for the child was exsanguinating in front of us.

Initially Marty laid the boy out with iv Ketamine, so I could do a full examination, which worried me still further, as there was an audible chest fistula, through which red blood was pouring into the chest drain I had just inserted. Marty told me that we had just two units of compatible blood, so it was to be a race against time. I had to open the chest. There was no option if I was to save this child's life.

My God ! How we do these things, almost as if by magic. In two minutes I had the chest wall open and an obstetric self-retractor deep in the wound. This exposed the pleural cavity, which was full of blood. I could just see what was left of the right middle lobe of the lung, and it was not much, just a bloody mess of crushed tissue through which blood was pouring. Using a No 2 chromic gut suture on a big needle and large abdominal packs, after an anxious few minutes I managed to get control of the bleeding and thus stabilise the blood pressure.

At the head of the operating table Marty was looking happier as the blood flowing from the wound diminished. We were on the last unit of blood by then, so good haemostasis was going to be essential. Ana was learning fast how to be a good scrub nurse and was cool as a cat as she handed me the instruments and prepared the sutures. Ansela, the female doctor of our team was opposite me at the table. She never seemed to get flustered and was always a calming spirit. Shwarma was standing by, acting as a runner and giving Ana occasional advice, and young Palu the nurse assistant was mopping blood off the floor.

I breathed a big sigh of relief, inserted two chest drains and closed the thoracotomy incisión. Then I looked around me, and suddenly realised that I was the only male, surrounded by five women. Not only that, but apart from Shwarma, these women were just young girls, half my age. Neither Ana nor Marty were over 30 years old, and neither had previous experience of this most demanding life-and-death surgery. But they had been magnificent and never faltered, as had everyone. If the operation was a success, it was down to them. No surgeon ever works alone.

It was another reason I had decided to do one more mission with MSF. I had never worked with better people. Almost all the volunteers were young, and all were inspired, competent and altruistic. Not one of them was doing the job for the money. (After my six months in Mannar, 800 euros was added to my bank account by MSF) Most people work to earn money, but those I met in the field from MSF were very different. Like me, they did it for their beliefs, and that made a very big difference. To me it was inspiring.

With this good thought in mind I turned back to our patient, Thomas, whom Marty had extubated, and was now breathing by himself. I quickly checked that the water seals under the chest drains were working well. Then we sent him back to the paediatric ward, still more dead than alive, but at least his vital signs were stable and there was practically no further bleeding from the chest. There was nothing else I could do, but I felt anxious at that moment, knowing how slim this young child's chances were.

In these treacherous war zones, sometimes no matter what we did or how hard we tried, the patient died in spite of our best efforts.

Afterwards, with Ansela, who had assisted me very well, I sat and sweated in the humid air of the surgeon's room whilst I wrote up the notes, filled out the data sheet and tried to collect myself. Our reward for our efforts was a luke-warm bottle of Fanta, brought by Shwarma.

It had been a tricky operation, and lots could have gone wrong. But everyone, from Palu the nursing assistant to Shwarma, who always came to help, day or night whenever the going got rough, to Marty the anaesthetist and Ana, my most able scrub nurse, all of us really did work like a well-oiled machine.

Thomas was with us for over two months, as post-operatively he developed a thoracic fistula. Eventually I had to go back into this chest and close the fistula. But one week before I was due to leave Mannar, we discharged Thomas, more or less in one piece and breathing reasonably well.

I underwrote the celebration party we held later, and Shwarma and Ansela organised the great feast. Ana and Marty came dressed in beautiful silk sharis which Shwarma had helped them buy. It was a fitting conclusion to a successful operation and helped to bond us even closer.

All this was part and parcel of my life as a general surgeon at war, and there would never ever be an end to all the new clinical challenges, for they come in every shape and form, some of which are extraordinary in their rarity and complexity.

On Courage

I should also say a word about courage, which also comes in many shapes and forms. Every one of us MSF volunteers was courageous in some way, for we all knew there was a real risk of death or injury in the course of our work. But some had another form of courage.

I have previously mentioned Steve, my project coordinator at Danané. He was the first person I ever met who lived with an EpiPen strapped to his body, because he had total, 100% allergy to all nuts, and was working in Danané, where the peanut was king.

The second such person I met was Ana, who arrived on this tropical island for six months with me, where our diet was always and every day some form of fish. Ana had 100% total allergy to all fish!

The coincidence was almost unbelievable. Yet both these MSF volunteers did their professional work every day, seemingly oblivious of the deadly risks surrounding them.

On three occasions during my six months at Mannar I had to save Ana from fatal anaphylactic shock, and the last time, very shortly before I left, her immune system had become so depleted that she was close to dying. It cost MSF 10,000$ to have her emergency evacuated and flown to Columbo in an Army helicopter for intensive care. She took more than three months to recover in Spain, suffering a long period of depression. Then she did another mission in Nicaragua.

That is what I mean when I talk of courage. It is not just the instant fear of death. It is the constant, daily awareness that every breath, every sip and every mouthful may be the last. I have never forgotten these two brave friends, and am still very much in touch with them. Both have come to visit me and my donkey in Andalucia, and I feel that for ever we shall truly be blood brothers and sisters.

Soon after Steve visited me in Spain he was posted to Somalia – always one of the most dangerous places on earth to be. From then on, for more than four years I had no word from him, which I found strange.

Only two years later did I find out what had happened. He had been kidnapped by one of the warring Somali factions, shot in the leg and badly injured, and then held captive for eight dreadful months. After his reléase he understandably fell into depression from which he also took months to recover.

We all knew the story of young Pierre, a 25 -year- old Parisian engineer who was the first of our PPD group to be sent on a mission – to Mogadishu, Somalia, as a WatSan specialist. His parents even flew from Paris to join our celebrations in Amsterdam. But within a week Pierre was dead. Blown to pieces by an RPG – rocket-propelled grenade, to those who know about these deadly weapons. It was shocking news to all of us, but Pierre was just the first of three dear young friends I know who have given their lives for MSF.

Exploring Mannar by Bike

Even though I was on-call at Mannar day and night for six months, there were times when life became almost normal, and then Giovanni and I used to jump onto cranky old push bikes and explore the island. There was much of interest to see in this remote part of northern Sri Lanka, but where I always ended up was on the silver-sanded beach which stretched for miles, bordered by a line of waving coconut palms – and there was never a tourist in sight.

This was one of the undoubted benefits of MSF. Trips to exotic places, guaranteed free of any tourists – a very rare event these days when global tourism has become a curse in every country. As things were at Mannar, the only humans on the beach were the Tamil fishermen repairing their fishing nets and their boats. They were always happy to see me, and I used to spend much time with them, learning about what went on in Mannar, apart from the war. I biked all over the island during my six months, and was always well received by the villagers, who were the most hospitable of people, in spite of being so visibly poor.

Mannar was a very religious community, over 80% of whom were Christians. The rest were a mixture of Buddhists, Sikhs, Hindus and others. One of my enduring memories is sitting in a tiny Buddhist temple with the MSF gang during a religious ceremony to which we had been invited. Opposite us was sitting a platoon of heavily armed Singalese soldiers in their camouflage battle dress, all looking rather dangerous. It was not the sort of thing I was used to seeing at the Church of St Marys, Warbleton back in East Sussex.

It was at another religious ceremony of Hindi initiates that I first saw humans walking on red-hot coals. I saw the whole process, from the lighting of the coals to the 25 initiates boldly walking over them. Then, to our further astonishment a crowd of onlookers also began to walk over the burning coals. They all shouted at us in the MSF gang to come and do the same. 'There's nothing to it', they cried as they bounced over the shimmering coals, laughing their heads off. I had heard of this strange phenomenon before, and even seen film of it, but to see it live was highly impressive.

Being exposed to other cultures was one of the things which made MSF appealing to so many of us volunteers. It wasn't just the interesting nature of our work. It was also the opportunity to live within another very different culture and to enjoy its benefits, of which there were many in Mannar.

The pisciculture was one big benefit for all of us except Ana. At least once a week we drove up to the fish market in the MSF pickup and bought some huge fish fresh out of the sea. Othman and Costa then prepared it for us back at the residence on the glowing barbecue. There was also tropical fruit in profusion – pineapple, banana and papaya were always on our table and coconuts were two a penny, often used by Prakish, our excellent cook, to create yet another prawn curry.

Even though Africa was such a rich continent, my diet there was never as rich and varied as it was in Sri Lanka. Every part of the Lankans' culture was refined and had been for thousands of years. Not just the food, but art in all its forms, from jewellery and the semi-precious stones which abounded in Sri Lanka, to the sophisticated Kandy dances and music they all enjoyed. It all seemed to me to be streets ahead of African culture, which was essentially subsistence in most of the parts I ever visited over a 30 – year span.

To Kandy and Sigiriya

During six months at Mannar, Ana and I were able to have a long weekend off duty on only two occasions, and we made the most of it. First, in August we went to Kandy to see the Esala Perahera, the Festival of the Golden Tooth. This has become world famous now for its beauty and sophistication. Imagine 60 elephants, each one carrying a 12-volt battery on board, dressed in huge cloths of the finest embroidered silk and lit up like Blackpool Promenade in high season, surrounded by a throng of fire-dancers with blazing faggots swirling around their heads.

It was a magnificent sight for me and Ana, who was still recovering from her latest anaphylactic reaction. We stayed on the main street in the up-market Victoria Hotel, for a very cheap price. We were about the only tourists in Kandy at that time, because of the war, and prices had become negotiable. Our bedroom had a balcony which over-looked the street where all the action of the religious parade took place, and we spent the whole night being dazzled by the illuminating entertainment.

We also visited the Botanical Gardens, set up by the colonial British in the 1800s, and still today a beautiful place. The extensive gardens were full of every imaginable plant and spice tree. To see the bark on a living cinnamon tree was for me a significant moment, for I use a lot of this and many other such spices in my own cuisine.

Kandy was a fine town, whose centre-piece was a large lake on which a flock of pelicans were floating. It was at over 1000 altitude and had been a popular resort during the colonial era. Until the civil war it had been an important centre of tourism, but we saw very few visitors during our visit.

On our second weekend of freedom Ana and I went to Sigirya, one of the ancient cities of Sri Lanka, and another major tourist destination – until the civil war drove the tourists away. It is dominated by a huge rock, formed of a solid volcanic lava, 200 metres high, and is thought to originally have been a retreat for Buddhist monks and pilgrims since the first century BC.

Around 1450 AD King Kassapa developed the site and created a series of water gardens and rock gardens. He used hydraulic pressure to drive fountains which are still in working order today. Ascending the rock there were beautiful frescoes of buxom, semi-naked women painted on the rock face, which were hundreds of years old. On the flat surface at the very top of the rock there were magnificent views of the surrounding jungle. There was also evidence of what had once been the residence of the king, including a large water cistern carved out of the rock.

Ana and I stayed at the up-market Sigirya Village lodge, where we were welcomed like long-lost relatives. We found ourselves almost the only guests in this beautifully designed lodge, set in the verdant jungle which surrounded Sigirya. We spent three days there, enjoying a standard of luxury which normally we could never have afforded. But now every tourist lodge was desperate for clients, and the normal rates had been slashed.

As we entered the twin bedroom, we saw the two beds covered with frangipani flowers, which immediately took me straight back to my first night in Africa in 1964. The sweet smell of the flowers was unforgettable, and Ana, who had never seen frangipani before agreed.

Ana wanted to visit a game park, of which there are several in Sri Lanka. So, from Sigiriya we took a taxi to Minneriya National Park and spent most of a day being driven around whilst we admired herds of elephants and antelope, jackals and mongoose and a vivid variety of birds. Ana had never been out of Madrid and was mesmerised by all the wildlife. For me, the sight of iridescent peacocks running wild was something I had never seen in Africa.

On our way back, we made a small diversion to another ancient city, Dambulla, to see the Royal Rock Temple. This is a collection of five caves of which the Temple of the Royal King was the most spectacular, being filled by two big statues of the kings, Valagamba and Nissanka Malla. The walls were covered with the most beautifully painted frescoes, centuries old but still brilliant.

It was here that I saw my only genuine snake charmer. As we descended the steps from the caves, there sat a ragged man playing a flute, with a round grass basket beside him from which rose a hooded cobra, swaying to the sound of the music. It was a memorable sight which I had seen depicted in books, but to witness it in the flesh was outstanding.

The snake charmer at Dambulla

There was no doubt, Sri Lanka was a rich country with a very long and substantial history and in spite of the on-going war, was still proud of all its rich culture. During our five days at Sigirya we had both seen and learned a lot, enough to convince me to re-visit this beautiful island if I ever had the chance.

After this brief but well-earned break it was hard for us both to return to Mannar, knowing what awaited us there, but the following day we were back in the swing of it. On the male ward I found a tree-tapper who had fallen out of his tree, suffering an anterior dislocation of his right shoulder. None of the four doctors knew how to reduce the dislocation, so I decided to make it a teaching experience, and invited them and Rosalind, our resident medical student, to the OT.

I invited the patient onto the operating table, where Marty sedated him with diazepam and pethidine in order to relax his muscles. Then I demonstrated the 'foot in armpit' technique, where, by placing the ball of one's foot in the axilla and putting traction along the arm, the head of the humerus usually pops back into the glenoid cavity of the scapula and thus restores the joint.

Then I enquired of my group of expectant medics, "Right, who's going to do the honours?", but I already knew. I pointed my finger at Rosalind the medical student, which surprised everyone. But she was game.

"You can do this just as well as the others", I said, encouraging her. And indeed, she did very well. After she had demonstrated a full range of movements of the joint, all four doctors applauded, and Ansela gave Rosalind an embrace. Then I showed Rosalind and the others how to fold and tie the important post-operative sling. Once again, I made Rosalind fix it to the patient. By now she was smiling all over her face, and I knew she would never forget this moment. It was exactly what Jack had done for me at the Hôpital Central in Ebolowa in 1965 – but I had not even started medical school then, as I explained to Rosalind.

The miracle of Margaret

Of all my patients at Mannar, Margaret was the one I shall never forget. Mostly for the hours and hours I had spent operating on her wounded body. She was yet another abused woman who had self-immolated with kerosene, and had presented three months before with 70% 3rd degree burns over her upper body.

From her chin to her umbilicus was an open sheet of infected tissue, which took weeks of daily dressings to clean up. Then I started grafting skin. As I could only retrieve skin from her lower body, mostly her thighs, the area I could cover at any time was limited, and sometimes the grafts became infected in spite of all our efforts.

Ana was the absolute queen of burns dressings and spent hours with Margaret, always with a nurse in training by her side. Ana had such a gentle touch it was a pleasure to watch her at work, for the pain caused by burns is terrible, and a dressing change was always an excruciating nightmare for these patients.

In the end we worked out a routine for Margaret, giving her pethidine and diazepam before each dressing change, but after nearly three months I had yet to free and then graft the massive contraction which had forced her chin onto her sternum and made it impossible to eat. We fed her by tube and with a teaspoon, but I knew that eventually I would have to brave the neck contractions.

Shortly before we were due to leave Ana begged me to sort Margaret's neck out. Otherwise, she said, she will surely die of starvation, and I knew it was true. After six months working at the side of this wonderful young Spanish nurse, she knew there was nothing I could refuse her. So, I began a three-hour operation which taxed me to the limit. We knew there would be some bleeding, but when I incised the right carotid artery by mistake, which had become completely embedded in dense scar tissue, everything went red.

The jet of blood blinded Shwarma and Ana who were assisting me and turned Marty, who was gassing, pale. I was terrified as well, and stuck my fist in Margaret's neck whilst a nurse rushed to get some 5 O sutures.

If I am completely honest, I have to say that I had delayed this necessary operation because of fear. I knew it would be extremely difficult because scar tissue always alters the normal anatomy and makes dissection very difficult and dangerous – as I was now confirming.

Averil Mansfield in Liverpool and Bob Gumpert in Brighton taught me much about vascular surgery, but I would never call myself a vascular surgeon. However, I did know how to conjoin blood vessels. It was very delicate work and it took me an hour to repair the artery, by which time I was sweating profusely.

It took another two hours to clear all the scar tissue below the chin and stop most of the bleeding, by which time Marty had infused two units of blood. Two days later we removed the dressings in the operating theatre and everything looked good. It usually takes between a week and 10 days for the necessary granulation tissues to form, and a week later we were all looking at some healthy granulations.

"Go on, Doc", said Ana. "Vamos! Let's go!" So we took Margaret to the OT once again – hopefully for the last time. I started slicing the skin off Margaret's left lateral thigh. Ana and Shwarma took the skin and laid it flat on paraffin gauze until I had cut enough partial thickness grafts to cover the exposed area. By the time we finished, Margaret's neck would have won no beauty contests, but the scarred area was now completely free and covered with skin. We could even flex her neck for the first time.

Then we started praying. Praying that my grafts would not become infected. This time I even used prophylactic antibiotics to minimise the chances. But at the first dressing, three days later I could see that one corner was looking suspect.

"Ana", I said, "get the papaya going!" I could not take a single chance with this patient, as I was leaving Mannar very soon and who knows what would happen to Margaret's grafts then.

I had started using papaya in Kenya to treat infected burns, once I found out that it contained papain, a proteolytic enzyme that seemed to really eat up infected tissue. And that is what I had taught Ana and the other nurses to use. As in Africa, papaya grew all over Mannar Island and was virtually free, so it made an ideal medicament.

Margaret had six days of daily papaya dressings, and on my last ward round before the new MSF surgeon arrived, we all applauded when we saw a clean and healing skin graft. Then Margaret did an amazing thing. She threw her arms out to me and embraced me. Then she grabbed a banana and stuck it in her mouth and started chewing it, laughing like a drain. And so were we all.

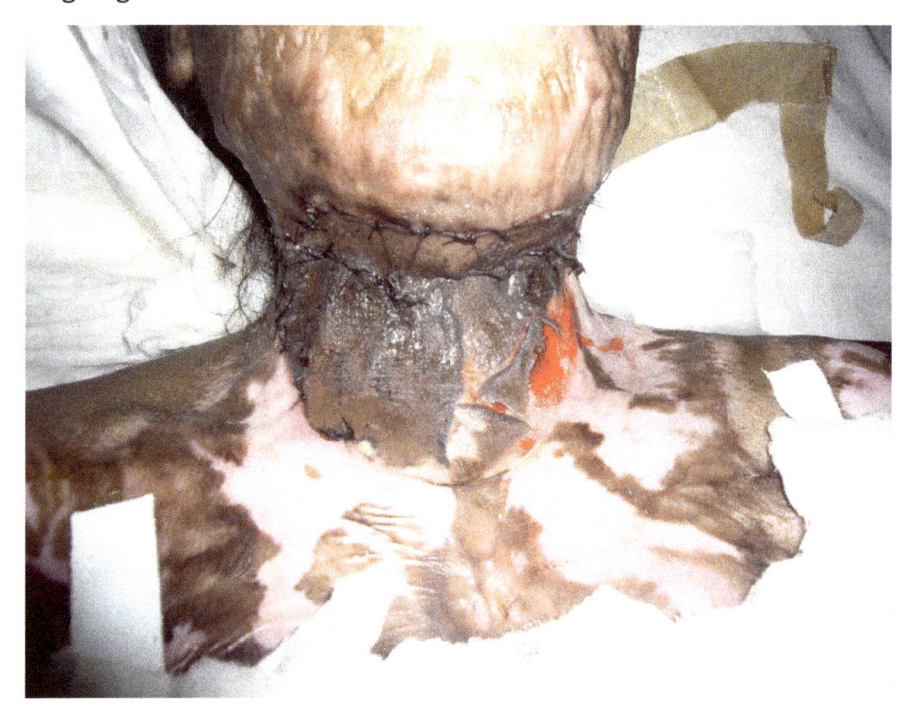

My last operation at Mannar – Margaret can eat again

To Ansela, Pryah, Rosalind, Ana and all the others it was like a miracle to see this patient eating normally again. When I took my last look down the long ward as I exited for the last time, I saw all the women laughing and waving their hands at me. That was a fine conclusion to my six months in Mannar.

I had been fortunate to be working with a very good team, and I knew I would miss them all when I left. Even our surgical outpatient clinics were always a pleasure for the variety of pathology which appeared in front of us, and I always used them as a teaching forum for Rosalind and my medical team.

With my team in surgical outpatients

Back in Spain a month later I received an email from Ansela saying that Margaret had been discharged from hospital, eating normally once again. I celebrated with a large gin and tonic whilst musing on the long hours I had spent operating on her. It was a wonderfully satisfying outcome to what had been a horrendous surgical problem.

The crash evacuation of Ana after her third anaphylactic episode was the only thing which dampened our farewell celebrations. I was sincerely sad to say goodbye to all the fine people I had worked with, and the small but beautiful island of Mannar, so troubled by civil war.

After almost six months of constant on-call I was beginning to tire of the constant surgical demands, much as I enjoyed them. I had forgotten that at nearly 65 years of age I was twice as old as most of my MSF companions. I was not too sad when my time came to leave, and hand over to the incoming surgeon, Carlos, a senior cardio-thoracic surgeon from Buenos Aires.

The Last of the General Surgeons

I had set aside three days for the handover and began with a gentle 0830h Ward round, as usual with Rosalind, Ansela and her three medical companions. Having completed the ward round, I turned to Carlos to ask how he had found things.

I found him looking slightly pale around the gills, and speechless. By the time I was back in Barcelona, Carlos was on his way back to open chests in Buenos Aires, and Mannar was once again without a surgeon. None of the Singalese doctors trained at Colombo medical school had any wish to visit the war-ravaged north, and MSF had found it impossible to find any surgeon with the necessary experience and qualifications.

We general surgeons are indeed a dying breed. I am one of the very last, but even as I write this, now aged 74, I am still performing general surgery, this time in Andalucia, for when I did finally retire from active duty with MSF in 2008, I sold half my precious surgical travelling kit to Juan, our local vet – on the understanding that he would employ me as first assistant now and then.

Today, my clients are domestic animals, and the occasional donkey. The anatomy and the surgery are very similar to any human, but these days there are no exploding mortars and flying RPGs to accompany my surgical endeavours. Just the sound of the endless waves of the Mediterranean lapping onto the shores of the Costa Tropical.

3 VOYAGES

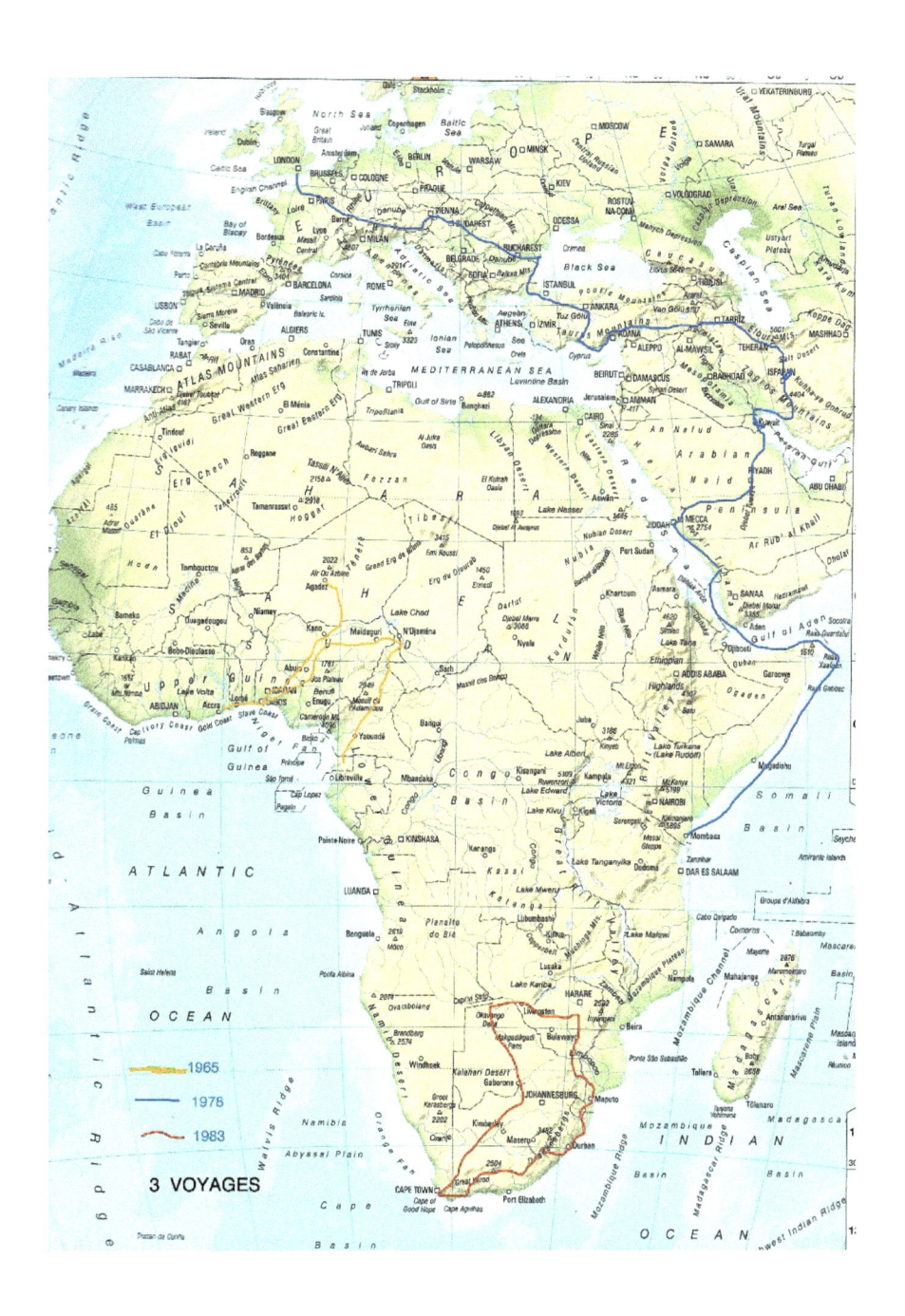

1965
1978
1983

20. EPILOGUE

Having traversed my life through this book, I am presently pondering on what it was that sent me on my long medical trajectory and kept me on the straight and narrow for over 50 years of my life as a physician, surgeon and teacher. I clearly remember the genesis of that seed. It was the day in 1960, aged 14, when I walked out of the cinema in Hailsham having just enjoyed "The World of Suzie Wong". At that moment I suddenly knew, for still unfathomable reasons, that I was going to become a surgeon.

Many medical students become physicians, but few of them become surgeons. It is one thing to cure a patient with a week´s course of antibiotics. But when the patient´s life is balanced on the tip of a 23 Swan and Morton scalpel blade poised a millimetre above the femoral vein, and catastrophic haemorrhage awaits the unsteady hand, it is another thing entirely.

Tom Wolfe expresses this unique ability in his book, "The Right Stuff". This epic tale describes the evolution of the world's first astronauts. From the first jet fighter pilots of the Second World War to the test pilots of the rocket-powered Bell X-1, which in 1947 was the first plane to exceed the speed of sound.

"Only surgeons can compare", were his words. He was talking about a certain type of ability and courage.

I shall never be able to adequately understand what the force was that drove me to become a surgeon, nor where it came from. I do know that it was critical to me being successful in my work, and I shall always be grateful for the fulfilling life it has allowed me to enjoy. I gratefully acknowledge the kindness, generosity and altruism of my many teachers who taught me the intricate skills of surgery and allowed this spirit to evolve, directing it to its highest purpose.

It was during my years in Africa that I began to develop my interest in public health, and preventive and social medicine. Even though I was a surgeon at heart, I began to realise the great importance of preventive medicine. The more I learned, the more I became interested. As Dr David Morley, at that time a primary health care doctor, said to me one day in 1968 at the Wesley Guild Mission hospital at Ilesha during the Biafran civil war, "As a surgeon you may save 10 lives in a day, but I can save 100!"

That is one of the joys of a career in medicine. There is no end to the range of disciplines to enjoy, from war surgery to public health. I have enjoyed many, including teaching which, now aged 75 I still do every week at my local District General Hospital, teaching scientific and medical English to my Spanish colleagues.

In the West, the ancient Greeks were some of the people who gave credence to the life I have led as a doctor, and expounded its moral justification, including religious and spiritual aspects. Even before them, in the East, Siddhartha Gautama (563 – 483 BC) and his disciples were spreading the word of Buddha and his philosophies of the good life, from Nepal to India and Sri Lanka and thence to China. Ayurvedic medicine was also widely practised then. The oldest hospital in the world where any form of rational medicine was practised was discovered at Mihintale in northern Sri Lanka. It is over 3000 years old.

Hippocrates (460 – 377 BC) taught the ethos of medicine, later collated in his Oath. This embodied his philosophy of the practice of medicine. It includes all moral aspects including the abuse of privilege, inappropriate sexual behaviour and even euthanasia and abortion. Repeating this solemn oath in unison with the whole class was a prerequisite to obtaining a formal degree in Medicine and Surgery in 1971 when I qualified. Today this ritual has been more or less forgotten, which I believe to be to the detriment of the profession.

A strong professional moral code is essential, because we healers and medical practitioners have absolute power over peoples´ lives, and temptation is always around. I was disappointed to find the American students I taught in Texas, USA, to be so driven by the thought of the money they could make from practising medicine. They also lacked much sense of altruism, such an important quality in the care of others. Today, in the richest country in the world, the poorest 30% of the population of the USA have no access to health care.

Re-reading those words of Hippocrates and Buddha written so long ago, I realise that they have marked and governed every aspect of my life as a doctor and a teacher. They are the foundation of everything I have been taught in medicine over many years. All doctors need a moral code they can constantly refer to.

The Greeks also designed their healing sanctuaries in harmonious surroundings. They believed that a healthy natural environment was an important component of the healing process, as well as drama, music and art. This is a concept which I completely agree with.

It was Aristotle who gave a name to this harmonious way of life : *eudaimonia*, derived from the Greek, *eu* – good, and *daimon* – the spirit. The Buddhists of Asia also have a word with similar meaning – *dharma* – which includes the teachings of the Buddha, and all the concepts of the Greeks *eudaimonia*. The *dharma* also includes powerful processes for influencing the mind, including meditation and mindfulness, both of which have recently appeared in the orthodox Western medical lexicon.

I believe that my original HALO project in Hailsham was similar in nature and ethos to that of the ancient Greeks. Empathy with the patients and kindness, were instrumental in its success. The neutral but pleasant ambiance of the Leisure Centre created a healing environment. The fact that HALO has progressed and expanded nation-wide is proof enough that my concept was valid, and that there is still a need for this type of therapy. In 1989 when I initiated the HALO project, my ideas were considered unorthodox. It has taken more than 20 years for them to become a normal part of orthodox practice, as ´GP Referral to Exercise´. Medicine and social health will always continue to evolve, even as civilisations wax and wane from century to century.

In the 14th century AD, it was the Moroccan poet, philosopher and physician, Ibn al Khatib who discovered the mode of spread of the plague known as the Black Death, which was then ravaging all of Europe and beyond. This devastating plague which caused so many millions of deaths was caused by a tiny microbe, Yersinia pestis. Seven centuries later another global plague is devastating the world, already causing over five million deaths in just two years. This present-day plague is caused by an even more tiny microbe, the corona virus. Yet, after seven centuries of evolution and development, it is surprising that we humans have learned so little about how to competently manage these existential threats. In particular, the behaviour of human beings.

During the 17th century AD, the Quakers defined Health as "a balance of Mind, Body and Spirit". It was a Quaker surgeon, Joseph Lister, the father of antisepsis, who said in 1865, "a feeling heart is the first requisite of a surgeon".

To me it is shocking that over 300 years later, since the World Health Organisation issued the Declaration of Alma Ata in 1978, for political reasons there is no longer any recognition of the importance of the Spirit within the global definition of health. Yet I believe that spirit is always with us.

During my years in Africa, I found much evidence of belief in the spirit and the spirits, which were often invoked to cure illness, and sometimes even to cause it (see Chapter 9). The Kisii tribe, who live near Lake Victoria in Kenya, used to perform fenestration of the skull in order to allow bad spirits to escape. I found the most remarkable example in The Congo in 1975 when I was physician to the King of the Bakuba. His dreams were interpreted by a cohort of priests and advisors. But those dreams were then made carnate, in the form of geometric patterns woven into reed mats, and that is unique in the world.

When I drove into the Catholic mission hospital at Morija, Lesotho, in February 1984 to see my wife and Anna Palesa, my new-born child, I was astonished and delighted to hear Marvin Gaye singing 'Sexual Healing'. This great song lifted my spirits, as well as making me smile. My music and my guitar have always been with me on this long voyage. They have given voice to my spirit and comforted me when I was down. They have also entertained many patients in the hospitals I have worked in over the years, and possibly even helped to shorten the in-patient stay of some of them. Music touches the soul of every human being.

The last contribution I made to the new Machabeng hospital in Lesotho was to plant 36 rose bushes in between the wards. I wanted my African patients to see something natural and beautiful when they looked out of the window of their ward, as well as the hospital garden which was already producing vegetables.

The Italian nuns at the Nazareth hospital just north of Nairobi, where at one time I used to do a day's voluntary surgery each week, went one better. They had a farm next door to the hospital, managed by the retired nuns. Their fat black and white cows grazed contentedly on the verdant Kikuyu hillsides, so the patients were never short of milk. But my reward was a big, two-kilo, home-made cheese every week.

There is a relationship between a harmonious environment and the healing process. Which must be why, 2,500 years after the Greeks, the British NHS has also started once again planting gardens in its hospital grounds.

Nothing is new. All of us humans are destined to suffer illness and injury, which is why the collective history of medicine remains so relevant. A new plague has arrived, one which is taxing the resources of all humanity, and after so many deaths we are still uncertain about the outcome.

Meanwhile, I have a full and happy life to contemplate, as well as much satisfaction from my memories of a career in Medicine in all its forms, some of which I have shared with you.

As the Dali Lama says, "We are here only to help others". Whilst I strongly adhere to this belief, it has never stopped me having fun. And I know of no better way of helping others than the practice of medicine and its teaching.

Condensing the Good Life in Three Images

Always Travel in Style

Celebrate every moment in life

Refresh the spirit daily with music

Lightning Source UK Ltd.
Milton Keynes UK
UKHW050656101022
410222UK00011B/114